S

Family Violence

Withdrawn

Issues In Children's and Families' Lives

AN ANNUAL BOOK SERIES

Senior Series Editor

Thomas P. Gullotta, *Child and Family Agency, Connecticut*

Editors

Gerald R. Adams, *University of Guleph, Ontario, Canada*

Earl H. Potter III, *U.S. Coast Guard Academy, Connecticut*

Robert L. Hampton, *Connecticut College, Connecticut*

Roger P. Weissberg, *University of Illinois at Chicago, Illinois*

Drawing upon the resources of Child and Family Agency of Southeastern Connecticut, one of this nation's leading family service agencies, **Issues in Children's and Families' Lives** is designed to focus attention on the pressing social problems facing children and their families today. Each volume in this series will analyze, integrate, and critique the clinical and research literature on children and their families as it relates to a particular theme. Believing that integrated multidisciplinary approaches offer greater opportunities for program success, volume contributors will reflect the research and clinical knowledge base of the many different disciplines that are committed to enhancing the physical, social, and emotional health of children and their families. Intended for graduate and professional audiences, chapters will be written by scholars and practitioners who will encourage the reader to apply their practice skills and intellect to reducing the suffering of children and their families in the society in which those families live and work.

Volume 1: Family Violence: Prevention and Treatment
LEAD EDITOR: Robert L. Hampton
CONSULTANTS: Vincent Senatore, *Child and Family Agency, Connecticut*; Ann Quinn, *Connecticut Department of Children, Youth, and Family Services, Connecticut*

Family Violence

Prevention and Treatment

EDITORS

Robert L. Hampton,

Thomas P. Gullotta,

Gerald R. Adams, Earl H. Potter III,
and Roger P. Weissberg

Vol. 1

Issues in Children's and Families' Lives

SAGE Publications

International Educational and Professional Publisher
Newbury Park   London   New Delhi

For information address:

SAGE Publications, Inc.
2455 Teller Road
Newbury Park, California 91320

SAGE Publications Ltd.   ℓ 5 2 8 8 6
6 Bonhill Street
London EC2A 4PU
United Kingdom

GATESHEAD
COLLEGE
LEARNING
RESOURCES
UNIT

SAGE Publications India Pvt. Ltd.
M-32 Market
Greater Kailash I
New Delhi 110 048 India

Printed in the United States of America

Library of Congress Cataloging-in-Publication Data

Main entry under title:

Family violence : prevention and treatment / edited by Robert L.
    Hampton . . . [et al.].
        p. cm.–(Issues in children's and families' lives : v. 1)
    Includes bibliographical references and indexes.
    ISBN 0-8039-5246-5 (cl).–ISBN 0-8039-5247-3 (pb)
    1. Family violence–United States–Prevention. 2. Family
violence–Treatment–United States.   I. Hampton, Robert L.
II. Series.
HQ809.3.U5F344   1993
362.82'92–dc20   93-14801

93 94 95 96 10 9 8 7 6 5 4 3 2

Sage Production Editor: Diane S. Foster

Contents

This volume is dedicated to John and Kelly Hartman, who chose philanthropy over personal gain, who saw communities profiting from their involvement rather than individuals, and who saw in the Hartman Conference and this book series the hope for change that can exist when caring people take action.

Series Introduction

This volume begins a new Sage book series devoted to issues of concern affecting children and their families. It is appropriate that Child and Family Agency of Southeast Connecticut be the force behind this and future volumes.

Tracing its history to 1809, the agency and its auxiliary membership has never wavered in its mission of serving children and their families within the context of their community. In recent years, the Agency has redefined itself from being solely a provider of quality service to becoming a laboratory for testing programs and promising new approaches for working with children and their families. To achieve this goal, it became important to do more than initiate successful home-based intensive family preservation programs or school-based health centers. To reach this goal, it became important to link our efforts with those in other academic disciplines, other practice fields, and other institutional settings. To effect this goal, the Agency joined with the John and Kelly Hartman Foundation to establish a national biennial conference on children and their families. It established, with the New York Gimbel Foundation and the *Journal of Primary Prevention*, a biennial national award to recognize promising new scholars and practitioners concerned with applying their knowledge to easing the pain too many children are experiencing in a society that seems to have forgotten that its future is its youth. It established a network of distinguished scholars who willingly lend their talents to these efforts.

It is with warmth and affection that my thoughts now drift back 8 years ago to a old fashioned front porch stoop conversation that Alva Gahagan and I had in which together we dreamed these possibilities. She, John and Kelly Hartman, and the many fine board members of Child and Family Agency have enabled those dreams. Were it not for the support, advice, guidance, and patience of Ross Johnson, Pat Rogerson, Bob Hampton, Ward Johnson and others, this book series would not have been brought to fruition. This wish to generate new approaches for improving the chances of children growing up in healthier environments would not have been realized. This developing center for applied preventive interventions would have remained an unfulfilled fantasy.

In the coming years the other editors in this series, Gerald Adams, Robert Hampton, Earl Potter, Roger Weissberg and I hope to contribute information that will assist scholars and practitioners in their search for solutions to easing the distress that for too many children across this country has become commonplace. We long for the day when every child is wanted; every family belongs; every individual's contribution is valued; and peace—not violence—is pandemic.

THOMAS P. GULLOTTA
Senior Series Editor

Preface

Acts of violence between members of the same family are an age-old phenomenon. There have been periods of heightened public and political awareness of family violence. Although acknowledged as a subject of public concern, research, theory, and practice in this field is less than three decades old. The research has delineated the nature and scope of family violence; however, our understanding of the antecedents and consequences remains incomplete.

The chapters in this volume are all testimony to the rapid expansion of knowledge on family violence. They attempt to summarize the best of current scholarship by family violence researchers from many specialties. They also address the issues of prevention and treatment within each of the subfields. The contributors were carefully selected from a variety of disciplines and reflect different approaches. The diverse perspectives brought to bear on the subject by professionals from many disciplines add to the richness of this volume.

Richard Gelles provides an overview of research, theory, and current controversies in the field. Joel Milner and Julie Crouch build on the more general theoretical overview presented in Chapter 1 by reviewing recent etiological models specific to physical child abuse. They also discuss the reported consequences of physical abuse in a development context. Jon Conte challenges us to address two important questions in his chapter on child sexual abuse: (a) What are the data supporting what we know about child sexual abuse? (b) Is belief based more on emotional and other psychological principles that meet our needs as professionals than on real data?

Responses to child maltreatment are presented by Theodore Stein, focusing on legal responses; Gary Blau, Mary Butteweg Dall, and Lynette Anderson, on treatment and assessment; and Donna Harrington and Howard Dubowitz, on preventive responses.

Three chapters deal with aspects of couple violence. Christopher Murphy and Michele Cascardi discuss the often neglected area of research: psychological violence in marriage. Their review suggests that psychological aggression and physical aggression are distinct yet correlated phenomena. The chapter by Robert Hampton and Alice Coner-Edwards focuses on physical and sexual violence in marriage. They include a discussion of conditional responses by police and health care professionals to battered women. One of the main points that can be inferred from the work of Edward Gondolf is that male batterers do not easily fall into a simple composite profile and that batterer counseling is not a unified venture.

Three areas of growing concern are also addressed in this volume: abuse of the elderly, ethnic diversity, and substance abuse. Frances Boudreau provides a list of important policy recommendations for those in the field of elder abuse. Jo-Ellen Asbury looks at research on families of color and discusses its implications for interventions. Finally, Heather Hayes and James Emshoff look at the bidirectional relationship between substance abuse and family violence.

Students will find the volume an essential introduction to a complex set of issues related to family violence research, treatment, and intervention. Experienced practitioners will find the volume helpful in updating their knowledge base and expanding their repertoire of treatment approaches.

Acknowledgments

Many people have contributed to the making of this book. The authors of the chapters were the key contributors. They come from different academic disciplines; however, they share a common field of work and inquiry. This book would not have been possible without them.

I want to thank Tom Gullotta, CEO of the Child and Family Agency of Southeastern Connecticut, series editor, and personal friend, for his attention to detail and deadlines and support of this project. Moreover, I want to thank him and all those involved in planning this series for placing the topic at the beginning. I would also like to thank my research assistants: Emily Cusic, Jennifer Fuss, Alisa Kreger, Sarah Robson, and Kristin Rizzo. A special word of praise is appropriate for Beverly G. Kowal, who suffered through countless revisions and missed deadlines while maintaining a hectic administrative office. Without her commitment, the project would have failed. Finally, I want to thank Cathy, Robyn, Conrad, and Nana, my wife, daughter, son, and mother, for their patience and understanding.

ROBERT L. HAMPTON

• CHAPTER 1 •

Family Violence

RICHARD J. GELLES

The rapid increase in public awareness of child abuse, sexual abuse, wife abuse, and other forms of family violence has led professionals and lay people alike to conclude that family violence is a new phenomenon that has increased to epidemic proportions in the last decade or so. Although family violence receives considerably more attention today, it has been a part of the family throughout its history, not only in families in the United States but in England, Western Europe, and many other countries and societies around the globe. The history of Western society is one in which women and children have been subjected to unspeakable cruelties. In ancient times, infants had no rights until the right to live was bestowed upon them by their fathers, typically as part of some formal cultural ritual (Radbill, 1980). When the right to live was withheld, infants were abandoned or left to die. Although we do not know how often children were killed or abandoned, we do know that infanticide was widely accepted among ancient and prehistoric cultures. Infants could be put to death because they cried too much, because they were sickly or deformed, or because they had some perceived imperfection. Girls, twins, and the children of unmarried women, for example, were special targets (Robin, 1982).

AUTHOR'S NOTE: This chapter was prepared as part of the work of the University of Rhode Island Family Violence Research Program. A complete list of publications is available on request. I want to thank Jody Brown, Debbie Levesque, and Heidi Recksiek, members of the Family Violence Research and Practice Work Group, who provided helpful comments and suggestions.

1

Infanticide continued through the eighteenth and nineteenth centuries; children born out-of-wedlock continue to run the greatest risk of infanticide even today.

Killing children was not the only form of harm inflicted by generations of parents. Since prehistoric times, children have been mutilated, beaten, and maltreated. Such treatment was not only condoned, it was often mandated as the most appropriate child-rearing method. Children were hit with rods, canes, and switches. Our forefathers in colonial America were implored to "beat the devil" out of their children (Greven, 1991).

The subordinate status of women in America and in most of the world's societies is well documented. Because physical force and violence are the last resort to keep subordinate groups in their place, the history of women in European and American societies has been one in which women have been victims of physical assault (Dobash & Dobash, 1979; Gordon, 1988; Pleck, 1987). A Roman husband could chastise, divorce, or kill his wife. Blackstone's codification of English common law in 1768 asserted that husbands had the right to "physically chastise" an errant wife, provided that the stick was no thicker than his thumb; thus the "rule of thumb" was born. In 1824, a Mississippi court set the precedent for allowing corporal punishment of wives by husbands. This precedent held for more than 40 years (Davidson, 1978).

Siblings have also been the victims of family violence. The first case of family violence described in the Bible is Cain killing Abel. There has been less historical and current interest in sibling violence or violence toward men compared with concern with violence toward children and women in families. In part, this is because social concern for victims of family violence is tied to the perceived powerlessness and helplessness of the victims. Thus there is greater social concern for violence toward infants and young children than violence toward adolescents or adult men.

Discovering Family Violence

The historical treatment of children is not entirely bleak. Children in Mesopotamia, 6,000 years ago, were protected by a patron goddess. The Greeks and Romans established orphan homes and some historical accounts also mention the existence of foster care for children. Child protection laws were legislated as long ago as 450 B.C. (Radbill, 1980). The Renaissance was the beginning of a new morality regarding children, who were seen as a dependent class in need of the protection of society. The Enlightenment of the eighteenth century brought children increased attention and services. For example, the London Foundling Hospital, founded during this time, not only provided pediatric care but was also the center of the moral reform movement on behalf of children (Robin, 1982). The hospital was the center of a campaign to control the consumption of gin, which was seen as the root cause of many problems that affected families and children.

In the United States, the case of Mary Ellen Wilson, an illegitimate child born in 1866 in New York City, is usually singled out as the turning point in concern for children's welfare. Mary Ellen's foster parents beat and neglected her. The legend of the case goes on to note that Henry Berge, founder of the Society for the Prevention of Cruelty to Animals, intervened on behalf of Mary Ellen and the courts accepted the case because she was a member of the animal kingdom. In reality, the court reviewed the case because the child needed protection. Mary Ellen Wilson was removed from her foster home and placed in an orphanage. Her foster mother was imprisoned for a year, and the case received detailed press coverage for months. In December 1874, the New York Society for the Prevention of Cruelty to Children was founded (Nelson, 1984; Robin, 1982). This was the first formal organization that focused on child maltreatment in the United States.

Technology paved the way for the renewed modern concern for child abuse. Pediatric radiologists described a number of cases of children who had multiple long bone fractures and subdural hematomas and speculated that such injuries might have been inflicted by the children's parents (Caffey, 1946; Woolley & Evans, 1955). By 1962, the physician C. Henry Kempe and his colleagues were certain that many of the injuries they were seeing and the healed fractures that appeared on X-rays had been intentionally inflicted by parents (Kempe, Silverman, Steele, Droegemueller, & Silver, 1962). The article Kempe and his colleagues wrote, which presents a number of case examples of child abuse and coined the term *battered child syndrome,* became the bench mark of the public and professional "rediscovery" of child abuse.

There was no Mary Ellen for battered women, no technological breakthroughs to uncover years of broken jaws and broken bones, no medical champion to capture public and professional attention. Concern with the abuse of women ebbed and flowed with feminism; when feminism was active and influential, interest in violence toward women was high, and, when feminism ebbed as a social movement, so did social concern for battered women (Gordon, 1988). Although there were a variety of efforts throughout history to define violence against women as a social problem, the modern identification of wife abuse was a grassroots effort (Pleck, 1987). Attention was drawn to the problem of wife battering by the women themselves. Women's groups began to organize safe houses and battered wife shelters in the United States in 1972. In 1975, the National Organization for Women created a task force to examine wife battering. This was 10 years after public attention was focused on child abuse.

The Development of
Family Violence Research

Family violence was not initially identified as a holistic problem; rather, like peeling away the skin of an onion, specific violent intimate relationships were uncovered one at a time. In time, the term *family violence* was applied to a broader concept of maltreatment that included harmful, but not necessarily physically violent, acts.

Physical child abuse (or violence toward children) received much of the clinical and research attention in the early 1960s. Gradually, the study of child abuse broadened beyond the early narrow conceptualization of the battered child syndrome (Kempe et al., 1962) to include other forms of maltreatment, including neglect. The study of child abuse was further broadened in the late 1970s and early 1980s to include study of the extent, causes, and consequences of sexual abuse. This expansion was primarily the result of efforts by feminists to focus attention on the broad spectrum of victimization of women. Feminists and the women's movement in general were also responsible for identifying the problem of wife abuse in the early 1970s. Finally, abuse and maltreatment of the elderly were identified as a social problem in the late 1970s, primarily by advocates for the elderly.

The study of family violence "is balkanized." Each field has its own "experts," funding sources, and even scholarly journals. Students of wife abuse rarely communicate with, or even read the works of, students of child abuse, and vice versa. A possible exception to this "balkanization" is the efforts of feminists who conceptualized the victimization of women across the age span as the central problem worthy of study.

The substantive focus of research on family violence broadened as the field developed. Research on family violence in the 1960s, and especially in the 1970s, focused mainly on three major topics: (a) the extent of family violence, (b) factors associated with family violence, and (c) causal explanations. Research in the 1980s and 1990s was less heavily weighted toward measuring the extent of family violence and more concerned with assessing the changing rates of violence and abuse in the home. Research on factors related to violence continued but was augmented by extensive examination of the consequences of being a victimized child or woman. There was some advance in theory testing and building, but few tests of theories of family violence have been carried out. The greatest emphasis of current family violence research is the examination of the effectiveness of treatment programs in reducing the incidence of family violence.

Issues of Research Methodology

Data on child abuse, wife abuse, and family violence come from three major sources: (a) clinical samples, (b) official report data, and (c) social surveys. Each source has certain advantages and specific weaknesses that influence both the nature and the generalizability of the findings derived from the research.

One of the most frequent sources of data on family violence continues to be *clinical studies* carried out by psychiatrists, psychologists, and counselors. This is primarily due to the fact that these investigators have the most direct access to cases of family violence. The clinical setting (including hospital emergency rooms and battered woman shelters) provides access to extensive in-depth information about particular cases of violence. Studies of wife abuse and violence toward women have relied heavily on samples of women who seek help at battered woman shelters (Dobash & Dobash, 1979; Giles-Sims, 1983; Pagelow, 1981; Walker, 1979). Such samples are important because they are often the only way of obtaining detailed data on the most severely battered women. Such data are also necessary to study the impact of intervention programs.

The most common data source for research on child abuse and child sexual abuse are *official reports*. The establishment of mandatory reporting laws for suspected cases of child abuse and neglect in the late 1960s and early 1970s made case-level and aggregate-level data on abuse available to researchers. Official report data, however, are limited to cases that fall under the investigation mandate of state agencies. In most states, such reporting is limited to abuse by family or quasi-family members (e.g., teachers). The American Association for Protecting Children (a division of the American Humane Association) collected data on officially reported child abuse and neglect from each state between 1976 to 1987 (see American Association for Protecting Children, 1988, 1989). The federal government sponsored two national surveys of officially reported child maltreatment (Burgdorf, 1980; National Center on Child Abuse and Neglect, 1988). In contrast, there has not been a tradition of officially reporting spouse abuse, with the exception of three states that collect data on spouse abuse. The *Uniform Crime Reports* provide data on criminal family violence and family homicide, but these are limited to instances of family violence that are reported to the police.

The use of *social surveys* to study family violence has been constrained by the low base rate of most forms of abuse and family violence and the sensitive and taboo nature of the topic. Some investigators cope with the problem of the low base rate by employing purposive or nonrepresentative sampling techniques to identify cases. A second approach has been to use available large groups of subjects. Students of courtship violence have made extensive use of survey research techniques using college students as subjects (Cate, Henton, Christopher, & Lloyd, 1982; Henton, Cate, Koval, Lloyd, & Christopher, 1983; Laner, 1983; Makepeace, 1981, 1983). Murray Straus and I carried out two national surveys on family violence in 1976 and 1985. We conducted telephone interviews with a nationally representative sample of 2,143 respondents in 1976 and 6,002 respondents in 1985 (Gelles & Straus, 1988; Straus & Gelles, 1986; Straus, Gelles, & Steinmetz, 1980). Karl Pillemer and David Finkelhor (1988) interviewed a representative sample of 2,020 community-dwelling elderly persons in the Boston metropolitan area for their study on the prevalence of elder abuse. Diana Russell (1984) examined sexual victimization by surveying 930 San Francisco women, while Dean Kilpatrick and his associates examined rape in marriage and other forms of sexual assault with a telephone sample of 391 women (Kilpatrick, Best, Saunders, & Veronen, 1988).

Another source of survey data on violence between intimates is the victimization data collected in the annual National Crime Survey (NCS). The U.S. Justice Department has published two reports on intimate violence based on the data collected by the NCS (U.S. Department of Justice, 1980, 1984). In addition, the NCS provides yearly data on rape. There has been considerable criticism of the NCS rape data, however, especially in light of the fact that the NCS has not directly asked respondents whether they have been victimized by rape. The question used to measure rape victimization has been, "Did anyone *try* to attack you in some other way?" This question is asked after a series of specific questions about criminal victimization, for example, being a victim of an assault, burglary, robbery, or the like.

Each of the major data sources has its own validity problems. Clinical data cannot be used to generalize information on the incidence or frequency of family violence and on the strength of factors associated with violence. Such samples are never representative, and few investigators gathering data from clinical samples employ appropriate comparison groups. Official records suffer from variations in definitions, differing reporting and recording practices, and biased samples of violent and abusive behaviors and persons (Finkelhor & Hotaling, 1984; Weis, 1989; Widom, 1988). In addition, official report records tend to be limited to a small set of variables. Data needed to answer key research, practice, or policy questions are often not included in official data sets. Self-report surveys have a number of significant limitations. The low base rate of intimate violence requires large samples, which, in turn, limits the amount of data that can be collected. The biases of social survey data on intimate violence include inaccurate recall, differential interpretation of questions, and intended and unintended response error (Weis, 1989). Some social surveys are limited by low response rates (e.g., Russell, 1984). The NCS data are limited because the minimum age for respondents is 14; thus the NCS data allow no estimates of violence toward young children. The reported rates of intimate violence in the NCS are smaller than in other self-report surveys. This could be because the respondents are interviewed in the home, perhaps within earshot of the perpetrator (Weis, 1989). Also, because the NCS measures "criminal violence," respondents may fail to report intimate violence that they do not view as criminal. As noted earlier, with regard to rape, there is no direct question to measure victimization.

The most common research design for the study of family violence has been the cross-sectional nonexperimental design. Longitudinal and experimental studies of family violence are rare.[1]

Theoretical Approaches to Family Violence

The first people to identify a problem often shape how others will perceive it (Nelson, 1984). The initial conceptualizations of family violence were developed in the study of battered children in the early 1960s. Descriptions of battered children portrayed abuse and violence between intimates as a rare event, typically caused by the psychopathology of the offender. The perception of the abuser as suffering from some form of psychopathology has persisted, in part because the first conceptualization of family violence was the guiding framework for the work that followed. The psychopathological or psychiatric conceptualization has also persisted because the tragic picture of a defenseless child, woman, or grandparent subjected to abuse and neglect arouses the strongest emotions in clinicians and others who see and/or treat the problem of intimate violence. There frequently seems to be no rational explanation for harming a loved one, especially one who appears to be helpless and defenseless.

Family violence has been approached from three general theoretical levels of analysis: (a) the intraindividual level of analysis, or the psychiatric model, (b) the social-psychological level of analysis, and (c) the sociological or sociocultural level of analysis.

The psychiatric model focuses on the offender's personality characteristics as the chief determinants of violence and abuse of intimates, although some applications focus on the individual personality characteristics of the victims (see, for example, Shainess, 1979; Snell, Rosenwald, & Robey, 1964). The psychiatric model includes theoretical approaches that link personality disorders, character disorders, mental illness, alcohol and substance abuse, and other intra-individual processes to acts of family violence.

The social-psychological model assumes that violence and abuse can best be understood by careful examination of the external environmental factors that affect the family, the family organization and structure, and the everyday interactions between intimates that are precursors to acts of violence. Theoretical approaches that examine family structure, stress, the transmission of violence from one generation to the next, and family interaction patterns fit the social-psychological model.

The sociocultural model provides a macro level of analysis. Violence is examined in light of socially structured variables such as inequality, patriarchy, or cultural norms and attitudes about violence and family relations.

Six Theories of Family Violence

General Systems Theory

Straus (1973) and Jean Giles-Sims (1983) developed and applied a social system approach to explain family violence. Here, violence is viewed as a system product rather than the result of individual pathology. The family system operations can maintain, escalate, or reduce levels of violence in families. General systems theory describes the processes that characterize the use of violence in family interactions and explains the way in which violence is managed and stabilized. Straus (1973) argues that a general systems theory of family violence must include at least three basic elements: (a) alternative courses of action or causal flow, (b) the feedback mechanisms that enable the system to make adjustments, and (c) system goals. Straus (1973) developed eight propositions to illustrate how general systems theory relates to family violence:

1. Violence between family members has many causes and roots. Normative structures, personality traits, frustrations, and conflicts are only some.
2. More family violence occurs than is reported.
3. Most family violence is either denied or ignored.
4. Stereotyped family violence imagery is learned in childhood from parents, siblings, and other children.
5. The family violence stereotypes are continually reaffirmed for adults and children through ordinary social interactions and the mass media.
6. Violent acts by violent persons may generate positive feedback; that is, these acts may produce desired results.
7. Use of violence, when contrary to family norms, creates additional conflicts over ordinary violence.
8. Persons who are labeled violent may be encouraged to play out a violent role, either to live up to the expectations of others or to fulfill their own self-concept of being violent or dangerous.

Giles-Sims (1983) elaborated Straus's basic model and identified six temporal stages that lead to wife battering. The six stages are:

1. establishing the family system,
2. the first incidence of violence,
3. stabilization of violence,
4. the choice point,
5. leaving the system, and
6. resolution or more of the same.

Resource Theory

The resource theory of family violence assumes that all social systems (including the family) rest to some degree on force or the threat of force. The more resources—social, personal, and economic—a person can command, the more force he or she can muster. According to William Goode (1971), however, the more resources a person actually has, the less he or she will actually use force in an open manner. Thus a husband who wants to be the dominant person in the family, but has little education, has a job low in prestige and income, and lacks interpersonal skills, may choose to use violence to maintain the dominant position. In addition, family members (including children) may use violence to redress a grievance when they have few alternative resources available.

An Ecological Perspective

James Garbarino (1977) and Jay Belsky (1980) have proposed an "ecological model" to explain the complex nature of child maltreatment. The model rests on three levels of analysis: the relationship between the organism and environment, the interacting and overlapping systems in which human development occurs, and environmental quality. The ecological model proposes that violence and abuse arise out of a mismatch of parent to child and family to neighborhood and community. The risk of abuse and violence is greatest when the functioning of the children and parents is limited and constrained by developmental problems. Children with learning disabilities and social or emotional handicaps are at increased risk for abuse. Parents under considerable stress, or who have personality problems, are at increased risk for abusing their children. These conditions are worsened when social interaction between the spouses or the parents and children heighten the stress or make the personal problems worse. Finally, if there are few institutions and agencies in the community to support troubled families, then the risk of abuse is further raised. Garbarino (1977) identifies two necessary conditions for child maltreatment. First, there must be cultural justification for the use of force against children. Second, the maltreating family is isolated from potent family or community support systems.

Sociobiology Theory

A sociobiological, or evolutionary, perspective of family violence suggests that violence toward human or nonhuman primate offspring is the result of the reproductive success potential of children and parental investment. The theory begins with the statement that natural selection is the process of differential reproduction (Daly & Wilson, 1980). Natural selection measures an organism's success and is solely determined by reproductive success. Males can be expected to invest in offspring when there is some degree of parental certainty (how confident the parent is that the child is his own genetic offspring), while females are also inclined to invest under conditions of parental certainty. Parental solicitude, Martin Daly and Margo Wilson (1980) argue, is discriminative. Parents recognize their offspring and avoid squandering valuable reproductive effort on someone else's offspring. Thus, Daly and Wilson conclude, "we should expect parental feelings to vary as a function of the prospective fitness value of the child in question" (1985, p. 197). Parental feelings are seen as more readily and more profoundly established with one's own offspring than in cases where the parent-offspring relationship is artificial. Thus, "when people are called upon to fill parental roles toward unrelated children, we may anticipate an elevated risk of lapses of parental solicitude" (Daly & Wilson, 1985). Children not genetically related to the parent (e.g., step-children, adopted or foster children) or children with low reproductive potential (e.g., handicapped or retarded children) are at the highest risk for infanticide and abuse (Burgess & Garbarino, 1983; Daly & Wilson, 1980; Hrdy, 1979). Risk is also high where there is a lack of bonding between parent and child and where paternity is uncertain (Burgess, 1979). Large families can dilute parental energy and lower attachment to children, thus increasing the risk of child abuse and neglect (Burgess, 1979).

Barbara Smuts (1992) has applied an evolutionary perspective to male aggression against females. Smuts agrees with Daly and Wilson (1988) and Burgess and Draper (1989) that male aggression against females often reflects male reproductive striving. Both human and nonhuman male primates are postulated to use aggression against females to intimidate females so that they will not resist future male efforts to mate with them and to reduce the likelihood that females will mate with other males. Thus males use aggression to control female sexuality to males' reproductive advantage. The frequency of male aggression varies across societies and situations depending on the strength of female alliances, the support women can receive from their families, the strength and importance of male alliances, the degree of equality in male-female relationships, and the degree to which males control the economic resources within a society. Male aggression toward females, both physical violence and rape, is high when female alliances are weak, when females lack kin support, when male alliances are strong, when relationships are unbalanced, and when males control societal resources.

Exchange/Social Control Theory

Gelles (1983) elaborated on the basic propositions of an exchange theory of aggression and developed an exchange/social control model of family violence that proposes that wife abuse and child abuse are governed by the principle of costs and rewards. Drawing from exchange theory, Gelles (1983) notes that violence and abuse are used when the rewards are higher than the costs. Drawing from social control theories of delinquency, he proposes that the private nature of the family, the reluctance of social institutions and agencies to intervene—in spite of mandatory child abuse reporting laws—and the low risk of other interventions reduce the costs of abuse and violence. The cultural approval of violence as both expressive and, in the case of disciplining children, instrumental behavior, raises the potential rewards for violence.

Patriarchy and Wife Abuse

The previous models of family violence have been different only in degrees. They tend to examine individuals and family relations in their search for the explanation for family violence. The final model is quite different. Dobash and Dobash (1979), Pagelow (1984), and Yllo (1983) see wife abuse as a unique phenomenon that has been obscured and overshadowed by what they refer to as the "narrow" focus on domestic violence. The theory's central thesis is that economic and social processes operate directly and indirectly to support a patriarchal (male-dominated) social order and family structure. The central theoretical argument is that patriarchy leads to the subordination and oppression of women and causes the historical pattern of systematic violence directed against wives.

Patriarchy finds the source of family violence in the society and how it is organized, as opposed to within individual families or communities.

Controversies in the Study of Family Violence

Thirty years after the publication of Kempe and his colleagues' (1962) ground-breaking article on child abuse, considerable research and theory development has occurred in the study of family violence. There are now more than five scholarly journals devoted to one or more aspects of family violence. The growth in the volume of articles published on the various facets of family violence is perhaps unprecedented in the social sciences (Straus, 1992). We now have data on almost every aspect of the extent, correlates, consequences, treatment, and prevention of family violence.

Despite the enormous growth of professional and public interest in child abuse, wife abuse, sexual abuse, elder abuse, emotional abuse, and other forms of family violence, the field is far from unified and there is no single dominant theory or body of data that guides the investigation of and efforts to treat and prevent family violence. In fact, a number of significant controversies have emerged in the study of family violence. This section reviews some of the more significant controversies and differences of opinion and interpretation of data and theory.[2]

Are Women Violent?

Abused Husbands: Fact or Myth?

Data from the earliest studies of spousal violence detected violence by women toward their husbands (see, for example, Gelles, 1974). These early data were dismissed, however, by those whose main goal was to use incidence data to prove that the problem of abuse and battering was a significant public health problem for women in our society. With the publication of the results of the First National Family Violence Survey (Steinmetz, 1977-1978; Straus, 1977-1978; Straus et al., 1980), however, the question of whether males were victims as well as offenders became a major controversy. Murray Straus, Suzanne Steinmetz, and I found that women reported high levels of violence toward their husbands. In fact, the data indicated that the rate of violence was the same or even higher than that reported for male-to-female violence. We qualified our findings by noting that much of the female violence appeared to be in self-defense and that females, because of their size and strength, appeared to inflict less injury than male attackers. Finally, we noted that the apparently similar rates were probably the result of a methodological artifact whereby females were more likely to report offenses and males more likely to report victimization than vice versa. Nevertheless, the reaction against these data was swift and emotional. Straus and Steinmetz were, and continue to be, subjected to vitriolic and personal attacks, including bomb scares and death threats (Straus, 1990). More reasonable critics of the data on violence by women have focused on the deficits of the main measure of violence, the Conflict Tactics Scales, and the limitations of positivistic, quantitative social science for studying the victimization of women (Berk, Berk, Loseke, & Rauma, 1983; Dobash & Dobash, 1979; Okun, 1986; Pleck, Pleck, Grossman, & Bart, 1977-1978; Stark & Flitcraft, 1983; Yllö, 1988). Straus (see, for example, Stets & Straus, 1990) continues to maintain that women are frequent users of violence in their relationships with men, that women sometimes initiate acts of violence, and that women frequently cause injury.

Is Violence Transmitted Intergenerationally?

One of the most consistent and persistent findings from research on physical child abuse is the so-called intergenerational transmission of violence. The intergenerational transmission of violence proposition, simply stated, is that children who have been physically abused tend to grow up to be abusive adults. Researchers generally recognize that intergenerational transmission is probabilistic and that not all abused children grow up to be abusive.

Joan Kaufman and Edward Zigler (1987) have argued that the intergenerational transmission hypothesis is overstated. They have analyzed the available research on physical child abuse and find that the best empirical data available suggest that only 30% of abused children will go on to become abusive adults. Kaufman and Zigler conclude that it is time for researchers to set aside the "intergenerational myth" and cease asking, "Do abused children become abusive parents?" and ask, instead, "Under what conditions is the transmission of abuse likely to occur?"

Although a 30% transmission rate is not even the majority of abused children becoming abusers, the rate of abuse among formerly abused children is considerably higher than the overall societal rate of between 2% and 3%. Nevertheless, the intergenerational transmission theory is often simplistically presented and viewed as a single-cause, deterministic explanation for abuse. A more sophisticated, multidimensional model of abuse is needed to explain child abuse.

Is Child Abuse Overreported?

Thirty years ago, after the publication of Kempe and his colleagues' (1962) article on the battered child syndrome, considerable effort was put into establishing mandatory child abuse reporting laws. The assumption behind these laws was that child abuse was detected but not reported to child welfare agencies by physicians, psychologists, teachers, and those in contact with children. If abuse was detected, those who suspected abuse were reluctant to report cases for fear of legal problems arising out of allegations of false reports. Mandatory reporting laws provided legal protection for those making reports of suspected abuse and thus were thought to motivate professionals and the public alike to report child maltreatment cases to child protection agencies.

Those who framed the early reporting laws assumed that child abuse could be accurately detected and that children would be better served if their abuse were reported to appropriate and well-trained professionals.

Over the last 30 years, the definition of maltreatment in mandatory reporting laws has been broadened, more groups and individuals have been mandated as reporters, and the laws have been strengthened by implementing penalties for failure to report and protections against accusations of false reporting. Not a surprise, the number of reports has increased dramatically. Douglas Besharov (1985, 1990) argues that child abuse is now "overreported." Too many false or inaccurate reports are received. These reports consume considerable time and resources of child protection agencies and reduce the time and attention that could be provided to valid and serious cases of abuse.

David Finkelhor (1990) believes that there is no reliable empirical evidence to support the claim that abuse is overreported. Not only is there a question about whether there are too many reports of child abuse, but there is also the question of whether such reports are biased. A third perspective is offered by the pediatrician Eli Newberger (1985), who notes that poor and minority individuals are more likely to be accurately and inaccurately reported for child maltreatment, while more affluent families who abuse their children often escape detection. Thus Newberger avoids the debate about overreporting and argues that the entire child protection system is biased against lower-class and minority families and thus fails to meet its overall objectives of providing protection to all maltreated children.

Are Child Sexual Abuse Prevention Programs Effective?

With the discovery of the extent of sexual abuse, there was considerable effort put into developing sexual abuse prevention programs. Many programs were developed and implemented in schools and aimed at school-aged populations. Program developers felt that school-aged children were the most vulnerable to sexual exploitation and sexual abuse and that abuse could be prevented if children knew how to identify and thwart attempts to sexually victimize them. Although a massive number of publications have extolled the effectiveness of school-based prevention programs, some critics, such as N. Dickon Reppucci and Jeffrey Haugaard (1989), argue that the available evidence indicates only limited support for the efficacy of sexual abuse prevention programs. While there is evidence for some statistically significant improvements, such as more assertive actions by children when approached by strangers, as a result of the programs, Reppucci argues that increases are slight.

The Battered Woman Syndrome: Are Battered Women Helpless?

A cornerstone of early research on wife abuse is Lenore Walker's (1979) conceptualization of the battered woman syndrome and the notion that women who are battered suffer from "learned helplessness." Both conceptualizations are significant elements of the "battered woman defense" offered to explain why some women kill their husbands in self-defense. In addition, the notion of the battered woman's syndrome and "learned helplessness" has been used to explain why battered women choose to remain with abusive husbands. There are some questions about whether the syndrome exists, whether battered women do indeed suffer from "learned helplessness," and whether these conceptualizations paint an inaccurate picture of helpless women. Gelles and Straus (1988) found that the vast majority of women who were assaulted by their husbands had left their homes for some period of time. The typical battered wife is hardly passive; she actively seeks to prevent further victimization and is handicapped not by her own psychological limitations but by the lack of concrete and effective remedies available from agencies of social control and other social institutions.

Does Mandatory Arrest Deter Wife Abusers?

Twenty years ago, the typical police response to domestic assault was either indifference or attempts to calm the situation down, either by removing the offender or by counseling the offender and the victim. A field experiment conducted by Lawrence Sherman and Richard Berk (1984) helped change the way police departments handle domestic assault. Sherman and Berk (1984) found that, when police randomly assigned one of three interventions—(a) arrest, (b) separation, or (c) mediation—the arrest intervention resulted in the lowest recidivism rate. Arrested husbands were least likely to be violent again compared with husbands who were separated or husbands with whom the police mediated. The results of the Sherman and Berk study, along with a successful and a costly lawsuit by a battered woman against the Torrington, Connecticut, Police Department (*Thurman v. City of Torrington,* 1985), resulted in hundreds of police departments across the country adopting mandatory arrest or presumptive arrest policies for misdemeanor-level domestic assault. Mandatory arrest policies require police to arrest the offender for misdemeanor assault, while presumptive policies allow the police to make an arrest without a complaint by the victim (felony assault cases allow police to make arrests without complaints).

It seemed, for the moment, that an effective broad-based prevention policy had been found that would reduce the toll of wife abuse. Subsequent to the Sherman and Berk study, however, the National Institute of Justice funded six replications of the original study. The results of the replications challenge the findings from the Minneapolis experiments. In two locations, exact replication of the original study failed to find a deterrent value in arresting assaultive husbands (Dunford, Huizinga, & Elliott, 1990; Hirschell, Hutchinson, & Dean, 1990). In another city, arrest deterred only those men who were employed (Sherman et al., 1991). Thus arrest, in and of itself, does not appear to be a magic bullet that can prevent a substantial proportion of wife abuse. On the other hand, arrest appears to be no less effective than other forms of police intervention.

Summary

One overriding factor that influences the study and consideration of family violence is the emotional nature of both research and practice. Few other areas of inquiry and practice generate the strong feelings and reactions that child abuse, child sexual abuse, wife abuse, elder abuse, and courtship violence generate. Even the most grotesque case examples fail to adequately capture the devastating physical and psychological consequences of physical abuse. Clinicians not only must face difficult and complex cases, but they often are frustrated by the inadequate conceptual, clinical, and service resources they can bring to bear on behalf of victims, offenders, and/or families. Amidst the emotional and frustrating nature of research and clinical work with violent families, there is a tendency to look for and latch onto simple explanations and solutions.

There are no simple answers or "cheap fixes." The relative recency of family violence as an area of study, and the fact that the first decade of research was dominated by a psychopathology model of the causation, has resulted in the limited level of theoretical development of the field. Yet, despite the rather primitive level of theory building and theory testing, one conclusion is inescapable: No one factor can explain the presence or absence of family violence. Characteristics of the child, parent, family, social situation, and community are related to which children are abused and under what conditions. Individual emotional states of caretakers, psychological characteristics, and community factors, such as cultural attitudes regarding violence, are moderated and influenced by family structure and family situations. Although there are indeed multiple factors related to abuse of children, all operate through the structure and function of the family group. In addition, power and control are common features of nearly all forms of family violence, especially violence and abuse of women. Thus interventions and prevention efforts need to be aimed at both the importance of control and power and the functions of the family system if family violence is to be effectively treated and prevented.

Currently, the vast majority of programs, such as shelters, crisis day-care centers, police intervention programs, and parent support groups, aimed at dealing with family violence are treatment programs that are implemented *after* the abusive incident. What are needed, and what have not been attempted on any large scale, are services that would prevent violence and abuse before they begin. But such prevention programs require sweeping changes in both the society and the family. After the conclusion of our national survey of family violence, Murray Straus, Suzanne Steinmetz, and I proposed the following steps for the *prevention of violence*:

1. Eliminate the norms that legitimize and glorify violence in the society and the family. The elimination of spanking as a child-rearing technique, the institution of gun control to get deadly weapons out of the home, the elimination of the death penalty and corporal punishment in schools, and the elimination of media violence that glorifies and legitimizes violence are all necessary steps.

2. Reduce violence-provoking stress created by society. Reducing poverty, inequality, and unemployment and providing for adequate housing, feeding, medical and dental care, and educational opportunities are steps that could reduce stress in families.

3. Integrate families into a network of kin and community. Reducing social isolation would be a significant step that would help reduce stress and increase the abilities of families to manage stress.

4. Change the sexist character of society. Sexual inequality, perhaps more than economic inequality, makes violence possible in homes. The elimination of men's work and women's work would be a major step toward equality in and out of the home.

5. Break the cycle of violence in the family. This step repeats the message of Step 1: Violence cannot be prevented as long as we are taught that it is appropriate to hit the people we love. Physical punishment of children is perhaps the most effective means of teaching violence, and eliminating it would be an important step in violence prevention.

These proposals call for such fundamental changes in society and family life that many people resist them and argue that they could not work. But not making such changes continues the harmful and deadly tradition of family violence.

Notes

1. For a complete review of the methodological and design issues in the study of family violence, see Gelles (1989) and Weis (1989).

2. For a complete examination of both sides of these and other controversies, see Gelles and Loseke (1993).

References

American Association for Protecting Children. (1988). *Highlights of official child neglect and abuse reporting, 1986.* Denver, CO: American Humane Association.

American Association for Protecting Children. (1989). *Highlights of official child neglect and abuse reporting, 1987.* Denver, CO: American Humane Association.

Belsky, J. (1980). Child maltreatment: An ecological integration. *American Psychologist, 35,* 320-335.

Berk, R. A., Berk, S. F., Loseke, D. R., & Rauma, D. (1983). Mutual combat and other family violence myths. In D. Finkelhor, R. Gelles, M. Straus, & G. Hotaling (Eds.), *The dark side of the families: Current family violence research* (pp. 197-212). Beverly Hills, CA: Sage.

Besharov, D. (1985). Right versus rights: The dilemma of child protection. *Public Welfare, 43,* 19-46.

Besharov, D. (1990). *Recognizing child abuse: A guide for the concerned.* New York: Free Press.

Burgdorf, K. (1980). *Recognition and reporting of child maltreatment.* Rockville, MD: Westat.

Burgess, R. L. (1979, April). *Family violence: Some implications from evolutionary biology.* Paper presented at the annual meetings of the American Society of Criminology, Philadelphia.

Burgess, R. L., & Draper, P. (1989). The explanation of family violence: The role of biological, behavioral, and cultural selection. In L. Ohlin & M. Tonry (Eds.), *Family violence: Crime and justice: A review of research* (Vol. 11, pp. 59-116). Chicago: University of Chicago Press.

Burgess, R. L., & Garbarino, J. (1983). Doing what comes naturally? An evolutionary perspective on child abuse. In D. Finkelhor, R. Gelles, M. Straus, & G. Hotaling (Eds.), *The dark side of the families: Current family violence research* (pp. 88-101). Beverly Hills, CA: Sage.

Caffey, J. (1946). Multiple fractures in the long bones of infants suffering from chronic subdural hematoma. *American Journal of Roentgenology, Radium Therapy, and Nuclear Medicine, 58,* 163-173.

Cate, R. M., Henton, J. M., Christopher, F. S., & Lloyd, S. (1982). Premarital abuse: A social psychological perspective. *Journal of Family Issues, 3,* 79-90.

Daly, M., & Wilson, M. (1980). Discriminative parental solicitude: A biosocial perspective. *Journal of Marriage and the Family, 42,* 277-288.

Daly, M., & Wilson, M. (1985). Child abuse and other risks of not living with both parents. *Ethology and Sociobiology, 6,* 197-210.

Daly, M., & Wilson, M. (1988). *Homicide.* New York: Aldine de Gruyter.

Davidson, T. (1978). *Conjugal crime: Understanding and changing the wifebeating pattern.* New York: Hawthorn.

Dobash, R. E., & Dobash, R. (1979). *Violence against wives.* New York: Free Press.

Dunford, F. W., Huizinga, D., & Elliott, D. S. (1990). The role of arrest in domestic assault: The Omaha Police Experiment. *Criminology, 28,* 183-206.

Finkelhor, D. (1990). Is child abuse overreported? The data rebut arguments for less intervention. *Public Welfare, 48,* 23-29.

Finkelhor, D., & Hotaling, G. (1984). Sexual abuse in the national incidence study of child abuse and neglect: An appraisal. *Child Abuse Neglect: The International Journal, 8,* 23-33.

Garbarino, J. (1977). The human ecology of child maltreatment. *Journal of Marriage and the Family, 39,* 721-735.

Gelles, R. J. (1974). *The violent home: A study of physical aggression between husbands and wives.* Beverly Hills, CA: Sage.

Gelles, R. J. (1983). An exchange/social control theory. In D. Finkelhor, R. Gelles, M. Straus, & G. Hotaling (Eds.), *The dark side of families: Current family violence research* (pp. 151-165). Beverly Hills, CA: Sage.

Gelles, R. J. (1989). Methodological issues in the study of domestic violence. In G. R. Patterson (Ed.), *Depression and aggression in family interaction* (pp. 49-74). Hillsdale, NJ: Lawrence Erlbaum.

Gelles, R. J., & Loseke, D. R. (1993). *Current controversies on family violence.* Newbury Park, CA: Sage.

Gelles, R. J., & Straus, M. A. (1988). *Intimate violence.* New York: Simon & Schuster.

Giles-Sims, J. (1983). *Wife-beating: A systems theory approach.* New York: Guilford.

Goode, W. (1971). Force and violence in the family. *Journal of Marriage and the Family, 33,* 624-636.

Gordon, L. (1988). *Heroes of their own lives: The politics and history of family violence.* New York: Viking.

Greven, P. (1991). *Spare the child: The religious roots of punishment and the psychological impact of physical abuse.* New York: Knopf.

Henton, J. M., Cate, R. M., Koval, J., Lloyd, S., & Christopher, F. S. (1983). Romance and violence in dating relationships. *Journal of Family Issues, 4,* 467-482.

Hirschell, J. D., Hutchinson, I. W., III, & Dean, C. W. (1990). The failure of arrest to deter spouse abuse. *Journal of Research in Crime and Delinquency, 29,* 7-33.

Hrdy, S. B. (1979). Infanticide among animals: A review classification, and examination of the implications for reproductive strategies of females. *Ethology and Sociobiology, 1,* 13-40.

Kaufman, J., & Zigler, E. (1987). Do abused children become abusive parents? *American Journal of Orthopsychiatry, 57,* 186-192.

Kempe, C., Silverman, F. N., Steele, B. F., Droegemueller, W., & Silver, H. K. (1962). The battered-child syndrome. *Journal of the American Medical Association, 181,* 17-24.

Kilpatrick, D. G., Best, C. L., Saunders, B. E., & Veronen, L. J. (1988). Rape in marriage and dating relationships: How bad is it for mental health? *Annals of the New York Academy of Sciences, 528,* 335-344.

Makepeace, J. M. (1981). Courtship violence among college students. *Family Relations, 30,* 97-102.

Makepeace, J. M. (1983). Life events stress and courtship violence. *Family Relations, 32,* 101-109.

National Center on Child Abuse and Neglect. (1988). *Study findings: Study of national incidence and prevalence of child abuse and neglect: 1988.* Washington, DC: U.S. Department of Health and Human Services.

Nelson, B. J. (1984). *Making an issue of child abuse: Political agenda setting for social problems.* Chicago: University of Chicago Press.

Newberger, E. H. (1985). The helping hand strikes again: Unintended consequences of child abuse reporting. In E. H. Newberger & R. Bourne (Eds.), *Unhappy families,* pp. 171-178. Littleton, MA: PSG Publishing.

Okun, L. (1986). *Women abuse: Facts replacing myths.* Albany: State University of New York Press.

Pagelow, M. (1981). *Women battering: Victims and their experiences.* Beverly Hills, CA: Sage.

Pagelow, M. (1984). *Family violence.* New York: Praeger.

Pillemer, K., & Finkelhor, D. (1988). The prevalence of elder abuse: A random sample survey. *The Gerontologist, 28,* 51-57.

Pleck, F. (1987). *Domestic tyranny: The making of American social policy against family violence from colonial times to the present.* New York: Oxford University Press.

Pleck, E., Pleck, J. H., Grossman, M., & Bart, P. B. (1977-1978). The battered data syndrome: A comment on Steinmetz's article. *Victimology, 3-4,* 680-683.

Radbill, S. A. (1980). A history of child abuse and infanticide. In R. Helfer & C. Kempe (Eds.), *The battered child* (3rd ed., pp. 3-20). Chicago: University of Chicago Press.

Reppucci, N. D., & Haugaard, J. J. (1989). Prevention of child sexual abuse: Myth or reality. *American Psychologist, 44,* 1266-1275.

Robin, M. (1982). Historical introduction: Sheltering arms: The roots of child protection. In E. H. Newberger (Ed.), *Child abuse* (pp. 10-41). Boston: Little, Brown.

Russell, D. (1984). *Sexual exploitation: Rape, child sexual abuse, and workplace harassment.* Beverly Hills, CA: Sage.

Shainess, N. (1979). Vulnerability to violence: Masochism as process. *American Journal of Psychotherapy, 33,* 174-189.

Sherman, L. W., & Berk, R. A. (1984). The specific deterrent effects of arrest for domestic assault. *American Sociological Review, 49,* 261-272.

Sherman, L. W., Schmidt, J. D., Rogan, D. R., Gartin, P. R., Cohn, E. G., Collins, D., & Bacich, A. (1991). From initial deterrence to long-term escalation: Short-custody arrest for poverty ghetto domestic violence. *Criminology, 29,* 821-850.

Smuts, B. (1992). Male aggression against women: An evolutionary perspective. *Human Nature, 3,* 1-44.

Snell, J., Rosenwald, R., & Robey, A. (1964). The wifebeater's wife: A study of family interaction. *Archives of General Psychiatry, 11,* 107-113.

Stark, E., & Flitcraft, A. (1983). Social knowledge, social policy, and the abuse of women: The case against patriarchal benevolence. In D. Finkelhor, R. Gelles, M. Straus, & G. Hotaling (Eds.), *The dark side of families: Current family violence research* (pp. 330-348). Beverly Hills, CA: Sage.

Steinmetz, S. K. (1977-1978). The battered husband syndrome. *Victimology, 2,* 499-509.

Stets, J., & Straus, M. A. (1990). Gender differences in reporting marital violence and its medical and psychological consequences. In M. A. Straus & R. J. Gelles (Eds.), *Physical violence in American families: Risk factors and adaptations in 8,145 families* (pp. 501-514). New Brunswick, NJ: Transaction.

Straus, M. A. (1973). A general systems theory approach to a theory of violence between family members. *Social Science Information, 12,* 105-125.

Straus, M. A. (1977-1978). Wife beating: How common and why? *Victimology, 2,* 443-458.

Straus, M. A. (1990). The Conflict Tactics Scales and its critics: An evaluation and new data on validity and reliability. In M. A. Straus & R. J. Gelles (Eds.), *Physical violence in American families: Risk factors and adaptations in 8,145 families* (pp. 49-73). New Brunswick, NJ: Transaction.

Straus, M. A. (1992). Sociological research and social policy: The case of family violence. *Sociological Forum, 7,* 211-237.

Straus, M. A., & Gelles, R. J. (1986). Societal change and change in family violence from 1975 to 1985 as revealed in two national surveys. *Journal of Marriage and the Family, 48,* 465-479.

Straus, M. A., Gelles, R. J., & Steinmetz, S. K. (1980). *Behind closed doors: Violence in the American family.* New York: Anchor/Doubleday.

Thurman v. City of Torrington, 595 F. Supp. 1521 (USDC, No. H-84-120, June 25, 1985).

U.S. Department of Justice. (1980). *Intimate victims: A study of violence among friends and relatives.* Washington, DC: Government Printing Office.

U.S. Department of Justice. (1984). *Family violence.* Washington, DC: Bureau of Justice Statistics.

Walker, L. E. (1979). *The battered woman.* New York: Harper & Row.

Weis, J. G. (1989). Family violence research methodology and design. In L. Ohlin & M. Tonry (Eds.), *Family violence* (pp. 117-162). Chicago: University of Chicago Press.

Widom, C. S. (1988). Sampling biases and implications for child abuse research. *American Journal of Orthopsychiatry, 58,* 260-270.

Woolley, P., & Evans, W. (1955). Significance of skeletal lesions resembling those of traumatic origin. *Journal of the American Medical Association, 158,* 539-543.

Yllö, K. (1983). Using a feminist approach in quantitative research. In D. Finkelhor, R. Gelles, M. Straus, & G. Hotaling (Eds.), *The dark side of families: Current family violence research* (pp. 277-288). Beverly Hills, CA: Sage.

Yllö, K. (1988). Political and methodological debates in wife abuse research. In K. Yllö & M. Bograd (Eds.), *Feminist perspectives on wife abuse* (pp. 28-50). Newbury Park, CA: Sage.

CHAPTER 2

Physical Child Abuse

JOEL S. MILNER

JULIE L. CROUCH

This chapter, which provides an introduction to the topic of physical child abuse, begins with a description of explanatory models and theories. The discussion of models builds on the more general theoretical overview presented in Chapter 1. Two organizational models and several recent etiological models specific to physical child abuse are summarized. The discussion of models concludes with the application of a human information processing model to physical child abuse. Throughout this chapter, an emphasis is placed on child abuse models because of their importance as conceptual frameworks for research and treatment.

Following the discussion of models, a representative literature review is provided. Physical child abuse factors from different ecological levels (e.g., perpetrator, family, and society) are described. While the review reveals varying levels of support for the different physical child abuse models, the review does indicate that multiple factors from different ecological levels contribute to child abuse. The last major section describes the effects of physical child abuse. In the description of victim effects, an attempt is made to place the reported consequences of abuse in

AUTHORS' NOTE: Preparation of this chapter was supported in part by National Institute of Mental Health Grant MH 34252 to Joel S. Milner. Correspondence concerning this chapter should be addressed to Joel S. Milner, Family Violence Research Program, Department of Psychology, Northern Illinois University, DeKalb, IL 60115-2892.

a developmental context. This orientation emphasizes the possibility that physical child abuse may have different short- and long-term consequences as a function of the child's developmental level at the time of the assault.

Theoretical Considerations

Numerous models have been developed to describe factors that contribute to physical child abuse. Examples of different models are presented in Table 2.1 and additional discussions of these and other models are available elsewhere (e.g., Azar, 1991; Tzeng, Jackson, & Karlson, 1991). One early model had its beginnings in an article by Kempe, Silverman, Steele, Droegemueller, and Silver (1962), which described the clinical characteristics of physical child abuse. As part of this description, Kempe et al. listed psychiatric characteristics believed to be common to perpetrators. These descriptions formed the basis for what today is referred to as the psychiatric model of physical child abuse.

Although subsequent research has supported the view that perpetrators vary on a variety of psychological dimensions, less than 10% of all physical child abusers have psychiatric disturbances. An early competing perspective is found in the sociological model promulgated by Gil (1970). This model was radically different than the psychiatric approach because it focused on sociological factors (e.g., economic conditions, societal values, social systems), instead of perpetrator factors, as causing physical child abuse.

A limitation of these early models is that they only included factors from single domains or ecological levels (i.e., individual, society). In addition, the psychiatric and sociological models were unidirectional and hence did not allow for the possibility of interactions between putative causal factors. In response to these problems, a number of authors developed multidomain, multifactor interactional models.

Early interactional models were organizational models that were guides to the domains of factors thought to be important in the description and explanation of physical child abuse. Two of the best known and most useful organizational models, the ecological model and the transactional model, are described in the next section. Following the description of these organiza-

Table 2.1 Examples of Physical Child Abuse Models/Theories

Early Single Factor Models:
    Psychiatric Model (Kempe et al., 1962)
    Sociological Model (Gil, 1970; Giovannoni & Billingsley, 1970)

Early Multifactor Organizational Models:
    Three-Component Theory (Schneider et al., 1972)
    Social-Psychological Theory (Gelles, 1973)
    Social-Situational Model (Parke & Collmer, 1975)
    Symbiosis Theory (Justice & Justice, 1976)
    Social-Interaction Theory (Burgess, 1979)
    Ecological Model (Belsky, 1980)
    Transactional Model (Cicchetti & Rizley, 1981)

Biological Models:
    Sociobiological Theory (Burgess & Garbarino, 1983; Daly & Wilson, 1981)
    Neuropsychological Theory (Elliott, 1988)

Learning Models:
    Two-Factor Theory (Vasta, 1982)
    Social Learning Theory (Tzeng et al., 1991)

Social/Cultural Models:
    Resource Theory (Goode, 1971)
    Culture Theory (Gelles & Straus, 1979)
    Social Systems Theory (Gil, 1987)

Interactional Models:
    Family Systems Theory (Straus, 1973)
    Choice Theory (Nye & McDonald, 1979)
    General Stress Theory (Farrington, 1980, 1986)
    Three Factor Theory (Lesnik-Oberstein et al., 1982)
    Situational Theory (Wiggins, 1983)
    Cognitive Developmental Model (Newberger & Cook, 1983)
    Encounter Theory (Zimrin, 1984)
    Cognitive Behavioral Model (Twentyman et al., 1984)
    Coercion Theory (Stringer & LaGreca, 1985)
    Social Cognitive Model (Azar, 1986, 1989; Azar & Siegal, 1990)
    Attachment Theory (Aber & Allen, 1987; Egeland & Erickson, 1987)
    Transitional Model (Wolfe, 1987)
    Social Information Processing Model (Milner, in press)

tional models, several current models that attempt to provide additional specification of variables that contribute to physical child abuse are described. Although much progress has been made, it should be noted that the field still lacks adequately validated models of physical child abuse.

Organizational Models

Ecological Model

Belsky (1980) has provided a comprehensive ecological model of physical child abuse. This organizational model describes the ecological levels thought to be important in understanding physical child abuse. Belsky's model, which is an extension of Bronfenbrenner's (1977) ecological model of human development, contains four domains or categories of factors. These domains include individual factors (ontogenic level), family factors (microsystem level), community factors (exosystem level), and cultural factors (marcosystem level). Although this model does not describe which specific factors cause physical child abuse, the model is important because it organizes the different domains of contributing factors and expands the focus of previous models.

Transactional Model

Building on an awareness that factors from different ecological levels contribute to physical child abuse, Cicchetti and Rizley (1981) provided an organizational model that included both contributing and protective factors at three ecological levels. In the transactional model, factors are classified along two dimensions. The first dimension describes two major types of influence on the likelihood of child abuse: potentiating or compensatory. The second dimension describes the temporal nature of the influence: transient or enduring.

Potentiating and compensatory conditions are combined with transient and enduring conditions so that four types of factors are defined. Potentiating factors that are transient are called *challengers,* whereas potentiating factors that are enduring are referred to as *vulnerability* factors. Compensatory factors that are transient are labeled *buffers,* while compensatory factors that are enduring are viewed as *protective* factors.

These four types of factors are thought to exist at the individual, family, and societal levels. Factors from each ecological level are believed to be bidirectional and interactive. In the simplest application of this model, physical child abuse is predicted to occur when potentiating conditions override compensatory conditions.

Examples of Recent Models

Three recent models of physical child abuse are summarized in this section. The first model, the transitional model, provides a description of the development of parent-child conflict through three stages and includes potentiating and compensatory factors from several ecological levels. The second model, a cognitive-behavioral model, describes with greater specificity perpetrator and child-related factors that are thought to cause physical child abuse. The third model, a social information processing model, provides a greater focus on factors within the abusive parent and presents a framework for developing more specificity in explaining perpetrator-related cognitive factors that contribute to physical child abuse.

Transitional Model

Wolfe (1987) has proposed a transitional model that describes how severe parent-child conflict, including physical child abuse, develops. Within this model, stress is viewed as a key element that serves to increase the likelihood of conflict within the family system. The transitional model is composed of three stages and includes multiple destabilizing and compensatory factors. The stages are not discrete but overlap and represent an ongoing development of parent-child conflict.

Stage one describes factors that contribute to a reduction in the parent's stress tolerance and ability to inhibit aggression. Destabilizing factors include the presence of stressful life events and inadequate preparation for parenting. Parental behaviors at this stage represent marginal attempts to cope with life's stressors and to manage his or her child's noncompliant behaviors. Compensatory factors include economic stability and social supports, which can moderate the impact of stress.

Stage two begins when the parent significantly fails to manage life stress and his or her child's behavior. During this stage, the parent becomes increasingly reactive to stressful events, attributes responsibility for negative behavior to the child, views the child as deliberately defiant, and perceives a loss of control. Stage two occurs when stressful life events and limited coping skills result in abusive parenting. Compensatory factors at this stage include parental acquisition of new coping skills and improvements in the child's behavior.

Stage three describes the situation where the parent develops patterns of continuous arousal and physical child abuse. During this period, the parent is confronted with multiple stressful stimuli and is ineffective in coping with these stressful events. The pattern of arousal and blaming the child is more frequent. Feelings of hopelessness may appear. The parent increases the intensity and frequency of his or her aggressive behavior in an attempt to regain control. Compensatory factors at this stage include the parent developing dissatisfaction with the increasingly severe physical punishment, child compliance following nonaversive discipline, and community intervention. At stage three, however, compensatory factors are viewed as having a minimal impact on the habitual pattern of child abuse that has developed.

Cognitive-Behavioral Model

Twentyman and his associates (e.g., Morton, Twentyman, & Azar, 1988; Twentyman, Rohrbeck, & Amish, 1984) have proposed a four-stage cognitive-behavioral model of physical child abuse. Key elements of this model are unrealistic parental expectations and misattributions of negative intent, which are viewed as mediators of abusive behavior. In stage one, the parent develops and maintains unrealistic expectations of the child. In stage two, the child behaves in a manner inconsistent with the parent's expectations. In stage three, the parent misattributes the child's behavior to negative intent (e.g., desire to annoy the parent) on the part of the child. In stage four, the parent overreacts and engages in excessive and severe punishment of the child.

Azar (1986, 1989) has expanded the original conceptualization of the cognitive-behavioral model by suggesting additional deficits in three core areas: parental cognitions, parental impulse control, and parent-child interactions. The levels of family stress and social support are also seen as important factors. Further, Azar and Siegal (1990) have recently argued that physical child abuse, which occurs at different stages in the child's development, may not always be associated with the same perpetrator deficits. For example, unrealistic expectations may be a significant perpetrator deficit during any developmental period, while a lack of certain parenting skills (e.g., reasoning and explaining) may be more detrimental at specific developmental stages (e.g., adolescence).

Social Information Processing Model

Although not designed to explain physical child abuse, a social skills model described by McFall (1982) has been used to guide the development of a social information processing model of physical child abuse (Milner, in press). The application of a social skills model to physical child abuse is intended to increase our understanding of physical child abuse perpetrator cognitions and their relationship to parental behavior. Three cognitive stages of social information processing are described, which lead to a fourth cognitive/behavioral stage of response execution. The three cognitive stages include *perceptions* of social behavior; *interpretations, evaluations,* and *expectations* that give meaning to social behavior; and the *response selection* process. The fourth stage involves *response implementation* and *monitoring.* Each stage of this social information model is believed to be affected by preexisting cognitive schema, involving beliefs and values held by the parent.

Stage one (perceptions) of this social information processing model states that abusers, compared with nonabusers, have perceptual distortions and biases in the representation of the child and the child's behavior. It is proposed that physical child abusers tend to be less attentive and/or are less aware of social events in their environment. With respect to situational factors, it is proposed that abusers experience more distress, which negatively affects their perceptions.

Stage two (interpretations, evaluations, and expectations) of the model states that abusers, compared with nonabusers, display differences in their interpretations and evaluations of children's behavior and expectations of children's compliance. Abusers interpret noncompliant child behavior as having more hostile intent and evaluate the behavior as being more wrong or blameworthy. Abusers also make inaccurate predictions of child compliance following different types of transgressions and disciplinary techniques. As predicted for perceptions at stage one, interpretations, evaluations, and expectations are believed to become more distorted and biased as distress levels increase.

Stage three (response selection) of the model states that abusers, compared with nonabusers, process information differently, which affects their response choice. This processing difference is viewed as a contributing factor to the response selection decision, separate from the contributions of distorted and biased cognitions. It is proposed that abusers are less likely to use situational information in their evaluation of children's behavior. Thus, even if social information is perceived and interpreted correctly, the abuser tends to ignore important information during this processing stage. For example, an abusive parent may be aware of mitigating events related to a child's transgression, but, because of his or her processing style, the mitigating information (e.g., big brother bumped little Johnny and caused Johnny to spill the milk) has less impact on the parent's disciplinary decision. This processing style allows the abuser to maintain explanations of the child's behavior that are consistent with his or her own rigidly held cognitive distortions and biases, which justify more power-assertive behavior. Finally, but most important, the response selection process is limited by the number and types of response choices that are available. Parental skill deficits obviously set limits on the response choice outcome.

Stage four (response implementation and monitoring) describes the parent's ability to adequately implement a parenting skill and the associated ability to monitor and modify his or her behavior as needed. Numerous factors may affect the parent's ability to implement and monitor his or her behavior. For example, cognitive factors (e.g., such as expectations of child noncompliance) may reduce the likelihood that a disciplinary technique will be carefully implemented or monitored by the parent. Further, higher levels of parental distress can negatively affect the parent's ability to implement or continue a disciplinary strategy (such as explaining to a child). Failure to achieve child compliance as a result of the parental behavior used at this stage serves to confirm the parent's biases and distortions, increasing the likelihood that power-assertion techniques will be used in the future.

The question remains as to where this social information processing style and cycle originate. While data are generally lacking, this style may originate as a consequence of early social learning. Chilamkurti and Milner (in press) demonstrated that several of the cognitive biases and distortions described in the social information processing model exist in high risk parents, compared with low risk parents; further, children in each risk group displayed cognitive styles similar to their respective parents. Thus parental cognitions may be passed on to the children and may mediate, in part, the intergenerational transmission of abuse. Finally, to adequately explain physical child abuse, the social information processing model must be embedded in a comprehensive model that includes contributing and compensatory factors from other ecological levels.

Selected Review of the Physical Child Abuse Literature

As previously noted, models of physical child abuse tend to be either broad organizational models or relatively specific explanatory models limited to a few constructs. The following review uses the broader perspective of the organizational models to provide a multidomain focus for the summary of the physical child abuse literature. As outlined in Table 2.2, this review will describe perpetrator, family, and sociological characteristics believed to be associated with the physical abuse of children.

Perpetrator Characteristics

Biological factors. The role of perpetrator neurological and neuropsychological factors in physical child abuse remains unclear. To date, there has been little research on the topic, and extant research has not demonstrated a casual relationship between neurological and neuropsychological factors and physical child abuse. Elliott (1988), nevertheless, has indicated that abusers' "neurological handicaps" have been overlooked. Elliott believes that "patchy" cognitive deficits (e.g., limited vocabulary and slowness of thought), related to minimal brain dysfunction, decrease parents' ability to adequately cope with family- and child-related problems, increasing the likelihood of physical child abuse. In addition, Milner and McCanne (1991) speculated that in some cases a childhood history of physical assault may

Table 2.2 Examples of Perpetrator, Family, and Sociological Characteristics

Perpetrator Characteristics:
    Biological factors
        neurological and neuropsychological factors
        physiological reactivity
        physical health problems
    Cognitive/affective characteristics
        self-esteem and ego strength
        perceptions, attributions, and evaluations of child behavior
        expectations of child behavior
        life stress/distress
        depression
        other psychological factors
    Behavioral characteristics
        alcohol and drug use
        social isolation
        parent-child interactions
        parental disciplinary strategies
        inadequate coping skills
Family Characteristics:
        conflict, little support in family of origin
        marital discord
        poor communication skills
        verbal and physical conflict
        value the use of force
        lack of cohesion
        isolation
        child factors
Sociological Characteristics:
    Perpetrator demographics
        nonbiological parent
        single parent
        age
        education level
        childhood history of abuse
    Family demographic characteristics
        lack of resources
        large number of children
    Social isolation
    Multiple environmental stressors
    Culturally sanctioned use of force

produce neurological and neuropsychological deficits that contribute to the intergenerational transmission of physical child

abuse. Additional discussions of the possible role of neurological and neuropsychological factors in physical child abuse are provided elsewhere (e.g., Elliott, 1988; Milner & McCanne, 1991).

Compared with the information available on neurological and neuropsychological characteristics, more data are available on psychophysiological differences between abusers and nonabusers. On the theoretical level, Knutson (1978) has suggested that abusers have a hyperreactive trait. Supporting this view, Wolfe, Fairbank, Kelly, and Bradlyn (1983) found that abusers had large increases in skin conductance and respiration rates in response to both stressful and nonstressful mother-child interactional scenes. Frodi and Lamb (1980) found that abusers, relative to nonabusers, were more physiologically reactive to a crying child. Further, abusers showed physiological reactivity to a smiling child, while nonabusers did not, leading Frodi and Lamb to conclude that the abusers found both the crying and the smiling child aversive. Similar increased physiological reactivity to crying (Crowe & Zeskind, 1992; Pruitt & Erickson, 1985) and smiling (Pruitt & Erickson, 1985) infants has been reported in high risk, childless adults, which suggests that some adults may enter the parent-child relationship with increased autonomic reactivity to child stimuli. One recent study supports the view that high risk parents also show increased reactivity to non-child-related stimuli. Casanova, Domanic, McCanne, and Milner (1992) found greater and more prolonged physiological reactivity in high risk parents, compared with low risk parents, following the presentation of two different stressful non-child-related stimuli.

Despite study limitations and inconsistent results, most investigators conclude that abusers show increased physiological reactivity to child-related stimuli. Even if these conclusions are valid, it still must be demonstrated that the autonomic changes are causally related to physical child abuse. Further, if autonomic changes are causally related to abuse, the manner in which they interact with other variables must be determined.

Although infrequently studied, several researchers indicate that perpetrators, compared with nonabusers, have more physical handicaps and health problems (Conger, Burgess, & Barrett, 1979; Lahey, Conger, Atkeson, & Treiber, 1984). Abusers also report more physical handicaps and health problems on the Child Abuse Potential Inventory (Milner, 1986). The extent to which these physical concerns are real or perceived, however, needs further investigation. Steele and Pollock (1974) report that abusers suffer from more psychosomatic illnesses; thus reported health complaints may be associated with other psychological conditions.

Cognitive/affective factors. As a group, physical child abusers have low self-esteem and poor ego strength (e.g., Friedrich & Wheeler, 1982; Milner, 1988). Low self-esteem has been linked to negative parental perceptions of child behavior (e.g., Mash, Johnston, & Kovitz, 1983) and to an inability to cope with stress (e.g., McCubbin, Cauble, & Patterson, 1982). Other research indicates that physically abusive parents have negative perceptions of their children, including the perception that their children are intentionally disruptive, disobedient (e.g., Helfer, McKinney, & Kempe, 1976; Wood-Shuman & Cone, 1986), and annoying (Bauer & Twentyman, 1985). Two recent studies found that abusers rate their children as more problematic (Mash et al., 1983), as being more aggressive, as having more conduct disorders, as being more active, and as having less intellectual ability (Reid, Kavanagh, & Baldwin, 1987) than comparison children. In these two studies, however, independent raters did not observe the differences reported by the abusive parents, suggesting an abuser evaluation bias.

Differences in attributions have been reported for abusive parents. Physically abusive parents perceive their children's negative behavior as due to internal and stable factors and their children's positive behavior as due to external and unstable factors (Larrance & Twentyman, 1983). Comparison parents display the opposite attributional style. With respect to the evaluation of wrongness, high risk parents, relative to low risk parents, have been reported to assign a greater degree of wrongness to child transgressions overall and to minor transgressions in particular (Chilamkurti & Milner, 1991).

Abusive and high risk parents have also been observed to have more unrealistic expectations of their children. The literature suggests that in some cases child expectations are too high and in other cases expectations are too low (Kravitz & Driscoll, 1983; Perry, Wells, & Doran, 1983; Twentyman & Plotkin, 1982). Research suggests that some reported differences may be due to the type of measure used and the type of expectation evaluated (Azar, Robinson, Hekimian, & Twentyman, 1984). Research also indicates that differences in parental expectations may occur even when the same measure is studied. For example, Chilamkurti and Milner (in press) found high risk parents, compared with low risk parents, had higher expectations for child compliance following discipline for minor child transgressions and lower expectations for child compliance following discipline for serious transgressions.

In most physical child abuse models, stress is seen as a central etiological factor. Stress is viewed as increasing the likelihood that the parent with limited resources will react in an aggressive manner toward his or her children. Supporting this contention, Schellenbach, Monroe, and Merluzzi (1991) reported that, while high risk parents are more aroused, controlling, punishing, and rejecting of their children, stress increases the magnitude of these behaviors.

It is unclear if abusers experience more environmental stressors, as some researchers report (Straus, 1980), or if they merely perceive more events as stressful and experience more distress. In a study where abusers and matched comparison parents were used, the amount of environmental stress did not differ between the two groups (Gaines, Sandgrund, Green, & Power, 1978). The presence of high levels of distress in abusers is supported, however, by studies indicating that abusers show more physiological reactivity to child and non-child-related stimuli (Casanova et al., 1992; Frodi & Lamb, 1980). It is also important to note that high levels of distress are related to reports of health-related problems and to depression.

Since an early report by Gil (1970), numerous studies have indicated that parental depression is associated with physical child abuse. As with other factors, it is unclear if depression is a marker variable or if it is causally related to child abuse. It has been reported, however, that depressed mothers are unaffectionate, distant, irritable, and punitive with their children, which may result in a lower threshold for perceived child misbehavior and more punitive reactions to child behavior (Lahey et al., 1984).

In addition to depression, abusers and high risk parents have been reported to have higher levels of state and trait anxiety (e.g., Aragona, 1983), to exhibit more anger and less assertiveness (e.g., Mee, 1983), and to indicate more loneliness (e.g., Milner, 1986). High risk and abusive parents have an external locus of control (e.g., Stringer & LaGreca, 1985), which may be associated with the clinical observation that some abusers blame their children for the abuse. Abusers also have been reported to be defensive (Milner, 1986), to deny knowledge of child injury (Rivara, Kamitsuka, & Quan, 1988), and to have less empathy (e.g., Steele, 1987) for their children. While these personality characteristics are descriptive of the abuser, again it is unclear which factors are marker factors and which are causal factors in physical child abuse.

Behavioral characteristics. Although alcohol use has been related to the likelihood and severity of assault in the general aggression literature (e.g., Taylor & Leonard, 1983), a review of the child abuse literature suggests that alcohol consumption is only modestly related to physical child abuse (Black & Mayer, 1980; Leonard & Jacob, 1988). Nevertheless, alcohol use still may be an important factor under some conditions. For example, alcohol use may be associated with the more severe types of physical child abuse. Because alcohol has been reported to negatively affect cognitive processing abilities in normal subjects, it may exacerbate any cognitive deficits that exist in abusers. Further, in individuals for whom alcohol use and depression coexist, the level of dysfunction has been observed to increase (Bland & Orn, 1986).

Abusers report social isolation, albeit, as previously noted, some research using matched comparison groups indicates that the actual number of social contacts may not be significantly different. Abusers therefore may simply perceive more social isolation and experience more loneliness. These characteristics may be related to their perceptions that others cannot be trusted or depended upon (Milner, 1986).

Studies support the contention that abusive parents exhibit highly aversive parent-child interactional patterns. For example, abusive mothers engage in more negative interactions and are less supportive of their children (Burgess & Conger, 1978). They display more verbal and nonverbal aggression and provide less positive verbal and nonverbal support (Bousha & Twentyman, 1984). Not only do abusers spend less time in positive interactions with their children (e.g., instructing, praising, and playing), they respond less often to their children's initiations of interactions (Kavanagh, Youngblade, Reid, & Fagot, 1988). Abusers display less emotional responsiveness (Egeland, Breitenbucher, & Rosenberg, 1980), use less age-appropriate stimulation (Dietrich, Starr, & Kaplan, 1980), are less responsive to temporal changes in their children's behavior (Aragona, 1983), and fail to modify their behavior in response to their children's behavior (Crittenden, 1981).

Most studies support the conclusion that abusive parents use more physical punishment to control their children than comparison parents. Abusers use assaultive (e.g., hitting, grabbing, and pushing) behavior (Lahey et al., 1984) and punitive strategies more often and use reasoning strategies less frequently (e.g., Chilamkurti & Milner, in press; Kelley, Grace, & Elliott, 1990; Oldershaw, Walters, & Hall, 1986; Trickett & Kuczynski, 1986). Abusers may use punishment more often because they view punishment as more effective than reasoning techniques (Trickett & Susman, 1988).

Familial Characteristics

Abusers report more deprivation, hostility, and abuse in their families of origin. Perpetrators of abuse also report less social support from parents, adults, siblings, and peers during childhood. Several authors have reported that parents who received childhood physical abuse but who do not continue the cycle of violence are parents who have received social support during childhood or adulthood (Caliso & Milner, 1992; Egeland, Jacobvitz, & Sroufe, 1988; Hunter & Kilstrom, 1979; Milner & Caliso, 1991). Congruent with these findings, higher levels of childhood social support are associated with lower adult scores on the Child Abuse Potential Inventory (Milner, Robertson, & Rogers, 1990).

Families in which physical child abuse occurs have more family and marital distress. The family members have poor or distorted communication patterns. There are role confusions, power imbalances, a lack of trust, and a greater likelihood of spouse abuse and multiple forms of child maltreatment. Not surprising therefore is the finding that abusive families report more conflict and less cohesion and expressiveness (Mollerstrom, Patchner, & Milner, 1992). With respect to child discipline, the family in which abuse occurs tends to value physical punishment (Trickett & Susman, 1988).

Historically, certain child characteristics and child problems were viewed as increasing the likelihood of physical child abuse by contributing to negative parent-child interactions (e.g., Friedrich & Boriskin, 1976). Child-related characteristics and problems include the premature child, the low birth weight child, the child with physical handicaps, and the child with a difficult temperament. Further, most social-interactional models of child abuse include the child as a significant component in the model. At the least, the child is viewed as contributing to the level of stress in the parents' environment, thereby increasing the likelihood of physical abuse. While, historically, the child victim has been viewed as playing a major role in the abuse event, recent critical reviews of the literature have questioned the degree to which the child contributes to the abuse (e.g., Ammerman, 1991).

Sociological Characteristics

Since Gil's (1970) initial development of the sociological model, a broad array of social factors related both to the perpetrator and to social systems have been associated with physical child abuse. As with factors at other ecological levels, it remains unclear which of the sociological factors are marker variables and which are causal variables.

With respect to perpetrator demographic characteristics, abusers are more often single, young, poorly educated, and report a childhood history of observing and/or receiving abuse. They are negatively affected by multiple environmental stressors, which are often related to family demographic factors (e.g., crowded living environment, large number of children, occupational difficulties; Milner & Chilamkurti, 1991). Some researchers view the lack of economic resources as a central factor in child abuse. Research indicates that important covariates of lower income include lower perpetrator intelligence, lower educational status, single-parent status, lower level of personal health, and higher levels of personal distress and psychopathology (Herrenkohl, Herrenkohl, Toedter, & Yanushefski, 1984).

While lack of resources acts as a contributing factor, the presence of resources appears to act as a compensatory factor. For example, higher family income has been related to higher levels of affectionate behavior, communication skills, and positive parent-child interactions (Herrenkohl et al., 1984). Thus income level appears to be a marker variable for either contributing and compensatory factors that affect parent-child interactions. It has been suggested that negative demographic conditions set the stage for the intergenerational transmission of child abuse because these conditions make it difficult for the parent to teach the child how to adequately function (Gabinet, 1983).

Developmental Effects of Physical Child Abuse

Consistent with the organizational models discussed above (e.g., Belsky, 1980; Cicchetti & Rizley, 1981), the life span perspective emphasizes that the developing individual is embedded in, and dynamically interactive with, a social context (Lerner, 1988). According to this view, the course of development remains relatively plastic throughout life, and changes in either the individual or the context may serve to alter the developmental course of the individual-context system (Lerner, 1988).

With respect to understanding the development of the physically abused child, the life span perspective serves to warn against expecting simple, direct relationships between the receipt of abuse and particular forms of sequelae (Starr, MacLean, & Keating, 1991). Rather, as noted by Starr et al., the receipt of physical abuse must be viewed as one of many factors from various ecological levels (i.e., ontogenic, microsystem, exosystem, and macrosystem factors), each of which simultaneously influences the development of the abused child. Each factor may be viewed as increasing (potentiating factors) or reducing (compensatory factors) the risk of developmental difficulties in the physically abused child (Cicchetti, 1989). According to a life span perspective, the developmental impact of physical abuse may be viewed as depending not only on the chronicity and severity of the abuse but also on the developmental level of the child at the time of the assault and the balance of current and future potentiating and compensatory factors.

The following is a summary of empirical findings related to the effects of physical abuse across the life span. While the information has been organized according to broad developmental stages, it should be noted that currently there are insufficient data to directly link the emergence and persistence of particular sequelae to specific life stages. The developmental framework used here is intended only to suggest the importance of considering the impacts of abuse from a life span perspective.

Physical Sequelae:
Risk Across the Life Span

At any point in development, a potential sequelae of physical abuse is bodily damage to the victim. Kempe et al. (1962), in their description of the "battered child syndrome," suggested a relationship between the receipt of physical abuse and certain physical symptoms in the child, such as subdural hematoma, fracture of long bones, multiple soft tissue injuries, poor skin hygiene, malnutrition, and poor general health. Of course, the most severe sequelae of physical abuse is death. It is estimated that 715 children in the United States died as a result of being physically abused in 1990 (Daro & McCurdy, 1991). Unfortunately, this statistic is probably an underestimate due to inadequate investigation procedures and underreporting of suspected maltreatment in cases of child fatalities (Daro & McCurdy, 1991).

In addition, victims of physical abuse are at risk for neurological and neuropsychological impairments that may result in detrimental effects across the life span. With the exception of accidental trauma (e.g., car accidents), most cases of infant head trauma are the results of physical abuse (Rivara et al., 1988). Elliott (1988) noted that damage or disorder in the nervous system may impair cognition, perception, and behavior and hence may play a role in determining the developmental effects of physical abuse. Lewis, Shanok, Pincus, and Glaser (1979) proposed that damage to the central nervous system as a result of physical abuse may contribute to the cognitive and behavioral difficulties (e.g., impulsivity, attention disorders, learning disabilities) often exhibited by abused children. While noting that additional evidence is needed, Milner and McCanne (1991) suggested that, when present, neuropsychological consequences of physical child abuse may extend into adulthood.

Early Childhood

One of the earliest observable differences between physically abused children and their nonabused counterparts is the manner in which they respond to their caretaker when under stress. Research has suggested that physically abused infants, compared with nonabused children, demonstrate higher frequencies of less secure attachments to their primary caretakers (Crittenden & Ainsworth, 1989; Egeland & Sroufe, 1981). At 12 months of age, physically abused children, after being left alone in a strange situation and then reunited with their caretaker, tended to avoid contact and maintain distance from their parent. In contrast, securely attached children after exposure to a strange situation directly approached and sought proximity with their caretaker (Egeland & Sroufe, 1981). Research in the area of early social development has suggested that patterns of infant-mother interaction may be related to the child's subsequent development in a number of areas. For example, certain aspects of the quality of infant-mother interaction have been reported to be significantly related to the child's later intellectual and linguistic abilities (Bee et al., 1982).

Middle and Late Childhood

Intellectual deficits. Physically abused children, in comparison with their nonabused counterparts, have been reported to earn lower scores on tests of general intellectual abilities during childhood (Barahal, Waterman, & Martin, 1981; Elmer & Gregg, 1967; Hoffman-Plotkin & Twentyman, 1984; Vondra, Barnett, & Cicchetti, 1990). Also, research has suggested that physically abused children suffer from specific deficits in linguistic abilities (Morgan, 1979; Vondra et al., 1990). It should be noted, however, that other environmental variables that often coexist with physical abuse (e.g., impoverished environment, concurrent neglect) may also contribute to the intellectual deficits observed in physically abused children (Bee et al., 1982; Elmer, 1977; Vondra et al., 1990).

Affective and behavioral problems. By middle childhood, physically abused children have been reported to exhibit a number of affective and behavioral difficulties, including acute anxiety, depression, sleep disturbance, self-destructive behavior, low self-esteem, social detachment, hyperactivity, excessive aggression, and noncompliance (Egeland & Sroufe, 1981; Green, 1978a, 1978b; Kaufman & Cicchetti, 1989; Kazdin, Moser, Colbus, & Bell, 1985; Straker & Jacobson, 1981). There is also evidence that a direct relationship exists between the severity of abuse to which the child is exposed (i.e., received and/or observed) and the degree of child maladjustment. That is, increasing severity of received or observed abuse appears to be related to higher levels of emotional and behavioral dysfunction (Fantuzzo et al., 1991; Kaufman & Cicchetti, 1989; Kazdin et al., 1985).

Perhaps the most frequently cited behavioral sequelae of physical child abuse is the prevalence of externalizing behavior problems, such as excessive aggressiveness, hyperactivity, conduct problems, and delinquency (Hoffman-Plotkin & Twentyman, 1984; Widom, 1989; Wolfe & Mosk, 1983). Kaufman and Cicchetti (1989) reported that children who were physically abused, as compared with children who received other forms of maltreatment, were rated by their peers as significantly more aggressive. Of interest, Wolfe and Mosk (1983) reported no significant differences in behavior problems and social competencies between abused children and nonabused children from high distress families. These authors concluded that the abused child's social and behavioral development may be more a function of general family interaction patterns than isolated abusive episodes.

While externalizing behavior problems have received a great deal of attention in the literature on physically abused children, these children also have been reported to demonstrate higher levels of internalizing behaviors (e.g., withdrawal, self-destructiveness) as compared with nonabused children (Green, 1978b; Kaufman & Cicchetti, 1989). Kaufman and Cicchetti noted that the relationship between physically abused children's use of aggression and withdrawal as coping strategies is unclear; some children demonstrate both behavioral tendencies and other children display a preference for one versus the other response strategy.

Physically abused children have been reported to be significantly less empathic than nonabused children (Main & George,

1985; Straker & Jacobson, 1981). For example, abused children have been reported to react to distressed peers with physical attacks, fear, or anger, while the predominant response of their nonabused counterparts appeared to be one of concern (Main & George, 1985). Differences between physically abused and nonabused children in empathic ability have been reported to disappear, however, when levels of intellectual abilities are controlled (Frodi & Smetana, 1984).

Social cognition. Physically abused children also appear to differ from their nonabused counterparts in the area of social cognition. Specifically, abused children have been reported to have less confidence in their ability to affect events (i.e., more external locus of control), a decreased understanding of social roles (Barahal et al., 1981), hostile attributional styles, and aggressive approaches to problem solving (Dodge, Bates, & Pettit, 1990).

A recent study of the relationship between children's and their mothers' social cognitions reported that children of mothers who were likely to abuse (i.e., high risk for abuse) evaluated conventional (e.g., disobeying family rules) and personal transgressions (e.g., wearing wrinkled clothes) as more wrong compared with evaluations made by children of low risk mothers (Chilamkurti & Milner, in press). While the two groups differed in their relative evaluations, both groups of children adopted patterns of evaluation that paralleled their mother's style of evaluating transgressions. This finding suggests that children may internalize certain parental social cognitions, and such cognitions may affect the child's assessment of the appropriateness of responding with aggression.

Adolescence

There is a general paucity of research related to the abused child's development during adolescence. It is important to note that some cases of adolescent physical abuse are simply the continuation of abuse that began in childhood, while others represent a deterioration of parent-child interactions as the child becomes an adolescent (Lourie, 1979). Families in which physical abuse emerges only as the child becomes an adolescent appear to be different than families in which preadolescent children are abused (Garbarino, 1989). For example, Garbarino (1989) noted that the literature on adolescent abuse indicates that lower social economic class appears to play a smaller role as a risk factor in adolescent maltreatment as compared with preadolescent physical abuse (i.e., adolescent abuse is more equally distributed across socioeconomic classes). Also, parents who physically abuse their adolescents, as compared with parents who abuse their preadolescent children, are less likely to have been abused themselves as children (Garbarino, 1989). As these findings suggest, physical abuse that emerges only in adolescence presents a number of ecological features that differentiate it from cases of preadolescent victimization, and research specifically focused on each phenomenon is needed.

Adulthood

General adaptation. Long-term, deleterious effects of the receipt of physical child abuse have not been consistently demonstrated (Widom, 1989). For example, Martin and Elmer (1992), in their 23-year follow-up of individuals who were severely physically abused as children, reported a broad range of adaptation among their—now adult—sample. According to these authors, some individuals appeared to be functioning adequately (i.e., raising families, remaining employed, and maintaining social relationships), while others exhibited exceptional difficulties in coping (i.e., depression, feelings of isolation, substance abuse). Although general measures of aggressiveness did not appear elevated for this group of adults who had experienced physical abuse as children, Martin and Elmer noted that these individuals did present more suspiciousness and resentment compared with normals. In contrast, other studies have noted a relationship between the receipt of physical child abuse and adult levels of anger and aggression (Briere & Runtz, 1990).

It should be noted that, in the Martin and Elmer (1992) study, many subjects from the original 1963 sample were unavailable at the time of the 23-year follow-up. Further, the unavailable subjects had been rated (at the outset of the study in 1963) as having more difficulties than those subjects who were available at the time of the follow-up. Due to the unavailability of some of the more disturbed subjects at the time of follow-up, Martin and

Elmer noted that their study may underestimate the deleterious impact of physical child abuse on later adult functioning.

Increased delinquent/criminal behavior. Research exploring the relationship between the receipt of childhood physical abuse and later delinquent or violent criminal activity has produced contradictory reports (Widom, 1989). An example of a study that appears to support a relationship between receipt of childhood physical abuse and later adult risk of criminality is the McCord (1983) prospective study. McCord (1983) assessed the quality of interaction between 232 males and their respective parents (classifying each child as loved, rejected, abused, or neglected) and then followed this group over a 40-year period. The results of this prospective study revealed that men who had been physically abused, neglected, and/or rejected as children, as compared with those who were loved, were at a higher risk of becoming alcoholic, mentally ill, or involved in criminal activity. Because the experiences of abuse, neglect, and rejection are not mutually exclusive, it is difficult to discern any distinct contribution of the receipt of physical abuse to the increased risk of antisocial behavior reported in the McCord study.

Intergenerational transmission of physical abuse. In its most general form, the intergenerational transmission of aggression hypothesis states that patterns of violent behavior are passed from one generation to the next. With reference to physical child abuse, this hypothesis suggests that victims of childhood physical abuse are more likely to abuse their own children.

Although intuitively appealing, the intergenerational transmission of physical abuse has been received critically by many researchers. Kaufman and Zigler (1987) integrated the findings of a number of studies related to the intergenerational transmission of abuse and estimated that only 30% of parents with a childhood history of abuse go on to abuse their own children. Current findings suggest a higher likelihood of abuse by parents if the parents themselves were abused as children. Research also indicates, however, that the majority of adults who abuse their children were not abused in their own childhoods (Widom, 1989). Research has suggested that concurrent or subsequent social support for the victim of childhood physical abuse may serve to buffer the intergenerational transmission of physical abuse (Caliso & Milner, 1992; Egeland, Jacobvitz, & Sroufe, 1988; Hunter & Kilstrom, 1979; Milner & Caliso, 1991; Milner et al., 1990). In their review of the literature on perpetrator characteristics, Milner and Chilamkurti (1991) suggested that, in cases of intergenerational transmission of abuse, a childhood experience of abuse may act as a marker variable for other factors (e.g., family dysfunction) that may more directly affect the probability of subsequent perpetration of physical child abuse.

Conclusion

Although still in the early stages of development, research in the area of physical child abuse has produced a growing body of knowledge related to the characteristics of the abusive parent and the effects of abuse on the child victim. Increased sophistication of explanatory models of physical child abuse has contributed significantly to this progress. The breadth of consideration added by newly developed multidomain, bidirectional models, as well as the specificity gained through models such as the social information processing model of physical child abuse, mark conceptual advances in the field. Each of the more recent models described in this chapter holds promise as an important guide for future research. Despite steady advances in knowledge and increasing sophistication of models, continued research in the area of physical child abuse remains of paramount importance as a means of informing prevention and treatment efforts.

References

Aber, J. L., & Allen, J. P. (1987). Effects of maltreatment on young children's socioemotional development: An attachment theory perspective. *Developmental Psychology, 23,* 406-414.

Ammerman, R. T. (1991). The role of the child in physical abuse: A reappraisal. *Violence and Victims, 6,* 87-101.

Aragona, J. A. (1983). Physical child abuse: An interactional analysis (Doctoral dissertation, University of South Florida, 1983). *Dissertation Abstracts International, 44,* 1225B.

Azar, S. T. (1986). A framework for understanding child maltreatment: An integration of cognitive behavioural and developmental perspectives. *Canadian Journal of Behavioural Science, 18,* 340-355.

Azar, S. T. (1989). Training parents of abused children. In C. E. Schaefer & J. M. Briesmeister (Eds.), *Handbook of parent training* (pp. 414-441). New York: John Wiley.

Azar, S. T. (1991). Models of child abuse: A metatheoretical analysis. *Criminal Justice and Behavior, 18,* 30-46.

Azar, S. T., Robinson, D. R., Hekimian, E., & Twentyman, C. T. (1984). Unrealistic expectations and problem-solving ability in maltreating and comparison mothers. *Journal of Consulting and Clinical Psychology, 52,* 687-691.

Azar, S. T., & Siegal, B. R. (1990). Behavioral treatment of child abuse: A developmental perspective. *Behavior Modification, 14,* 279-300.

Barahal, R. M., Waterman, J., & Martin, H. P. (1981). The social cognitive development of abused children. *Journal of Consulting and Clinical Psychology, 49,* 508-516.

Bauer, W. D., & Twentyman, C. T. (1985). Abusing, neglectful, and comparison mothers' responses to child-related and non-child-related stressors. *Journal of Consulting and Clinical Psychology, 53,* 335-343.

Bee, H. L., Barnard, K. E., Eyres, S. J., Gray, C. A., Hammond, M. A., Spietz, A. L., Snyder, C., & Clark, B. (1982). Prediction of IQ and language skill from perinatal status, child performance, family characteristics, and mother-infant interaction. *Child Development, 53,* 1134-1156.

Belsky, J. (1980). Child maltreatment: An ecological integration. *American Psychologist, 35,* 320-335.

Black, R., & Mayer, J. (1980). Parents with special problems: Alcoholism and opiate addiction. *Child Abuse & Neglect, 4,* 45-54.

Bland, R. C., & Orn, H. (1986). Psychiatric disorders, spouse abuse, and child abuse. *Acta Psychiatrica Belgica, 86,* 444-449.

Bousha, D. M., & Twentyman, C. T. (1984). Mother-child interactional style in abuse, neglect, and control groups: Naturalistic observations in the home. *Journal of Abnormal Psychology, 93,* 106-114.

Briere, J., & Runtz, M. (1990). Differential adult symptomatology associated with three types of child abuse histories. *Child Abuse & Neglect, 14,* 357-364.

Bronfenbrenner, U. (1977). Toward an experimental ecology of human development. *American Psychologist, 32,* 513-531.

Burgess, R. (1979). Project interact: A study of patterns of interaction in abusive, neglectful and control families. *Child Abuse & Neglect, 3,* 781-791.

Burgess, R. L., & Conger, R. D. (1978). Family interaction in abusive, neglectful, and normal families. *Child Development, 49,* 1163-1173.

Burgess, R. L., & Garbarino, J. (1983). Doing what comes naturally? An evolutionary perspective on child abuse. In D. Finkelhor, R. J. Gelles, G. T. Hotaling, & M. A. Straus (Eds.), *The dark side of families: Current family violence research* (pp. 88-101). Beverly Hills, CA: Sage.

Caliso, J. A., & Milner, J. S. (1992). Childhood history of abuse and child abuse screening. *Child Abuse & Neglect, 16,* 647-659.

Casanova, G. M., Domanic, J., McCanne, T. R., & Milner, J. S. (1992). Physiological responses to non-child-related stressors in mothers at risk for child abuse. *Child Abuse & Neglect, 16,* 31-44.

Chilamkurti, C., & Milner, J. S. (in press). Perceptions and evaluations of child transgressions and disciplinary techniques in high- and low-risk mothers and their children. *Child Development.*

Cicchetti, D. (1989). How research on child maltreatment has informed the study of child development: Perspectives from developmental psychopathology. In D. Cicchetti & V. Carlson (Eds.), *Child maltreatment: Theory and research on the causes and consequences of child abuse and neglect* (pp. 377-431). New York: Cambridge University Press.

Cicchetti, D., & Rizley, R. (1981). Developmental perspectives on the etiology, intergenerational transmission, and sequelae of child maltreatment. *New Directions for Child Development, 11,* 31-55.

Conger, R. D., Burgess, R. L., & Barrett, C. (1979). Child abuse related to life change and perceptions of illness: Some preliminary findings. *Family Coordinator, 28,* 73-78.

Crittenden, P. M. (1981). Abusing, neglecting, problematic, and adequate dyads: Differentiating by patterns of interaction. *Merrill-Palmer Quarterly, 27,* 201-218.

Crittenden, P. M., & Ainsworth, M. D. (1989). Child maltreatment and attachment theory. In D. Cicchetti & V. Carlson (Eds.), *Child maltreatment: Theory and research on the causes and consequences of child abuse and neglect* (pp. 432-463). New York: Cambridge University Press.

Crowe, H. P., & Zeskind, P. H. (1992). Psychophysiological and perceptual responses to infant cries varying in pitch: Comparison of adults with low and high scores on the Child Abuse Potential Inventory. *Child Abuse & Neglect, 16,* 19-29.

Daly, M., & Wilson, M. I. (1981). Child maltreatment from a sociobiological perspective. *New Directions for Child Development, 11,* 93-112.

Daro, D., & McCurdy, K. (1991). *Current trends in child abuse reporting and fatalities: The results of the 1990 Annual Fifty State Survey* (Working Paper No. 808). Chicago: National Center on Child Abuse Prevention Research.

Dietrich, K. N., Starr, R. H., & Kaplan, M. G. (1980). Maternal stimulation and care of abused infants. In T. M. Field, S. Goldberg, D. Stern, & A. M. Sostek (Eds.), *High-risk infants and children* (pp. 25-41). New York: Academic Press.

Dodge, K. A., Bates, J. E., & Pettit, G. S. (1990). Mechanisms in the cycle of violence. *Science, 250,* 1678-1683.

Egeland, B., Breitenbucher, M., & Rosenberg, D. (1980). Prospective study of the significance of life stress in the etiology of child abuse. *Journal of Consulting and Clinical Psychology, 48,* 195-205.

Egeland, B., & Erickson, M. F. (1987). Psychologically unavailable caregiving. In M. R. Brassard, R. Germain, & S. N. Hart (Eds.), *Psychological maltreatment of children and youth* (pp. 110-120). New York: Pergamon.

Egeland, B., Jacobvitz, D., & Sroufe, L. A. (1988). Breaking the cycle of abuse. *Child Development, 59,* 1080-1088.

Egeland, B., & Sroufe, A. (1981). Developmental sequelae of maltreatment in infancy. *New Directions for Child Development, 11,* 77-92.

Elliott, F. A. (1988). Neurological factors. In V. B. Van Hasselt, R. L. Morrison, A. S. Bellack, & M. Hersen (Eds.), *Handbook of family violence* (pp. 359-382). New York: Plenum.

Elmer, E. (1977). A follow-up study of traumatized children. *Pediatrics, 59,* 273-279.

Elmer, E., & Gregg, G. S. (1967). Developmental characteristics of abused children. *Pediatrics, 40,* 569-602.

Fantuzzo, J. W., DePaola, L. M., Lambert, L., Martino, T., Anderson, G., & Sutton, S. (1991). Effects of interparental violence on the psychological adjustment and competencies of young children. *Journal of Consulting and Clinical Psychology, 59,* 258-265.

Farrington, K. (1980). Stress and family violence. In M. Straus & G. Hotaling (Eds.), *Social causes of husband-wife violence.* Minneapolis: University of Minnesota Press.

Farrington, K. (1986). The application of stress theory to the study of family violence: Principles, problems, and prospects. *Journal of Family Violence, 1,* 131-147.

Friedrich, W. N., & Boriskin, J. A. (1976). The role of the child in abuse: A review of the literature. *American Journal of Orthopsychiatry, 46,* 580-590.

Friedrich, W. N., & Wheeler, K. K. (1982). The abusing parent revisited: A decade of psychological research. *Journal of Nervous and Mental Disease, 170,* 577-587.

Frodi, A. M., & Lamb, M. E. (1980). Child abusers' responses to infant smiles and cries. *Child Development, 51,* 238-241.

Frodi, A. M., & Smetana, J. (1984). Abused, neglected, and nonmaltreated preschoolers' ability to discriminate emotions in others: The effects of IQ. *Child Abuse & Neglect, 8,* 459-465.

Gabinet, L. (1983). Child abuse treatment failures reveal need for redefinition of the problem. *Child Abuse & Neglect, 7,* 395-402.

Gaines, R., Sandgrund, A., Green, A. H., & Power, E. (1978). Etiological factors in child maltreatment: A multivariate study of abusing, neglecting, and normal mothers. *Journal of Abnormal Psychology, 87,* 531-540.

Garbarino, J. (1989). Troubled youth, troubled families: The dynamics of adolescent maltreatment. In D. Cicchetti & V. Carlson (Eds.), *Child maltreatment: Theory and research on the causes and consequences of child abuse and neglect* (pp. 685-706). New York: Cambridge University Press.

Gelles, R. J. (1973). Child abuse as psychopathology: A sociological critique and reformulation. *American Journal of Orthopsychiatry, 43,* 611-621.

Gelles, R. J., & Straus, M. A. (1979). Determinants of violence in the family: Toward a theoretical integration. In W. R. Burr, R. Hill, F. I. Nye, & I. L. Reiss (Eds.), *Contemporary theories about the family* (pp. 549-581). New York: Free Press.

Gil, D. G. (1970). *Violence against children.* Cambridge, MA: Harvard University Press.

Gil, D. G. (1987). Maltreatment as a function of the structure of social systems. In M. R. Brassard, R. Germain, & S. N. Hart (Eds.), *Psychological maltreatment of children and youth.* New York: Pergamon.

Giovannoni, J. M., & Billingsley, A. (1970). Child neglect among the poor: A study of parental adequacy in families of three ethnic groups. *Child Welfare, 49,* 196-204.

Goode, W. J. (1971). Force and violence in the family. *Journal of Marriage and the Family, 33,* 624-636.

Green, A. H. (1978a). Psychopathology of abused children. *Journal of the American Academy of Child Psychiatry, 17,* 92-103.

Green, A. H. (1978b). Self-destructive behavior in battered children. *American Journal of Psychiatry, 135,* 579-582.

Helfer, R. E., McKinney, J., & Kempe, R. (1976). Arresting or freezing the developmental process. In R. E. Helfer & C. H. Kempe (Eds.), *Child abuse and neglect: The family and the community* (pp. 134-163). Cambridge, MA: Ballinger.

Herrenkohl, E. C., Herrenkohl, R. C., Toedter, L., & Yanushefski, A. M. (1984). Parent-child interactions in abusive and non-abusive families. *Journal of the American Academy of Child Psychiatry, 23,* 641-648.

Hoffman-Plotkin, D., & Twentyman, C. T. (1984). A multimodal assessment of behavioral and cognitive deficits in abused and neglected preschoolers. *Child Development, 55,* 794-802.

Hunter, R. S., & Kilstrom, N. (1979). Breaking the cycle in abusive families. *American Journal of Psychiatry, 136,* 1320-1322.

Justice, B., & Justice, R. (1976). *The abusing family.* New York: Human Sciences Press.

Kaufman, J., & Cicchetti, D. (1989). Effects of maltreatment on school-age children's socio-emotional development: Assessments in a day-camp setting. *Developmental Psychology, 25,* 516-524.

Kaufman, J., & Zigler, E. (1987). Do abused children become abusive parents? *American Journal of Orthopsychiatry, 57,* 186-192.

Kavanagh, K. A., Youngblade, L., Reid, J. B., & Fagot, B. L. (1988). Interactions between children and abusive versus control parents. *Journal of Clinical Child Psychology, 17,* 137-142.

Kazdin, A. E., Moser, J., Colbus, D., & Bell, R. (1985). Depressive symptoms among physically abused and psychiatrically disturbed children. *Journal of Abnormal Psychology, 94,* 298-307.

Kelley, M. L., Grace, N., & Elliott, S. N. (1990). Acceptability of positive and punitive discipline methods: Comparisons among abusive, potentially abusive, and nonabusive parents. *Child Abuse & Neglect, 14,* 219-226.

Kempe, C. H., Silverman, F. N., Steele, B. F., Droegemueller, W., & Silver, H. K. (1962). The battered child syndrome. *Journal of the American Medical Association, 181,* 105-112.

Knutson, J. F. (1978). Child abuse as an area of aggression research. *Journal of Pediatric Psychology, 3,* 20-27.

Kravitz, R. I., & Driscoll, J. M. (1983). Expectations for childhood development among child-abusing and nonabusing parents. *American Journal of Orthopsychiatry, 53,* 336-344.

Lahey, B. B., Conger, R. D., Atkeson, B. M., & Treiber, F. A. (1984). Parenting behavior and emotional status of physically abusive mothers. *Journal of Consulting and Clinical Psychology, 52,* 1062-1071.

Larrance, D. T., & Twentyman, C. T. (1983). Maternal attributions and child abuse. *Journal of Abnormal Psychology, 92,* 449-457.

Leonard, K. E., & Jacob, T. (1988). Alcohol, alcoholism, and family violence. In V. B. Van Hasselt, R. L. Morrison, A. S. Bellack, & M. Hersen (Eds.), *Handbook of family violence* (pp. 383-406). New York: Plenum.

Lerner, R. M. (1988). Personality development: A life-span perspective. In E. M. Hetherington, R. M. Lerner, & E. M. Perlmutter (Eds.), *Child development in life-span perspective* (pp. 21-46). Hillsdale, NJ: Lawrence Erlbaum.

Lesnik-Oberstein, M., Cohen, L., & Koers, A. J. (1982). Research in the Netherlands on a theory of child abuse: A preliminary report. *Child Abuse & Neglect, 6,* 199-206.

Lewis, D. O., Shanok, S. S., Pincus, J. H., & Glaser, G. H. (1979). Violent juvenile delinquents: Psychiatric, neurological, psychological, and abuse factors. *The American Journal of Child Psychiatry, 18,* 307-319.

Lourie, I. S. (1979). Family dynamics and the abuse of adolescents: A case for a developmental phase specific model of child abuse. *Child Abuse & Neglect, 3,* 967-974.

Main, M., & George, C. (1985). Responses of abused and disadvantaged toddlers to distress in agemates: A study in the day care setting. *Developmental Psychology, 21,* 407-412.

Martin, J. A., & Elmer, E. (1992). Battered children grown up: A follow-up study of individuals severely maltreated as children. *Child Abuse & Neglect, 16,* 75-87.

Mash, E. J., Johnston, C., & Kovitz, K. (1983). A comparison of the mother-child interactions of physically abused and nonabused children during play and task situations. *Journal of Clinical Child Psychology, 12,* 337-346.

McCord, J. (1983). A forty year perspective on effects of child abuse and neglect. *Child Abuse & Neglect, 7,* 265-270.

McCubbin, H. I., Cauble, A. E., & Patterson, J. M. (1982). *Family stress, coping and social support.* Springfield, IL: Charles C Thomas.

McFall, R. M. (1982). A review and reformulation of the concept of social skills. *Behavioral Assessment, 4,* 1-33.

Mee, J. (1983). *The relationship between stress and the potential for child abuse.* Unpublished thesis, Macquarie University, Australia.

Milner, J. S. (1986). *The Child Abuse Potential Inventory: Manual* (2nd ed.). Webster, NC: Psytec Corporation.

Milner, J. S. (1988). An ego-strength scale for the Child Abuse Potential Inventory. *Journal of Family Violence, 3,* 151-162.

Milner, J. S. (in press). Social information processing and physical child abuse. *Clinical Psychology Review.*

Milner, J. S., & Caliso, J. A. (1991, March). *Childhood physical abuse, childhood social support, and adult child abuse potential.* Paper presented at the meeting of the Southeastern Psychological Association, New Orleans.

Milner, J. S., & Chilamkurti, C. (1991). Physical child abuse perpetrator characteristics: A review of the literature. *Journal of Interpersonal Violence, 6,* 345-366.

Milner, J. S., & McCanne, T. R. (1991). Neuropsychological correlates of physical child abuse. In J. S. Milner (Ed.), *Neuropsychology of aggression* (pp. 131-145). Norwell, MA: Kluwer Academic.

Milner, J. S., Robertson, K. R., & Rogers, D. L. (1990). Childhood history of abuse and adult child abuse potential. *Journal of Family Violence, 5,* 15-34.

Mollerstrom, W. W., Patchner, M. A., & Milner, J. S. (1992). Family functioning and child abuse potential. *Journal of Clinical Psychology, 48,* 445-454.

Morgan, S. R. (1979). Psycho-educational profile of emotionally disturbed abused children. *Journal of Clinical Child Psychology, 8,* 3-6.

Morton, T. L., Twentyman, C. T., & Azar, S. T. (1988). Cognitive-behavioral assessment and treatment of child abuse. In N. Epstein, S. E. Schlesinger, & W. Dryden (Eds.), *Cognitive-behavioral therapy with families* (pp. 87-117). New York: Brunner/Mazel.

Newberger, C. M., & Cook, S. J. (1983). Parental awareness and child abuse: A cognitive-developmental analysis of urban and rural samples. *American Journal of Orthopsychiatry, 53,* 512-524.

Nye, F. I., & McDonald, G. W. (1979). Family policy research: Emergent models and some theoretical issues. *Journal of Marriage and the Family, 41,* 473-485.

Oldershaw, L., Walters, G. C., & Hall, D. K. (1986). Control strategies and noncompliance in abusive mother-child dyads: An observational study. *Child Development, 57,* 722-732.

Parke, R. D., & Collmer, C. W. (1975). Child abuse: An interdisciplinary analysis. In E. M. Hetherington (Ed.), *Review of child development research* (Vol. 5, pp. 509-590). Chicago: University of Chicago Press.

Perry, M. A., Wells, E. A., & Doran, L. D. (1983). Parent characteristics in abusing and nonabusing families. *Journal of Clinical Child Psychology, 12,* 329-336.

Pruitt, D. L., & Erickson, M. T. (1985). The Child Abuse Potential Inventory: A study of concurrent validity. *Journal of Clinical Psychology, 41,* 104-111.

Reid, J. B., Kavanagh, K., & Baldwin, D. V. (1987). Abusive parents' perceptions of child problem behaviors: An example of parental bias. *Journal of Abnormal Child Psychology, 15,* 457-466.

Rivara, F. P., Kamitsuka, M. D., & Quan, L. (1988). Injuries to children younger than 1 year of age. *Pediatrics, 81,* 93-97.

Schellenbach, C. J., Monroe, L. D., & Merluzzi, T. V. (1991). The impact of stress on cognitive components of child abuse potential. *Journal of Family Violence, 6,* 61-80.

Schneider, G., Pollock, C., & Helfer, H. C. (1972). The predictive questionnaire: A preliminary report. In R. E. Helfer & C. H. Kempe (Eds.), *Helping the battered child and his family* (pp. 271-282). Philadelphia: Lippincott.

Starr, R. H., MacLean, D. J., & Keating, D. P. (1991). Life-span developmental outcomes of child maltreatment. In R. H. Starr & D. A. Wolfe (Eds.), *The effects of child abuse and neglect* (pp. 1-32). New York: Guilford.

Steele, B. (1987). Psychodynamic factors in child abuse. In R. E. Helfer & R. S. Kempe (Eds.), *The battered child* (4th ed., pp. 81-114). Chicago: University of Chicago Press.

Steele, B. F., & Pollock, C. B. (1974). A psychiatric study of parents who abuse infants and small children. In C. H. Kempe & R. E. Helfer (Eds.), *The battered child* (2nd ed., pp. 103-147). Chicago: University of Chicago Press.

Straker, G., & Jacobson, R. S. (1981). Aggression, emotional maladjustment, and empathy in the abused child. *Developmental Psychology, 17,* 762-765.

Straus, M. A. (1973). A general systems theory approach to a theory of violence between family members. *Social Science Information, 12,* 105-125.

Straus, M. A. (1980). Stress and child abuse. In C. H. Kempe & R. E. Helfer (Eds.), *The battered child* (3rd ed., pp. 86-103). Chicago: University of Chicago Press.

Stringer, S. A., & LaGreca, A. M. (1985). Correlates of child abuse potential. *Journal of Abnormal Child Psychology, 13,* 217-226.

Taylor, S., & Leonard, K. (1983). Alcohol and human physical aggression. In R. Green & E. Donnerstein (Eds.), *Aggression: Theoretical and empirical reviews* (pp. 77-101). New York: Academic Press.

Trickett, P. K., & Kuczynski, L. (1986). Children's misbehaviors and parental discipline strategies in abusive and nonabusive families. *Developmental Psychology, 22,* 115-123.

Trickett, P. K., & Susman, E. J. (1988). Parental perceptions of child-rearing practices in physically abusive and nonabusive families. *Developmental Psychology, 24,* 270-276.

Twentyman, C. T., & Plotkin, R. C. (1982). Unrealistic expectations of parents who maltreat their children: An educational deficit that pertains to child development. *Journal of Clinical Psychology, 38,* 497-503.

Twentyman, C. T., Rohrbeck, C. A., & Amish, P. L. (1984). A cognitive-behavioral model of child abuse. In S. Saunders, A. M. Anderson, C. A. Hart, & G. M. Rubenstein (Eds.), *Violent individuals and families: A handbook for practitioners* (pp. 87-111). Springfield, IL: Charles C Thomas.

Tzeng, O. C., Jackson, J. W., & Karlson, H. C. (1991). *Theories of child abuse and neglect.* New York: Praeger.

Vasta, R. (1982). Physical child abuse: A dual-component analysis. *Developmental Review, 2,* 125-149.

Vondra, J. I., Barnett, D., & Cicchetti, D. (1990). Self-concept, motivation, and competence among preschoolers from maltreating and comparison families. *Child Abuse & Neglect, 14,* 525-540.

Widom, C. S. (1989). Does violence beget violence? A critical examination of the literature. *Psychological Bulletin, 106,* 3-28.

Wiggins, J. A. (1983). Family violence as a case of interpersonal aggression: A situational analysis. *Social Forces, 62,* 102-123.

Wolfe, D. A. (1987). *Child abuse: Implications for child development and psychopathology.* Newbury Park, CA: Sage.

Wolfe, D. A., Fairbank, J. A., Kelly, J. A., & Bradlyn, A. S. (1983). Child abusive parents' physiological responses to stressful and non-stressful behavior in children. *Behavioral Assessment, 5,* 363-371.

Wolfe, D. A., & Mosk, M. D. (1983). Behavioral comparison of children from abusive and distressed families. *Journal of Consulting and Clinical Psychology, 51,* 702-708.

Wood-Shuman, S., & Cone, J. D. (1986). Differences in abusive, at-risk for abuse, and control mothers' descriptions of normal child behavior. *Child Abuse & Neglect, 10,* 397-405.

Zimrin, H. (1984). Child abuse: A dynamic process of encounter between needs and personality traits within the family. *The American Journal of Family Therapy, 12,* 37-47.

• *CHAPTER 3* •

Sexual Abuse of Children

JON R. CONTE

The sexual abuse of children by older persons has captured significant public and professional attention. Although there has been reference to adult/child sexual contact throughout history, it is only within the last decade and a half that there has been widespread and consistent attention given to the subject. Early professional literature tended to be concerned with the incest taboo (see, e.g., White, 1948), descriptions of samples of abused children (e.g., Weiss, Rogers, Darwin, & Dutton, 1955), case studies describing the emotional impact of sexual abuse on children (see, e.g., Bender & Gruett, 1952), or descriptions of the characteristics of adults who sexually use children (e.g., Peters, 1976).

While it has been difficult for the public and professionals to recognize that older persons abuse children, since Kempe's (Kempe, Silverman, Steele, Droegemueller, & Silver, 1962) classic paper, "The Battered Child Syndrome," there has been more or less general acceptance of physical child abuse as a real problem of childhood. It is not clear as this chapter is being written in 1992 that sexual abuse of children is as generally accepted as a real problem of childhood as physical abuse is or, at least, that childhood sexual abuse is understood as it really is. Currently, media reports and television talk shows are making much of stories about individuals falsely accused of sexual abuse. More critically, elsewhere, I have argued that much of what professionals have believed over the years about childhood sexual abuse has turned out with additional experience and research to be incorrect (see, e.g., Conte, 1991). While this is an old theme in my writing, the editors of this volume have charged me with preparing a general overview of child sexual abuse for this audience. I cannot meet this charge without rehashing both what we don't know and what we know. Therefore, in the pages that follow, I discuss why accurate knowledge is so difficult in this area, outline the subareas of knowledge that make up childhood sexual abuse, and illustrate what we know in several of these subareas.

Why Is Knowledge Development So Difficult?

If the reader will accept as fact (for the moment) my assertion that as a field we in childhood sexual abuse have often tended to believe things at one point in time that only a few years later we realized were inaccurate, understanding why this has happened will, I believe, tell us important things about our field and about how to be more effective professionals in childhood sexual abuse. There are a number of factors that make up the "why."

Methodological Weaknesses

In many aspects of practice and knowledge, childhood sexual abuse has been a relatively new area of interest. As a result, there has not yet been a long tradition of research upon which to build. In fact, in a number of areas, much of the early professional writings were not based on research at all. A presumably well-meaning and competent professional with good intentions puts his or her clinical observation to paper and that observation is then taken as fact by countless other professionals. For example, early literature on incest suggested that one of the reasons that incest occurred was that mothers switched roles with their daughters (e.g., Justice & Justice, 1979). The incest victim took over many of their mother's responsibilities, such as care for younger siblings, housecleaning, and emotional support of and eventually sexual relations with her father. This view was consistent with "family views of incest," which believed that incest was a family problem in which every member of the family participated in the development and maintenance of the incest (for discussion, see Conte, 1986). Treatment programs tried to change role reversal between mothers and daughters and tried to restructure the family so that mother and father acted like mother and father and children were children.

As appealing as this idea may have been, there was not then nor is there today any data that support that *role reversal* is in fact a characteristic of most incest families or that it is a major reason that incest takes place. Clinically, it is just as likely that, as a consequence of having sex with her father, a child develops heightened emotional awareness and sensitivity to her father as a self-protection strategy (e.g., so that she can try to anticipate when her abuse may take place by judging his moods).

There are also many methodological reasons that the original observation of role reversal may have been incorrect or biased. The observations, because they were not carried out using research measurement where the reliability and validity of measurement (observation) was known, may have been inaccurate or wrong. The observations may have been accurate for the cases the original professional knew about but may have been *unrepresentative* of all or most incest cases. There are numerous areas within childhood sexual abuse knowledge that appear to have suffered because of methodological weaknesses such as these (see below).

Strong Emotional Valence

Elsewhere (Conte, 1991), I have argued that as a field we have also tended to believe things that served to make it easier for us to work in this area. Because sexual abuse of children involves and stimulates powerful human emotions and behaviors, such as sex, power, coercion, physical and emotional pain, and involves older persons who often have positions of responsibility in our families and other social institutions, recognition of sexual abuse and what sexual abuse is requires that as people we confront aspects of living that are difficult for us (e.g., sex).

Perhaps my favorite example of how our knowledge has been based more on denial and minimization is the idea that incest is a unique form of child sexual abuse. A key aspect of this belief has been the idea that incest fathers sexually abuse only their own children and by so doing are giving expression to a family problem. Preliminary data have seriously challenged this core belief about incest. Abel, Becker, Cunningham-Rathner, Mittelman, and Rouleau (1988) indicate that 49% of the incestuous fathers and stepfathers referred for outpatient treatment at their clinics abused children outside of the family at the same time they were abusing their own children (18% of these men were raping adult women at the same time they were sexually abusing their own children). While replication of these data is critical in understanding how generalizable they are, the data do raise question about the validity of the assumption that the initial referral diagnosis (e.g., father/stepfather incest) has any significance in understanding the nature of the incest father's or stepfather's problem.

Why was it easier for so many professionals to believe that incest was different than other kinds of sexual abuse of children? I ask you the reader to consider the possibility that one of the reasons was that it is too emotionally difficult to imagine that a *father* would really be a *sexual offender.* The image of *father* carries great personal, emotional, and psychological significance for many of us. Our relationships with or memories of our own fathers are often complex and can be ambivalent. It can just be easier for us to resolve the complex psychological tension that results from confronting the fact that fathers have sex with their children to somehow regard it as something different than sexual abuse and the fathers as something other than *pedophiles* or *sexual offenders* (i.e., incest offenders).

I ask that you to keep in mind these two questions then as you read the rest of this chapter: (a) What are the data supporting what we know about child sexual abuse? (b) Is belief based more on emotional and other psychological principles that meet our needs as professionals than on real data?

Child Sexual Abuse: The Knowledge Domains

Definitions

Definitions of sexual abuse of children tend either to focus on the adults who sexually use children (see *Diagnostic and Statistical Manual of Mental Disorders,* III-R, American Psychiatric

Association, 1987) or describe the nature of the sexual use of children. Nature of abuse has been described along three dimensions: *age difference* of 5 years or more between child and offender, *specific sexual behavior* (e.g., exhibitionism, voyeurism, kissing, foundling, fellatio or cunnilingus, penetration of the vagina, anus, or mouth with sexual organs or objects, and photography—either taking pictures of the child or exposing the child to pornographic materials), and *sexual intent* wherein the intent of the behavior is the sexual gratification of the adult. It is assumed that a child cannot give *informed consent* to sexual contact with an adult because the young child may not know what she or he is consenting to and because the child does not have the power to decline involvement (Finkelhor, 1979).

The application of these dimensions (age difference, specific sexual behaviors, and sexual intent) presents few problems in the majority of cases, where there is little room for doubt (e.g., penile penetration of the vagina or anus). In some cases, however, it can be quite difficult to determine the *intent* of the behavior. For example, a 3-year-old child describes what sounds like her grandfather's limited (a few times) touching of her labia (no penetration). The grandfather, who has cared for the child on a number of occasions, indicates that he was checking for a diaper rash (which the child has in fact had during the time the grandfather took care of the child). It is not clear if his behavior has the intent of "grooming" (see Conte, Wolf, & Smith, 1989) the child for more specific sexual behavior, does in fact serve as a form of sexual gratification, or is what the child's grandfather says it is.

Another potential problem of definition in some cases is that there is little current information available about the range of sexual behaviors generally regarded as acceptable in families or how these vary by culture or subgroup. (For an exception, see Rosenfeld et al., 1979; for an excellent current review, see Korbin, 1990.) Certainly, families vary in attitudes about nudity, privacy, touching, or kissing family members. There are no Western cultures that proscribe adult-child sexual contact as appropriate behavior.

In most cases of sexual abuse, these matters will be of little consequence because there is no doubt about the behavior (e.g., having a small child sit unclothed on a unclothed penis and rocking back and forth). There are cases, however, where these questions are of considerable importance in deciding whether the behavior is sexual abuse, inappropriate, perhaps even representing poor judgment, or a variation within acceptable bounds of adult-child contact. Often these difficult cases will involve vague descriptions of behavior by young, developmentally delayed, or extremely terrorized children, with possible, but not absolutely certain, indicators (e.g., stress symptoms in the child).

Incidence Estimates

In their comprehensive and thoughtful review of studies on the incidence and prevalence of child sexual abuse, Peters, Wyatt, and Finkelhor (1986) report that estimates of the prevalence range from 6% to 62% for females and from 3% to 31% for males. They point out that this variation may be accounted for by a number of methodological factors, such as differences in definitions of abuse, sample characteristics, interview format (e.g., in-person versus phone interview), and number of questions used to elicit information about abuse experience. While these would seem to be quite plausible reasons for the variation in estimates of incidence and prevalence, there has been no real research on these methodological factors. Hence it is not completely clear what accounts for the variation among studies.

There are a number of problems created by the variation and the magnitude of the problem as described by these figures. Even if one only takes the lowest estimates, it is clear that sexual abuse of children is a common experience of childhood and affects a large number of children. Indeed, the numbers appear so large that they serve to create a sense of disbelief about the problem and make it easier for some to turn away from the problem as impossibly large. The variation in estimates and the resulting disagreement in professional and media reports on child sexual abuse, although potentially understandable due to methodological factors, such as those discussed by Peters et al. (1986), also tends to create a sense of irritation in those, especially policy-makers and professionals, who hear the varying estimates. This can serve to support a sense that the problem may be overestimated or that there is much "hype" surrounding the problem. In time, it is likely that surveys of the general population (that is, not clinical samples or regionally biased samples) using tested survey methodologies will provide additional information about the rate of childhood sexual abuse.

Knowledge Domains

No scholar has yet fully categorized child sexual abuse knowledge. There are, no doubt, many ways to organize such knowledge, and knowledge domains do overlap. Most critically, knowledge from a wide range of social and behavioral sciences, although not strictly thought of as "child sexual abuse" knowledge, is important in understanding various aspects of child sexual abuse. For the time, I suggest that you view current sexual abuse knowledge and knowledge development activities as falling within the following areas.

The Nature and Extent of Sexual Abuse

This includes studies that describe the characteristics of various samples of victim, offenders, their families, and the relationship among these. This includes information about age, race, gender, the relationship between offender and victim, the specific acts and behaviors making up the abuse, or associated social, psychological, or other characteristics (e.g., degree of social isolation of the victim). Knowledge in this area includes information about how victims experience sexual abuse (see, e.g., Summit, 1983), abuse of special populations of children, such as boys (see, e.g., Friedrich, Beilke, & Urquiza, 1988) or very young children (see, e.g., MacFarlane, Cockriel, & Dugan, 1990), or the types of sexual behavior children are exposed to (see, e.g., Kercher & McShane, 1983).

An important thing to bear in mind when reading these descriptive reports is how the sample was drawn or created. Most descriptive reports describe a sample of children or adults seen in a community agency or clinic. These "clinical samples" may or may not be similar to all abused children or adults abused in childhood. The *representativeness* of the sample is often not known and hence *generalizations* should be made cautiously.

This should not be taken as major criticism of these studies. Indeed, *description* (describing what is) is the first task of science. The large number of descriptive studies carried out over the last 10 to 15 years have helped us understand many things about the nature and extent of sexual abuse of children.

For example, there has been some effort to identify factors that increase children's risk for sexual abuse. The ability of professionals and parents to identify factors that increase a child's risk for sexual abuse would be immensely useful in protecting children from sexual victimization. Finkelhor and Baron (1986) conclude in their comprehensive review that it is currently not clear what factors increase children's risk for sexual abuse. It appears that girls are at greater risk, although boys are also victimized. Girls are more likely to be victimized if they have somehow been separated from their mothers (e.g., ever lived away from mother, mother ill or disabled) or if they report poor relationships with their mothers. As the authors note, these factors may be consequences of sexual abuse as much as risk factors.

There have also been efforts to describe the types of behavior to which children have been exposed. For example, Erickson, Walbek, and Seely (1988) present relatively specific sexual behavior descriptions for a sample of 229 sexual offenders against male and female children. *Vaginal contact* occurred in 42% of female cases, *anal contact* in 33% of male and 10% of female cases, *offender oral* in 41% of male and 19% of female cases, *victim oral* in 29% of male and 17% of female, *offender fondle* in 43% of male and 54% of female, and *victim fondle* in 8% of male and 7% of female cases.

There have been a number of descriptive reports based on victims that have described the specific sexual behaviors to which the child was exposed, although different studies have employed somewhat different definitions for the sexual behaviors examined. Kendel-Tackett and Simon (1987), in their description of 365 adults sexually abused in childhood, report that 64% experienced fondling from the waist up; 92%, fondling from the waist down; 48%, oral sex; 19%, attempted intercourse; 10%, simulated intercourse; 44%, intercourse; and 9%, anal intercourse. Kercher and McShane (1983) describe the sexual behaviors a sample of 619 children were exposed to: 19%, exhibitionism by perpetrator; 42%, fondling by perpetrator; 39%, heterosexual intercourse; 6%, homosexual intercourse; 14%, oral sex on victim; 14%, oral sex on perpetrator; 8%, perpetrator masturbates self; 2%, photographing child nude or in sexual act; 2%, prostitution of victim; 2%, sale/distribution of erotic material to victim; and 3%, sexual performance by child.

A number of investigators have explored the relationship between the victim and offender and the specific type of sexual behaviors constituting the sexual abuse. For example, using data on child victims, Kercher and McShane (1983) found significant differences for 3 of 9 sexual behaviors (reported above). Intrafamilial sexual abuse cases were more likely to include fondling and heterosexual intercourse and less likely to include exhibitionism than extrafamilial sexual abuse cases. One wonders whether the lower reporting of exhibitionism in family cases reflects a greater tolerance for nudity in families or than between nonrelated adults and children. In her sample of adults abused as children, Russell (1984) examined the degree of seriousness of the sexual abuse by the relationship between victim and offender. *Very serious* sexual abuse included completed or attempted vaginal, oral, or anal intercourse, cunnilingus, anilingus; *serious* sexual abuse included completed and attempted genital fondling, simulated intercourse, and digital penetration; and *less serious* sexual abuse included completed and attempted acts of sexual touching of buttocks, thighs, legs or other body parts, clothed breasts, or genitals, or kissing. Of the incest cases, 23% involved very serious, 41% serious, and 36% less serious abuse; 53% of nonincestuous abuse consisted of very serious, 27% serious, and 20% less serious sexual abuse.

Sexual Offenders

There has been a long and productive tradition spanning more than two decades of effort to understand sexual offenders. There have been a wide range of knowledge development activities. For example, an early and ongoing effort has been to characterize the sexual offender. This has also been an area especially marked by the field's tendency to believe things at one point in time that only a few years later look not to be accurate. For example, some attention has been directed toward the identification of psychological characteristics of offenders (e.g., profiles on psychological tests). Clinically, although men are far more often identified as the sexual offender, females are known to sexually abuse children. Offenders of virtually all ages and sociodemographic characteristics have been identified. To date, there has been no psychological profile or set of psychological characteristics that discriminate between men who have and men who have not had sex with children (see Armentrout & Hauer, 1978; Langevin, Handy, Russon, & Day, 1985; Quinsey, 1983).

Early on, it was thought that offenders were either fixated or regressed (Groth, Hobson, & Gary, 1982). The *fixated* offender was thought to have a primary sexual orientation toward children; this interest usually begins in adolescence, there appears no precipitating event associated with the onset of the orientation, and male victims are primary targets. The *regressed* offender develops a primary sexual orientation to age-mates; the sexual involvement with a child is a clear change in interest and behavior, comes about usually at a time of stress, may be more episodic, and female victims are primary targets.

This model was primarily developed on an incarcerated sample of sexual offenders. Men in prison may be quite psychologically distinct from men with the same problem who are not in prison. To date, no empirical evidence exists for the accuracy of the topology to classify adult sexual offenders. Indeed, community therapists report that many offenders have characteristics of both the regressed and the fixated offender. It appears that the largest group of offenders is a mixed group combining certain of the characteristics of both fixated and regressed. For example, in the sample of offenders described by Abel et al. (1988), of the 159 incestuous offenders referred for sexual abuse of a daughter, 12% had abused nonrelated male children, 49% had abused nonrelated female children, and 19% had raped adult females. (Another example of what now appears to be an unhelpful classification concept is that all offenders are either incest offenders or pedophiles. This issue was briefly touched upon above. For additional readings, see Conte, 1991.)

Sexual Arousal

A hallmark of research on sexual offenders has been a long tradition of methodological research to develop assessment procedures and measures (see, e.g., Marshall, Laws, & Barbaree, 1990). Among the most controversial assessment devices developed out of this tradition of research is penile plysmography (see Earls & Marshall, 1983). This procedure involves a male subject, in the privacy of a lab or clinic, placing a mercury-encased-in-rubber strain gauge around the base of his penis. The subject is then shown slides or videos of different types of sexual partners (e.g., same-age opposite sex partners, young male children, adolescent—11-13—females) or listens to audiotaped descriptions of different kinds of sexual encounters (e.g., consenting nonviolent sex with an opposite sex, same-age partner; nonconsenting, violent sex with a male child). The strain gauge is sensitive to small increases in the circumference of the penis and percentage of arousal is recorded by the plysmograph.

This assessment procedure has been the subject of considerable debate. On the face of it, it presents an intuitively obvious measure of sexual arousal in males. It runs counter to a long-held believe about incest, that "incest is the sexual expression of nonsexual needs" (for discussion, see Conte, 1985). It is increasingly being used as an assessment device in community settings and often with men who deny sexual abuse charges. Earls (1991), in an excellent review, points to the many problems with the use of penile plysmography in forensic evaluations with men who deny abuse. Some of these include the following: Some men who engage in deviant sexual behavior may not demonstrate deviant arousal in the lab and some men (although it appears few) may demonstrate deviant arousal in the lab and not abuse children. Because, however, it is also clear that the self-report of sexual offenders is likely to be unreliable (Abel, Becker, Murphy, & Flanagan, 1981; Marshall & Christie, 1981; Quinsey, 1984; Quinsey, Steinman, Bergersen, & Holmes, 1975), evaluations of men accused of sexual abuse when done for the legal system are going to be inherently limited. Another concern about lab assessments is that not all men respond sexually in the laboratory (e.g., 22% of child molesters and 34% of incest offenders in Marshall, Barbaree, & Christophie, 1986, and 80% of subjects in Hall, Proctor, & Nelson, 1988, were able to inhibit sexual arousal).

Currently available research suggests that many men do respond differentially to various sexual stimuli (e.g., slides of sexual partners varying by age or sex or audiotaped descriptions of various sexual behaviors). Some studies have found that sexual arousal measures can discriminate between violent and less violent offenders (see, e.g., Abel, Barlow, Blanchard, & Guild, 1977; Hall et al., 1988; Quinsey & Chaplin, 1988). And child molesters respond differentially to adult and child stimuli, with more arousal to child stimuli (both male and female children). A sample of normals selected from the community and nonsexual offenders responded only to adult, consenting stimuli (Quinsey & Chaplin, 1988).

Nonetheless, as a knowledge development or research tool, the importance of the study of sexual arousal is clear. For example, a number of studies have examined the sexual arousal of incest fathers and stepfathers. Quinsey, Chaplin, and Carrigan (1979) evaluated 9 incestuous and 7 nonincestuous child molesters and found that incestuous (father or stepfather) offenders exhibited more appropriate (i.e., adult) sexual arousal than nonincestuous child molesters. Abel et al. (1981) found that incest offenders were sexually aroused to children. Marshall et al. (1986) evaluated 40 child molesters, 21 incest offenders, and 22 normal controls. The normals demonstrated minimal arousal to children (under age 12), slight arousal to children 12-14, and a dramatic increase with substantial arousal to children 14 years and older. Child molesters showed considerable arousal to children, with the largest amount of arousal to 9-year-olds, decreasing arousal to 11-, 12-, and 13-year-olds, and a gradually increasing arousal from 14- to 24-year-olds. The findings that child molesters are aroused to children and adults is surprising and not consistent with other research. Incest offenders more closely parallel normals, although they showed no dramatic arousal increase to children over 14 (as did normals). There were significant differences between normals and incest offenders in the magnitude of their arousal to 14- to 24-year-olds, with the incest offenders showing less arousal to older persons.

These data are contradictory and limited but nonetheless illustrate the importance of basing practice and practice knowledge on *what is known* and not on *what is believed or hoped*. What has been learned from studies on sexual arousal must be viewed in the context of the methodological problems or issues presented in the research. This is true of all research-based knowledge. For example, as Marshall et al. (1986) point out, many studies have mixed natural fathers, stepfathers, and adoptive fathers in a single incest sample. It may well be that the level of arousal to children will vary across these subsamples. Other problems in the studies of sexual arousal in incestuous and nonincestuous offenders include small sample sizes, selection of nonrepresentative samples or samples of unknown representativeness, lack of raters blind to the hypotheses, and lack of control groups (Avery-Clark, O'Neil, & Laws, 1981).

Consequences of Abuse

One of the largest literature areas in child sexual abuse has been that concerning the effects of sexual abuse in childhood on children (often referred to as the initial effects) and on adults abused in childhood (long-term effects). This research area has become increasing sophisticated and moved from early clinical and anecdotal reports where the effects of impacts of abuse are described in the lives of a small number of subjects to studies using multiple measures with control or comparison groups to the group of sexually abused children. (For recent reviews, see Starr & Wolfe, 1991.)

A wide range of emotional and behavioral problems have been identified with child sexual abuse. These include learning difficulties, sexual promiscuity, runaway behavior, somatic complaints, and sudden changes in behavior (Burgess, Groth, & McCausland, 1981); hysterical seizures (Goodwin, Simms, & Bergman, 1979); phobias, nightmares, and compulsive rituals (Weiss et al., 1955); self-destructive or suicidal behavior (Carroll, Schaffer, Spensley, & Abramowitz, 1980; DeYoung, 1982; Yorukoglu & Kempe, 1966). Much of this literature has consisted of clinical, anecdotal reports of relatively small samples. Rarely have assessments of the psychological or social functioning of victims been aided by measurement. Most reports have failed to include comparison groups or other control procedures. Cases have not been consistently described so that the substance use of one patient and the relationship difficulties of another is outlined. It is not clear what substance use there is in the second case or what relationship difficulties are present in the first case.

Recent reports have tended to employ actual measurement of subject functioning and often employ comparison or other control procedures. These recent studies have tended to describe differences in psychological functioning between children who have sexual abuse histories and those who do not. For example, Gomes-Schwartz, Horowitz, and Sauzier (1985) compared 156 sexually abused children with the norms provided for the Louisville Behavior Checklist (LBC) and found that the preschool children (N = 30) were rated as more pathological than the normative group on 10 of the 16 behavioral dimensions of the LBC (e.g., infantile aggression, fear, immaturity, cognitive disability, and prosocial deficit). Comparison of the abused children with the norms for a group of children receiving mental health services revealed that abused children exhibited less overall pathology and fewer specific difficulties than norms derived from the clinically referred children. School-age sexually abused children (N = 58) exhibited significantly more pathology on every dimension of the LBC (infantile aggression, hyperactivity, antisocial behavior, aggression, social withdrawal, sensitivity, fear, inhibition, academic disability, immaturity, learning disability, normal irritability, neurotic behavior, and psychotic behavior, somatic behavior, and prosocial deficits such as lack of social skills). School-age sexually abused children exhibited less problematic functioning on 11 of 16 LBC dimensions than other children in mental health treatment. As is generally recognized, the comparison of samples with standardized norms can be quite problematic because it is often not known in what ways the sample significantly varies from the samples used to the develop the norms. Another problem created for some professionals and students of child sexual abuse is that the names of some of the factors or dimensions of behaviors measured by the LBC (and other multi-item, multifactor measures) are abstract. For example, what is normal *irritability* or *sensitivity*?

Several recent studies have employed comparison groups. For example, Conte and Scheruman (1987) compared a sample of 369 victims of sexual abuse aged 4 to 17 years old with a comparison group of 318 children who had not been abused. On a 110-item parent-completed behavior checklist (Child Behavior

Profile), sexually abused children were found to display significantly more dysfunction on 12 dimensions (concentration problems, aggressive, withdrawn, somatic complaints, character personalty style—nice or pleasant disposition, too anxious to please—antisocial behavior, nervous/emotional, depression, behavioral regression, body image/self-esteem problems, fear, and symptoms of posttraumatic stress). (See also Gomes-Schwartz, Horowitz, & Cardarelli, 1990; Lipovsky, Saunders, & Murphy, 1989; Mannarino, Cohen, & Gregor, 1989; Wolfe, Gentile, & Wolfe, 1989.)

Available data indicate that sexual abuse in childhood is associated with a variety of negative social, emotional, behavioral, and physical problems. Sexually abused children appear to function differently than do children who have not been abused and those identified as problematic for nonsexual abuse reasons (e.g., physical abuse, psychiatric hospitalization). There is disagreement on the nature of these differences and some disagreement across studies on the specific problems associated with abuse. Some of the differences in findings across studies may result from different investigators employing different measures of functioning or in differences in the characteristics of samples. Some studies continue to examine effects in relatively small samples and comparison groups are often not comparable on many dimensions in addition to the sexual abuse/not sexual abuse one of major interest. As Berliner and Wheeler (1987) have pointed out, much of the literature has been atheoretical or lacking in conceptualization of the effects of sexual abuse with clear diagnostic or therapeutic implications. Studies vary considerably in the behavioral specificity employed in the description of victim functioning, and comparison across studies is often impossible.

Increasingly, investigators have sought to identify factors (e.g., who the offender was, what type of sexual behavior the child was exposed to) accounting for variation in the effect of abuse. Understanding what factors increase risk for more serious impact or effects of abuse can be helpful in identifying victims at greatest need for treatment and (depending on the type of risk factor) may help direct treatment. Finkelhor (1986) reports that there is considerable disagreement among the handful of studies about which factors are associated with more negative effects. In a recent, excellent review, Berliner (1991) suggests that the following are associated with a more serious or negative impact: longer duration, force, and closer relationship between victim and offender. Parental support and belief of the child appear to be associated with less negative effects. Some factors (such as age) have not been shown to be consistently associated with more negative effects.

Assessment of Children
for Possible Abuse

There has been a great deal of research on various aspects of how adults come to a decision about whether a child has been abused or not. This issue occupies a great deal of professional time and concern. It is the subject of heated debate in courts, disagreement among professionals, and controversial news reports. Some of the research that informs this area of practice includes information about the differences between "true" and "false" allegations (see, e.g., DeYoung, 1986; Everson & Boat, in press-a; Green, 1986; Johnson & Foley, 1984; Rosenfeld et al., 1979); the use of anatomically correct or anatomically detailed dolls (e.g., Boat & Everson, 1986; Everson & Boat, in press-b; Gabriel, 1985; Jampole & Weber, 1987; White, Strom, Santilli, & Halpin, 1986); interviewing child victims (see, e.g., Jones & McQuiston, 1985; Spaulding, 1987); children as witnesses (see, e.g., Benedek & Schetky, 1986, 1987a, 1987b; Goodman, 1984; Goodman, Aman, & Hirschman, 1987; Goodman & Rosenberg, 1987; and medical evaluations of children (see, e.g., Cantwell, 1987).

It is quite obvious that the professional assessment of whether a child has been sexually abused, whether correct or not, has profound implications for the child, the child's loved ones, and the adult (if identified) who may have abused the child. Although a professional opinion about whether a child has been abused is generally not admissible in criminal court (see Melton & Limbers, 1989), such opinions are used in family and juvenile court proceedings, child protection investigations, and mental health assessments. In many cases, the decision is not all that difficult (e.g., an older child—4 years and older—making relatively clear descriptions of sexual contact with an older person).

In other cases (e.g., those involving young children making vague or unclear statements or seriously traumatized children), the determination of abuse can be extremely difficult.

Recently, it has become increasingly clear that *belief* plays a role in determining whether a child has been abused. For example, if an evaluator believes that children who are abused are usually exposed to a seduction or grooming process directed by the offender and a particular child describes no grooming process, the evaluator may tend to disbelieve the child's report even though it is known that some children are abused without any grooming behaviors on the part of the offender (Berliner & Conte, 1990).

The role of belief is important in the assessment of children who may have been abused and is only now being studied. Everson and Boat (1990), in a study of CPS workers, report that workers who believe that children make false reports are more likely to have encountered reports that they judged to be false. While the direction of influence is not clear (did belief influence behavior or behavior belief?), this study points to the strong possibility that what professionals believe influences the action they take on cases. A concern about professional belief is that what professionals believe may in fact be incorrect. In a survey of 212 professionals across the United States, Conte, Sorenson, Fogarty, and Dalla Rosa (1991) report that some professional knowledge (especially about sexual offenders) is at variance with the research literature. Illustrative of this point is the analysis of Berliner and Conte (in press), who point out that several recent reports have documented that professionals often believe allegations of childhood sexual abuse arising in divorce/custody disputes are less likely to be true (Conte et al., 1991; Thoenes & Tjaden, 1990). There is not a single empirical study that has documented that, in fact, false cases of sexual abuse are more likely to arise in divorce/custody cases. Belief may or may not be based on scientifically verified knowledge.

Another aspect of determining whether a child has been abused that has received recent research attention is the use of anatomical dolls as an interview aid with children who may have been abused. The dolls have been recommended as a communication device whereby a child could demonstrate for an adult what the child could not say. It was argued that very young children and all children with language problems (e.g., developmentally disabled children) could demonstrate with dolls what they could not say. At no point were dolls ever intended to be a diagnostic tool. The use of anatomically correct dolls has received an inordinate amount of attention, in part because the fact of their genitalia have made them atypical. Research has demonstrated that young children (3 and 5) are no more suggestible when interviewed with anatomically correct dolls than with regular (nonanatomical) dolls (Goodman & Clarke-Stewart, 1991). A number of studies have documented that both abused and not-abused children exhibit behaviors with the dolls (e.g., demonstrating sexual behavior) thought to be suggestive of sexual abuse, although overwhelmingly the proportion of abused children exhibiting such behavior is greater than for those not abused (Everson & Boat, 1990; Jampole & Weber, 1987). For example, inspection of the table summarizing data in Jampole and Weber (1987) indicates that the only behaviors that some not abused children did not exhibit were the demonstration of intercourse between the dolls and the demonstration of oral sex between the dolls. For example, of 7 children who penetrated the genitals of the dolls with their fingers, 5 were in the abused group.

Other research has indicated that not-abused young children (e.g., 10% of 3-year-olds and 80% of 5-year-olds) refer to the dolls and their sexual parts after a doll interview (Boat, Everson, & Holland, 1990); 37% of the mothers of these not-abused children reported behavioral sequelae in their children following the doll interview. Sexual behavior with the dolls in the presence of an adult in not-abused children is more likely in lower SES black males (Everson & Boat, 1990). Other research has examined not-abused children's (3- to 8-year-olds) labels for sex-related body parts (Schor & Sivan, 1989). Boat and Everson (1988) describe the level of training of professionals in the use of the dolls (e.g., at the time of the research, less than 50% of CPS and law enforcement personnel had even minimal training).

There are a number of important questions not yet addressed by the research. With the exception of those in Boat and Everson (1988), there are no data on how the dolls are actually used in practice. It is currently not clear what prior exposure to sexually explicit material (either in vivo observation of parents or media) has (if any) on children's demonstrations with dolls. It is clear that behaviors vary by race (Everson & Boat, 1990). It is not currently known the extent to which family values about touching and bodies or psychological characteristics of the child (e.g., degree of assertiveness or inquisitiveness or IQ) may interact with children's reactions to the dolls. Given that more than 50% of parents in Schor and Sivan (1989) do not have separate names for sex-related body parts, it would not be surprising to find some variation in children's knowledge or reactions to the anatomical dolls. Whether these are of sufficient magnitude to influence an assessment is currently only a matter of speculation. Although there are a number of well-designed and well-executed studies dealing with anatomical dolls, there are virtually no data available on the reliability of adult descriptions or conclusions based on the dolls. It is not always clear from research reports what variation has existed among observers about whether children exhibited certain behaviors. Sometimes children exhibit behaviors in interaction with the dolls that may or may not be "indicative" depending on the observer. Estimates of the reliability (interobserver) or accuracy of such judgments seem to be a key piece of information not currently available. It is quite likely that professionals will vary on the nature of their judgments depending on training.

Notwithstanding these issues, there is an emerging research literature that supports the careful and informed use of the dolls as an aid in the assessment of children who may have been abused. For example, dolls may be used with children to determine what terms are used by a child to refer to what body parts. A child may describe touching of a certain body part or describe a behavior that is not known to the evaluator (e.g., "bumping" for intercourse). Asking the child to demonstrate what part of the body was touched or what "bumping" looks like with the dolls is a good use for this tool. Research on the anatomical dolls illustrates how research can build findings over time that inform practice. As a result, professional use of the dolls today can be more knowledge based than when the dolls first appeared on the professional market.

Prevention of Sexual Abuse

There has been considerable attention paid by the public and processionals to programs (e.g., in-school training programs, television shows, books) to prevent sexual abuse in childhood. As Conte, Rosen, and Saperstein (1987) have suggested, there are a set of core assumptions upon which most sexual abuse prevention efforts rest: Many children do not know what sexual abuse is, that sexual touch need not be tolerated, that adults want to know about sexual touching by older persons, and that it is possible to tell about sexual abuse to have it cease. Children can be taught knowledge (e.g., the difference between a safe and unsafe touch or who to tell about abuse) and skills (e.g., how to assertively say "no" to unwanted touch) that will be useful in preventing or escaping their own abuse.

These assumptions underpin a large number of programs and materials designed to help children prevent or escape sexual abuse (for reviews, see Kolko, 1988; Tharinger et al., 1988; Wurtele, 1987). There are differences among these programs and materials in terms of the range of material presented, the time it takes to deliver the message to the child, the concepts or words used to describe the concepts, the location in which the material is presented (e.g., home or school), the format of presentation (e.g., video, instruction by adult trainers, printed matter), the degree to which the child interacts with the materials (e.g., reads a book, listens and asks questions of an instructor, observes a model demonstrating a prevention behavior and then role-plays the skills), and occupation of the trainer. With the exception of the value of modeling and rehearsal of skills, little is known about how important these alternatives are in the prevention effort.

Notwithstanding this variation, most prevention material consists of the key concepts outlined by Conte et al. (1987). These include the concept that children own their *own bodies* and therefore can control access to their bodies; there is a *touch continuum*, which recognizes that there are different kinds of touches (e.g., safe and unsafe); *secrets about touching* can and should be told; children have a range of individuals in their *support systems* whom they can tell about touching problems; some programs encourage children to *trust their own feelings* so that, when a situation feels uncomfortable or strange, they should tell someone; and they can learn *how to say* "no!"

There has been a considerable amount of research addressing various aspects of prevention programs (for reviews, see Conte

& Fogarty, 1990; Finkelhor & Strapko, 1987; Kolko, 1988; Tharinger et al., 1988; Wurtele, 1987). The ability of children to learn prevention concepts (i.e., knowledge gains) has been found in evaluations of several different programs using a variety of training formats (Binder & McNeil, 1987; Conte, Rosen, Saperstein, & Shermack, 1985; Downer, 1984; Garbarino, 1987; Harvey, Forehand, Brown, & Holmes, 1988; Plummer, 1984; Wolfe, MacPherson, Blount, & Wolfe, 1986; Wurtele, Kast, Miller-Perrin, & Kondrick, 1989; Wurtele, Marrs, & Miller-Perrin, 1987). Most evaluations assess learning directly following the education program but only a few have instituted a follow-up assessment to look at "long-term" knowledge retention. Harvey and colleagues (1988) found that, at a 7-week follow-up, children in the treatment condition had retained the knowledge gains found at posttest and scored significantly higher than controls at the follow-up assessment.

Although evaluations have generally found overall knowledge gains following prevention program implementation, there is evidence that some concepts are more difficult to learn than others. For example, at least one study empirically supported the notion that children have an easier time learning concrete than abstract concepts (Conte et al., 1985). Similarly, Gilbert and his colleagues report that preschoolers had difficulty explaining the abstract idea of why specific touches would create specific feelings and could not give examples of why feelings about a touch might change (Gilbert et al., 1988). These same children had difficulty learning which secrets to keep (e.g., secrets about a surprise party) and which to report (e.g., secrets about touching).

Another difficult concept included in most prevention curricula is that someone familiar to the child can be the perpetrator of sexual assault. Some evaluations have found that, even after training, children have a difficult time understanding that a family member or someone they know could try to abuse them (Wurtele et al., 1987) and have difficulty knowing what to do if approached by someone known (Plummer, 1984). Although it was found that the percentage of incorrect responses to the question, "Do kids ever have touching problems with people they know and like?" decreased from 62% at pretest to 11% after training, this was still the most difficult item at posttest. Other studies have also found substantial posttraining increases on this concept (Kenning, Gallmeier, Jackson, & Plemons, 1987; Swan,

Press, & Briggs, 1985), but it continues to be a difficult one for children and adults in our society. Another concept found difficult to learn in two studies is that the victim is not to blame (Plummer, 1984; Wolfe et al., 1986). This is understandable following a program in which we are at once describing sexual touch as "bad" or "inappropriate" and inviting children to take responsibility for their bodily integrity while presenting sexual touch as the "adult's fault." The implied message may be that "it is your fault" if sexual touching occurs, because you should know it's bad and now you should know how to escape it.

Behavioral Strategies:
Say "No," Get Away, Tell Someone

Prevention education programs typically teach children to follow three strategies in a "dangerous" or sexually abusive situation. Children are taught to say "no," to get away from the assailant or dangerous situation, and to report the incident to a trusted adult. Many evaluations have assessed the learning of these skills using multiple choice, true/false, or yes/no questions such as this one: "If an older child touched your private parts, would you tell?" (Binder & McNeil, 1987; Conte et al., 1985; Plummer, 1984; Wolfe et al., 1986).

Another method of assessing the three behavioral rules has involved presenting scenarios including appropriate and inappropriate touch and asking the child what should be done in such a situation (Borkin & Frank, 1986; Harvey et al., 1988; Hill & Jason, 1988; Kenning et al., 1987; Kolko, Moser, Litz, & Hughes, 1987; Thiesse-Duffy et al., 1987; Wurtele et al., 1989; Wurtele, Marrs, & Miller-Perrin, 1987). For example, in one study children were asked: "What if you are having fun wrestling with your cousin, and all of a sudden your cousin starts grabbing and feeling your private parts. Is there anything wrong with this situation?" (from the WIST; Wurtele et al., 1987). Assessments of this kind have the advantage of requiring a child to apply prevention knowledge rather than just reciting it. Again, although it is not certain that success on such measures is correlated with prevention behaviors in real life situations, results of these behavioral assessments have been promising.

Unanticipated Consequences

As attention to programs aimed at empowering children to prevent their own sexual victimization increases, so does the fear that these same programs may be hastily instituted, harmful to children, and create a false sense of security to members of our society. Researchers have attempted to address concerns that program participation may be harmful to children by evaluating immediate behavioral changes or increases in fear and anxiety. Using these outcomes to measure effects, evaluations have generally found positive results (Binder & McNeil, 1987; Kenning et al., 1987; Miltenberger & Thiesse-Duffy, 1988; Wolfe et al., 1986). Binder and McNeil (1987) found no significant increases in behavior problems recorded by parents' ratings after prevention programs in a 5- through 12-year-old sample but did find a decrease in 3 of 18 problem behaviors. Miltenberger and Thiesse-Duffy (1988) found no new behavioral problems, nightmares, or other lasting emotional reactions according to parent reports but nearly a third of the children were "a little more scared" and more than two thirds were more cautious.

Overall, it appears that the sexual abuse prevention education programs evaluated to date have generally achieved the goals of teaching prevention knowledge and skill acquisition. It remains to be seen if these gains will be retained over time and will be useful to a child in a potential assault situation. It also appears that curricula employing concrete concepts, and an interactive learning experience, including rehearsal and modeling, will be most effective. Although the goal of exposing abuse needs to be more systematically assessed, current data do not support this desired program effect. Fears that prevention programs will have negative consequences on the child, such as increasing anxiety or creating behavioral problems, don't seem to be supported by the data—generally speaking. There are currently no research data indicating whether children can actually use this knowledge to prevent, escape, or avoid their own abuse. This clearly is the prevention research question for the next decade.

And, yet, in the face of these generally positive results, arguments continue to be offered that children should not be expected to protect themselves, that it is the responsibility of parents to protect children, and that little can really be done to make the battle between a child and an adult sexually interested in that child at all a fair one. I know of none in the field of sexual abuse prevention who disagrees with these points. Sexual abuse prevention programs were never conceived of as the best way to prevent abuse. But, for the time, they may be the best or only way to try.

Sexual abuse took place for generations within the homes and under the "supervision" of parents. If the critics of prevention think they have a better way to protect children, to help adults protect children, or to equalize the battle between children and sexual offenders, then let them offer their programs and their research data. Until then, to stop prevention programs that have amassed this amount of research support is to give in to an ideological battle of unclear dimensions.

Final Note

The development of knowledge about the nature, effects, assessment, and prevention of childhood sexual abuse has been dramatic. It is clear that there are many questions yet to be addressed about childhood sexual abuse. It is also clear that an increasing number of students, professionals, and the public in general are concerned about this problem. It remains the responsibility of students and professionals to be sure that what they believe about sexual abuse is in fact what is true and accurate. In the long run, knowledge must inform what can be done to help sexually abused children and to end sexual abuse in the future.

References

Abel, G., Barlow, D. H., Blanchard, E. B., & Guild, D. (1977). The components of rapists' sexual arousal. *Archives of General Psychiatry, 34,* 895-903.

Abel, G., Becker, J., Cunningham-Rathner, J., Mittelman, M., & Rouleau, J. L. (1988). Multiple paraphiliac diagnoses among sex offenders. *Bulletin of the American Academy of Psychiatry and the Law, 16*(2), 153-168.

Abel, G., Becker, J., Murphy, W., & Flanagan, B. (1981). Identifying dangerous child molesters. In R. Stuart (Ed.), *Violent behavior: Social learning approaches to prediction, management and treatment* (pp. 116-137). New York: Brunner/Mazel.

American Psychiatric Association. (1987). *Diagnostic and statistical manual of mental disorders* (3rd ed., rev.). Washington, DC: Author.

Armentrout, J. A., & Hauer, A. L. (1978). MMPIs of rapists of adults, rapists of children, and non-rapist sex offenders. *Journal of Clinical Psychology, 34,* 330-332.

Avery-Clark, C., O'Neil, J., & Laws, D. R. (1981). A comparison of intrafamilial sexual and physical child abuse. In M. Cook & K. Howells (Eds.), *Adult sexual interest in children.* London: Academic Press.

Bender, L., & Gruett, A. (1952). A follow-up report on children who had atypical sexual experiences. *American Journal of Orthopsychiatry, 22,* 825-837.

Benedek, E., & Schetky, D. (1986). The child as a witness. *Hospital and Community Psychiatry, 37*(12), 1225-1229.

Benedek, E., & Schetky, D. (1987a). Problems in validating allegations of sexual abuse. Part 1: Factors affecting perception and recall of events. *Journal of the American Academy of Child and Adolescent Psychiatry, 26,* 912-915.

Benedek, E., & Schetky, D. (1987b). Problems in validating allegations of sexual abuse. Part 2: Clinical evaluation. *Journal of the American Academy of Child and Adolescent Psychiatry, 26,* 916-921.

Berliner, L. (1991). Effects of sexual abuse on children. *Violence Update, 1*(10), 1, 8, 10-11.

Berliner, L., & Conte, J. (1990). The process of victimization: The victims' perspective. *Child Abuse & Neglect, 14,* 29-40.

Berliner, L., & Conte, J. (in press). Sexual abuse evaluations: Conceptual and empirical obstacles. *Child Abuse & Neglect.*

Berliner, L., & Wheeler, J. R. (1987). Treating the effects of sexual abuse on children. *Journal of Interpersonal Violence, 2,* 1415-1434.

Binder, R., & McNeil, D. (1987). Evaluation of a school-based sexual abuse prevention program: Cognitive and emotional effects. *Child Abuse & Neglect, 11,* 497-506.

Boat, B., & Everson, M. (1986). *Using anatomical dolls: Guidelines for interviewing young children in sexual abuse investigations* (Training manual). North Carolina Department of Human Resources.

Boat, B., & Everson, M. (1988). Interviewing young children with anatomical dolls. *Child Welfare, 62,* 337-352.

Boat, B. & Everson, M.

Boat, B., Everson, M., & Holland, J. (1990). Maternal perceptions of nonabused young children's behavior after the children's exposure to anatomical dolls. *Child Welfare, 69,* 389-400.

Borkin, J., & Frank, L. (1986). Sexual abuse prevention for preschoolers: A pilot program. *Child Welfare, 65*(1), 75-82.

Burgess, A. W., Groth, A. N., & McCausland, M. P. (1981). Child sex initiation rings. *American Journal of Orthopsychiatry, 51*(1), 110-119.

Cantwell, H. (1987). Update on vaginal inspection as it relates to child sexual abuse in girls under thirteen. *Child Abuse & Neglect, 11,* 545-546.

Carroll, J., Schaffer, C., Spensley, J., & Abramowitz, S. I. (1980). Family experiences of self-mutilating patients. *American Journal of Psychiatry, 137*(7), 852-853.

Conte, J. (1985). Clinical dimensions of adult sexual use of children. *Behavioral Sciences and the Law, 3*(4), 341-354.

Conte, J. (1986). Child sexual abuse and the family: A critical analysis. *Journal of Psychotherapy and the Family, 2*(2), 113-126.

Conte, J. (1991). The nature of sexual offenses against children. In C. Hollin & K. Howells (Eds.), *Clinical approaches to sex offenders and their victims* (pp. 11-34). New York: John Wiley.

Conte, J., & Fogarty, L. (1990). Programs for children on child abuse. *Education and Urban Society, 22*(3), 270-284.

Conte, J., Rosen, C., & Saperstein, L. (1987). An analysis of programs to prevent the sexual victimization of young children. *The Journal of Primary Prevention, 6*(3), 141-155.

Conte, J., Rosen, C., Saperstein, L., & Shermack, R. (1985). An evaluation of a program to prevent the sexual victimization of young children. *Child Abuse & Neglect, 9,* 319-328.

Conte, J., & Scheruman, J. (1987). Factors associated with an increased impact of child sexual abuse. *Child Abuse & Neglect, 11,* 201-211.

Conte, J., Sorenson, E., Fogarty, L., & Dalla Rosa, J. (1991). Evaluating children's reports of sexual abuse: Results from a survey of professionals. *American Journal of Orthopsychiatry, 61*(3), 428-437.

Conte, J., Wolf, S., & Smith, T. (1989). What sexual offenders tell us about prevention. *Child Abuse & Neglect, 13*(2), 293-302.

DeYoung, M. (1982). *The sexual victimization of children.* Jefferson, NC: McFarland.

DeYoung, M. (1986). A conceptual model for judging the truthfulness of a young child's allegation of sexual abuse. *American Journal of Orthopsychiatry, 56,* 550-559.

Downer, A. (1984). *Evaluation of talking about touching.* Seattle, WA: Committee for Children. (Available from the author in care of the Committee for Children)

Earls, C. M. (1991). The relationship of sexual arousal to sexual assault. *Violence Update, 2*(1), 1, 8, 10-11.

Earls, C., & Marshall, W. L. (1983). The current state of technology in the laboratory assessment of sexual arousal patterns. In J. G. Greer & I. R. Stuart (Eds.), *The sexual aggressor: Current perspectives on treatment.* New York: Reinhold.

Erickson, W. D., Walbek, N. H., & Seely, R. K. (1988). Behavior patterns of child molesters. *Archives of Sexual Behavior, 17,* 77-86.

Everson, M., & Boat, B. (1990). Sexualized doll play among young children: Implications for the use of anatomical dolls in sexual abuse evaluations. *Journal of the American Academy of Child and Adolescent Psychiatry, 29,* 736-742.

Everson, M., & Boat, B. (in press-a). False allegations of sexual abuse by children and adolescents. *Journal of the American Academy of Child and Adolescent Psychiatry.*

Everson, M., & Boat, B. *Putting the anatomical doll controversy in perspective: An examination of the major uses and related criticisms.* Unpublished manuscript, University of North Carolina, Chapel Hill.

Finkelhor, D. (1979). *Sexually victimized children.* New York: Free Press.

Finkelhor, D. (1986). *A sourcebook on child sexual abuse*. Beverly Hills, CA: Sage.

Finkelhor, D., & Baron, L. (1986). High risk children. In D. Finkelhor (Ed.), *A sourcebook on child sexual abuse* (pp. 60-88). Beverly Hills, CA: Sage.

Finkelhor, D., & Strapko, N. (1987). Sexual abuse prevention education: A review of evaluation studies. In D. Willis, E. Holder, & M. Rosenberg (Eds.), *Child abuse prevention*. New York: John Wiley.

Friedrich, Beilke & Urquiza. (1988). Behavior problems in young sexually abused boys: A comparison study. *Journal of Interpersonal Violence, 3*(1), 21-28.

Gabriel, R. (1985). Anatomically correct dolls in the diagnosis of sexual abuse in children. *Journal of the Melanie Klein Society, 3*(2), 40-51.

Garbarino, J. (1987). Children's response to a sexual abuse prevention program: A study of the Spiderman comic. *Child Abuse & Neglect, 11,* 143-148.

Gilbert, N., Daro, D., Duerr, J., et al. (1988). *Child sexual abuse prevention: Evaluation of educational materials for preschool programs* (Grant No. 90-CA-1163). Unpublished manuscript, Family Welfare Research Group, School of Social Welfare, University of California, Berkeley, for the Department of Health and Human Services, National Center on Child Abuse and Neglect.

Gomes-Schwartz, R., Horowitz, J., & Cardarelli, A. (1990). *Child sexual abuse: The initial effects*. Newbury Park, CA: Sage.

Gomes-Schwartz, B., Horowitz, J., & Sauzier, M. (1985). Severity of emotional distress among sexually abused preschool, schoolage and adolescent children. *Hospital and Community Psychiatry, 36,* 503-508.

Goodman, G. (Ed.). (1984). The child witness [Special issue]. *Journal of Social Issues, 40*(2).

Goodman, G., Aman, C., & Hirschman, J. (1987). Child sexual and physical abuse: Children's testimony. In S. J. Ceci, M. P. Toglia, & D. F. Ross (Eds.), *Children's eyewitness memory* (pp. 1-23). New York: Springer-Verlag.

Goodman, G., & Clarke-Stewart. (1991). Suggestability in children's testimony: Implications of sexual abuse investigation. In J. Doris (Ed.), *Suggestability of children's recollection* (pp. 92-105). Washington, DC: APA Press.

Goodman, G., & Rosenberg, M. (1987). The child witness to family violence: Clinical and legal considerations. In D. Sonkin (Ed.), *Domestic violence on trial*. New York: Springer-Verlag.

Goodwin, J., Simms, M., & Bergman, R. (1979). Hysterical seizures: A sequel to incest. *American Journal of Orthopsychiatry, 49,* 698-703.

Green, A. (1986). True and false allegations of sexual abuse in child custody disputes. *Journal of the American Academy of Child Psychiatry, 25,* 449-456.

Groth, N. A., Hobson, W., & Gary, T. (1982). The child molester: Clinical observations. In J. Conte & D. Shore (Eds.), *Social work and child sexual abuse*. New York: Haworth.

Hall, G., Proctor, W. C., & Nelson, G. M. (1988). Validity of physiological measures of pedophilic sexual arousal in a sexual offender population. *Journal of Consulting and Clinical Psychology, 56,* 118-122.

Harvey, P., Forehand, R., Brown, C., & Holmes, T. (1988). The prevention of sexual abuse: Examination of the effectiveness of a program with kindergarten-age children. *Behavior Therapy, 19*(3), 429-435.

Hill, J. H., & Jason, L. A. (1988). An evaluation of a school-based child sexual abuse primary prevention program. *Community Psychologist*, pp. 36-88.

Jampole, L., & Weber, K. (1987). The assessment of behavior of sexually abused and nonsexually abused children with anatomically correct dolls. *Child Abuse & Neglect, 11*, 187-192.

Johnson, M., & Foley, M. (1984). Differentiating fact from fantasy: The reliability of children's memory. *Journal of Social Issues, 40*, 33-50.

Jones, D., & McQuiston, M. (1985). *Interviewing the sexually abused child.* Denver, CO: C. Henry Kempe National Center for the Prevention and Treatment of Child Abuse and Neglect.

Justice, B., & Justice, R. (1979). *The broken taboo.* New York: Human Sciences.

Kempe, C. H., Silverman, F. N., Steele, B. F., Droegemueller, W., & Silver, H. K. (1962). The battered child syndrome. *Journal of the American Medical Association, 181*, 4-11.

Kendel-Tackett, K. A., & Simon, A. F. (1987). Perpetrators and their acts: Data from 365 adults molested as children. *Child Abuse and Neglect: The International Journal, 11*, 237-246.

Kenning, M., Gallmeier, T., Jackson, T., & Plemons, S. (1987). *Evaluation of child sexual abuse prevention programs: A summary of two studies.* Paper presented at the Third National Conference on Family Violence, University of New Hampshire.

Kercher, G., & McShane, M. (1983). *The prevalence of child sexual abuse victimization in an adult sample of Texas residents.* Huntsville, TX: Sam Houston State University. (mimeo)

Kolko, D. J. (1988). Educational programs to promote awareness and prevention of child sexual victimization: A review and methodological critique. *Clinical Psychology Review, 8*, 195-209.

Kolko, D., Moser, J., Litz, J., & Hughes, J. (1987). Promoting awareness and prevention of child sexual victimization using the Red Flag/Green Flag program: An evaluation with followup. *Journal of Family Violence, 2*, 11-35.

Korbin, J. E. (1990). Child sexual abuse: A cross cultural view. In K. Oates (Ed.), *Understanding and managing child sexual abuse* (pp. 42-58). Philadelphia: W. B. Saunders.

Langevin, R., Handy, L., Russon, A. E., & Day, D. (1985). Are incestuous fathers pedophilic, aggressive or alcoholic? In R. Langevin (Ed.), *Erotic preference: Gender, identity, and aggression in men.* Hillsdale, NJ: Lawrence Erlbaum.

Lipovsky, J. A., Saunders, B. E., & Murphy, S. M. (1989). Depression, anxiety and behavior problems among victims of father-child sexual assault and non-abused siblings. *Journal of Interpersonal Violence, 4*, 452-468.

MacFarlane, Cockriel, & Dugan. (1990). Treating young victims of incest. In K. Oates (Ed.), *Understanding and managing child sexual abuse* (pp. 149-177). Philadelphia: W. B. Saunders.

Mannarino, A. P., Cohen, J. A., & Gregor, M. (1989). Emotional and behavioral difficulties in sexually abused girls. *Journal of Interpersonal Violence, 4*, 452-468.

Marshall, W. L., Barbaree, H. E., & Christophie, D. (1986). Sexual offenders against female children: Sexual preferences for age of victims and type of behavior. *Canadian Journal of Behavioral Science, 18*, 424-439.

Marshall, W. L., & Christie, M. M. (1981). Pedophilia and aggression. *Criminal Justice and Behavior, 8,* 145-158.

Marshall, W. L., Laws, D. R., & Barbaree, H. E. (Eds.). (1990). *Handbook of sexual assault: Issues, theories and treatment of the offender.* New York: Plenum.

Melton, G., & Limbers, S. (1989). Psychologists involvement in cases of child maltreatment: Limits of role and expertise. *American Psychologist, 44,* 1225-1233.

Miltenberger, R. G., & Thiesse-Duffy, E. (1988). Evaluation of home-based programs for teaching personal safety skills to children. *Journal of Applied Behavioral Analysis, 21,* 81-87.

Peters, J. (1976). Children who are victims of sexual assault and the psychology of offenders. *American Journal of Psychotherapy, 30,* 398-421.

Peters, S. D., Wyatt, G. E., & Finkelhor, D. (1986). Prevalence. In D. Finkelhor (Ed.), *Sourcebook on child sexual abuse* (pp. 15-39). Beverly Hills, CA: Sage.

Plummer, C. (1984). *Preventing sexual abuse: What in-school programs teach children.* Paper presented at the Second National Conference on Family Violence, University of New Hampshire.

Quinsey, V. L. (1983). Prediction of recidivism and the evaluation of treatment programs for sex offenders. In S. N. Verdon-Jones & A. A. Keltner (Eds.), *Sexual aggression and the law.* Simon Fraser University, Criminology Research Center.

Quinsey, V. L. (1984). Sexual aggression: Studies of offenders against women. In D. Weisstub (Ed.), *Law and mental health: International perspectives.* New York: Pergamon.

Quinsey, V. L., & Chaplin, T. (1988). Penile responses of child molesters and normals to descriptions of encounters with children involving sex and violence. *Journal of Interpersonal Violence, 3,* 259-274.

Quinsey, V. L., Chaplin, T. C., & Carrigan, W. F. (1979). Sexual preferences among incestuous and nonincestuous child molesters. *Behavior Therapy, 10,* 562-565.

Quinsey, V. L., Steinman, C. M., Bergersen, S. G., & Holmes, T. F. (1975). Penile circumference, skin conductance, and ranking responses of child molesters and "normals" to sexual and nonsexual visual stimuli. *Behavior Therapy, 6,* 213-219.

Rosenfeld, A., Nadelson, C., Krieger, M., et al. (1979). Incest and sexual abuse of children. *Journal of the American Academy of Child Psychiatry, 16,* 327-339.

Russell, D. E. (1984). *Sexual exploitation: Rape, child sexual abuse and work place harassment.* Beverly Hills, CA: Sage.

Schor, D., & Sivan, A. (1989). Interpreting children's labels for sex-related body parts of anatomically explicit dolls. *Child Abuse & Neglect, 13,* 523-531.

Spaulding, W. (1987). *Interviewing child victims of sexual exploitation.* Washington, DC: National Center for Missing and Exploited Children.

Starr, R. H., & Wolfe, D. A. (Eds.). (1991). *The effects of child abuse and neglect: Issues and research.* New York: Guilford.

Swan, H. L., Press, A. N., & Briggs, S. L. (1985). Child sexual abuse prevention: Does it work? *Child Welfare, 64*(4), 395-405.

Summit, R. C. (1983). The child sexual abuse accommodation syndrome. *Child Abuse & Neglect, 7*(2), 177-193.

Tharinger, D. J., et al. (1988). Prevention of child sexual abuse: An analysis of issues, educational programs, and research findings. *School Psychology Review, 17*(4), 614-634.

Thiesse-Duffy, E., Miltenberger, R., Kozak, C., et al. (1987). *Assessment of third graders' knowledge of personal safety skills and initial program evaluation.* Paper presented at the 13th Annual American Bar Association Convention, Nashville, TN.

Thoenes, N., & Tjaden, P. (1990). The extent, nature, and validity of sexual abuse allegations in custody/visitation disputes. *Child Abuse & Neglect, 14*, 151-163.

Weiss, J., Rogers, E., Darwin, M., & Dutton, C. (1955). A study of girl sex victims. *Psychiatric Quarterly, 29*, 1-2.

White, L. A. (1948). The definition and prohibition of incest. *American Anthropologist, 50*, 416-435.

White, S., Strom, G., Santilli, G., & Halpin, B. (1986). Interviewing young sexually abused victims with anatomically correct dolls. *Child Abuse & Neglect, 10*, 519-540.

Wolfe, D. A., MacPherson, T., Blount, R., & Wolfe, V. V. (1986). Evaluation of a brief intervention for educating school children in awareness of physical and sexual abuse. *Child Abuse & Neglect, 10*, 85-92.

Wolfe, V. V., Gentile, C., & Wolfe, D. A. (1989). The impact of sexual abuse on children: A PTSD formulation. *Behavior Therapy, 20*, 215-228.

Wurtele, S. K. (1987). School-based sexual abuse prevention programs: A review. *Child Abuse & Neglect, 11*, 483-495.

Wurtele, S. K., Kast, L. C., Miller-Perrin, C. L., & Kondrick, (1989). A comparison of programs for teaching personal safety skills to preschoolers. *Journal of Consulting and Clinical Psychology, 57*, 505.

Wurtele, S. K., Marrs, S., & Miller-Perrin, C. (1987). Practice makes perfect: The role of participant modeling in sexual abuse prevention programs. *Journal of Consulting and Clinical Psychology, 55*, 599-602.

Yorukoglu, A., & Kempe, J. P. (1966). Children not severely damaged by incest with a parent. *Journal of American Academy of Child Psychiatry, 55*, 111-124.

CHAPTER 4

Psychological Aggression and Abuse in Marriage

CHRISTOPHER M. MURPHY

MICHELE CASCARDI

Defining Abuse and Aggression

The study of aggression has a long and varied history. Traditionally, scholars have described the origins of aggressive behavior in natural selection (Darwin & Wallace, 1858/1970), characterizing aggression as an instinctual trait (James, 1890) or instinctual energy (Freud, 1920/1959). In contrast to this social science heritage, the study of abusive behavior emerged more recently in parallel with the battered women's movement and feminist victimology (Dobash & Dobash, 1979; Martin, 1976; Schecter, 1982). Given these historical and political distinctions, this chapter separates psychological aggression and abuse, highlighting research strategies and findings unique to each approach.

Although aggression has been conceptualized in many ways, most U.S. social scientists define it as behavior intended to produce injury or harm (e.g., Dollard, Doob, Miller, Mowrer, & Sears, 1939). Finer discriminations include bodily modes of expression (e.g., verbal versus physical aggression), interpersonal styles of expression (e.g., passive/indirect aggression versus direct

AUTHORS' NOTE: Preparation of this chapter was supported by NIMH Grant MH 42488 to K. Daniel O'Leary and Peter Neidig. Original research presented was supported by NIMH Grant MH 35340 to K. Daniel O'Leary and Alan Rosenbaum.

aggression), or functional significance (e.g., instrumental versus expressive or irritable aggression).

Definitions of abuse also vary considerably. While abuse, like aggression, generally implies harmful intentions, abuse usually refers to harmful or potentially harmful effects of behavior as well. Similar to most ethological formulations of aggression (Eibl-Eibesfeldt, 1989; Petrovich, 1990), abuse is usually defined within interpersonal and social contexts characterized by power or dominance relations. Thus abuse connotes excessive or exploitative expressions of power or dominance, as in the abuse of children by adults. The study of adult relationship abuse has emphasized subjective experiences associated with being the target of aggression. Operational definitions of aggression, like those in the widely used Conflict Tactics Scale (Straus, 1979), generally do not include such features or, when they do, impose different assumptions about power and dominance (e.g., assuming gender neutrality rather than gender inequality).

Interpersonal and Social Context

As noted in feminist reviews (e.g., Breines & Gordon, 1983), common problems arise from inadequate appreciation of interpersonal and social contexts in the definition and measurement of aggression. For example, communication theorists demonstrate how similar behaviors can be playful or aggressive depending on the frame, or "metacommunication" context (Bateson, 1972). Subtle shifts in voice tone, posture, or facial expression can render the same phrase "harmless ribbing" in one context and "character assault" in another.

Similarly, some behaviors may only become abusive in the context of violence or intimidation. For example, anger expressed as sarcasm or verbal hostility may be experienced as annoying or disheartening in the context of a healthy relationship. The same behavior may take on a very threatening, frightening meaning, however, if it has been previously accompanied by physical assault or threat of assault.

To add even greater complexity, the same or similar behavior may be abusive in certain social contexts, and not in others. For example, therapists have begun to examine the importance of ethnicity in the family (McGoldrick, Pearce, & Giordano, 1982).

Some behaviors that may be acceptable or even normative within certain ethnic or cultural contexts (e.g., loud expressions of negative emotions) may be perceived as verbal abuse in other ethnic or cultural contexts.

Power Structure of the Relationship

Another contextual feature concerns power relations, especially within the family. Differences in role definition, often reflecting power differences between individuals, alter the meaning of behavior. For example, when aggression occurs in a relatively symmetrical relationship, as in a boxing match or between two siblings of roughly equal age and strength, it is not generally considered abusive. Aggressive behavior is likely to be considered abusive if it takes place in a relationship that is asymmetrical by tradition (e.g., parent and child), so that a perpetrator and victim can be identified. Note, also, that aggressive behavior itself may alter the symmetry of a relationship, so that abuser and victim roles emerge over time.[1] In contemporary Western societies, a tradition of male domination in the family, men's relatively greater size, weight, and violence training, and the economic oppression of women (particularly single and divorced mothers) typically yield quite different effects for aggressive actions performed by a man toward a female partner than vice versa (Murphy & Meyer, 1991).

Given the ethological and behaviorist traditions in research on aggression, we associate this term with objective assessment from the perspective of an observer (or "outsider") who imputes hostile intent to others' behavior with the goal of discovering universal generalizations. Given the activist and feminist traditions in conceptualizing abuse, we associate this term with assessment of the subjective meaning of potentially harmful events from an empathic, or "insider," perspective, with the goal of understanding behavior in its social, cultural, and historical contexts (e.g., the gendered relations of power). This distinction between abuse and aggression should help clarify the usefulness of different research methods (Murphy & O'Leary, 1992) and help integrate knowledge developed by traditional academic social scientists with knowledge developed by social activists in the battered women's movement.[2]

Topography, or Consequences of Behavior?

Researchers in the field of child maltreatment have generally defined psychological abuse in terms of its effects, claiming that psychological harm is the essential common theme in the varieties of abuse (e.g., physical, emotional, sexual; Garbarino, Guttman, & Seeley, 1986; Grusec & Walters, 1991). Researchers studying adult relationships, however, have generally considered psychological abuse as one category of abusive behavior, like sexual coercion or physical abuse (Sonkin, Martin, & Walker, 1985). Similarly, the present review defines "psychological" abuse and aggression based on the form of behavior expressed rather than the consequences intended or produced (i.e., in contrast to physical abuse and aggression). Further clarity will arise from existing research on this topic. Because this is a relatively new area of research (Tolman, 1992), the chapter provides considerable detail for each topic covered.

Assessment

Overview

The distinction between abuse and aggression highlights important trends in this new area of research. The prototypical studies employing the "relationship abuse" perspective are in-depth, qualitative, or clinical interview studies of battered women (e.g., Hoffman, 1984; Walker, 1979). The prototypical studies using the "relationship aggression" approach are national representative surveys of U.S. households that employ an objective checklist of aggressive behaviors (Straus & Gelles, 1990; Straus, Gelles, & Steinmetz, 1980). Some studies integrate aspects of these two approaches, employing a variety of new assessment strategies with various samples.

Qualitative Research Strategies

In-depth, qualitative, and clinical studies have helped identify basic themes in the experience of abused partners, primarily battered women. Although different interviewers have different styles, employ different strategies, and draw from different samples, there is remarkable consistency in the basic descriptions offered. By virtually all accounts, abusive behavior represents an attempt to control, dominate, or gain power over one's partner (Pence, 1989; Ptacek, 1988).

Forms and Subtypes of Psychological Abuse

In general, psychological abuse can be said to operate through three major pathways: It instills fear, increases dependency, and/or damages self-esteem. Scholars have presented various conceptual schemes to describe the specific varieties of psychological abuse. Most researchers have included some variant of the following general categories: *Isolation/restriction* efforts to track, monitor, and control the partner's activities and social contacts; *humiliation/degradation,* efforts to denigrate, ridicule, or degrade the partner; *threats* to harm self, partner, friends, relatives, pets, and so on; *property violence,* damage or destruction of personal property; *jealousy and possessiveness,* accusations or recriminations of infidelity; and *economic deprivation,* attempts to control finances unilaterally or increase financial dependency. Some accounts also include *male privilege,* demands of subservience or adherence to rigid sex roles; *emotional withholding,* refusals to provide emotional contact or support; and *minimization and denial,* efforts to downplay the extent or impact of violence or abuse, often through questioning the partner's perceptions, feelings, or sanity. Further description and subtypes can be found in work by Hoffman (1984), Marshall (personal communication, 1991, see note 4), Pence (1989), Sonkin et al. (1985), and Tolman (1992).

Two further subtypes of abuse often go together with the above but are not considered in the current review because they have somewhat different associated research traditions: *manipulation, or abuse of children* and *sexual coercion and violence.*

Strengths and Weaknesses of Qualitative Studies

In-depth, qualitative interview studies of battered women have offered very important insights. These accounts have helped accentuate the subtlety and complexity of psychological abuse, uncovering a central theme of domination and control and many variations of abusive behavior. These efforts have helped to highlight the often devastating effects of psychological abuse, including the disorientation and self-doubt associated with tactics of mind control (Andersen, Boulette, & Schwartz, 1991) and the extreme terror experienced by many battered women. Qualitative studies have offered an integrative framework to understand how physical and psychological abuse operate in tandem to establish domination and control.

Researchers, however, need to be very careful not to overgeneralize findings from specific settings and specific populations to other settings and populations. The experiences of battered women in shelters may differ in important ways from other samples and settings, like distressed nonviolent marriages, marital and family clinic samples, or general population samples (O'Leary & Murphy, 1992). Similar psychologically aggressive or controlling behaviors may be experienced very differently in the context of a mutually satisfactory nonviolent relationship, a distressed nonviolent relationship, or a violent relationship. The unstructured format of qualitative interviewing is well suited to uncover patterns of experience and behavior. Some research questions, however, demand more structured data collection (e.g., when aggregating data from multiple interviewers) or a briefer format (e.g., when surveying large samples).

Quantitative Research Strategies

The "relationship aggression" approach, focused on objective assessment of hostile behaviors, has helped to identify the prevalence of psychologically aggressive acts in populations outside of domestic violence facilities. In addition, large-scale studies have begun to examine correlates of psychological aggression as well as associations between physical and psychological aggression.

Behavior Checklist Measures

The most widely used measure of relationship aggression is Straus's (1979) Conflict Tactics Scale (CTS), an 18-item behavior checklist designed to assess three conflict resolution strategies: reasoning, verbal aggression, and physical aggression. Factor analyses consistently locate a dimension labeled psychological aggression, as distinct from physical aggression (Barling, O'Leary, Jouriles, Vivian,

& MacEwen, 1987). This factor contains some items that reflect verbal aggression (e.g., "insulted or swore at partner") and some that are nonverbal (e.g., "stomped out of the room or house or yard").

The CTS was designed for large-scale survey studies of violence in various family relationships (interspousal, parent-child and sibling), which have dramatized the remarkable prevalence of violence in the American family (Straus et al., 1980). With respect to many other research problems, however, the CTS has important limitations as a measure of psychological aggression (and physical aggression as well). The items were not derived from qualitative understanding of the subjective experience of people in violent relationships (Stets, 1991). As a result, the measure equates behaviors that may have very different intentions and very different effects, particularly in light of cultural, ethnic, and social class norms governing the expression of hostility in the family and the gendered relations of power in marriage (Breines & Gordon, 1983; Murphy & Meyer, 1991). In addition, the CTS was not designed primarily to assess psychological aggression and therefore contains relatively few such items and no further breakdown of its forms or subtypes.

Other measures have attempted to redress some of these imperfections. The Index of Spouse Abuse (ISA; Hudson & McIntosh, 1981) was designed for use with clinical samples. It contains a checklist of behaviors, roughly similar to the CTS, that fall into two factors: physical abuse (11 items) and nonphysical abuse (19 items). The authors provide a weighting scheme to reflect normative perceptions of the seriousness or severity of the scale items.

O'Leary and Curley (1986) developed a measure of spouse-specific aggression (SSAG), as distinguished conceptually from spouse-specific assertion. This measure includes 12 items reflecting both passive aggression (e.g., "I'll often give my mate the 'silent treatment' when I am mad at him/her") and direct psychological aggression (e.g., "I often say nasty things to my mate, especially when I'm angrily discussing something with him/her"). Subjects endorse the items as personal tendencies rather than reporting on the frequency of specific behaviors.

Strengths and Weaknesses

These three measures all appear to assess a general domain of psychological aggression in adult relationships. Each can be administered in questionnaire format in 5-10 minutes. They all meet general psychometric standards for internal consistency and have shown predicted correlations with various criteria. The ISA and SSAG measures have some apparent advantages over the CTS with respect to psychological aggression. Both have more items, which may increase reliability. One attempts to index the severity of aggressive behaviors (ISA). The other includes items to assess passive aggression and does not ask respondents to recall the frequency of specific behaviors (SSAG).[3]

All of these measures share certain limitations. They assess a relatively small sample of psychologically aggressive behaviors (or styles) with no further breakdown of subscales or subtypes. Behavior checklists also require some questionable assumptions, namely, that respondents interpret the meaning of items in a relatively consistent fashion (e.g., what is considered "yelling," "insulting") and that they can accurately recall the frequency of such acts. When assorted behaviors are abstracted and grouped into discrete scale items, some potentially important aspects of personal experience may be lost or distorted. These measures do not take into account the effects of aggression or the subjective experience of the meaning and severity of aggression. These may reflect critical aspects of definition and assessment, particularly with respect to psychological abuse.[4]

Incorporating Qualitative Insights
Into Quantitative Assessments

Some recent assessments of psychological abuse incorporate insights from qualitative research into a more structured assessment format. Tolman (1989) specified 58 abusive behaviors in a self-report questionnaire called the Psychological Maltreatment of Women Inventory (PMWI). Items were drawn from existing measures and developed from the clinical and qualitative literatures on battered women. The PMWI excludes items involving physical contact, threats of violence, or aggression toward objects. Although the items represent several abuse subtypes, factor analysis uncovered only two subscales: "Dominance-Isolation" and "Emotional-Verbal." The author found high internal consistency for the subscales but low agreement between spouses' reports. While the PMWI is the most comprehensive questionnaire measure of psychological abuse to date, the current subscales may not adequately reflect the different forms of abuse described by battered women. The other criticisms of behavior checklist measures of abuse (described above) in general apply to the PMWI as well.

Marshall (personal communication, 1991) has been very concerned with how researchers and respondents may have different conceptions of abusive behavior. She presents respondents with a dictionary of definitions for 44 categories of psychological abuse and then combines an interview and self-report questionnaire to assess the various categories of abuse.[5]

Folingstad and colleagues also have interviewers interpret or categorize experiences described by battered women (Folingstad, Rutledge, Berg, Hause, & Polek, 1990). From semistructured phone interviews, they coded women's experiences into several predetermined categories of psychological abuse, along with information about the frequency of abuse in each category and the perceived severity of pain that each caused. These interview methods allow battered women to describe their own experiences and reactions in an open-ended fashion, yet the methods categorize and quantify information for statistical analysis as well.

Response Bias

One persistent issue in the assessment of relationship abuse concerns the tendency to bias responses in a socially desirable fashion (Arias & Beach, 1987; Saunders, 1991). With regard to interpartner violence, some evidence suggests that perpetrators are more likely than victims to provide inaccurate, socially desirable reports (Riggs, Murphy, & O'Leary, 1989). Partners may disagree in reports of violence for many reasons, including different definitions of behaviors or terms, errors in memory, conscious dissimulation, or unconscious self-deception (Paulhus, 1984; Riggs et al., 1989). Some researchers have begun to document ways that batterers minimize or deny their violence and its consequences (Dutton, 1986; Ptacek, 1988). Initial evidence suggests that aggressive men may underreport physical violence and blame the partner to maintain or enhance self- esteem (Murphy, Cascardi, Ginsburg, & O'Leary, 1991; Waltz, Babcock, Jacobson, & Gottman, 1991). Psychological abuse seems to follow a similar pattern. Men admit to less abuse than their partners report (Tolman,

1989). Further research may clarify determinants of reporting biases and may help inform clinical efforts to reduce denial and promote assumption of responsibility for abusive behavior.

Research Findings

Prevalence of Psychological Aggression in Marriage and Cohabiting Relationships

Table 4.1 contains prevalence estimates for a set of psychologically aggressive behaviors from the Conflict Tactics Scale (Straus, 1979) in different samples. For distressed partners seeking marital therapy, 89%-97% have enacted each aggressive behavior during the preceding 12 months. More than two thirds of engaged partners reported that these aggressive behaviors occurred in the year prior to marriage. The high rates were not surprising for the marital clinic group. For the engaged couples, however, who generally report a high level of satisfaction in their relationships, the normative nature of psychological aggression was somewhat surprising (physical aggression is also very common in dating relationships and engaged couples; Arias, Samios, & O'Leary, 1987; O'Leary et al., 1989).

Rates from a representative survey of U.S. households are considerably lower than newlywed and clinical samples, with somewhere between 30% and 60% of spouses reporting each behavior in Table 4.1 (Stets, 1990). In part, this may be due to differences in the way aggression was assessed. The national figures rely on reports from one partner only, and the other studies combine both spouses' reports about each partner's aggression. Perhaps more important, however, is the reduction of aggressive behavior over the life span observed both within and outside the family (Hirschi & Gottfredson, 1983; Suitor, Pillemer, & Straus, 1990). Negative correlations between age and psychological aggression on the CTS (in the .25-.40 range) were observed for both men and women in the two national family violence surveys (Suitor et al., 1990). The relatively high rates among newlyweds may reflect age-specific norms for relationship aggression.

In contrast to aggressive behavior surveys, Lebov-Keeler and Pipes (1990) examined self-definitions of psychological abuse

Table 4.1 Yearly Prevalence Estimates for Psychologically Aggressive Behaviors (in percentages)

Behavior (during a disagreement or conflict)	Marital Therapy Clinic (N = 187)[a]		Engaged Couples (sexes combined) (N = 398)[a]	National Survey[b] (N = 1,461 males; 1,909 females)	
	M → F	F → M		M → F	F → M
Insulted or swore at partner[c]	94	92	77	43	54
Did or said something to spite partner	94	95	67	44	54
Stomped out of the room, house, or yard	90	89	74	33	39
Sulked or refused to talk about an issue	97	97	87	52	58

NOTES: M → F = male to female aggression; F → M = female to male aggression.
a. Data are from Barling et al. (1987). Estimates combine both partners' reports; that is, husband and wife each report on their own and their partners' behavior; N = number of couples.
b. Stets (1990); estimates by self-report only.
c. In the national survey, this item was shortened to "insulted partner."

for female college students in exclusive heterosexual relationships using the following definition:

> Being psychologically abused means that your boyfriend *repeatedly* used one or more of the above verbal and/or nonverbal tactics [from the CTS] with the result that you *frequently* feel hurt or fearful, or feel badly about yourself following his use of these tactics. (p. 36, emphasis in original)

Of 175 women surveyed, 11% identified themselves as psychologically abused on this basis.

Other research has examined the prevalence of psychological abuse in violent relationships. In general, physically abusive men engage in a wide variety of psychologically abusive activities. Folingstad et al. (1990) located women with a history of physical abuse through advertisements, shelters, and social service agencies. Of 234 women interviewed, 99% reported experiencing at least one type of emotional abuse at some time during the marriage. More specifically, 90% reported having experienced ridicule/verbal harassment, 79% experienced restriction (behaviors designed to isolate them or restrict their activities), 74% experienced threats of abuse, 73% experienced severe jealousy or possessiveness, 59% experienced property damage, and 48% experienced threats to change or end the marriage. In addition, the abuse was very frequent for most women studied. For restriction, jealousy/possessiveness, and ridicule/harassment, more than 60% of the women who had experienced each form of abuse reported that it occurred at least once a week.

Tolman (1989) administered 58 items covering a wide range of psychologically abusive behaviors to more than 200 women at shelter intake. A very high proportion of the women reported that each behavior had occurred at least once in the past 6 months. Very few items were endorsed by less than half of the women, and the vast majority of items were endorsed by more than three fourths of them.

Some example item endorsement frequencies are as follows: partner called her names (86%); swore at her (95%); insulted her in front of others (85%); ordered her around (89%); criticized her housework (82%); gave her the silent treatment (87%); acted irresponsibly with money (83%); monitored her time (85%); did not allow her to socialize with friends (79%) or see family (60%); restricted her use of the car (54%) or telephone (56%); tried to blame her for causing the violence (90%); said her feelings were irrational or crazy (90%); tried to convince her that she was crazy (55%); threatened to have her committed (33%); and kept her from medical care (29%) (Tolman, 1989, p. 165).

Men's reporting rates at batterers' program intake were considerably lower than women's rates at shelter intake. Although only a small number of those studied were from the same marriages, there was relatively little correspondence between partners' reports. Even so, the men reported perpetrating a wide range of psychologically abusive behaviors (Tolman, 1989).

In sum, available studies support the clinical impression that psychological and physical abuse go hand in hand (Sonkin et al., 1985; Walker, 1979). Note, however, that some forms of psychological aggression are found in the vast majority of relationships, whether or not physical abuse is present. Future studies might compare the frequency and patterns of psychological abuse in violent versus distressed nonviolent relationships to identify how violence or the threat of violence alters the perception and effects of psychological abuse and to examine the possible role of psychological abuse in the development of physical abuse.

Associations With Physical Aggression

Several cross-sectional studies have documented a moderate to strong correlation between measures of psychological aggression and physical aggression (Straus, 1974; Straus et al., 1980). By claiming that verbal aggression increases the likelihood of physical violence, Straus (1974) used these correlations to argue against "ventilationist" therapies that promote openly hostile expression of feelings to "let off steam."

Longitudinal associations between psychological aggression and physical aggression further support Straus's point. Murphy and O'Leary (1989) found that prior levels of psychological aggression predicted initial reports of physical aggression during the first 2½ years of marriage. Marital satisfaction did not significantly predict physical aggression longitudinally, even though it was correlated with physical aggression cross-sectionally. These findings support the idea that an escalating process of coercive attempts to control one's partner over months or years often precedes the initiation of physical aggression. At least early on in marriage, a decline in general satisfaction with the relationship may be a by-product of coercive interactions rather than a cause.

Figure 4.1 details the longitudinal association between psychological and physical aggression early in marriage, presenting the probability of physical aggression at an ensuing longitudinal assessment (either 6 months or 1 year later) for married partners who had not reported physical aggression at any earlier assessments. Subjects with the highest levels of psychological aggression were most likely to report physical aggression at the ensuing assessment. Of subjects in the top 10% on the psychological aggression scale, 30% to 50% reported physical aggression at the next assessment. None of the subjects in the lowest 10% on the measure of psychological aggression ever reported physical aggression at the next assessment.

An important question that arises from these strong associations is whether psychological and physical aggression reflect different manifestations of a single psychological process (or an arbitrary division of a single relationship aggressiveness variable). Factor analyses from a variety of samples suggest that psychological and physical aggression, as measured by the CTS and other scales, form distinct latent variables (Barling et al., 1987; Shepard & Campbell, 1992).

Along these lines, Stets (1990) examined whether psychological and physical aggression could be best represented by a "two-stage" process of escalation or as different thresholds along a single continuum of aggression. To make this case, she examined two patterns of correlates: One pattern optimally distinguished nonaggressive individuals from psychologically aggressive but nonviolent individuals; the other pattern optimally distinguished psychologically aggressive individuals from physically aggressive individuals. Because these patterns were different, she argued in favor of a "two-stage" escalation process for psychological and physical aggression rather than a single underlying process with different thresholds. While this evidence does not strictly refute the notion of one single underlying dimension or process, it suggests that there is something to gain by separating psychological and physical aggression in research on putative causes or correlates of these behavior patterns.

In sum, research has documented widespread use of psychological coercion in physically violent relationships. Available evidence suggests that psychological aggression and physical aggression are distinct yet correlated phenomena. Longitudinal research suggests an escalation process from psychological to physical aggression early on in relationships.

Other Correlates and Presumed Causes

A few studies have specifically identified correlates of psychological abuse, and other information is available from research on physical abuse. In the national family violence surveys, for both men and women, levels of psychological aggression were correlated with an index of marital conflict, husbands' alcohol consumption (in one of two surveys described by Suitor et al., 1990), verbal aggression outside of the home, and approval of the use of physical aggression (Stets, 1990).

In a community study of psychological abuse, women's relationship satisfaction was negatively correlated with male partners' use

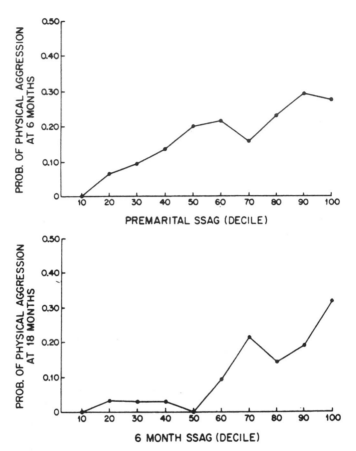

Figure 4.1 Predicting First Reports of Physical Aggression Longitudinally from Psychological Aggression in Early Marriage

NOTE: Assessments were conducted 6 weeks prior to marriage and 6, 18, and 30 months into marriage. Predictive patterns were similar for husbands and wives, who are combined in the figures. The top figure includes data from 380 individuals, the middle figure, from 268 individuals, and the figure on p. 101, from 191 indivduals. SSAG = Spouse-Specific Aggression Scale. For further description of the study, see Murphy and O'Leary (1989).

of emotional control tactics. In addition, women's decisions to leave a relationship were associated with male partners' attempts to control or degrade them (Vitanza, Walker, & Marshall, 1990).

Other correlates have been found within college dating relationships. Longer relationships with more frequent contact appear to have somewhat elevated rates of psychological aggression (Mason

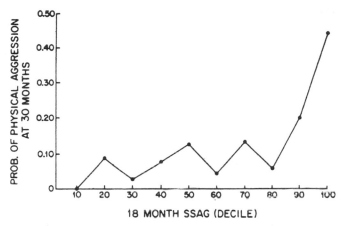

Figure 4.1 Continued

& Blankenship, 1987; Stets, 1991). In one study, stressful life events were associated with women's psychological aggression (both experienced and perpetrated), but not men's (Mason & Blankenship, 1987). Witnessing interparental violence predicted psychological abuse for males, but not females, in Stets's (1991) study of college students, but it apparently predicted psychological aggression by females, but not males, in national survey data (Stets, 1990).[6] With the possible exception of interpersonal control (discussed below), all of these associations appear to be of relatively small magnitude (r's less than .30).

Interpersonal control appears to be correlated with levels of psychological abuse in dating relationships (Stets, 1991). Stets (1991) defined interpersonal control as "the act of managing or regulating another's thoughts, feelings or actions" (p. 98), that is, as actual control by one member of a couple over the other's behavior. Unfortunately, this approach may cast the controlling effects of abuse as presumed causes.[7]

As an alternative, some researchers postulate a stable, preexisting personality trait reflecting the motivation to influence others and labeled "need for power." This trait can be assessed independent of relationship behavior through a projective test (Winter, 1973). In a college dating sample, males' need for power was associated with their use of physical aggression but not with psychological aggression (Mason & Blankenship, 1987). The need for power discriminated male batterers from a mixed sample of discordant and happily married contrast men and was highly correlated with the level of physical violence within the sample of batterers (Dutton & Strachan, 1987). Further research on the motivational dynamics of control in relationships may provide an integrative understanding of the various forms of abusive behavior.

Gender Differences

As with behavior checklist measures of physical aggression, psychological aggression generally appears to be reciprocal in relationships. There are moderate to high correlations between levels reported by relationship partners (O'Leary & Curley, 1986; Stets, 1991), and men and women report roughly equal rates. When differences are observed, women report having engaged in slightly higher rates of psychologically aggressive behavior than men (Stets, 1990). When self-definitions (e.g., reports of having been attacked or assaulted, police call records) or consequences (e.g., injuries) are studied, physical aggression no longer appears "reciprocal" but highly gender specific, perpetrated by males in 85%-95% of heterosexual cases (Berk, Berk, Loseke, & Rauma, 1983; Schwartz, 1987).

Psychological abuse may similarly prove to be more male perpetrated when self-definitions or consequences are examined or when more extremely abusive samples are studied. In one study of college students, males and females reported perpetrating similar levels of psychological abuse, but females reported having sustained more abuse than males. In addition, self-esteem was negatively correlated with sustained psychological abuse, but only for females (Stets, 1991).

In extremely violent samples, abuse appears less reciprocal. Sabourin (1991) asked battered women in a shelter to describe specific violent episodes. Raters coded the women's verbal aggression and the severity of men's violence from these accounts. She found that the more violent a man was during an incident, the less verbally aggressive the woman was.

Effects

Many women perceive psychological abuse to be more painful and damaging than physical abuse. Walker (1979) began her interview studies by equating battering with physical violence but later downplayed this distinction because so many women claimed that psychological abuse was more harmful. From interviews with more than 120 battered women, she stated that most "described incidents involving psychological humiliation and verbal harassment as their worst battering experiences, whether or not they had been physically abused" (Walker, 1979, p. xv). Along similar lines, Folingstad et al. (1990) sampled more than 200 women with a history of physical abuse and found that 72% rated psychological abuse as having had a more severe impact on them than physical abuse.

Folingstad and colleagues (1990) also asked women which form of emotional abuse was the worst one for them. Of all those who had experienced ridicule/harassment, 51% rated it the worst type of emotional abuse (this represented 46% of the total sample). Of those who had experienced threats of abuse, 20% rated it the worst (15% of the total sample); of those experiencing jealousy, 17% rated it the worst (12% of the sample); for restriction, 13% (10% of the sample); for threats to change the marriage, 12% (6% of the sample), and for damage to property, 8% (4% of the sample). Attacks on self-esteem and self-concept appear to be even more painful and damaging than attempts to provoke fear and intimidation. Most likely, there is a synergistic effect on self-esteem when women are also isolated from social supports or encouraged to feel responsible for the violence. Because these data were gathered retrospectively, they may also reflect women's efforts to sort out long-lasting effects of the more insidious forms of abuse.

Relatively little research has examined specific effects of psychological abuse, because it is usually seen as inseparable from physical abuse (Walker, 1979) or as part of relationship conflict in general (e.g., Peterson, 1983). Thus it is possible that many of the effects commonly observed in battered women are due to psychological abuse or combined effects with physical abuse. Commonly described sequelae of abuse include alcohol problems (Bergman, Larsson, Brismar, & Klang, 1987), posttraumatic stress disorder (Houskamp & Foy, 1991), and low self-esteem or depression (Cascardi & O'Leary,1992; Walker, 1984).

Clinical accounts often focus attention on the ways that abuse can systematically erode self-esteem, creating confusion, self-blame and self-doubt (e.g., Nicarthy, 1986; Walker, 1979). Some of these effects may depend upon subtle psychological cues from batterers, friends, relatives, authorities, or the culture at large. For example, women often wonder if what they are experiencing is in fact abuse, after having been convinced that they "deserved" it, that they "provoked" it, or that "it was not that bad." Abusive men commonly try to convince a partner that she is "crazy," question her view of events or reality, and minimize the degree or effects of violence (Dutton, 1986; Tolman, 1989). Unfortunately, health professionals may reinforce these notions, often failing to diagnose the cause of injuries in cases of spouse assault and often providing battered women with a diagnosis and medication but not social service or shelter referrals (Kurz & Stark, 1988).

Some authors have compared battered women to prisoners of war (Romero, 1985) or political hostages (Graham, Rawlings, & Rimini, 1988). Romero (1985) noted many similarities between strategies used to brainwash POWs in Korea and patterns of psychological and physical abuse. Both involve concerted efforts to produce terror, dependency, and debility in the context of a life-and-death situation over an extended period of time. Like hostages in life-threatening situations, battered women sometimes display intense attachments to their captors (called "traumatic bonding") and efforts to protect captors from outside intervention (Dutton & Painter, 1981; Graham et al., 1988).

Future Research Directions

Several important directions for future research might bolster efforts to prevent domestic violence. First, more information is needed about psychological aggression and abuse in nonviolent relationships, in early stages of relationship formation, and in youthful samples. Much of the available knowledge derives from samples where violence and many forms of psychological abuse have been present for a considerable period of time. It appears that potentially dangerous and self-limiting relationship patterns often begin in adolescence and/or early adulthood, and escalating coercive processes begin very early on in relationships. More information is needed about the use of different tactics of control and abuse over time within specific relationships and across relationships within individual life histories to further illuminate patterns of coercive escalation and desistance.

Second, more research is needed to understand and clarify the specific effects of psychological aggression and abuse for men and women, within both violent and nonviolent relationships and in both same- and different-sex relationships. We have argued that the various forms of psychological abuse have general effects: namely, to damage self-esteem, produce fear, and/or increase dependency. Further attention to both general and specific effects of psychological abuse may help clarify obstacles that battered women face in escaping violent relationships and may suggest additional strategies for public education about early detection of abuse. Research on how men and women define, perceive, and experience effects of psychological aggression and abuse may prove helpful for future intervention efforts, because many abusive individuals experience themselves as deeply attacked, threatened, or vulnerable in intimate relationships (Coleman, 1992; Dutton, 1988a; Murphy, Scott, Meyer, & O'Leary, 1992).

Finally, further research should examine the patterns and development of abuse in the life course of male batterers. Patterns of psychological abuse often highlight motivational factors that, in turn, indicate pathways for prevention or intervention. Such research may complement efforts to identify subgroups of batterers and determine the best available interventions for different groups (Dutton, 1988b; Saunders, 1992).

Implications for Prevention and Intervention

Innovative programs for public education, primary prevention, and early intervention for relationship violence are sorely needed, given that legal interventions, educational programs, and psychotherapy have demonstrated somewhat limited success in halting interpartner violence to date. Intervention studies suggest that even when physical violence ends, threats and other forms of psychological abuse often remain (Hamberger & Hastings, 1988; Tolman & Bhosley, 1991). Such interventions may offer only marginal improvement in victims' lives (Eisikovits & Edleson, 1989). In addition, psychological coercion and threats may eventually reescalate to physical assault.

Emerging understanding of psychological abuse and increasing knowledge about risk factors for wife assault may soon allow researchers and activists to detect teenagers at high risk to become batterers. What, then, might be done? Based on the research reviewed in this chapter, we would make the following recommendations.

1. Continue to increase public awareness through education and focused media campaigns about domestic violence. Because the theme of power and control is so central to abusive behavior, efforts to examine and change related belief systems may be particularly relevant. Education may promote personal responsibility for abusive behavior and clearly communicate the criminal nature of domestic assault. In addition, media campaigns might attempt to change attitudes and increase public discourse about the sense of entitlement, "rights," and power conferred by sexual intimacy or marriage. Other educational efforts may help individuals to identify and address abusive patterns early on in relationships, emphasizing attacks on self-esteem, tactics of intimidation, and unhealthy promotion of dependency. Healthier alternatives could be stressed, including means to achieve open dialogue and negotiation, ways to promote mutual growth, clarification and acceptance of differences, and ways to detect and end unhealthy relationships.

2. Further develop and promote relationship enhancement/early prevention programs. One working hypothesis is that abusive relationships tend to become increasingly asymmetrical over time, as dominance strategies escalate and become entrenched. By the time many batterers are seen for treatment, power dynamics in the relationship are so distorted and the situation is so dangerous that couples' therapy (which in general is a more powerful form of intervention than individual therapy for relationship-based problems) cannot be undertaken unless the batterer makes significant individual changes first. Perhaps early on in relationships, there is more potential for conjoint efforts to interrupt coercive cycles, improve communication patterns, increase mutual trust, and promote equality.

Related research suggests that a 15-hour premarital program to improve communication and problem solving, clarify expectations, and promote satisfying activities can significantly affect the quality of marriage several years later (Markman, Floyd, Stanley, & Storaasli, 1988). It remains to be seen whether similar efforts might also prevent abuse and violence or whether additional program strategies might be needed to prevent abuse.

3. Continue to stress the role of psychologically abusive behavior and tactics of power and control in intervention programs with batterers. To end violence in the long run and improve victims' lives, intervention efforts must focus on psychological abuse as well as physical violence. In addition to learning new behaviors, abusive partners may need to alter the motivations underlying extreme coercive and controlling behavior. Most intervention models for batterers emphasize only one side of this picture: behavior change or motivational dynamics of power and control. As of yet, very little is known about the effectiveness of batterers' treatment programs, and available evidence contains many contradictory findings. Careful research and program development are critical priorities.

Summary

Psychological abuse in intimate adult relationships represents an important new area of inquiry. Psychologically aggressive or hostile acts occur in the vast majority of intimate relationships and are distinguished from physical aggression both conceptually and empirically. An escalating pattern of psychological aggression may precede the emergence of physical aggression early on in relationships. Diverse and profound forms of psychological abuse are commonly experienced by battered women, who generally report that it is more painful and damaging than physical abuse. Most forms of psychological abuse attack self-esteem, increase dependency, and/or provoke fear. Further research on psychological abuse may help refine prevention and early intervention strategies for adult relationship violence.

Notes

1. We use terms like *abusive relationships* or *abusive partners* despite criticisms that they ignore the overwhelmingly gender-linked patterns whereby males abuse females (Breines & Gordon, 1983). Recent interest in battering and abuse in homosexual relationships (Coleman,

1992; Island & Lettelier, 1991) and the prevalence of aggressive behavior reported by females (Straus et al., 1980) suggest a need for terms that do not invariably assume gender-linked roles for victims and perpetrators.

2. The reader may notice a similarity between these descriptions and the linguistic/anthropological distinction between emic and etic approaches (Pike, 1967). Emic approaches understand behavior through its internal relations with other aspects of one specific cultural system. Etic approaches attempt to compare behavior across different cultural systems from a perspective external to any specific culture. Unfortunately, careful analysis suggests confusion when the emic/etic distinction is applied to problems in psychology, particularly in distinguishing among approaches, constructs, and measures (Jahoda, 1983; Serpell, 1990). For this reason, we employed specific criteria rather than this general framework to distinguish between abuse and aggression.

3. Despite the extensive work on severity weighting, we would not generally recommend the ISA as a measure of relationship aggression. Very few items actually assess physical abuse, and some items are not face valid (e.g., "my partner screams and yells at me" is listed as a physical abuse item).

4. An interesting anecdote relayed by Linda Marshall exemplifies these limitations of behavior checklists. When asked "Does your partner restrict your use of the phone?" a research participant replied "no." Upon further inquiry, the interviewer discovered that this was because she never used the phone, having stopped several years earlier as a result of her partner's abuse and threats.

5. Copies of the dictionary defining the 44 types of psychological abuse are available from Linda Marshall at the University of North Texas.

6. Correlates from Stets's (1990) study were presented in a multivariate prediction context. We assumed that variables with highly significant beta weights also had significant univariate correlations (a safe assumption unless there were strong suppression or moderator effects in the regression equation).

7. In addition, Stets's measure of interpersonal control contained items that might be considered forms of psychological abuse. For example, disagreement with the statement "my partner is free to go wherever s/he wants to go even though I may not approve" may reflect isolation or restriction.

References

Andersen, S. M., Boulette, T. R., & Schwartz, A. H. (1991). Psychological maltreatment of spouses. In R. T. Ammerman & M. Hersen (Eds.), *Case studies in family violence* (pp. 293-327). New York: Plenum.

Arias, I., & Beach, S. R. H. (1987). Validity of self-reports of marital violence. *Journal of Family Violence, 2,* 139-149.

Arias, I., Samios, M., & O'Leary, K. D. (1987). Prevalence and correlates of physical aggression during courtship. *Journal of Interpersonal Violence, 2,* 82-90.

Barling, J., O'Leary, K. D., Jouriles, E. N., Vivian, D., & MacEwen, K. E. (1987). Factor similarity of the Conflict Tactics Scales across samples, spouses, and sites: Issues and implications. *Journal of Family Violence, 2,* 37-54.

Bateson, G. (1972). *Steps to an ecology of mind.* San Francisco: Chandler.

Bergman, B., Larsson, G., Brismar, B., & Klang, M. (1987). Psychiatric morbidity and personality characteristics of battered women. *Acta Psychiatrica Scandinavica, 76,* 678-683.

Berk, R. A., Berk, S. F., Loseke, D. R., & Rauma, D. (1983). Mutual combat and other family violence myths. In D. Finkelhor, R. J. Gelles, G. T. Hotaling, & M. A. Straus (Eds.), *The dark side of families* (pp. 191-212). Beverly Hills, CA: Sage.

Breines, W., & Gordon, L. (1983). The new scholarship on family violence. *Signs: Journal of Women in Culture and Society, 8,* 490-531.

Cascardi, M., & O'Leary, K. D. (1992). Depressive symptomatology, self- esteem and self blame in battered women. *Journal of Family Violence, 7,* 249-259.

Coleman, V. E. (1992, August). *Breaking silence about lesbian battering: New directions in domestic violence theory.* Paper presented at the American Psychological Association, Washington, DC.

Darwin, C., & Wallace, A. R. (1970). The Linnean Society Papers. In P. Appleman (Ed.), *Darwin: A Norton critical reader* (pp. 81-97). New York: Norton. (Original work published 1858)

Dobash, R. E., & Dobash, R. (1979). *Violence against wives: A case against the patriarchy.* New York: Free Press.

Dollard, J., Doob, L., Miller, N., Mowrer, O., & Sears, R. (1939). *Frustration and aggression.* New Haven, CT: Yale University Press.

Dutton, D. G. (1986). Wife assaulters' explanations for assault: The neutralization of self-punishment. *Canadian Journal of Behavioral Science, 18,* 381-390.

Dutton, D. G. (1988a). *The domestic assault of women.* Newton, MA: Allyn & Bacon.

Dutton, D. G. (1988b). Profiling of wife assaulters: Preliminary evidence for a trimodal analysis. *Violence and Victims, 3,* 5-29.

Dutton, D., & Painter, S. L. (1981). Traumatic bonding: The development of emotional attachments in battered women and other relationships of inter- mittent abuse. *Victimology, 6,* 139-155.

Dutton, D. G., & Strachan, C. E. (1987). Motivational needs for power and spouse-specific assertiveness in assaultive and nonassaultive men. *Violence and Victims, 2,* 145-156.

Eibl-Eibesfeldt, I. (1989). *Human ethology.* New York: Aldine de Gruyter.

Eisikovits, Z. C., & Edleson, J. L. (1989). Intervening with men who batter: A critical review of the literature. *Social Service Review, 63,* 384-414.

Folingstad, D. R., Rutledge, L. L., Berg, B. J., Hause, E. S., & Polek, D. S. (1990). The role of emotional abuse in physically abusive relationships. *Journal of Family Violence, 5,* 107-120.

Freud, S. (1959). *Beyond the pleasure principle* (J. Strachey, Trans.). New York: Bantam. (Original work published 1920)

Garbarino, J., Guttman, E., & Seeley, J. W. (1986). *The psychologically battered child.* San Francisco: Jossey-Bass.

Graham, D. L. R., Rawlings, E., & Rimini, N. (1988). Survivors of terror: Battered women, hostages and the Stockholm Syndrome. In K. Yllö & M. Bograd (Eds.), *Feminist perspectives on wife abuse* (pp. 217-233). Beverly Hills, CA: Sage.

Grusec, J. E., & Walters, G. C. (1991). Psychological abuse and childrearing belief systems. In R. H. Starr & D. A. Wolfe (Eds.), *The effects of child abuse and neglect* (pp. 186-202). New York: Guilford.

Hamberger, L. K., & Hastings, J. E. (1988). Skills training for treatment of spouse abusers: An outcome study. *Journal of Family Violence, 3,* 121-130.

Hirschi, T., & Gottfredson, M. (1983). Age and the explanation of crime. *American Journal of Sociology, 89,* 552-584.

Hoffman, P. (1984). Psychological abuse of women by spouses and live-in lovers. *Women and Therapy, 3,* 37-47.

Houskamp, B. M., & Foy, D. W. (1991). The assessment of post traumatic stress disorder in battered women. *Journal of Interpersonal Violence, 6,* 367-375.

Hudson, W. W., & McIntosh, S. R. (1981). The assessment of spouse abuse: Two quantifiable dimensions. *Journal of Marriage and the Family, 43,* 873-888.

Island, D., & Lettelier, P. (1991). *Men who beat the men who love them.* Binghamton, NY: Haworth.

Jahoda, G. (1983). The cross-cultural emperor's conceptual clothes: The emic-etic issue revisited. In J. B. Deregowski, S. Dziurawiec, & R. C. Annis (Eds.), *Explorations in cross-cultural psychology* (pp. 19-37). Amsterdam: Swets & Zeitlinger.

James, W. (1890). *The principles of psychology* (Vol. 2). New York: Henry Holt.

Kurz, D., & Stark, E. (1988). Not-so-benign neglect: The medical response to battering. In K. Yllö & M. Bograd (Eds.), *Feminist perspectives on wife abuse* (pp. 249-266). Newbury Park, CA: Sage.

Lebov-Keeler, K., & Pipes, R. B. (1990, August). *Psychological abuse among college women in exclusive heterosexual dating relationships.* Paper presented at the American Psychological Association, Boston.

Markman, H. J., Floyd, F. J., Stanley, S. M., & Storaasli, R. D. (1988). Prevention of marital distress: A longitudinal investigation. *Journal of Consulting and Clinical Psychology, 56,* 210-217.

Martin, D. (1976). *Battered wives.* New York: Pocket Books.

Mason, A., & Blankenship, V. (1987). Power and affiliation motivation, stress and abuse in intimate relationships. *Journal of Personality and Social Psychology, 52,* 203-210.

McGoldrick, M., Pearce, J. K., & Giordano, J. (Eds.). (1982). *Ethnicity and family therapy.* New York: Guilford.

Murphy, C. M., Cascardi, M., Ginsburg, E., & O'Leary, K. D. (1991, November). *Responsibility attributions for aggression in dating relationships.* Paper presented at the Association for the Advancement of Behavior Therapy, New York.

Murphy, C. M., & Meyer, S. L. (1991). Gender, power and violence in marriage. *Behavior Therapist, 14,* 95-100.

Murphy, C. M., & O'Leary, K. D. (1989). Psychological aggression predicts physical aggression in early marriage. *Journal of Consulting and Clinical Psychology, 57,* 579-582.

Murphy, C. M., & O'Leary, K. D. (1992). *Research paradigms, values and spouse abuse.* Manuscript submitted for publication.

Murphy, C. M., Scott, E., Meyer, S. L., & O'Leary, K. D. (1992, November). *Emotional vulnerability patterns in partner assaultive men.* Paper presented at the Association for the Advancement of Behavior Therapy, Boston.

Nicarthy, G. (1986). *Getting free: A handbook for women in abusive relationships* (2nd ed.). Seattle, WA: Seal.

O'Leary, K. D., Barling, J., Arias, I., Rosenbaum, A., Malone, A., & Tyree, A. (1989). Prevalence and stability of physical aggression between spouses: A longitudinal analysis. *Journal of Consulting and Clinical Psychology, 57,* 263-268.

O'Leary, K. D., & Curley, A. D. (1986). Assertion and family violence: Correlates of spouse abuse. *Journal of Marital and Family Therapy, 12,* 281-289.

O'Leary, K. D., & Murphy, C. M. (1992). Clinical issues in the assessment of spouse abuse. In R. T. Ammerman & M. Hersen (Eds.), *Assessment of family violence* (pp. 26-46). New York: John Wiley.

Paulhus, D. L. (1984). Two-component models of socially desirable responding. *Journal of Personality and Social Psychology, 46,* 598-609.

Pence, E. (1989). Batterer programs: Shifting from community collusion to community confrontation. In P. I. Caesar & L. K. Hamberger (Eds.), *Treating men who batter* (pp. 24-50). New York: Springer.

Peterson, D. R. (1983). Conflict. In H. H. Kelley et al., *Close relationships* (pp. 169-219). New York: Freeman.

Petrovich, S. B. (1990). Aggression, violence and violence prevention: An ethological perspective. In L. J. Hertzberg, G. F. Ostrum, & J. R. Field (Eds.), *Violent behavior: Vol. 1. Assessment and intervention* (pp. 3-26). Great Neck, NY: PMA.

Pike, K. L. (1967). *Language in relation to a unified theory of the structure of human behavior* (2nd ed.). The Hague, the Netherlands: Mouton.

Ptacek, J. (1988). Why do men batter their wives? In K. Yllö & M. Bograd (Eds.), *Feminist perspectives on wife abuse* (pp. 133-157). Newbury Park, CA: Sage.

Riggs, D. S., Murphy, C. M., & O'Leary, K. D. (1989). Intentional falsification in reports of interpartner aggression. *Journal of Interpersonal Violence, 4,* 220-232.

Romero, M. (1985). A comparison between strategies used on prisoners of war and battered wives. *Sex Roles, 13,* 537-547.

Sabourin, T. C. (1991). Perceptions of verbal aggression in interpersonal violence. In D. D. Knudsen & J. L. Miller (Eds.), *Abused and battered* (pp. 135-145). New York: Aldine de Gruyter.

Saunders, D. G. (1991). Procedures for adjusting self-reports of violence for social desirability bias. *Journal of Interpersonal Violence, 6,* 336-344.

Saunders, D. G. (1992). A topology of men who batter: Three types derived from cluster analysis. *American Journal of Orthopsychiatry, 62,* 264-275.

Schecter, S. (1982). *Women and male violence.* Boston: South End.

Schwartz, M. D. (1987). Gender and injury in spousal assault. *Sociological Focus, 20,* 61-74.

Serpell, R. (1990). Audience, culture and psychological explanation: A reformulation of the emic-etic problem in cross-cultural psychology. *The Quarterly Newsletter of the Laboratory of Comparative Human Cognition, 12,* 99-132.

Shepard, M. F., & Campbell, J. A. (1992). The Abusive Behavior Inventory: A measure of psychological and physical abuse. *Journal of Interpersonal Violence, 7,* 291-305.

Sonkin, D. J., Martin, D., & Walker, L. E. (1985). *The male batterer.* New York: Springer.

Stets, J. E. (1990). Verbal and physical aggression in marriage. *Journal of Marriage and the Family, 52,* 501-514.

Stets, J. E. (1991). Psychological aggression in dating relationships: The role of interpersonal control. *Journal of Family Violence, 6,* 97-114.

Straus, M. A. (1974). Leveling, civility, and violence in the family. *Journal of Marriage and the Family, 36,* 13-29.

Straus, M. A. (1979). Measuring intrafamily conflict and violence: The Conflict Tactics Scales. *Journal of Marriage and the Family, 41,* 75-88.

Straus, M. A., & Gelles R. J. (Eds.). (1990). *Physical violence in American families: Risk factors and adaptations in 8,145 families.* New Brunswick, NJ: Transaction.

Straus, M. A., Gelles, R. J., & Steinmetz, S. K. (1980). *Behind closed doors: Violence in the American family.* Garden City, NY: Anchor/Doubleday.

Suitor, J. J., Pillemer, K., & Straus, M. A. (1990). Marital violence in life course perspective. In M. A. Straus & R. J. Gelles (Eds.), *Physical violence in American families* (pp. 305-317). New Brunswick, NJ: Transaction.

Tolman, R. M. (1989). The development of a measure of psychological maltreatment of women by their male partners. *Violence and Victims, 4,* 159-177.

Tolman, R. M. (1992). Psychological abuse of women. In R. T. Ammerman & M. Hersen (Eds.), *Assessment of family violence* (pp. 291-310). New York: John Wiley.

Tolman, R. M., & Bhosley, G. (1991). The outcome of participation in a shelter-sponsored program for men who batter. In D. D. Knudsen & J. L. Miller (Eds.), *Abused and battered* (pp. 113-122). New York: Aldine de Gruyter.

Vitanza, S., Walker, F., & Marshall, L. L. (1990). *The effect of psychological abuse on women's relationships and health.* Unpublished manuscript, University of North Texas.

Walker, L. E. (1979). *The battered woman.* New York: Harper & Row.

Walker, L. E. (1984). *The battered woman syndrome.* New York: Springer.

Waltz, J., Babcock, J. C., Jacobson, N. S., & Gottman, J. M. (1991, November). *Husband and wife reports of interspousal violence: Sex differences in minimization.* Paper presented at the Association for the Advancement of Behavior Therapy, New York.

Winter, D. G. (1973). *The power motive.* New York: Free Press.

CHAPTER 5

Physical and Sexual Violence in Marriage

ROBERT L. HAMPTON

ALICE F. WASHINGTON CONER-EDWARDS

Considerable research on couple violence has been conducted over the past two decades. In this chapter, we consider research on physical and sexual violence between spouses, including the legal aspects, as well as clinical intervention and treatment. We explore the incidence and prevalence of marital rape and examine the consequences of family violence with reference to battered individuals as victims and survivors. Included is an analysis of the social systemic factors that affect the individual and the overall societal response to violence.

The research literature on marital violence has increased substantially during the past decade. The most notable of these studies were surveys conducted by Gelles (1988), Straus and Gelles (1986), Walker (1979), and Kilpatrick (1990), which found that a significant number of Americans experience serious acts of violence at the hands of family members. The authors note high rates of violence including sexual assaults and violence during pregnancy. They highlight the seriousness of the problem and the need for rethinking, redefining, and developing effective intervention techniques.

By definition, marital violence is a behavior pattern that occurs in physical, emotional, psychological, sexual, and economic forms developed to perpetuate intimidation, power, and control of the abusing spouse over the abused spouse. Definitions of *marital* and *violence*, when combined, raise questions and offer

113

explanations regarding the historically muted or inadequate societal response to the battered woman.

The *Oxford English Dictionary* (1982) defines *marital* as "pertaining to or relating to a husband." It defines *violence* as "acting with or using great physical force or strength in order to injure, control or intimidate others . . ., committing harm or doing destruction." From these definitions, it would follow naturally that *marital violence* is "the abuse of a spouse, usually a woman, to maintain control and power by the abuser, usually a man" (Dickstein, 1988; Gelles & Conte, 1990).

Women and children, not men, historically, have been the subject of inquiry or discussion on marital or family violence. Recent studies of family violence (Straus & Gelles, 1986; Walker, 1991) show that large numbers of women are likely to be the intended victims of men's violence, ranging from simple assault to homicides.

For many centuries, women have occupied low status and have commanded little respect in the social hierarchy. Such low standing made them the natural victims of a variety of impositions, including violence. In many instances, it led to an overt disregard for women in general. In this context, it is not surprising that many cultures did not have labels for spouse abuse; it was hidden, disguised, ignored, and accepted as "culturally consistent" behavior (Pirsig, 1991).

In a 1988 report, a Virginia medical college team of paleopathologists found that the incidence of fractures among women (30% to 50%) was much higher than among men (9% to 20%) in mummies that were 2,000 to 3,000 years old. According to Dickstein (1988), these were primarily skull fractures caused by lethal blows as a result of personal violence in peacetime. Also, in 508-548 A.D., the female coruler of the Byzantine Empire was active in women's causes including opposition to physical abuse of women by their husbands.

Early American laws perpetuated the low status and abuse of women. The old English common law doctrines permitted wife beating for curbing or changing wives' inappropriate behavior, as determined by husbands. One such law, which remained on the books until the end of the nineteenth century, was known as the "Rule of Thumb Law"; it permitted a husband to beat his wife with a stick no larger than the circumference of his thumb.

As recently as the 1970s, an old Pennsylvania town ordinance prohibited a husband from beating his wife after 10 p.m. on Sundays. Such actions were culturally consistent and representative of society's disregard for women. This historical disparity between men and women throughout society led to the women's movement of the 1960s; 1973 marked the official beginning of the current battered women's movement.

When battered women seek medical treatment today, physicians are far more likely to raise the possibility of physical abuse by the spouse than at any previous time in history. Although women still are reluctant to reveal their situations because of the stigmas attached, they are acknowledging the fact of their abuse more openly than ever before. Several factors could account for these positive changes. In 1981, the first "National Day of Unity" against domestic violence was observed. This observance continued annually until 1984, when several days in October were designated as Domestic Violence Awareness Week. In 1987, the week was expanded to include an entire month of observance by the National Coalition Against Domestic Violence. This organization of battered women, shelters, and support groups continually publicizes and educates the public about battering. Battering is recognized as a crime and many people now believe it has reached epidemic proportions.

Lethal Violence

Intrafamily homicide is the most severe consequence of family violence. In the United States from 1980 to 1984, approximately 25% of all one-on-one cases of murder and nonnegligent manslaughter—18,712 homicides—occurred between family members over the age of 18 (Browne, 1987; Straus, 1986a). Women were at greater risk of being killed by a male partner than by other family members or by any other persons outside the partnership (Frieze & Browne, 1989). Of homicides that occurred between heterosexual partners, 58% were women killed by their male partners: 42% were men killed by their female partners.

From 1976 through 1985, the spousal homicide rate in the United States was 1.6 per 100,000 married persons; wives' risk was 1.3 times as great as that of husbands (Mercy & Saltzman,

1989). African Americans accounted for 45.4% of all spousal homicide victims, and the rate of spousal homicides in that group was 8.4 times as high as that among whites.

Previous research has shown that female victims of marital homicide are more likely to be killed at home than elsewhere (Goetting, 1991; Mann, 1991). Using homicide data from Detroit in the early 1980s, Goetting found that almost 40% of homicides occurred in the bedroom, 21% in the living room, and 10% in the kitchen. Husbands were twice as likely as wives to kill in a bedroom. Nearly 60% of the homicides occurred on weekends.

The location of the homicide is important in the circumstances associated with the event (Rose & McClain, 1990). The home is not only the place where female victims are more likely to be killed but also the place where they are more likely to kill their marital partners (Goetting, 1991; Jurik & Winn, 1990; Rose & McClain, 1990). When women kill, they frequently do so during domestic conflicts or in retaliation for previous abuse (Browne, 1987; Goetting, 1991; Jurik & Winn, 1990; Mann, 1991). Several studies have shown that African Americans are overrepresented among female perpetrators (Block, 1988; Jurik & Winn, 1990; McClain, 1982-1983; Valdez & Nourjah, 1988).

Data on prior police contact suggest that family and intimate assaults occur in a context of repeated violence (Browne, 1987; Saltzman et al., 1990; Straus, 1986a). Thus intrafamily homicides are not unpredictable; they are the most severe consequence of domestic conflict.

The Incidence and Prevalence
of Physical Violence

Estimates of the incidence and prevalence of violence vary depending on how the problem is defined and how it is measured. For this discussion, *violence* is defined as an act performed with the intention, or perceived intention, of causing physical pain or injury to another person.

This definition contains two elements: act and intention. Regarding the first element, the act is clear-cut, as in the case of a husband who throws a knife at his wife. Although he misses and no one is injured, throwing a knife is a serious act of violence.

Defining violence on the basis of an act results in a higher estimate of incidence rates than when based on injuries.

Intention, the second element of the definition, is less easily defined: It suggests that the husband must act willfully toward his spouse in a manner that could cause pain or injury. In most instances, accidental injuries are not considered violence.

The true rates of spousal violence are unknown. Estimates based on community, clinic, or shelter samples have several weaknesses (see Gelles, this volume). In many instances, these estimates are based on an insufficient number of cases or on samples that represent special populations. Consequently, they can provide some specific information about the group from which they are drawn but cannot be used in producing overall estimates of the extent of spousal violence.

The National Family Violence Surveys are the only existing nationally representative studies of family violence (Gelles & Straus, 1988; Straus & Gelles, 1990). These surveys are a rich source of data on the nature, type, severity, and correlates of violence in the American family. Because the 1985 survey provides the most recent data, we use this information for our estimate of couple violence.

Of every 100 couples in a married or cohabiting relationship, 16 reported a violent incident during the year of the survey. This figure represents a negligible decrease in the proportion of couples experiencing violence between 1875 and 1985 (Straus & Gelles, 1986). When the 1985 rate is applied to the 54 million couples living in the United States in that year, the result is in an estimated 8.7 million couples who experienced at least 1 assault in 1985. The rate of overall violence is not the most important statistic because most of the assaults were relatively minor—pushing, slapping, shoving, or throwing things. More to the point, 63 of 1,000 couples reported serious assaults such as kicking, punching, biting, or choking. When this rate is applied to the number of couples in the United States, we estimated 3.4 million instances in which the violence was relatively likely to cause injury.

In contrast to the one-year incidence rates, prevalence rates are used to indicate the proportion of couples who experience a violent event over the course of their relationship. Approximately 30% of the couples had experienced at least one such event.

Physical Violence Against Women

Violence toward women by their male partners is part of contemporary family life. Although Straus and Gelles (1986) estimated that husband-to-wife violence had decreased by 6.6% between their 1975 and their 1985 surveys, they found that more than 11% of the women had experienced at least one act of violence during the study year.

The rate of severe violence by husbands also decreased, declining from 38 per 1,000 couples in 1975 to 30 per 1,000 couples in 1985. This 21% decrease is important because it represents a considerable number of couples. According to Straus and Gelles:

> If the 1975 rate for husband-to-wife severe violence had remained in effect, the application of this rate to the 54 million couples in the U.S. in 1985 is an estimate of a least 2,052,000 severely assaulted wives each year. . . . However, if there has been a 27 percent decrease in the rate, that translates to 1,620,000 beaten wives, which is 432,000 fewer than would have been the case if the 1975 rate prevailed. (1986, p. 470)

Violence Toward Husbands

Men's violence against their wives and lovers has been an appropriate focus for most research on couple violence. There is considerable debate about the degree of sexual symmetry in this type of violence (Dobash, Dobash, Wilson, & Daly, 1992). Some researchers believe that many of the methods used to detect family violence are inadequate. The Conflict Tactics Scales, for example, ignore sexual assaults and rapes. In addition, scholars have argued that claims of sexual symmetry in couple violence do not reflect sexually symmetrical motivation or action (Dobash et al., 1992). Finally, many feminist researchers believe that we cannot ignore the context, the nature, and the consequences of the violence, the role of obligations of each family member, and the different mechanisms or transactional sequences that lead to various forms of abuse (Bograd, 1988).

Because men are typically larger than their wives and usually have greater access to power, property, and prestige, they do not experience the same physical or social consequences of violence as do women. Also, a considerable proportion of wife-to-husband violence occurs in domestic conflict, either as a preemptive strike or in retaliation for previous abuse. These observations, however, do not alter the fact that husbands can be victims of domestic strife.

Data from the 1985 National Family Violence Survey reveal that slightly more than 4% of the wives surveyed reported they had engaged in violence toward their husbands (Gelles & Straus, 1988).

Ethnic and Racial Differences

Families of color have been victims of benign neglect in community-based studies of spousal violence. The first National Family Violence Survey (Straus, Gelles, & Steinmetz, 1980) was constrained by the small sample of African American families (n = 147) and by a limited sampling frame. The survey did not include enough Hispanic families for comparative analyses.

Violence Among African American Couples

The first National Family Violence Survey (Straus et al., 1980) is generally cited as the primary (and sole) source of data on the prevalence and incidence of spousal violence in African American families. Straus and his colleagues reported that African American husbands showed higher rates of overall and severe violence toward their wives than white husbands. In African American families, the rate of severe violence toward wives, or wife abuse, was 113 per 1,000, in contrast to 30 per 1,000 in white households. African American wives were nearly twice as likely as white wives to engage in acts of severe violence against their husbands (76 per 1,000 and 41 per 1,000, respectively).

In their analysis of these data, Cazenave and Straus (1979) found that embeddedness in primary networks is closely associated with rates of spousal slapping among African American couples; these rates were lower than among white couples. For African American couples, the number of years in the neighborhood, the number of children, and the number of nonnuclear family members in the household were associated with lower levels of spousal violence. In spite of the small sample size (n =

147), these data provided some important insights concerning violence in African American families. The study revealed that several variables must be examined to provide a thorough comparison. It also revealed that rates of violence among African Americans vary by family income, social class, and strength of social networks.

In assessing the effects of race on spousal violence, Lockhart and White (1989) and Lockhart (1991) found that a larger proportion of middle-class African American women than of middle-class white women reported violent treatment at the hands of their marital partners. On the basis of data gathered through a purposive sample in a major southeastern metropolitan area, Lockhart argued that African American couples were not inherently more violent than white couples. When higher levels of violence exist, they may be due in part to the particular social predicament of African Americans in American society. According to this reasoning, many African Americans, who have achieved middle-class positions only recently as a result of relatively recent changes in their lives, may have retained the norms, values, and role expectations of their lower SES developmental experiences (Lockhart, 1991). Aggressive and violent problem-solving strategies may be partially related to this background.

The second National Family Violence Survey was designed to address many of the shortcomings of previous research. A comparison of data from the two surveys revealed that, overall, husband-to-wife violence was unchanged between 1975 and 1985. Severe violence, or "wife beating," declined by 43.4%; however, these data revealed an increase in the rate of overall and severe wife-to-husband violence (Hampton, Gelles, & Harrop, 1989).

The limited research on African American spouse abuse reveals several relevant variables. These include occupation, income, embeddedness in social networks, unemployment, and violence in one's family of orientation (Asbury, 1987; Uzzell & Peebles-Wilkins, 1989). Although statistics suggest that African American families represent a significant portion of the violent families identified and served by agencies, this finding may reflect in part the actions of gatekeepers rather than racial differences in the type, nature, or severity of family violence (Hampton, 1987; Hampton & Newberger, 1985).

Violence Among Hispanic Couples

Data collected as part of the Los Angeles Epidemiologic Catchment Area (ECA) survey provide us with one of the most comprehensive studies of couple violence among Hispanics. To avoid problems associated with generalizing across Hispanic subgroups, the researchers limited their analyses to persons of Mexican descent. The sample included 1,243 Mexican American and 1,149 non-Hispanic whites (Sorenson & Telles, 1991).

No significant differences were found between non-Hispanic white and Mexican American families in lifetime rates of self-reported violence toward a spouse. Spousal violence rates for Mexican Americans born in Mexico and for non-Hispanic whites born in the United States were virtually equivalent (20.0% and 21.6%, respectively); rates were highest for Mexican Americans born in the United States (30.9%; Sorenson & Telles, 1991). This research also revealed a gender difference; the women reported higher rates of hitting or throwing things at their spouses/partners than the men.

One of the major findings of this study was that rates of spousal violence among Mexican Americans vary according to immigration status. Mexican Americans born in the United States reported rates 2.4 times higher than those born in Mexico. The researchers suggest that this difference may be related to cultural conflicts, in which members of later generations of immigrant families are exposed to discrepancies between their familial culture of origin and the dominant culture in which they reside (Sorenson & Telles, 1991).

Ethnic Comparison

The second National Family Violence Survey provides us with an opportunity to compare rates of couple violence for African Americans, non-Hispanic whites, and Hispanics. Table 5.1 shows that African American and Hispanic families had comparable rates of husband-to-wife violence (174 per 1,000 and 173 per 1,000, respectively). Whites reported lower rates of overall husband-to-wife violence and severe violence. The rate of severe assaults on wives in African American and Hispanic families, which can be considered a measure of wife beating, was more than double the rate in non-Hispanic white families.

Table 5.1 Annual Incidence Rates for Black, Non-Hispanic White, and Hispanic Couples

| Type of Violence[a] | Rate per 1,000 Couples[b] | | |
	Black	Non-Hispanic White	Hispanic
Husband to Wife:			
Any violence by male partner	174	108	173
Severe violence	71	30	73
Wife to Husband:			
Any violence by female partner	207	115	168
Severe violence	112	40	78

NOTES: a. Data in this table are based on separate analyses from the 1985 National Family Violence Survey. Independent comparisons of Hispanic-non-Hispanic white couples and black-white couples were conducted by Straus and Smith (1990) and Hampton and Gelles (in press). b. The Ns for this table are 3,690 non-Hispanic white families, 602 Hispanic families, and 580 black families.

Rates of overall wife-to-husband violence for Hispanic females were intermediate between those of African American and white females. Black women had the highest rates (207 per 1,000) and white women the lowest (115 per 1,000). A similar pattern holds for severe violence: African American women had the highest rates, followed by Hispanic and white women.

Straus and Smith (1990) found that, compared with white families, the higher rates of spouse abuse in Hispanic families reflect the economic deprivation, youthfulness, and urban residence of Hispanics. When these factors are controlled, no statistically significant difference exists between Hispanics and non-Hispanic whites.

Although income inequalities are a factor in explaining differences in rates of violence between African American and white families, controlling for income does not account exclusively for the racial disparity (Hampton & Gelles, in press; Hampton et al., 1989). There are several additional factors that must be considered in assessing domestic violence among African American couples (Hampton & Gelles, in press).

The Incidence and Prevalence of Marital Rape

The subject of marital rape has been popularized in the media as a result of several significant court cases in which efforts were made to criminalize this form of sexual assault. For most of our history, it was assumed that a husband could not rape his wife. This idea was based firmly in our assumptions that, under patriarchy, men are the undisputed heads of their households. Legal policies based on common law and on patriarchal attitudes have supported husbands in their notion that their wives—and their wives' bodies—belong to them (Pagelow, 1988). Marital rape is one of the least discussed and least researched areas of family violence.

Sociologists have given attention to the prevalence and legal status of marital rape and to public attitudes (Finkelhor & Yllö, 1985). Diana Russell (1982) was one of the first scholars to challenge the assumption that marital rape is simply another form of abuse suffered by battered wives. Of the 644 married women in her sample, 14% reported sexual assaults by husbands, 12% had been forced to have intercourse, and 2% had experienced other types of sexual assault. Sexual assaults by husbands were the most common kind of sexual assault reported, occurring more than twice as often as sexual assault by strangers. David Finkelhor and Kertsi Yllo (1985) interviewed 323 Boston-area women and found that nearly 10% had been forced to have sex with their husbands. According to Gelles and Straus (1988), 50 women per 1,000 each year reported that their husbands attempted to force them to have sex and 80 women per 1,000 were forced to have sex by their husbands.

In Russell's sample and others, researchers have found that some men batter their wives but do not rape them; some rape but do not batter them; and others do both (Bowker, 1983; Browne, 1987; Finkelhor & Yllö, 1985; Shields & Hanneke, 1983). The mixture of sexual and nonsexual violence in marriage may be the extreme point on a continuum of wife abuse because these victims may have experienced more severe forms of nonsexual violence and stronger reactions than have others (Bowker, 1983; Russell, 1982; Shields & Hanneke, 1983).

Most of the available conceptual knowledge of marital rape is based on surveys of battered women, rape crisis hot lines, and court cases. Although our theoretical knowledge of marital rape is limited, public professional awareness and research concern are growing. In addition, there is evidence (Gelles, 1987) to suggest that rape is a matter of concern in many marriages, whether or not it is connected with battering. Analysis of the definition of marital rape and of previously held views on its occurrence offer some conceptual understanding of this subject.

Definition of Marital Rape

Until the mid-1970s in the United States, marital rape was not a crime. With the advent of the women's movement of the 1970s, however, feminists forced society to reconsider this concept. Subsequently, social scientists began to investigate sexual assault, forced sex in marriage, and marital rape. Yet, by 1980, only three states had completely eliminated the marital rape exemption from their laws, and only five states had modified it. The rationale for this exemption was based in part on the traditional belief that marriage implied consent by the wife to have sexual relations with her husband whenever he desired them. Many women also felt it was their duty to have sex with their husbands even if they were not in the mood for sex. In many states, this implied consent exists as long as a couple is legally married.

Few women whose husbands have forced them to have sex define themselves as having been raped (Gelles, 1987). Most women view rape as something that happens primarily between strangers. Many women do not define even forceful sexual advances as assaultive when these acts are perpetrated by their husbands. According to Pagelow (1984), women who stated that they had not been raped said they had submitted to sexual demands to prevent beatings or out of fear of their partners. Several women in this study also reported physical assaults during sexual activity so severe that they were injured or lost consciousness; yet they did not define these acts as sexual assaults.

A more difficult issue is the case in which the wife does not view the behavior as problematic or as marital rape. Is it appropriate for the larger social order to intervene or to define the behavior as such? It has become easier, though still controversial, to intervene in a child's best interest in child abuse cases. It would be even more controversial to intervene in the case of marital rape when one or both spouses fail to define the behavior as rape.

Risk Factors for Marital Violence

Researchers and family violence experts agree consistently that several factors are related to various aspects of family violence. Gelles and Conte (1990) identified the following: the cycle of violence, low socioeconomic status, social and structural stress, social isolation, low self-concept, and psychopathology.

Parallel with the thinking by Gelles and other scholars, we identify two broad categories of antecedents to family and domestic violence: social and psychological antecedents. Social antecedents include limited access to goods and services, limited opportunities, social and structural constraints, estrangement and social isolation from others, and physical proximity of family members. The anger and despair generated by social structural constraints are acted out with those nearest and most vulnerable to scapegoating.

Psychological antecedents include blocked aspirations, unrestrained anger, faulty regulation of emotional closeness and distance, sadomasochistic relational patterns, intergenerational transmission of learned violence-prone behavior, and low self-esteem. Factors in these two broad sociological and psychological categories perpetuate the cycle of violence identified by Gelles, Walker, and others.

Structure of the Family

Physical and sexual violence in marriage perhaps are viewed most accurately as indicators of families in trouble. Many factors can place a family in jeopardy and lead to violence. This multiplicity of causes complicates the task of understanding the origins of couple violence.

Straus (1991) believes that one of the social causes of domestic violence is the high level of conflict that characterizes families. Much of this conflict is associated with factors that form the very foundation of family life in this country. According to Gelles and Straus (1979), these factors are involuntary membership, intensity of involvement, differences in gender and age, family privacy, range of activities and interests, the right to influence, and shared identity. These factors add up to produce a high level of conflict, which in turn increases the risk that one family member or another will try to prevail by using violence. As the amount of conflict increases, the assault rate also increases dramatically (Straus, 1991).

Gender Inequality

Wife abuse is not a rare and deviant phenomenon that results from the breakdown of family functioning. It is a predictable and common dimension of normal family life as that life is structured in our society (Bograd, 1988). Feminist scholars regard male dominance in overt and subtle forms as a major cause of family violence. In many respects, the feminist analysis of wife beating is a critique of patriarchy (Yllö & Straus, 1990).

Egalitarian couples have the lowest rates of violence, and husband-dominated couples have the highest rates of spouse abuse (Straus et al., 1980). Violence by husbands is associated with nonegalitarian decision making (Yllö & Straus, 1990). One can argue that, in male-dominated relationships, many husbands use physical and sexual violence as a way to maintain power. Also, in many instances where the husband is not dominant, men may resort to violence in response to perceived powerlessness.

Exposure to Violence in Family of Orientation

The theoretical rationale for the intergenerational transmission of spousal violence is derived from social learning theory. Simply stated, this proposition suggests that a disproportionate number of individuals who engage in physical assault against their wives were socialized in households in which they observed parental violence. Some studies indicate an association between observation of fathers hitting mothers and subsequent wife abuse (Caesar, 1988; Hampton & Gelles, in press; Pagelow, 1981; Rosenbaum & O'Leary, 1981; Straus et al., 1980).

Although one's experience with violence as a child is a powerful contributor to adult attitudes toward violence, this variable explains only a small percentage of the variance in couple violence. In most couples, behaviors observed in childhood are not transferred directly to the marital relationship.

Alcohol and Substance Abuse

Several studies report a strong association between substance abuse, especially alcohol, and marital violence (Browne, 1987; Hayes & Emshoff, this volume; Rosenbaum & O'Leary, 1981; Walker, 1984). Abusive men with a history of alcohol or drug problems are apt to abuse their spouses both when drunk and when sober. They tend to be violent more frequently and more severely when under the influence than men without such a history. They also are more apt to attack their partners sexually (Browne, 1987; Frieze & Knoble, 1980; Roy, 1977; Walker, 1984).

Consequences of Family Violence

The response to family violence on the part of battered individuals is negative and extensive. This response includes the development of general negative attitudes toward marriage and relationships and toward men. Psychosomatic reactions create alarming health problems. Depression and suicide attempts increase, with a corresponding increase in the use of drugs and alcohol. Social isolation, child battering, and retaliatory violence develop. Extramarital sex and loss of interest in sex increase and the family's structure and functions are eroded.

The literature on abused women reports poor psychological and emotional well-being among battered women who have sought help or refuge in a shelter or agency. These studies have shown that battered women frequently lack self-esteem (Rieker & Carmen, 1986; Roark & Vlahos, 1983) and suffer from feelings of loss and inadequacy (Turner & Shapiro, 1986), depression (Hilberman & Munson, 1977) and learned helplessness (Walker, 1979).

The second National Family Violence Survey included several psychological distress items with the intent of measuring the three aspects of mental health that have been mentioned as the result of experiencing violence: depression, stress, and somatic symptoms. Women who reported experiencing violence and abuse also reported higher levels of moderate and severe psychological distress. The multivariate analysis showed that violence made an independent and nonspurious contribution to the psychological distress experienced by women (Gelles & Harrop, 1989).

Battered Women as Survivors of Family Violence

The response of the social system to the battered woman's cry for help historically has been insufficient. We believe that this cry should mobilize an entire system of supports. Serious barriers and deficiencies exist, however, and these must be addressed if battered women are to receive help.

The literature contains two views of the consequences of family violence on battered women. According to the one view, the battered woman is an active survivor of an abusive situation; the second view categorizes her as a "helpless and passive victim" (Gondolf & Fisher, 1988). In the following discussion, we first consider the battered woman as a helpless and passive victim and use the concept of "learned helplessness" to illustrate the victimization process.

Walker (1979) suggests that repeated battering diminishes the woman's motivation to respond. As a result, women tend to be submissive in the face of intermittent punishments or abuse. As the abuse continues, the battered woman becomes immobilized, feels a loss of emotion about the battering experience, and begins to blame herself for the abuse inflicted upon her.

From a Freudian perspective, "learned helplessness" may be rooted in infancy, when the infant cries for attention to a wet diaper or an empty stomach and does not receive an immediate response. The infant is helpless and unable to change the situation. In the latency years, the child's exposure to family violence represents another, equally traumatic and uncontrollable situation. In adolescence, strict discipline bordering on violence continues the process. Even in young adult life, the socialization to violence may continue when the young husband is told that the way to control his domineering wife is to beat her. The woman learns to feel helpless at an early age and is socialized in later life for helpless relationships. Such learning and socialization can create a sadomasochistic, pain-inducing, pain-seeking expectation for the relationship.

Contrary to learned helplessness theory is the "survivor hypothesis" whereby the battered woman is viewed as an active survivor rather than as a helpless victim. Many battered women remain in abusive situations not because of passivity but because they have failed in attempts to escape. These women increase their help-seeking efforts in the face of increased violence. In a logical, consistent way, they try to assure protection and survival for themselves and their children. Such efforts supersede fear, giving up, depression, or the passivity of learned helplessness. The surviving battered woman is heroic, assertive, and persistent (Gondolf & Fisher, 1988).

This research, based on a comprehensive survey of more than 6,000 women in Texas shelters, provides the largest data base on the subject to date. The findings challenge the existing paradigm of learned helplessness; they offer new modes of thinking about victimization and survival, help seeking, battered women and their batterers, and the community system of resources and support services. The implications for clinical treatment and intervention are extensive.

Clinical Aspects

Sociological investigations represent the most prevalent attempts to understand the nature of marital violence. This situation is ironic because the practice professions have been asked most often to address the problems. Marital violence is a clinical matter; it moves beyond the exterior of the marriage, which deals with offspring, security, and caretaking. It emanates from the underlying architecture of the relationship and symbolizes the complex problems encountered by couples. Marriage is expected to provide all things to both spouses: love, sex, companionship, togetherness, and all other expressive and instrumental needs. A great deal is expected of each spouse; the greater the burden that is placed on the intimate relationship, the more stressed and fragile it becomes. Contemporary couples are trying to cope with vast and widespread societal changes. In addition, people bring disparate expectations and values to marriage. Dreams and visions often are based more on wishes and fantasies than on what reality can offer. As a result, it is no wonder that marital violence develops or that it originates perhaps as often in the intimate, emotional realm as in social structural and societal patterns. Couples become angry when unmet needs or unrealistic demands surface. Long-standing anger often is projected onto the partner, and violence erupts repeatedly in the marriage.

Experts in marital violence must wonder about the extent to which this violence is reported. They have made serious attempts to understand this complex nature of intimate relationships in developing effective clinical models simultaneously with the current social structural changes.

Assumptions About Battered Women

Why is there such an observable breakdown in the social support network designed to aid individuals in crisis? Family violence scholars have made several assumptions about battered woman. The first, based on a system of male dominance, is an insensitivity to the impact of the larger social order on individual problems. Second is the unquestioned belief that individual problems and family pathology are due to individual and family difficulties rather than to social structural constraints. Third, because of the privatization of family life, it is believed that families are expected to fend for themselves in obtaining adequate housing, child care, economic sufficiency, protection, employment, and support.

Thus the male-dominated, "masculine" approach to battering emphasizes a pathological analysis of problems, a medical model of treatment, and an autonomous family approach. To address the social problems and the consequences of family violence substantially and realistically, however, efforts toward a social structural assessment of the problem and toward an increase in the battered woman's social status and power are necessary. The social structural constraints cited earlier must be relaxed; the attitudes, thinking, actions, and resources of the social system must be mobilized to alter the position in which many women find themselves.

Simultaneous with the need for social structural assessment is the need for a thorough clinical assessment, particularly when family work or counseling of couples is indicated. Intense family violence nearly always involves serious and strong emotional reactions. Long-standing battering situations often produce clinical levels of depression, low self-concept, anger, and other underlying problems that require the understanding and the skills of capable clinicians. Clinical intervention, when coupled with systematic intervention, often can move individuals swiftly toward regaining stability.

Intervention

Interventions to aid physically abused children have the oldest history and originated in the medical community in the 1950s. Formal programs for victims of marital violence were established almost two decades later. In most cases, these programs assume that survivors of wife assault are adults and can make their own decisions. Among the crisis intervention services that have received considerable attention in the past decade are hospitals, the police, and treatment programs for male batterers. Because male batterers are being addressed elsewhere in this volume (see the chapter by Gondolf), we direct our attention to interventions by hospitals and the police.

Hospitals

Hospitals and medical personnel play important roles in recognizing, reporting, and treating victims. Although health care professionals frequently see cases of family violence, it is widely known that the abuse is often ignored or minimized, especially for women, and the victims are made into scapegoats or are not believed (Klingbeil, 1986).

The available data suggest that health care professionals treat a large number of women for injuries resulting from interpersonal violence. In a study of 1,793 women in Kentucky (Shulman, 1979), 1 woman in 10 had been physically assaulted by her partner during the year, and 79 of the assaults were serious enough to require medical attention: 43% percent of the injured women required treatment, and 44% of these individuals needed two or more treatments. Of those assaulted, 59% had sought treatment in a hospital emergency room. Employing these data to estimate spouse abuse, Straus (1986b) calculated an annual incidence rate of 4.4 injuries requiring medical attention per 100 married women in Kentucky.

Two hospital-based studies also concluded that battered women are seen frequently in emergency rooms. In a study conducted at a large general hospital emergency department in Detroit, 25% of the women examined were known victims of domestic violence (Goldberg & Tomlanovich, 1984). Similar results were reported by researchers in San Francisco, who concluded that 36% of admissions to the county trauma center resulted from interpersonal violence (Sumner, Mintz, & Brown, 1986).

There is also evidence that physicians frequently ignore the initial signs of battering. Flitcraft, Frazier, and Stark (1980) found that many women seen initially in emergency departments for inflicted injuries subsequently returned with inflicted injuries. Stark and Flitcraft (1985) found that only 1 battered woman in 25 was identified as battered in the emergency department they studied. McLeer and Anwar (1989) found that, when a protocol for identifying battered women was introduced to an emergency department, in which female trauma patients were asked whether they had been injured by someone, almost 30% of those patients were battered women.

Staff members' responses to victims vary on the basis on their medical specialty, their perception of the victim, and their training. Many medical personnel tend to focus on the injury itself while ignoring the process and the circumstances that produced it. Health care advocates for victims of wife abuse have proposed that health care personnel should learn to identify battered women and intervene on their behalf (Hampton, 1988).

A recent study (Kurz, 1990) produces two important additions to our discussion of battered women in health care settings. First, battered women who present to emergency departments have a diverse set of behavioral characteristics: The majority presented like other patients. A significant minority, 39%, had traits that medical staff found discrediting and difficult: 26% of this group had alcohol on their breath or had used drugs, while 13% were, as the medical literature suggests, "evasive." Although no stereotypical "abused woman" was found, this study suggests that health care personnel should be prepared to encounter many battered women who appear similar to other patients. The study also suggests that most abused women respond to direct questioning.

Second, an ongoing program of education and concrete intervention can produce positive responses to battered women (Kurz, 1990). This study suggests, however, that we cannot automatically assume that the presentation of information to health care personnel will lead to completed interventions. Health care personnel, like other professionals in the field, often give conditional responses to victims. Staff members are less responsive to women with discrediting attributes than to other patients. Sometimes they do not respond because they feel they do not have the time for interventions and often prefer to give priority to other cases. Occasionally, too, they do not regard responding to battered women as a central part of their medical role (Kurz, 1990).

The Police

One of the recommendations that emerged from the study by the Attorney General's Task Force on Family Violence (1984) was that the criminal justice system should become more actively involved in punishing perpetrators of domestic violence. In Law Enforcement Recommendation 2, the report states that, "consistent with state law, the chief executive of every law enforcement agency should establish arrest as the preferred response in cases of family violence" (p. 22).

Drawing heavily from the results of the Minneapolis police experiment, the attorney general's report called on police departments and criminal justice agencies to recognize battering as a criminal activity and to respond accordingly. This position was supported by the case of Tracy Thurman, a battered wife who had regularly sought assistance from the Torrington, Connecticut, police to protect her from attacks by her estranged husband. Thurman was battered severely and was left permanently injured in June 1983 while police officers stood by and did nothing. Subsequently, she filed a civil suit against the City of Torrington and 29 police officers (*Thurman v. City of Torrington,* 1985). Thurman won her case and later settled out of court for $1.9 million. Because of the ever-present threat of similar suits, a number of communities have adopted the policy of mandatory arrest in cases of family violence.

In general, police respond to domestic violence calls reluctantly and with a sense of futility (Berk & Loseke, 1980; Caputo, 1991; Elliot, 1989). Police intervention in these calls is often dangerous; the officers often fear that the violence will be redirected toward them.

Although arresting the perpetrator was the response preferred by many law enforcement agencies in the early 1980s, recent evidence sheds new light on this type of intervention

(Berk, Campbell, Klap, & Western, 1992; Pate & Hamilton, 1992; Sherman & Smith, 1992). If asked whether arrest influences the subsequent violence of those arrested, the answer is that, in general, it depends on the arrested person's stake in conformity (Sherman & Smith, 1992). Whereas arrest leads to a significant increase in subsequent assaults among unemployed suspects, it appears to have a deterrent effect among employed suspects (Pate & Hamilton, 1992).

On the basis of his assessment of data collected in seven National Institute of Justice experiments, Sherman (1992) found the following:

> Arrest increases domestic violence among people who have nothing to lose, especially the unemployed.
>
> Arrest deters domestic violence in cities with higher proportions of white and Hispanic suspects.
>
> Arrest deters domestic violence in the short run but escalates violence later in cities with higher proportions of unemployed African American suspects.
>
> A small but chronic portion of all violent couples produce the majority of domestic violence incidents.
>
> Offenders who flee before police arrive are deterred substantially by warrants for their arrest, at least in Omaha.

This study suggests that arrest as an intervention does not produce uniform results. In some cases, it can produce unintended negative consequences for victims. Consequently, this intervention is conditional and limited, as in the case of medical professionals.

Compassion Versus Control

Alvin Rosenfeld and Eli Newberger (1977), two physicians, described two competing philosophies that have been applied to treating child abuse. These philosophies are equally applicable to other forms of family violence.

A compassionate intervention may focus on mediation, education, training, and treatment. Often, it involves providing additional resources for the family. The agent of social control who applies a compassionate intervention is directed to approach each case with understanding and a nonpunitive outlook (Mederer & Gelles, 1989). Outcomes of the intervention are thought to be change of attitude, improved skills for coping with stress, and, ultimately, the cessation of wife battering. The underlying philosophy is humane and compassionate toward both the victim and the abuser (Rosenfeld & Newberger, 1977).

A control model is based on the assumption that deviant behavior is controlled when punishment is both certain and severe. Individuals in effect are coerced, threatened, and sanctioned into conformity, both formally and informally. Paternoster and Iovanni (1986) found that deterrence works primarily through informal processes; when these are controlled, perceptions of severity and certainty of punishment have no effect on deviant behavior. This threat of arrest and public exposure as a wife beater might deter potentially violent men from abusing their wives (Mederer & Gelles, 1989).

The control model involves aggressive use of intervention to limit and, if necessary, punish the perpetrator. Abusers are held accountable for their actions. Arrest and criminal prosecution of the aggressor are among the preferred options.

Mederer and Gelles (1989) discuss several advantages and disadvantages to interventions based on each philosophy. It is probably wise to heed the advice given by Rosenfeld and Newberger (1977); they suggest that effective treatment involves both compassion and control. This advice is supported by an empirical examination of the effectiveness of battered women's shelters (a compassionate approach) in preventing future battering (Berk, Newton, & Berk, 1986). The shelters appeared to have a beneficial effect; 8 of 10 women who stayed in shelters reported no new violence after they left the shelters. This appears to be the case when a survivor can actually take control of her life. For women who cannot take control of their lives, shelters either had no impact or, worse, triggered new episodes of violence for these women. Washburn and Frieze (1981) compared three groups of battered women: those who went to a shelter, those who filed orders of protection, and those who responded to an advertisement seeking subjects for a study of battered women. Women from the shelter were about twice as likely as the others to be unemployed. These women and those who filed protection orders tended to have experienced more severe violence, particularly marital rape. The women who filed protection orders felt the least powerful and defined their actions as helping themselves to change their situations.

It is possible to use control interventions (arrest, prosecution, and sentencing) to motivate perpetrators to participate in treatment programs. Diversion programs are another way of combining control and compassion (Mederer & Gelles, 1989). In an era when the police are the only institution that can command substantial public funds to combat domestic violence, it is important to recognize that control and compassion can be linked. In addition, domestic violence can be addressed more effectively through a wide range of nonpolice programs such as industrial policy, Head Start, and counseling and therapy for victims and batterers (Sherman, 1992).

In the best of all worlds, appropriate legal controls, humane support, and primary prevention programs to address wife abuse would be in place in all communities. These programs not only would address individual-level variables that might contribute to violent episodes but, also, where possible, would be concerned with social structural issues. In the final analysis, violence is a series of dynamic processes between perpetrators and survivors wherein one party ultimately wins and the other ultimately loses or in which a draw results. Because all parties are influenced by inner and outer dynamics, both groups are victims and need intervention and assistance. Violence is more than an overt act; it is the end product of complex psychological and social forces.

We cannot assume that simply presenting information to professionals in the field will lead to appropriate interventions. Hospitals and the police must continue, for example, to make referrals to battered women's programs, and vice versa. Only through cross-agency and cross-disciplinary efforts on many levels can we hope to reduce and eventually alleviate the pain and suffering related to marital violence.

References

Asbury, J. (1987). African-American women in violent relationships: An exploration of cultural differences. In R. Hampton (Ed.), *Violence in the black family: Correlates and consequences* (pp. 89-105). Lexington, MA: Lexington.

Attorney General's Task Force on Family Violence. (1984). *Final report.* Washington, DC: Government Printing Office.

Berk, R. A., Campbell, A., Klap, R., & Western, B. (1992). The deterrent effect of arrest: A Bayesian analysis of four field experiments. *American Sociological Review, 57*(5), 698-708.

Berk, R., & Loseke, D. (1980). Handling family violence: The situated determinants of police arrest in domestic disturbances. *Law and Society Review, 15*(2), 317-346.

Berk, R., Newton, P., & Berk, S. F. (1986). What a difference a day makes: An empirical study of the impact of shelters for battered women. *Journal of Marriage and the Family, 48,* 481-490.

Block, C. (1988). Lethal violence in the Chicago Latino community, 1965 to 1981. In J. F. Kraus, S. B. Sorenson, & P. D. Juarez (Eds.), *Proceedings from the Research Conference on Violence and Homicide in Hispanic Communities* (pp. 31-65). Los Angeles: UCLA Publication Services.

Bograd, M. (1988). Feminist perspectives on wife abuse: An introduction. In K. Ylló & M. Bograd (Eds.), *Feminist perspectives on wife abuse* (pp. 11-26). Newbury Park, CA: Sage.

Bowker, L. H. (1983). Marital rape: A distinct syndrome? *Social Casework: The Journal of Contemporary Social Work, 64,* 347-352.

Browne, A. (1987). *When battered women kill.* New York: Free Press.

Caesar, P. L. (1988). Exposure to violence in the families-of-origin among wife-abusers and maritally nonviolent men. *Violence and Victims, 3*(1), 49-63.

Caputo, R. K. (1991). Police classification of domestic-violence calls: An assessment of program impact. In D. D. Knudsen & J. L. Miller (Eds.), *Abused and battered* (pp. 147-152). New York: Aldine de Gruyter.

Cazenave, N., & Straus, M. (1979). Race, class network embeddedness and family violence: A search for potent support systems. *Journal of Comparative Family Studies, 10,* 281-299.

Dickstein, L. (1988). Spouse abuse and other domestic violence. *Psychiatric Clinics of North America, 2,* 611-625.

Dobash, R. P., Dobash, R. E., Wilson, M., & Daly, M. (1992). The myth of sexual symmetry in marital violence. *Social Problems, 39*(1), 71-91.

Elliot, D. (1989). Criminal justice procedures in family violence crimes. In L. Ohlin & M. Tonry (Eds.), *Family violence* (pp. 427-480). Chicago: University of Chicago Press.

Finkelhor, D., & Yllo, K. (1985). *License to rape: Sexual abuse of wives.* New York: Free Press.

Flitcraft, A., Frazier, W. D., & Stark, E. (1980). *Medical encounters and sequelae of domestic violence.* Final report to the National Institute of Mental Health, Bethesda, MD.

Frieze, I. H., & Browne, A. (1989). Violence in marriage. In L. Ohlin & M. Tonry (Eds.), *Family violence* (pp. 161-218). Chicago: University of Chicago Press.

Frieze, I. H., & Knoble, J. (1980, August). *The effects of alcohol on marital violence.* Paper presented at the annual meeting of the American Psychological Association, Montreal.

Gelles, R. J. (1987). *Family violence.* Newbury Park, CA: Sage.

Gelles, R. J. (1988). Violence and pregnancy: Are pregnant women at greater risk of abuse? *Journal of Marriage and the Family, 50,* 1045-1058.

Gelles, R. J., & Conte, J. (1990). Domestic violence and sexual abuse of children. *Journal of Marriage and the Family, 52,* 1045-1058.

Gelles, R. J., & Harrop, J. W. (1989). Violence, battering, and psychological distress among women. *Journal of Interpersonal Violence, 4*(4), 400-420.

Gelles, R. J., & Straus, M. A. (1979). Determinants of violence in the family: Toward a theoretical integration. In W. Burr et al. (Eds.), *Contemporary theories about the family* (Vol. 1, pp. 549-581). New York: Free Press.

Gelles, R. J., & Straus, M. A. (1988). *Intimate violence: The causes and consequences of abuse in the American family.* New York: Simon & Schuster (Touchstone).

Goetting, A. (1991). Patterns of marital homicide: A comparison of husbands and wives. In R. L. Hampton (Ed.), *Black family violence: Current research and theory* (pp. 147-160). Lexington, MA: Lexington.

Goldberg, W., & Tomlanovich, M. C. (1984). Domestic violence victims in the emergency department. *Journal of the American Medical Association, 251*(25), 3259-3264.

Gondolf, E. W., & Fisher, E. R. (1988). *Battered women as survivors.* Lexington, MA: Lexington.

Hampton, R. L. (1987). Race, ethnicity and child maltreatment: An analysis of cases recognized and reported by hospitals. In R. E. Staples (Ed.), *The black family essays and studies* (4th ed., pp. 178-191). Belmont, CA: Wadsworth.

Hampton, R. L. (1988). Physical victimization across the lifespan: Recognition, ethnicity, and deterrence. In M. Straus (Ed.), *Abuse and victimization: Across the life span* (pp. 203-222). Baltimore, MD: Johns Hopkins University Press.

Hampton, R. L., & Gelles, R. J. (in press). Violence toward black women in a nationally representative sample of black American families. *Journal of Comparative Family Studies.*

Hampton, R. L., Gelles, R. J., & Harrop, J. W. (1989). Is violence in black families increasing: A comparison of 1975 and 1985 national survey rates. *Journal of Marriage and the Family, 51,* 969-980.

Hampton, R. L., & Newberger, E. H. (1985). Child abuse incidence and reporting by hospitals: The significance of severity, class, and race. *American Journal of Public Health, 75*(1), 56-60.

Hilberman, E., & Munson, K. (1977). Sixty battered women. *Victimology, 2,* 460-470.

Jurik, N. C., & Winn, R. (1990). Gender and homicide: A comparison of men and women who kill. *Violence and Victims, 5,* 227-242.

Kilpatrick, D. (1990). *Violence as a precursor of women's substance abuse.* Paper presented at the annual meetings of the American Psychological Association, Boston.

Klingbeil, K. S. (1986). Interpersonal violence: A comprehensive model in a hospital setting from policy to program. In *Homicide, suicide, and unintentional injuries* (Department of Health and Human Services, Report of the Secretary's Task Force on Black and Minority Health, Vol. 5, pp. 245-263). Washington, DC: Government Printing Office.

Kurz, D. (1990). Interventions with battered women in health care settings. *Violence and Victims, 5*(4), 243-256.

Lockhart, L. L. (1991). Spousal violence: A cross-racial perspective. In R. L. Hampton (Ed.), *Black family violence: Current research and theory* (pp. 85-102). Lexington, MA: Lexington.

Lockhart, L., & White, B. (1989). Understanding marital violence in the black community. *Journal of Interpersonal Violence, 4*(4), 3-4.

Mann, C. R. (1991). Black women who kill their loved ones. In R. L. Hampton (Ed.), *Black family violence: Current research and theory* (pp. 129-146). Lexington, MA: Lexington.

McClain, P. D. (1982-1983). Black females and lethal violence: Has time changed the circumstances under which they kill? *Omega, 13*(1), 3-25.

McLeer, S., & Anwar, R. (1989). A study of battered women presenting in an emergency department. *American Journal of Public Health, 79*(1), 65-66.

Mederer, H., & Gelles, R. J. (1989). Compassion or control: Intervention in cases of wife abuse. *Journal of Interpersonal Violence, 4*(1), 25-34.

Mercy, J. A., & Saltzman, L. E. (1989). Fatal violence among spouses in the United States. *American Journal of Public Health, 79*, 595-599.

Oxford English Dictionary. (1982). London: Oxford University Press.

Pagelow, M. D. (1981). *Women-battering: Victims and their experiences.* Beverly Hills, CA: Sage.

Pagelow, M. D. (1984). *Family violence.* New York: Praeger.

Pagelow, M. D. (1988). Marital rape. In V. B. Van Hesselt, R. L. Morrison, A. S. Bellack, & M. Hersen (Eds.), *Handbook of family violence* (pp. 207-232). New York: Plenum.

Pate, A. M., & Hamilton, E. E. (1992). Formal and informal deterrents: Dade County experiment. *American Sociological Review, 57*(5), 691-697.

Paternoster, R., & Iovanni, L. (1986). The deterrent effect of perceived severity: A reexamination. *Social Forces, 64*(3), 751-770.

Pirsig, R. (1991). *LILA: An inquiry into morals.* New York: Bantam.

Rieker, P. P., & Carmen, E. H. (1986). The victim-to-patient process: The disconfirmation and transformation of abuse. *American Journal of Orthopsychiatry, 56*(3), 360-370.

Roark, M. L., & Vlahos, S. (1983). An analysis of the ego status of battered women. *Transactional Analysis Journal, 13*, 164-167.

Rose, H. M., & McClain, P. D. (1990). *Race, place and risk: Black homicide in urban America.* Albany: State University of New York Press.

Rosenbaum, A., & O'Leary, D. K. (1981). Marital violence: Characteristics of abusive couples. *Journal of Consulting and Clinical Psychology, 49*, 63-71.

Rosenfeld, A., & Newberger, E. (1977). Compassion versus control: Conceptual and practical pitfalls in the broadened definitions of child abuse. *Journal of the American Medical Association, 237*, 2086-2088.

Roy, M. (1977). A current survey of 150 cases. In M. Roy (Ed.), *Battered women: A psychosociological study of domestic violence* (pp. 25-44). New York: Van Nostrand.

Roy, M. (1982). Four thousand partners in violence: A trend analysis. In M. Roy (Ed.), *The abusive partner* (pp. 17-35). New York: Van Nostrand.

Russell, D. E. H. (1982). *Rape in marriage*. New York: Macmillan.

Saltzman, L. E., Mercy, J. A., Rosenberg, M. L., Elsea, W. R., Napper, G., Sikes, R. K., & Waxweiler, R. J. (1990). Magnitude and patterns of family and intimate assaults in Atlanta, Georgia, 1984. *Violence and Victims, 5,* 3-17.

Sherman, L. (1992). *Policing domestic violence*. New York: Free Press.

Sherman, L., & Smith, D. (1992). Crime, punishment, and stake in conformity: Milwaukee and Omaha experiments. *American Sociological Review, 57*(5), 680-690.

Shields, N. M., & Hanneke, C. R. (1983). Battered wives' reactions to marital rape. Rape in marriage: A sociological view. In D. Finkelhor, R. Gelles, G. Hotaling, & M. Straus (Eds.), *The dark side of families* (pp. 119-130). Beverly Hills, CA: Sage.

Shulman, M. A. (1979). *A survey of spousal violence against women in Kentucky* (Law Enforcement Assistance Administration Study 792701). Washington, DC: Government Printing Office.

Sorenson, S. B., & Telles, C. A. (1991). Self-reports of spousal violence in a Mexican-American and non-Hispanic white population. *Violence and Victims, 6*(1), 3-15.

Stark, E., & Flitcraft, A. (1985). Spouse abuse. In *Surgeon General's Workshop of Violence and Public Health: A sourcebook* (pp. SA1-SA43). Atlanta, GA: Center for Disease Control.

Straus, M. A. (1986a). Domestic violence and homicide antecedents. *Bulletin of the New York Academy of Medicine, 62,* 446-465.

Straus, M. A. (1986b). Medical care costs of intra-family assault and homicide to society. *Bulletin of the New York Academy of Medicine, 62,* 556-561.

Straus, M. A. (1991). Physical violence in American families: Incidence, rates, causes, and trends. In D. D. Knudsen & J. L. Miller (Eds.), *Abused and battered* (pp. 17-33). New York: Aldine de Gruyter.

Straus, M., & Gelles, R. (1986). Societal change and change in family violence from 1975-1985 as revealed by two national studies. *Journal of Marriage and the Family, 48,* 465-479.

Straus, M., & Gelles, R. (Eds.). (1990). *Physical violence in American families: Risk factors and adaptations in 8,145 families*. New Brunswick, NJ: Transaction.

Straus, M., Gelles, R., & Steinmetz, S. (1980). *Behind closed doors: Violence in American families*. Garden City, NY: Anchor/Doubleday.

Straus, M., & Smith, C. (1990). Violence in Hispanic families in the United States: Incidence rates and structural interpretations. In M. A. Straus & R. J. Gelles (Eds.), *Physical violence in American families: Risk factors and adaptations in 8,145 families* (pp. 341-368). New Brunswick, NJ: Transaction.

Sumner, B. B., Mintz, E. R., & Brown, P. L. (1986). Interviewing persons hospitalized with interpersonal violence-related injuries: A pilot study. In *Homicide, suicide, and unintentional injuries* (Department of Health and Human Services, Report of the Secretary's Task Force on Black and Minority Health, Vol. 5, pp. 267-317). Washington, DC: Government Printing Office.

Thurman V. City of Torrington, 595 F. Supp. 1521 (USDC No. H-84120, 1985).

Turner, S. F., & Shapiro, C. H. (1986). Battered women: Mourning the death of a relationship. *Social Work, 30,* 372-376.

Uzzell, O., & Peebles-Wilkins, W. (1989). Black spouse abuse: A focus on relational factors and intervention strategies. *Western Journal of Black Studies, 13,* 10-16.

Valdez, R. B., & Nourjah, R. (1988). Homicide in Southern California, 1966-1985: An examination based on vital statistics data. In J. F. Kraus, S. B. Sorenson, & P. D. Juarez (Eds.), *Proceedings from the Research Conference on Violence and Homicide in Hispanic Communities* (pp. 85-100). Los Angeles: UCLA Publication Services.

Walker, L. E. (1979). *The battered woman.* New York: Harper & Row.

Walker, L. E. (1984). *The battered woman syndrome.* New York: Springer.

Walker, L. E. (1991). *Abused mothers, infants and substance abuse.* Paper presented at the International Conference of Victimology, Onata, Spain.

Washburn, C., & Frieze, I. H. (1981, July). *Methodological issues in studying battered women.* Paper presented at the First National Conference for Family Violence Researchers, University of New Hampshire, Durham.

Yllö, K., & Straus, M. (1990). Patriarchy and violence against wives: The impact of structural and normative factors. In M. A. Straus & R. J. Gelles (Eds.), *Physical violence in American families: Risk factors and adaptations in 8,145 families* (pp. 383-400). New Brunswick, NJ: Transaction.

• *CHAPTER 6* •

Elder Abuse

FRANCES A. BOUDREAU

Elder Abuse as a
Growing Social Problem

Abuse of the elderly, like other forms of family violence, has become an increasingly visible aspect of American life. Although domestic elder abuse has come to be defined as a contemporary social problem, there is considerable evidence that abuse of the elderly, including patricide, has been present throughout history (Fischer, 1977; Smith, 1980; Stearns, 1986). Yet, today, the issue of maltreatment of the elderly elicits unparalleled public and professional attention. Wolf and Pillemer (1989), along with others, attribute this to a growing public awareness of other types of family violence as well as to the increased willingness of the state to intervene in family life to protect at-risk members.

This chapter addresses several related questions about elder abuse in the United States. How prevalent is such abuse, who are the abused, and who are the abusers? To what extent does contemporary research and theory explain the prevailing trends? Finally, what are some social policy issues and their implications for prevention and intervention?

Growth of the Older Population

One of the major factors making this historical period different than those preceding it is the sheer number of persons affected. First, there has been a tremendous growth in the elderly population during the twentieth century. Between 1920 and

1990, the average life expectancy in the United States increased from 54.8 to 80.4 years for females and from 53.6 to 73.5 years for males. Today, the elderly number almost 30 million persons and make up 12.7% of the population (U.S. Bureau of the Census, 1991). Second, not only has the number of people surviving to old age increased, but, more important, the elderly population is continuing to age. The "frail elderly," those 70 years of age and over, who are seen as the most vulnerable, are the fastest growing segment of the elderly population. In this regard, it may be argued that the problems facing modern societies are rather unique. Never before have the elderly, and especially the infirm elderly, constituted such a large proportion of the population. If we divide the older population into the younger-old (65 to 74) and the older-old (75 and over), we can see the effects of an aging older population more clearly. In 1960, only one third of the elderly population was over the age of 75. Projections estimate that, by the year 2000, people over the age of 75 will constitute almost 50% of the total elderly population (U.S. Bureau of the Census, 1991). Given sex differences in mortality rates, the majority of the frail elderly will be female.

Ironically, the fact that greater numbers of people live to reach old age is surely one of modern society's greatest achievements. Modern medical and technological advances mean, however, that a greater number of persons will spend longer periods of time in various stages of dependency, some in deteriorating physical and mental health. Because families continue to be the primary source of care for the dependent elderly, the increase in the number of persons surviving to old age is accompanied by increased pressures on family members who serve as caretakers. Although most families respect and nurture their aging members, it is clear that some respond with abuse or neglect.

The Prevalence of Elder Abuse

How widespread is abuse of the elderly? In 1989, at least 1.5 million elderly Americans were victims of abuse, an increase of approximately 500,000 per year since 1980 (U.S. House Select Committee on Aging, 1990a). It is estimated that the percentage of older persons being abused ranges from 4% to 10% (Callahan, 1988; Council on Scientific Affairs, 1987; Crystal, 1987; Powell

& Berg, 1987). It is difficult to make definitive assessments about the scope of the problem because the majority of cases go unreported and uninvestigated. Elder abuse is more hidden than other forms of family violence. The elderly often are isolated from mainstream society, having fewer outside contacts than younger persons. In fact, Kosberg (1988) believes that only 1 case in 6 is reported. Perpetrators of abuse generally deny the abuse, and those who are abused may be too embarrassed or afraid to report it. Some may internalize the blame believing that they are responsible for the abusive behavior of their abusers. Others may believe that suffering the consequences of occasional abuse is more desirable than dealing with the consequences of reporting it, such as being taken from their homes and placed into nursing homes. These difficulties notwithstanding, there is little question that the magnitude of the problem is increasing.

Conceptual and Methodological Issues

The research on elder abuse suffers from definitional and methodological problems. Not only is comparison of studies difficult, but the implementation of effective social intervention and the enactment of effective social policy are hindered by these flaws.

Definitional Problems

The question of how to define elder abuse is a subject of much controversy (see Kosberg, 1988; Pillemer & Finkelhor, 1988; Sprey & Matthews, 1989). The concept has a number of different meanings, each of which focuses research in different ways. In some studies, researchers use different categories of abuse, while, in others, dissimilar phenomena are subsumed under the same category (Wolf & Pillemer, 1989). Many of the categories are vague and subject to multiple interpretations. The most frequently used categories of abuse are summarized in Table 6.1.

One indication of the definitional problems is the diffuse nature of the concepts employed. Some researchers differentiate between *neglect* and *abuse,* while others subsume both under

Table 6.1 Most Frequently Used Categories of Elder Abuse

Categories	Descriptions
Physical abuse	Lack of personal care, lack of supervision, visible bruises and welts, repeated beatings, withholding of food
Psychological abuse	Verbal assaults, isolation, threats, inducement of fear
Financial/material abuse	Misuse, appropriation, or theft of money or property.
Unsatisfactory living environment	Unclean home, urine odor in home, hazardous living conditions
Violation of individual/ constitutional rights	Reduction of personal freedom/autonomy, involuntary commitment, guardianship, false imprisonment, "incompetence"

abuse. A working definition that includes only abuse will yield different findings than a definition that includes both abuse and neglect. Some studies differentiate between active and passive neglect. *Passive neglect*, sometimes referred to as benign neglect, occurs when caregivers are not aware they are harming the older person. *Active neglect* means causing intentional harm. Still other studies include self-neglect as an example of elder abuse. Some include sexual abuse under physical abuse, while others use a separate category. Also, the frequency and severity of abusive behavior included in a study has implications for the incidence and prevalence of elder abuse.

Methodological Problems

Definitional problems are compounded by different research methodologies and the use of nonrandom sampling procedures (see Callahan, 1988; Gold & Gwyther, 1989; Hamilton, 1989; Kosberg, 1988; Pillemer & Finkelhor, 1988). Some studies survey a sample of the elderly population, while others review agency case records or survey professionals working with the elderly (Lau & Kosberg, 1979; Sengstock & Liang, 1982). Still others (see Steinmetz, 1988) use in-depth interviews with caregivers. The majority of studies are descriptive and exploratory in nature, generally based on relatively small samples. Few are aimed at causal model testing (Hudson, 1986). A notable exception to this is a study conducted by Pillemer and Finkelhor (1988), which is based on a random sample of 2,020 noninstitutionalized elderly Boston residents.

Ethnicity is an important variable in understanding elder abuse that often is neglected. Where it is taken into account, there are so few cases that the data on minorities are excluded from analysis or subsumed in the larger sample. Thus research findings pertain generally to the white population.

Characteristics of
Abusers and Their Victims

Who are the abused, and who are the abusers? Several general conclusions may be drawn from the literature. First, abuse is not related to socioeconomic status but crosses social class lines. Second, abuse is more likely to occur among the elderly who live with a spouse, child, or other relative rather than those living alone. Third, abuse is a repetitive pattern rather than an isolated occurrence. Finally, the perpetrator of abuse typically is related to the victim, most frequently a spouse or child.

A profile of the typical perpetrator, victim, and most frequent types of domestic elder abuse can be distilled from a recent national survey of state adult protective service and aging agencies conducted by the National Aging Resource Center on Elder Abuse (NARCEA; U.S. House Select Committee on Aging, 1990b). Victims of elder abuse are most likely to be female and 75 years of age or over. The greater likelihood of older women being abused is at least partially a function of their life expectancy. The ratio of female victims to male victims is greater, however, than the ratio of female elderly to male elderly in the general population. For 1988, the ratio of female victims to male victims is 1.79, while the comparable figure for proportional population representation is 1.33. It may be that women are more likely to report abuse or that the consequences of abuse are more serious for females than males, thus the greater likelihood that it is reported. Adult children are the most likely perpetrators of abuse (30%) as compared with spouses (14.8%). The NARCEA report lists neglect as the most frequent type of domestic elder abuse (37.2%), followed by physical abuse (26.3%), financial/material exploitation (20%), and emotional abuse (11%).

These data are contradicted, however, by the results of some studies that find that the elderly are most often abused by their own spouses with men being at least as likely to be victims as females (see Pillemer & Finkelhor, 1988). In addition, these data indicate that physical abuse is the most frequent type of elder abuse with spousal abuse being the major form of physical violence. One of the difficulties with spousal abuse is, of course, the problem of distinguishing cases that involve long-standing patterns of abuse from those occurring because of the onset of problems associated with aging. The question must be asked: Do long-standing patterns of spousal abuse qualify as elder abuse simply because the participants have reached a specific chronological age? Clearly, there is a need to differentiate between these two types of spousal abuse.

General Theories of Elder Abuse

Theories about elder abuse are not easily codified into coherent frameworks. Research in this area has a relatively short history and therefore lacks theoretical integration. Most theories of elder abuse remain in a conjectural state. In general, elder abuse theories have concentrated on explanations for why it occurs, the conditions under which specific others abuse elders, the attributes of individuals and familial structures that induce abuse, and the prediction of high risk factors. Complex, and by no means consistent, the reasons elder abuse occurs are not easily analyzed. Elder abuse is multicausal, and no one theory appears to account for its existence. Rather, each perspective focuses on the different social and psychological forces involved. Several of the most commonly used theoretical perspectives are summarized here.

Intergenerational Transmission of Violence

The theory of intergenerational transmission of violence, which has its origins in social learning theory, is based primarily on research about other types of family violence (Pedrick-Cornell & Gelles, 1982). The theory focuses on the experience of growing up in an abusive home as an antecedent to violence. One learns to be violent in family settings, then uses this behavior as an adult. The theory suggests that the elder abuser is more likely to have been abused as a child or to have observed abusive behavior in the family. While this theory makes a great deal of sense and provides an explanatory model for other types of family violence, it has proved largely ineffective in predicting elder abuse (Galbraith, 1989). Although some early research supports the idea that, through abuse of the elderly, the caretaker continues a cycle of abuse begun earlier (see Steinmetz, 1978, 1981), later research has failed to provide support for this theory. It appears that elder abusers are no more likely to have been raised in families characterized by violence than non-abusers (Wolf & Pillemer, 1989).

Psychopathology

The basic premise of the psychopathological model is that abusers have personality problems and disorders that cause them to be abusive. Intraindividual pathologies such as mental illness or alcoholism are seen to render some individuals unable to control their aggression. Older family members, because of their proximity to the abusers, frequently become the objects of this aggressive behavior leading to abuse.

The psychopathological model appears to have greater explanatory power for elder abuse than for either child or spousal abuse. The influence of psychopathology on elder abuse is supported by numerous studies and appears to be implicated most frequently in cases of physical abuse and verbal aggression (see Hickey & Douglas, 1981; Wolf & Pillemer, 1989). Wolf, Strugnell, and Godkin (1982), for example, report that 31% of abusers had a history of psychiatric illness, while 43% had substance abuse problems. Although most of the research in this area is based on cases reported to social service agencies, the psychopathology of those abusing elders is supported both by surveys (see Finkelhor & Pillemer, 1987) and by interviews with perpetrators (see Anetzberger, 1987).

Dependency

A theoretical perspective associated primarily with social exchange theory focuses on the intricacies of dependency as a preface to elder abuse. According to exchange theory (Dowd, 1975; Homans, 1961), all human interaction is guided by attempts to maximize rewards and minimize costs, both material and nonmaterial. A major proposition of exchange theory is that interaction between two or more persons will be positively evaluated if all persons involved benefit equally from the exchange. Under these conditions, a mutually satisfying interdependence may emerge. Asymmetrical relationships are perceived as negative and frequently lead to differences in power. An imbalance in exchange processes increases the risk of elder maltreatment.

Two competing theories of the role of dependency in elder abuse have emerged from the social exchange perspective. The first focuses on the dependency of the victim on the perpetrator of abuse. The second focuses on the dependency of the perpetrator on the target of abuse. In both instances, dependency is seen to create an imbalance in exchange processes, increasing the risk of elder maltreatment.

The first model posits the thesis that abuse of the elderly is a consequence of the increasing dependency of older persons on their caretakers, usually an adult child, and is supported by several studies (Davidson, 1979; Quinn & Tomita, 1986; Steinmetz & Amsden, 1983). That the mutual exchange of instrumental and emotional support between elderly parents and their children affects the quality of their relationship is well documented (Cicirelli, 1983; Mancini & Bliezner, 1988). With the loss of mutual sharing of resources between parent and child, the quality of the relationship declines. The increasing costs of providing for the emotional, financial, and physical well-being of a parent without concomitant rewards may lead some children to perceive the exchange as unfair. With increasing dependency, the parent may engage in a variety of negative techniques (i.e., excessive demands or intrusion into personal affairs) in an attempt to maintain some control over the relationship, further exacerbating the negative quality of the exchange (Steinmetz, 1988). Thus the exchange imbalance may predispose some individuals to be abusive toward their elderly parents.

The second model puts forth the idea that those who abuse the elderly, most frequently adult children, are most likely to be dependent on the target of abuse for housing and financial assistance. Not only does this create an imbalanced exchange, it violates strongly held norms regarding independent adult behavior. From this perspective, abuse is a response to perceived powerlessness in exchange processes (Finkelhor, 1983). Thus abuse is used as a resource to establish control in an asymmetrical exchange. That perpetrators of abuse tend to be dependent on their victims, most specifically for economic support, is supported by a great deal of empirical evidence (see Anetzberger, 1987; Pillemer, 1985; Wolf & Pillemer, 1989; Wolf, et al., 1982).

Familial Stress

Familial stress is one of most widely used theories in explaining elder abuse and neglect. Stress theory is closely allied with conflict theory. From this perspective, the individual needs of some family members frequently come into conflict with the needs of other family members, leading to stress and instability. Steinmetz (1988), for example, points out that caregiving offspring often must cope with their parents' problems just when the needs of their nuclear families are the greatest. It is just such situations as these that led to the coining of the phrase the "sandwich generation," those middle-aged children caught between caring for the needs of multiple generations. Adult children frequently must make difficult choices in providing care for an elderly parent, involving such things as the decision to provide routine care, that may mean limiting one's career, or providing financial assistance, that may mean altering retirement planning or an inability to provide for children's college plans (Church, Siegal, & Foster, 1988).

Many families caring for elderly parents have limited economic resources. The costs associated with insufficient income, combined with the inherent stress of caring for an individual who requires a great deal of assistance, can sometimes become overwhelming, precipitating neglect or abuse (U.S. House Select Committee on Aging, 1991). This is illustrated dramatically by "granny dumping," a phenomenon recently given national attention on a CBS series. Some families, unable to cope with the stress of caring for an elderly relative, quite literally abandon them in hospital emergency rooms. Although highly sensationalized by the media, that the phenomenon exists at all points out that some families, logistically, emotionally, or economically, are ill-equipped to provide day-to-day constant care.

Federal and State
Responses to Elder Abuse

The fundamental idea that governments should establish policy and intervene in elder abuse has been firmly established. Federal and state activity in the area of elder abuse has been marked by more than a decade of legislative history. Many would argue, however, that support for intervention has been more symbolic than real.

Federal support for programs designed to ameliorate elder abuse and neglect have been unfunded or underfunded. Since 1981, the primary source of federal funding for state elderly and adult protective services has been the Social Services Block Grant. Since its inception, funding has been reduced by more than one third due to direct cuts and inflation. Furthermore, the funds are not marked specifically for the provision of services designed to prevent, identify, and treat elder abuse, making it an inadequate source of primary funding. The Older Americans Act of 1987 provided for a national program of identification and prevention of elder abuse. The act required area agencies on aging to assess the need for elder abuse prevention services and the extent to which this need was being met. Authorization for $5 million was granted to carry out the program in that year. To this date, however, no national program has been established because no funds have been appropriated to support it (U.S. House Select Committee on Aging, 1991).

In 1980, the Joint Congressional Hearings on Elder Abuse concluded with recommendations for adult protective service laws. A majority of states have adopted at least some of the proposed elements contained within this model law, including mandatory reporting: 43 states have enacted state statutes or adult protective service laws making it mandatory that members of certain professions report cases of elder abuse. Most states indicate that they are hampered in their efforts to implement these laws due to insufficient funding for increased services necessarily accompanying the change in law. In a study of a

Rhode Island agency charged with implementing a mandatory abuse law, for example, Wolf, Godkin, and Pillemer (1984) found that the investigation of abuse and neglect cases monopolized most of the agency time. Without increased financial support for additional personnel, the law had the effect of limiting services to the population it was designed to serve. Lack of funding, however, is not the only problem associated with the policy of mandatory reporting.

Laws governing mandatory reporting have the express purpose of protecting victims of elder abuse. Critics of mandatory reporting see the laws themselves as potential sources of abuse (Krauskopf & Burnett, 1983). Elder abuse statutes are patterned on child abuse statutes, which presume that persons, because of their age and circumstance, need protection. According to Krauskopf and Burnett (1983), not only does this reinforce ageism by infantalizing an entire elderly population, but it has the potential for diminishing an elderly person's autonomy. The inference to be drawn from mandatory reporting is that the older person is incompetent and unable to make the decision to report (Lee, 1986). While this may be true for some, it does not describe all victims of elder abuse, some of whom unfortunately make competent decisions to remain in abusive situations. Because statutory protections frequently take the form of state-initiated institutionalization or guardianship, the elderly may be reluctant to seek help from social service agencies. Indirect support for this comes from state data collected by the NARCEA (U.S. House Select Committee on Aging, 1990b). The data indicate that, on average, a greater number of elder abuse cases go unreported today than in previous years—this during the same period when estimates are that elder abuse and neglect are increasing rather than decreasing.

Policy Recommendations

Broadened Research Agenda

A number of significant implications for social policy can be drawn from the previous discussions. First, the current state of knowledge is limited. Although strides have been made in identifying some of the important variables involved in elder abuse and neglect, major gaps in knowledge remain to be filled. Although it has become axiomatic in essays of this type to state that additional research is needed, clearly this is the case. Questions of what type of social policy will best serve which constituency, and strategies for effective intervention, require moving beyond exploratory studies based on nonrandom samples. Estes and Freeman (1973) have noted that, in the absence of quality research and theory, social policymakers will rely upon whatever is available, regardless of the adequacy. Thus, for example, in 1978, following congressional hearings, the Administration on Aging funded two research projects. This bare skeleton of research findings became the foundation for new legislation and social policy, not because they provided comprehensive data and analyses but because they constituted the only data available (Cronin & Allen, 1982). Knowing, as we do, that the problem of elder abuse will continue to grow in U.S. society, now is the time to establish a comprehensive research agenda that can guide future social policies in this area.

What are the specific research needs on this agenda? First, as we've seen here, the field of elder abuse research suffers from a lack of definitional and conceptual clarity. Because, ultimately, scientific generalization rests upon comparison and replication, conceptual agreement within the field is essential. In addition, potentially contradictory evidence about who the most likely victims and perpetrators of abuse are needs to be addressed further. This can be done only through more broadly based research.

Second, I hope that the current array of small pilot studies will be replaced by appropriate national survey data. Pilot studies, while useful in suggesting areas for research and giving hints of the scope of the problem that exists, are not adequate for national policy formulation. Rather, a more mature survey approach is required to fully portray the events of concern to us here. This, of course, will require national levels of coordination and funding in the field of elder abuse.

Third, the United States is a highly pluralistic society composed of diverse ethnic, religious, and cultural communities. Social policy intervention in other areas, such as medical care, housing, and health, has shown that policy implementation must take account of the varieties of subcultures into which programs are inserted. The same considerations apply to the area of elder abuse. How do the general problems in this realm vary in different subcultures? How do variations, if they exist, affect policy implementation? Do different communities have different needs? Clearly, comparative research on subcultures is essential.

Fourth, the topic of elder spousal abuse requires greater clarification and investigation. Except for the Pillemer and Finkelhor study (1988), spousal abuse has received scant attention from the research community.

Differences and similarities between long-standing patterns of abuse and late-onset abuse need to be delineated to understand the different resources and patterns of intervention necessary in each type.

Evaluation Research

Another type of research agenda aimed at evaluating the implementation and impact of social policy is essential. Evaluation research will not only provide us with an assessment of the impact of policy on the lives of those persons it is designed to serve, it will allow for more rational allocation of extremely limited resources. Programs that are successful can be expanded, while those that are not can be discarded. Without this type of evaluation research, policy exists in a social vacuum. Evaluation research must be aimed also at determining whether or not, in the name of protecting the elderly, intervention strategies compound the problem of elder abuse by violating individual rights and autonomy.

Establishment of Local Shelters

The overwhelming majority of states express approval for the establishment of temporary emergency shelters for abused elderly similar to those now in existence for victims of spousal abuse. Not only would this provide an immediate place of safe transfer for impaired elders who are endangered by abuse, but this also could serve as a refuge to which the nonimpaired elderly could retreat on their own. Within this setting, self-help groups would be available to provide emotional support and generate ideas about ways to deal with abusive situations. Obviously, the establishment

and operation of emergency shelters would require some financial support from the federal government.

Provision of Services to Caretakers

Continued emphasis should be placed on providing services
that would alleviate family stress resulting from the need to care
for a dependent family member. The most successful intervention in elder abuse is prevention. There is agreement that the
provision of more social services such as home health care, adult
day care, homemaker services, home-delivered meals, and short-
term total care would lessen the burden on family caregivers and
help to prevent or ameliorate elder abuse and neglect related to
familial stress. Information about the availability of these community services should be broadly disseminated.

Family Counseling

Many advocate counseling prior to a family making the final
decision to take an elderly relative into their home. Families may
not be aware of the demands that caring for an elderly person,
particularly one who is impaired, will place upon them. Information about the physical, emotional, medical, and social needs
of the elderly person, and the variety of supportive services
available to assist them in their care of the elderly, will allow for
a more informed decision. It should also be recognized that all
families are not equally equipped to deal with the stress of
caregiving. Thus, for those who are reluctant to take on this role,
alternative avenues should be explored fully.

Increased Awareness of Service Providers

Finally, those who work with the elderly need to be cognizant
of the potential risk of abuse associated with the situation of
dependent relatives living with the elderly. Greater attention
needs to be paid to the provision of services that might have an
impact on preventing or reducing this type of risk. Wolf and
Pillemer (1989) suggest that exchange theory, used to explain
this type of abuse, can be an effective tool for intervention:

Either increase the rewards for reducing dependency on the elderly person or heighten the costs of engaging in abusive actions. This will require those professionals working in the field to devise innovative and tactful strategies for intervention to modify this high risk situation.

References

Anetzberger, G. J. (1987). *The etiology of elder abuse by adult offspring.* Springfield, IL: Charles C Thomas.

Callahan, J. J. (1988). Elder abuse: Some questions for policymakers. *The Gerontologist, 28,* 453-458.

Church, D. K., Siegal, M. A., & Foster, C. D. (1988). *Growing old in America.* Wylie, TX: Information Aids.

Cicirelli, V. G. (1983). Adult children's attachment and helping behavior to elderly parents: A path model. *Journal of Marriage and the Family, 45,* 815-825.

Council on Scientific Affairs. (1987). Elder abuse and neglect. *Journal of the American Medical Association, 257,* 966-971.

Cronin, C., & Allen, A. (1982). The uses of research sponsored by the Administration on Aging. In *Case study #5: Maltreatment and abuse of the elderly.* Washington, DC: Gerontological Research Institute.

Crystal, S. (1987). Elder abuse: The latest crisis. *Public Interest, 88,* 56-66.

Davidson, J. L. (1979). Elder abuse. In M. R. Block & J. D. Sinnott (Eds.), *The battered elder syndrome: An exploratory study* (pp. 49-55). College Park: University of Maryland, Center on Aging.

Dowd, J. J. (1975). Aging and exchange: A preface to theory. *Journal of Gerontology, 30,* 584-594.

Estes, C. L., & Freeman, H. E. (1973). Strategies of design and research for intervention. In R. H. Binstock & E. Shanas (Eds.), *Handbook of aging and the social sciences* (pp. 536-560). New York: Van Nostrand Reinhold.

Finkelhor, D. (1983). Common features of family abuse. In D. Finkelhor et al., (Eds.), *The dark side of families* (pp. 17-28). Beverly Hills, CA: Sage.

Finkelhor, D., & Pillemer, K. (1987, July). *Correlates of elder abuse: A case control study.* Paper presented at the Third National Conference for Family Violence Researchers, Durham, NH.

Fischer, D. H. (1977). *Growing old in America.* New York: Oxford University Press.

Galbraith, M. W. (1989). A critical examination of the definitional, methodological, and theoretical problems of elder abuse. In R. Filenson & S. R. Ingman (Eds.), *Elder abuse: Practice and policy* (pp. 35-42). New York: Human Sciences Press.

Gold, D. T., & Gwyther, L. P. (1989). The prevention of elder abuse: An educational model. *Family Relations, 38,* 8-14.

Hamilton, G. P. (1989). Preventing elder abuse: Using a family systems approach. *Gerontological Nursing, 15,* 21-26.

Hickey, T., & Douglas, R. L. (1981). Mistreatment of the elderly in the domestic setting: An exploratory study. *American Journal of Public Health, 71,* 500-507.

Homans, G. C. (1961). *Social behavior: Its elementary forms.* New York: Harcourt, Brace and World.

Hudson, M. F. (1986). Elder mistreatment: Current research. In K. A. Pillemer & R. S. Wolf (Eds.), *Elder abuse: Conflict in the family* (pp. 125-161). Dover, MA: Auburn House.

Kosberg, J. I. (1988). Preventing elder abuse: Identification of high risk factors prior to placement decisions. *The Gerontologist, 28,* 43-50.

Krauskoph, J. M., & Burnett, M. E. (1983). When protection becomes abuse. *Trial,* pp. 61-76.

Lau, E. A., & Kosberg, J. I. (1979). Abuse of the elderly by informal care providers. *Aging, 299,* 10-15.

Lee, D. (1986). Mandatory reporting of elder abuse: A cheap but ineffective solution to the problem. *Fordham Urban Law Journal, 14,* 725-771.

Mancini, J. A., & Bliezner, R. (1988). Aging parents and adult children: Research themes in intergenerational relations. *Journal of Marriage and the Family, 51,* 275-290.

Pedrick-Cornell, C., & Gelles, R. J. (1982). Elder abuse: The status of current knowledge. *Family Relations, 31,* 457-465.

Pillemer, K. A. (1985). The dangers of dependency: New findings on domestic violence against the elderly. *Social Problems, 33,* 146-158.

Pillemer, K., & Finkelhor, D. (1988). Prevalence of elder abuse: A random sample survey. *The Gerontologist, 28,* 51-57.

Powell, S., & Berg, R. C. (1987). When the elderly are abused: Characteristics and intervention. *Educational Gerontology, 13,* 71-83.

Quinn, M. J., & Tomita, S. K. (1986). *Elder abuse and neglect.* New York: Springer.

Sengstock, M. G., & Liang, J. (1982). *Identifying and characterizing elder abuse.* Detroit, MI: Wayne State University, Institute of Gerontology.

Smith, D. B. (1980). *Inside the great house: Planter family life in the 18th century Chesapeake society.* Ithaca, NY: Cornell University Press.

Sprey, J., & Matthews, S. H. (1989). The perils of drawing policy implications from research: The case of elder mistreatment. In R. Filenson & S. R. Ingman (Eds.), *Elder abuse: Practice and policy* (pp. 51-61). New York: Human Sciences Press.

Stearns, P. J. (1986). Old age family conflict: The perspective of the past. In K. A. Pillemer & R. S. Wolf (Eds.), *Elder abuse: Conflict in the family* (pp. 3-24). Dover, MA: Auburn House.

Steinmetz, S. K. (1978). Battered parents. *Society, 15,* 54-55.

Steinmetz, S. K. (1981). Elder abuse. *Aging, 315-316,* 6-10.

Steinmetz, S. K. (1988). *Duty bound: Elder abuse and family care.* Newbury Park, CA: Sage.

Steinmetz, S. K., & Amsden, D. J. (1983). Dependent elders, family stress and abuse. In T. H. Brubaker (Ed.), *Family relationships in later life* (pp. 173-192). Beverly Hills, CA: Sage.

U.S. Bureau of the Census. (1991). *Statistical abstract of the United States 1991* (11th ed.). Washington, DC: U.S. Department of Commerce.

U.S. House of Representatives, Select Committee on Aging. (1990a, December 10). *Elder abuse: Curbing a national epidemic* (Hearings). Washington, DC: Government Printing Office.

U.S. House of Representatives, Select Committee on Aging. (1990b, May 1). *Elder abuse: A decade of shame and inaction* (Hearings). Washington, DC: Government Printing Office.

U.S. House of Representatives, Select Committee on Aging. (1991, May 15). *Elder abuse: What can be done?* (Hearings). Washington, DC: Government Printing Office.

Wolf, R. S., Godkin, M. A. & Pillemer, K. A. (1984). *Elder abuse and neglect: Final report from 3 model projects and appendices.* Worchester: University of Massachuetts Medical Center, Center on Aging.

Wolf, R. S., & Pillemer, K. A. (1989). *Helping elderly victims: The reality of elder abuse.* New York: Columbia University Press.

Wolf, R. S., Strugnall, C. P., & Godkin, M. A. (1982). *Preliminary findings from three model projects on elderly abuse.* Worcester: University of Massachusetts Medical Center, Center on Aging.

CHAPTER 7

Violence in Families of Color in the United States

JO-ELLEN ASBURY

People of color constitute a growing proportion of the population of the United States. While minorities were 11.4% of the population (20.6 million) in 1960, they were 15.9% (nearly 40 million) by 1989. And it is projected that people of color will constitute 21.1% of the population (62.9 million) by 2025 (U.S. Bureau of the Census, 1991). As the minority population continues to grow in proportion to European Americans, interventions that apply theories and empirical studies based upon the experiences and norms of the majority group becomes less and less appropriate.

The experience of being a person of color in the United States is qualitatively different than that of being a member of the dominant culture. Minority group members tend to have lower incomes, lower educational attainment, and lower life expectancy (see Table 7.1). And they are the objects of prejudiced attitudes and discriminatory behaviors. Therefore any analysis of violence in families would be incomplete without an examination of how their unique background and experiences might influence the dynamics of intrafamilial violence. Such an analysis is a prerequisite to fully understanding the precipitating conditions and the nature of the violent behavior and to designing effective interventions. As cultures vary, so do familial roles and relationships. Any

AUTHOR'S NOTE: This work was supported by the Bethany College Faculty Development Fund.

Table 7.1 Selected Demographic Comparisons by Race*

Demographic Characteristics	Whites	Blacks	Other	Total Population
Percentage of population	84.1	12.4	3.5	100.0
Projected percentage of population by year 2025	78.9	14.6	6.5	100.0
Median income (in 1989 dollars)	35,975	20,209	23,446	343,213
			(Hispanics only)	
Number in poverty (in thousands)	4049	2077	1133	6784
			(Hispanics only)	
Percentage of group in poverty	7.8	27.8	23.4	10.3
			(Hispanics only)	
Percentage of all births in group to unmarried women	17.7	63.5		25.7
Median years of education for persons 25 years and older	12.7	12.4	12.0	12.7
			(Hispanics only)	
Life expectancy (in years)	M: 72.6	M: 65.2	M: 67.5	M: 71.8
	F: 79.1	F: 74.0	F :75.7	F: 78.5
			(Includes blacks)	

SOURCE: U.S. Bureau of the Census (1991).
NOTE: *Group labels are those of the Census Bureau, not the author. Individuals labeled "Hispanic" may be of any race. Numbers listed under "Other" include all minorities except blacks, unless otherwise stated.

intervention must be aware of and take those cultural differences into consideration (e.g., Gibbs & Huang, 1989; Thomas & Sillen, 1972; Zuniga, 1988).

Scope of the Chapter

While it is acknowledged that the minority groups in the United States include African Americans, Asian Americans, Native American Indians, and Hispanics, minority experiences have not been systematically addressed in past research (Hampton, 1987; Huang & Ying, 1989). Therefore the following addresses intrafamilial violence in all minority groups where information is available but does not profess to be a comprehensive treatment.

Minority Group Experiences
in the United States

Table 7.1 provides a very general overview of the status of minority group members in this country relative to the majority group. As previously mentioned, while their numbers in the population are increasing, their status is not. Minority group members make $12,000 to $15,000 less than European Americans. Not a surprise, a substantially greater proportion of their group (23%-27% versus roughly 8%) live below the poverty level. One, but certainly not the only, contributor to their numbers in poverty is the higher proportion of minority children born to single mothers. Further, minorities tend to complete fewer years of education (12.0 to 12.4 versus 12.7). And, as a final indicator of the precarious situation of minority group members, they can expect to die 5 to 7 years sooner than their majority group counterparts.

In addition to these grim realities, people of color also must confront the attitudes toward them held by members of the majority group. A recent *New York Times* article reports some of the findings from the National Opinion Research Center's General Social Survey ("Whites Retain Negative View," 1991). The survey found that 56% of European Americans thought African Americans were more prone to violence (than not) and 50% held this view of Hispanics. Of the respondents, 68% of European Americans thought that African Americans preferred living on welfare, and 74% thought this of Hispanics; 62% thought African Americans were less likely to be hardworking, while 74% held this view of Hispanics. And 53% thought African Americans were less intelligent, an opinion held by 55% regarding Hispanics. Such attitudes are likely to influence the ways in which people of color are treated as well as how their behaviors are interpreted.

Space does not permit a comprehensive review of the experiences of each minority group in the United States. So, an attempt is made to highlight those aspects of each culture that may have some bearing on the occurrence of or response to family violence.

African Americans

Although all minority groups discussed here have been the objects of discrimination, African Americans are unique in their history of more than 200 years of enslavement and being viewed as inferior human beings at best and property at worst. Although slavery legally ended more than 100 years ago, Akbar (1973) notes the continuing influence.

As Table 7.1 reflects, African Americans constituted 12.4% of the population of the United States in 1989. Their median income ($20,209), median level of education (12.4 years), and life expectancy (65.2 years for males, 74.0 for females) are all below the levels of the total population and that of European Americans. Approximately 28% of African Americans live in poverty (compared with about 8% of European Americans) and 63% of all African American births are to unmarried women—no doubt one of the major contributors to the large number living in poverty.

Moynihan (1965) described the African American family as a "tangle of pathology": female dominated, lacking in structure and stability, and badly in need of male role models. The fact that Moynihan (and others) would be led to such conclusions about the African American family is a perfect example of why an individual's cultural context must be understood before his or her behaviors can be.

While it is true that many African American families are headed (but not necessarily dominated) by women, one should not presume the absence of positive male role models for African American children or that such families are unstable or otherwise dysfunctional. As Stack (1974) illustrated, extended family networks are quite prevalent in African American communities; networks that often include individuals who are not strictly blood relations. What may appear as lack of structure from a European American perspective is actually an organized and effective response to difficult circumstances. Individuals in these networks tend to provide one other with the emotional support and goods and services necessary for survival and fulfill familial roles when a traditional nuclear family structure is vacant.

Hill (1972) writes of flexibility of roles as one of the strengths of black families, which Nobles (1980) traces back to their African roots. Children are likely to be reared without strict differences determined by sex and are likely to be reared to consider competence in interpersonal relationships more important than competence in dealing with the physical environment.

Given the oppression African Americans have had to endure, they are more likely to be suspicious and distrustful of outsiders, a predilection that may influence their tendency not to report incidents of family violence to individuals outside the family unit. Therefore they may use social services that are available in only the more extreme cases. So, available data may actually be more representative of those more extreme cases and not all cases of African American intrafamilial violence.

Asian Americans

Asian Americans[1] represent the fastest growing minority group in the United States (LaFromboise, 1992), totaling 3.7 million in 1980 (Zane, 1992). Of those persons over 25 years of age, 71.3% are high school graduates, with 13.4 median years of school completed. Yet, 11% of Chinese Americans are illiterate, which is 7 times the national average and 3 times that of blacks (Huang & Ying, 1989).

It has been suggested (Huang & Ying, 1989; Nagata, 1989) that Asian Americans have been inappropriately labeled the "model" or "problem-free" minority group. That is, non-Asians wrongly assume that Asian Americans have successfully assimilated into the dominate culture and therefore experience no additional problems as a result of their cultural heritage. On the contrary, while Asian Americans have the highest median family income among minorities, they are also underemployed and receiving lower wages than others doing comparable work (Huang & Ying, 1989; Nagata, 1989). This misperception may result in their intrafamilial difficulties being minimized.

Asian culture has been described as "face" oriented (Huang & Ying, 1989; Zane, 1992). Family appearance and status are extremely important, and group desires or priorities take precedence over those of the individual (Huang & Ying, 1989; Nagata, 1989). Extended families are often considered the primary family unit (Huang & Ying, 1989; Nagata, 1989). If violence were exhibited within the family, it might be difficult for an individual member to admit such a condition to outsiders, which might be perceived as bringing shame on the family.

Huang and Ying (1989) suggest that historically in Asian families role structure was hierarchial, with the father as the undisputed head. The mother's primary role was to serve the father and the children. Sons were highly valued in this patrilineal society. Of course, contemporary Asian families are only derivatives of these rigidly defined roles, but such a tradition may contribute to greater violence against women family members, who are not as highly valued.

Finally, some Asian Americans may have a language other than English as their primary one. This may serve as an additional barrier to effective intervention when one must interact with the dominant culture to receive help.

Hispanics

As Marin and Marin (1991) note, the term *Hispanic* is one of convenience used to refer to those who reside in the United States and trace their origins to Spain or one of the Spanish-speaking nations of Latin America. Marin and Marin (1991) note that not all accept this term in reference to themselves. It is also acknowledged that those from Spain have a different culture, history, and demography. The term connotes ethnicity, not race. Mexican Americans make up 63% of the Hispanic population (Ramirez, 1989).

As Table 7.1 shows, Hispanics also have a median income substantially below that of European Americans and a substantially larger proportion of their group in poverty. Their median level of education is lower, as is their life expectancy.

Marin and Marin (1991) review literature that suggests that Hispanics, like other minority groups already discussed, value a willingness to place the welfare of the group above those of the individual. Hispanics identify with and are attached to the nuclear and extended family and exhibit strong feelings of loyalty, reciprocity, and solidarity with family members. Thus Hispanics may exhibit reluctance to involve outsiders in familial conflicts.

Simpatía, according to Marin and Marin (1991), is a Hispanic cultural script that emphasizes the need for behaviors that promote smooth and pleasant social relationships. As such, simpatía encourages a certain level of conformity and empathy for the feelings of others and deemphasizes negative behaviors in conflictive circumstances; this may also inhibit their willingness to acknowledge and report violence in the family.

And, as with Asian Americans, Hispanics may have a primary language other than English, which may further inhibit their involvement with police or social service agencies.

American Indians

Those referred to as *American Indians* include all North American native people, including Alaskan Natives, Alutes, Eskimos, and Metis (mixed bloods; LaFromboise & Low, 1989). At least in part due to relocation and substandard living conditions, Indian people have perhaps the least enviable circumstances of all minority groups discussed here. LaFromboise and Low (1989) review literature about the contemporary American Indian experience. They note malnutrition, alcoholism rates 3.8 times higher than for other ethnic groups, suicide rates 2.3 times greater than other groups, and a life expectancy as low as 44 years. Berlin (1987) suggests that, while, traditionally, child abuse and neglect were foreign to Native American culture and traditions, such cases, coupled with parental alcoholism and depression, seem to be increasing.

While tribes differ, traditionally many live in relational networks that emphasize strong bonds of mutual assistance (LaFromboise & Low, 1989). Given their experiences, Native Americans may also exhibit a group loyalty and distrust of outsiders, which could result in not bringing incidents of family violence to the attention of legal or social service agents of the dominant culture, as Long (1986) has suggested.

Implications of U.S. Minority Experiences for the Study of Intrafamilial Violence

Gelles and Straus (1988) note that a multitude of factors are responsible for violence in families. Gelles (1972) indicates that families that have less education, lower occupational status, and lower income are more likely to experience stress and are less likely to have the resources and abilities to cope with that stress. Gelles (1972) suggests that violence is a response to the stress of particular structural and situational stimuli and that stress is differentially distributed across different social structures. Further, the greater the number of stressful events, the greater the rate of abuse (Gelles & Straus, 1988). In general, violent families are economically stressed; the parents were exposed to violence as children; and the parents are generally cut off from the community in which they live (Gelles & Straus, 1988).

While all families and family members experience stress, the above factors demonstrate that members of minority families are even more likely to experience the stressors that seem to contribute to family violence. In general, families of color are poorer, have less education, and—perhaps the ultimate reflection of the additional stress they encounter—lower life expectancy. Yet, the way this translates to intrafamial violence in not entirely known. A portion of this conceptual work has been done by Sampson (1987), who explores the relationship between African American male joblessness and urban violence (all forms).

Beyond structural stressors that seemingly influence the occurrence of violence in minority families are the attitudes held by majority group members of minorities. As noted earlier, some minority groups are viewed as having a greater predilection toward violence ("Whites Retain Negative View," 1991). One wonders to what extent such views become self-fulfilling—yet another unique aspect of the minority experience in the United States relative to intrafamilial violence.

Not only must cultural background experiences be considered in assessing factors that contribute to family violence, they also must be considered in designing effective interventions. We have seen that, for most people of color in the United States, identities and loyalties go beyond the traditional nuclear family. Extended family units are quite common, sometimes with networks encompassing individuals beyond blood relations. Loyalty to that family unit and suspicion of the dominant group—the agents of their oppression—are likely to complicate any given family member's acknowledging that violence is occurring and seeking help. And those who do seek help may be frustrated by interactions with individuals who do not understand their language, customs, or expectations.

Further, given this unwillingness to involve outsiders in family conflicts, perhaps only the severest cases may come forward, as Nagata (1989) has suggested relative to Japanese Americans. Therefore information that is available may be distorted.

Family Violence[2]

Given that, as stated above, the experience of minorities in violent families have not been systematically treated, the following review will be limited by that reality. Studies that do consider minority experiences often focus only on African Americans and sometimes Hispanics. Empirical studies devoted to an investigation of violence in Asian American and Native American families are rare. Therefore some conclusions about the contributing and inhibiting factors of violence in minority families remain speculative at best.[3]

Spousal Abuse

Previously, physical violence between marital or cohabiting partners was simply referred to as "wife beating." It has been acknowledged, however, that not all violence is husband to wife; wife-to-husband abuse also occurs (e.g., Lockhart & White, 1989). But, as Gelles and Straus (1988) and others have noted, women who physically abuse their husbands generally have been the victims of abuse themselves. While some may strike back to try to protect themselves during a specific violent episode, others may strike first, believing they are about to be beaten. Further, the larger average size and strength of males enables them to inflict greater damage when they physically assault their mates. Therefore the following discussion will focus primarily on husband-to-wife physical abuse. Though sexual assaults may accompany the physical abuse, investigations focusing solely upon sexual assaults within marriage are not common. This may be due in part to relatively recent legislative changes that acknowledge the legitimacy of claims of rape within marriage.

While some suggest that interspousal violence is more likely among minorities and the poor (e.g., Bowker, 1984), others have found no differences (Torres, 1987; Walker, 1979), particularly when one controls for social class (e.g., Lewis, 1987; Lockhart, 1987). Also, because many studies solicit participants from among domestic violence shelter clients, poor women are likely to be overrepresented in those data (Asbury, 1987).

The debate about the frequency with which husbands of different ethnic groups abuse their wives is beyond the scope of the current discussion and is to some extent irrelevant. Regardless of their numbers, women of all ethnic groups who are abused by their mates are in need of assistance. The point here is to explore the nature of the abuse and devise ways interventions can be made most effective, given the victim's cultural background and current circumstances.

Gelles and Straus (1988) describe the typical batterer as young (18-24) and poor, worrying about economic security and dissatisfied with his standard of living. Gelles and Straus note that, "while he tries to dominate the family and hold down what he sees as the husband's position of power, he has few of the economic or social resources that allow for such dominance" (p. 88). Typically, he has been married less than 10 years.

Roy (1982) somewhat corroborates this profile by reporting that 75% of the batterers in her study held blue-collar jobs. Roy also notes, however, that only 10% of the abusers in her study had any past criminal record, and most of those convictions were for past wife abuse. Thus the typical batterer is not a social deviant in other respects.

Gelles and Straus (1988) suggest that status inconsistency is also an important factor in the profile of an abusive husband. This situation occurs when a man's educational background is much higher than his occupational attainment. It may also occur when the husband does not have as much occupational or educational status as his wife. Given the lower median incomes reported in Table 7.1, this is likely to be an issue for males heading minority families.

Very little work has been directed specifically toward addressing the experience of women of color in abusive relationships. And, given the contributing factors outlined by Roy (1982) and Gelles and Straus (1988), such investigations are badly needed. Given that demographic information (see Table 7.1) shows that minorities are more likely to be poor, studies need to address the extent to which this condition affects the tendency for husbands to abuse their wives. Further, given past discriminatory hiring practices, minority males are more likely to occupy jobs beneath their level of preparation. So, the status inconsistency discussed by Gelles and Straus may warrant even greater consideration in assessing abuse between minority spouses.

Roy (1982) suggests that arguments over money, questions about the wife's fidelity, sexual problems, husband's alcohol use, arguments over children and whether or not the wife will work outside the home, pregnancy, and wife's alcohol use have been identified as catalysts for specific violent episodes. Whether or not these same factors—and in the same order of importance—contribute to violence against women of color, however, has yet to be determined. While minority women and their families are certainly at a greater disadvantage economically, different cultural traditions may nullify—or intensify—the detrimental effect of some factors.

For example, because African American women have typically been a part of the paid labor force, their employment is not likely to contribute to the stress that sometimes results in violence. If an Asian American woman's family is expected to be her first priority, however, her outside employment probably would result in additional stress. Further, there may be other factors thus far unidentified that contribute to the battering of minority women.

Not only must we consider cultural differences in analyzing factors that contribute to violence against women, but they are also important in understanding women's response to the abuse. For example, Torres (1987) found that Hispanic women were more tolerant in their attitudes toward abuse and in their perception of what constitutes abuse. Presumably, one's perception of an act will influence one's response to that act.

Peterson-Lewis, Turner, and Adams (1988) suggest that African American women may attribute the causes of their abuse to the larger society (externally, but not to the abuser) or internally. Therefore they may be less likely to involve the police because of their belief that African American males are more likely to be arrested and to be the victims of police maltreatment than their European American counterparts. Further, African American women might also rationalize that the abuse received from mates is merely a reflection of the treatment the men received from the dominant culture. Pejorative perceptions of African American women as stronger (physically and emotionally) than other women may add to the belief that they should endure the abuse. And African American women may succumb to a belief in media portrayals that suggests they may have few other options in terms of other relationships or economic survival. While Peterson-Lewis et al. (1988) focus on the experiences of African American women, they suggest that their attributional analysis may be adapted to women of all cultures.

Physical Child Abuse

The "rate" question (i.e., which group is abused more) seems even more prevalent in literature on violence against children. Countless studies (e.g,. Jason & Andereck, 1983; Johnson & Showers, 1985; Paulson, Coombs, & Landsverk, 1990; Polansky, Ammons, & Gaudin, 1985; Spearly & Lauderdale, 1983) report or attempt to estimate how frequently minority children are abused in comparison with European American children. Many of these studies provide little else by way of ethnic comparisons. Yet, despite the fact that so much effort has been devoted to these comparisons, no clear answer to the "rate" question has emerged.

Many studies estimate the rate by which children are abused by comparing the proportion of minorities in some type of clinical sample with their numbers in the general population of that city/county/state or with some other apparently appropriate comparison group (e.g., Jason & Andereck, 1983; Johnson & Showers, 1985; Polansky et al., 1985; Spearly & Lauderdale, 1983). While several authors acknowledge that such sources do not profess to be comprehensive, they do assume that these data are reasonably representative.

Literature reviewed by Daniel, Hampton, and Newberger (1983) and Hampton (1987), however, suggests that poor and minority children are more likely to be labeled "abused" than other children. That is, relevant professionals may be more likely to assume a child who is injured has been abused when that child is poor and of color. So, official records may be problematic, given the mechanism by which cases end up a part of those records.

Even if credible rate estimates were available, how useful would they be? Such comparisons encourage a superficial between-group analysis of basic descriptive statistics and reveal nothing about causal factors, the nature of violence against children, inhibitory factors, or effective intervention strategies. To truly understand *all* of the contextual factors that influence violence toward children, a within-group approach is needed. Of interest, while researchers refer to the importance of the ecological approach to research on child abuse (e.g., Spearly & Lauderdale, 1983), few seem to acknowledge that culture is an integral part of each child's environment.

A study by Johnson and Showers (1985) serves to illustrate the point. Among other things, Johnson and Showers report differences between African Americans and European Americans in types of injuries, implement of abuse, and location (on the victim) of the injury. Whether or not these differences suggest real differences in the nature of violence toward children (therefore dictating a within-group analysis) or "serendipity is a factor" (p. 213), as the authors suggest, is unclear. But the question does seem to warrant further investigation. One would not generalize across dissimilar groups for any other type of analyses. Why do we simply report rate differences and move on?

Polansky et al. (1985) provide another example. These researchers report having intentionally recruited relatively equal numbers of African American and European American neglectful and control families. Yet, no race differences (or similarities) are reported.

Though still a comparison of basic statistics across groups, Lampe (1984) at least moves beyond the question of which group is more often or more severely abused. He asked African American, Hispanic, and European American adults to rank the six worst crimes in order of seriousness. Of the respondents, 36% of European American, 28% of African American, and 19% of Mexican Americans mentioned child abuse. Lampe indicates that these percentages represent significant differences between all groups.

Lampe's study is interesting in the current context because it illustrates the differences in perspective across groups that must be considered, just as Torres (1987) demonstrated relative to perception of spouse abuse. That is, if parents of different ethnic groups have different perceptions of how serious it is to abuse children—or whether it can be considered a crime at all—their actions must be interpreted within that context. Long (1986) also suggests that cultures may differ in their definitions of abuse, which may markedly affect the manner in which the abuse can be assessed and treated.

Lassiter (1987) suggests that African American parents may use more severe forms of discipline because of their belief that only a well-disciplined family member will escape the problems that contributed to their poverty and that have the potential to keep their children in poverty. Reid (1984) makes a similar point regarding undocumented Spanish-speaking families.

Lampe (1984), Torres (1987), Long (1986), Lassiter (1987), and Reid (1984) all lend credence to basic social cognitive theory, which indicates that behaviors are often driven by perceptions. So, if groups differ in their perception of the justification or appropriateness of an act, their tendency to engage in that act will also differ. And any strategy designed to alter or prevent that behavior must take these perceptual differences into consideration.

A study by Daniel et al. (1983) is one notable exception to the comparison approach, which provides an analysis of child abuse of African American children. They indicate that abuse cases were more likely to also exhibit higher levels of social isolation, more geographic mobility, maternal childhood history of corporal punishment extending through adolescence, and generally more stressful living conditions. These authors note that, in many respects, these parents might also be considered victims themselves. Similar investigations of the experiences of other children of color are badly needed.

Child Sexual Abuse

Synthesizing information on the sexual abuse of minority children is as much if not more problematic than for the other forms of violence discussed here. Again, many studies compare abuse rates and little more. Further, generalizing across studies is difficult due to nonequivalent samples and nonequivalent methodologies. While one study reports findings based upon a clinical sample, another draws participants from the general population. Some studies have participants respond to closed-ended items, often embedded in a more general survey. Others use in-depth face-to-face interviews.

Pierce and Pierce (1984) rely on a sample of children and their families who were reported to a child abuse hot line. They report that African American victims were significantly younger than European American victims (X = 8.7 years versus X = 11.1 years), abuse was less likely to have been reported previously, and it was less likely for abuse to include oral sex or masturbation. African Americans were also more likely to be living at home when the case was closed or transferred. The abuse was more likely to be reported by a physician or the child's mother for blacks but by a social worker for white children.

Cupoli and Sewell (1988), who also report on a clinical sample, did not report a difference in the age of the victims when comparing African American and European American children but did indicate that Latin victims were somewhat older (10.2 years). Kercher and McShane (1984) randomly surveyed the general population of Texas. In response to one item near the end of their survey, which asked if the respondent had ever been sexually abused as a child, they report that Hispanic females are most likely to be the victims of sexual assault (21.7 per 100), followed by females of "other" races (16.6 per 100), African American females (10.4 per 100), and European American females (9.8 per 100).

Wyatt (1983) reports on interviews from a multistage probability sample of women ages 18-36 from Los Angeles County. In in-depth, face-to-face structured interviews, 62% of the women in Wyatt's study reported at least one incident of abuse as a child. Wyatt reports no ethnic differences in who reported having been abused, who reported more than one incident of abuse, or the type of abuse reported.

Contrary to Pierce and Pierce (1984), however, Wyatt found that African American women tended to be older (9-12 years versus 6-8 years) than European Americans. And African American women were more likely to have been abused in their own or the perpetrator's home and were more likely to be the victims of contact (versus noncontact) abuses.

It seems that few justifiable conclusions can be drawn regarding ethnic differences in sexual abuse, other than to suggest that more studies of the depth and representativeness of Wyatt's are needed.

Implications for Intervention

As stated at the beginning of this chapter, the experiences of minority group members in the United States are quite different than those of the majority. And those differences must be considered in devising strategies for prevention or intervention. Any recommendations, however, must be viewed as tentative at best, given that knowledge is limited by the quality of information available.

For guidance regarding successful interventions, sources that are most helpful are descriptions or evaluations of specific community-based programs. While one must question the generalizability of such endeavors, they do illustrate the advantages of culture-based efforts. In each of the following cases, programs were designed based upon intimate knowledge of and respect for the cultural heritage of the intended participants. Participants were able to interact with counselors to whom they could relate, and project goals were fashioned with appropriate community norms in mind.

Herrerias (1988) describes successes achieved by the MADRE Parent Education Program, which assumes a preventive approach with Hispanic parents. By targeting Hispanic women at risk of child abuse and neglect, and using bilingual/bicultural social workers, improvements were noted in parenting skills.

Maypole and Anderson (1987) propose a model for preventing substance abuse among African Americans. By incorporating the family and also the church—a particularly important institution in African American communities—Maypole and Anderson report greater success that seen in previous programs based in schools that were not culture specific.

Reid (1984) discusses the unique circumstances and perspectives of undocumented Spanish-speaking families. What may appear to be neglect to some may actually be the result of severe poverty. Reid also notes that what may appear to be abuse to some may actually be viewed by the parents as discipline that is an accepted part of their parental authority. Such differences in perception must be considered before foster care placements or other interventions are planned.

As these individual reports suggest, and as is discussed more generally by Derezotes and Snowden (1990), interventions must match services with client problems, encourage service use, and encourage community control of those services. One cannot accomplish this without an understanding of the background and experience of the intended clients. Derezotes and Snowden particularly note the importance of incorporating the existing network of opinion leaders in the community and recruiting and training appropriate staff for such services. Zuniga (1988) also notes the importance of culturally sensitive services, as does Bell (1987).

Carl Bell proposes a similar model to alleviate black-on-black violence. He suggests that interventions must take place on multiple levels. To develop community institutions and support systems into vehicles that will prevent black-on-black murder, a great deal of public consciousness-raising and education must be done. This awareness must be accomplished because services are not always available or the established black institutions such as black colleges, civil rights organizations, the black church, or beauty parlor/barber shops may need some support and guidance to adequately address the issue of violence. By using the community psychiatry principle of community development, the community psychiatrist or other provider can help the community in a way that respects that community's history, values, and needs.

Khatib (1980) draws a distinction between "Black Studies" and "the study of black people." The former, he suggests, strives for social change and approaches issues from the relevant cultural perspective. The latter, Khatib goes on to say, studies black people with the values, traditions, and perspectives of the majority group in mind. It seems we need to remind ourselves of Khatib's distinction and engage more in minority studies as opposed to the study of minority people.

Notes

1. Though referred to collectively, Zane noted that 20 distinct groups were included under this general rubric.

2. While a discussion of children who abuse parents might also be included here, only one study (Paulson et al., 1990) was discovered that addressed this issue in children of various ethnic groups.

3. Though beyond the focus of this chapter, much of the literature in this area addresses the frequency with which family members of various ethnic groups are abused. The reader is referred to Hampton, Gelles, and Harrop (1989) for information about African American families and to Straus and Smith (1990) for further information about Hispanic families.

References

Akbar, N. (1973). *The psychological legacy of slavery.* Unpublished manuscript, Norfolk State University, Norfolk, VA.

Asbury, J. E. (1987). African-American women in violent relationships: An exploration of cultural differences. In R. L. Hampton (Ed.), *Violence in the black family* (pp. 89-105). Lexington, MA: D. C. Heath.

Bell, C. C. (1987). Preventive strategies for dealing with violence among blacks. *Community Mental Health Journal, 23*(3), 217-228.

Berlin, I. N. (1987). Effects of changing Native American cultures on child development. *Journal of Community Psychology, 15,* 299-306.

Bowker, L. H. (1984). Coping with wife abuse: Personal and social networks. In A. R. Roberts (Ed.), *Battered women and their families* (pp. 168-191). New York: Springer.

Cupoli, J. M., & Sewell, P. M. (1988). One thousand fifty-nine children with a chief complaint of sexual abuse. *Child Abuse & Neglect, 12,* 151-162.

Daniel, J. H., Hampton, R. L., & Newberger, E. H. (1983). Child abuse and accidents in black families: A controlled comparative study. *American Journal of Orthopsychiatry, 53*(4), 645-653.

Derezotes, D. S., & Snowden, L. R. (1990). Cultural factors in the intervention of child maltreatment. *Child and Adolescent Social Work, 7*(2), 161-175.

Gelles, R. J. (1972). *The violent home.* Beverly Hills, CA: Sage.

Gelles, R. J., & Straus, M. A. (1988). *Intimate violence.* New York: Simon & Schuster.

Gibbs, J. T., & Huang, L. N. (1989). A conceptual framework for assessing and treating minority youth. In J. T. Gibbs, L. N. Huang, et al. (Eds.), *Children of color* (pp. 1-29). San Francisco: Jossey-Bass.

Hampton, R. L. (1987). Race, class and child maltreatment. *Journal of Comparative Family Studies, 18*(1), 113-126.

Hampton, R. L., Gelles, R. J., & Harrop, J. W. (1989). Is violence in black families increasing? A comparison of 1975 and 1985 national survey rates. *Journal of Marriage and the Family, 51*(4), 969-980.

Herrerias, C. (1988). Prevention of child abuse and neglect in the Hispanic community: The MADRE Parent Education Program. *Journal of Primary Prevention, 9*(1-2), 104-119.

Hill, R. (1972). *The strengths of black families.* New York: Emerson-Hall.

Huang, L. N., & Ying, Y-W. (1989). Chinese-American children and adolescents. In J. T. Gibbs, L. N. Huang, et al. (Eds.), *Children of color* (pp. 30-66). San Francisco: Jossey-Bass.

Jason, J., & Andereck, N. D. (1983). Fatal child abuse in Georgia: The epidemiology of severe physical child abuse. *Child Abuse & Neglect, 7*(1), 1-9.

Johnson, C. F., & Showers, J. (1985). Injury variables in child abuse. *Child Abuse & Neglect, 9*(2), 207-215.

Kercher, G. A., & McShane, M. (1984). The prevalence of child sexual abuse victimization in an adult sample of Texas residents. *Child Abuse & Neglect, 8*(4), 495-501.

Khatib, S. M. (1980). Black studies or the study of black people: Reflections on the distinctive characteristics of black psychology. In R. L. Jones (Ed.), *Black psychology* (2nd ed., pp. 48-55). New York: Harper & Row.

LaFromboise, T. (1992). In obligation to our people: Giving merit to cultural and individual differences. *Focus, 6*(1), 11-14.

LaFromboise, T. D., & Low, K. G. (1989). American Indian children and adolescents. In J. T. Gibbs, L. N. Huang, et al. (Eds.), *Children of color* (pp. 114-147). San Francisco: Jossey-Bass.

Lampe, P. E. (1984). Ethnicity and crime: Perceptual difference among blacks, Mexican Americans, and Anglos. *International Journal of Intercultural Relations, 8*(4), 357-372.

Lassiter, R. (1987). Child rearing in black families: Child-abusing discipline. In R. L. Hampton (Ed.), *Violence in the black family* (pp. 39-53). Lexington, MA: D. C. Heath.

Lewis, B. Y. (1987). Psychosocial factors related to wife abuse. *Journal of Family Violence, 2*(1), 1-10.

Lockhart, L. (1987). A reexamination of the effects of race and social class on the incidence of marital violence: A search for reliable differences. *Journal of Marriage and the Family, 49*(3), 603-610.

Lockhart, L., & White, B. H. (1989). Understanding marital violence in the black community. *Journal of Interpersonal Violence, 4*(4), 421-436.

Long, K. L. (1986). Cultural considerations in the assessment and treatment of intrafamilial abuse. *American Journal of Orthopsychiatry, 56*(1), 131-136.

Marin, G., & Marin, B. V. (1991). *Research with Hispanic populations.* Newbury Park, CA: Sage.

Maypole, D. E., & Anderson, R. B. (1987). Culture-specific abuse prevention for blacks. *Community Mental Health Journal, 23*(3), 135-139.

Moynihan, D. P. (1965). The tangle of pathology. In R. Staples (Ed.), *The black family: Essays and studies* (pp. 3-13). Belmont, CA: Wadsworth.

Nagata, D. K. (1989). Japanese American children and adolescents. In J. T. Gibbs, L. N. Huang, et al. (Eds.), *Children of color* (pp. 67-113). San Francisco: Jossey-Bass.

Nobles, W. W. (1980). Africanity: Its role in black families. *Black Scholar, 9,* 10-17.

Paulson, M. J., Coombs, R. H., & Landsverk, J. (1990). Youth who physically assault their parents. *Journal of Family Violence, 5*(2), 121-133.

Peterson-Lewis, S., Turner, C. W., & Adams, A. M. (1988). Attributional processes in repeatedly abused women. In G. W. Russell (Ed.), *Violence in intimate relationships* (pp. 107-130). New York: PMA.

Pierce, L. H., & Pierce, R. L. (1984). Race as a factor in the sexual abuse of children. *Social Work Research & Abstracts, 20*(2), 9-14.

Polansky, N. A., Ammons, P. W., & Gaudin, J. M. (1985). Loneliness and isolation in child neglect. *Social Casework, 66*(1), 38-47.

Ramirez, O. (1989). Mexican American children and adolescents. In J. T. Gibbs, L. N. Huang, et al. (Eds.), *Children of color* (pp. 224-250). San Francisco: Jossey-Bass.

Reid, A. S. (1984). Cultural difference and child abuse intervention with undocumented Spanish-speaking families in Los Angeles. *Child Abuse & Neglect, 8*(1), 109-112.

Roy, M. (1982). Four thousand partners in violence: A trend analysis. In M. Roy (Ed.), *The abusive partner* (pp. 17-35). New York: Van Nostrand.

Sampson, R. J. (1987). Urban black violence: The effect of male joblessness and family disruption. *American Journal of Sociology, 93*(2), 348-382.

Spearly, J. L., & Lauderdale, M. L. (1983). Community characteristics and ethnicity in the prediction of child maltreatment rates. *Child Abuse & Neglect, 7*(1), 91-105.

Stack, C. B. (1974). *All our kin.* New York: Harper & Row.

Straus, M. A., & Smith, C. (1990). Violence in Hispanic families in the United States: Incidence rates and structural interpretations. In M. A. Straus & R. J.

Gelles (Eds.), *Physical violence in American families* (pp. 341-367). New Brunswick, NJ: Transaction.

Thomas, A., & Sillen, S. (1972). *Racism and psychiatry.* Secaucus, NJ: Citadel.

Torres, S. (1987). Hispanic-American battered women: Why consider cultural differences? *Response, 10*(3), 20-21.

U.S. Bureau of the Census. (1991). *Statistical abstract of the United States 1991* (11th ed.). Washington, DC: U.S. Department of Commerce.

Walker, L. E. (1979). *The battered woman.* New York: Harper & Row.

Whites retain negative view of minorities, a survey finds. (1991, January 10). *New York Times,* p. C19.

Wyatt, G. E. (1983). The sexual abuse of Afro-American and White-American women in childhood. *Child Abuse & Neglect, 9*(5), 507-519.

Zane, N. (1992). Health status of Asian Americans. *Focus, 6*(1), 8, 10.

Zuniga, M. E. (1988). Assessment issues with Chicanas: Practice implications. *Psychotherapy, 25*(2), 288-293.

CHAPTER 8

Legal Perspectives on Family Violence Against Children

THEODORE J. STEIN

T his chapter will acquaint the reader with the legal framework for state intervention to protect children from harm and with issues pertaining to court intervention on behalf of abused and neglected children.

The foundation for child protection is found in state laws that require the reporting of known or suspected child abuse and neglect. The common elements of state laws that sanction action to protect children from intrafamilial violence[1] and violence committed by foster caretakers, including institutional caretakers and staff of day-care centers,[2] are reviewed. Next, statutory requirements that provide for services to protect children in their own homes and that provide for placement of children in out-of-home care are discussed.

Safeguarding from harm children who are at risk of abuse or neglect and those who have been abused or neglected may require intervention by the courts. Issues pertaining to court intervention are covered, including (a) standard of proof, (b) evidence, (c) juvenile court jurisdiction, (d) representation for children in juvenile court proceedings, and (e) child testimony.

Child Abuse and Neglect Reporting Laws

The elements of reporting laws differ state by state (see, generally, Myers & Peters, 1987). In general, they define as mandated reporters all professionals who come into contact with children, such as social service, medical, psychiatric, psychological, educational, day-care, and law enforcement personnel. Reporting is required whenever a mandated reporter has knowledge of or reasonable cause to believe a child is being neglected or physically or sexually abused.

Most states define *abuse* and *neglect* in their statutes but definitions vary in their specificity. *Physical abuse* refers generally to a physical injury caused by other than accidental means that causes or creates a substantial risk of death, disfigurement, impairment of physical health, or loss or impairment of function of any bodily organ. Sexual abuse provisions may cover specific acts, such as vaginal intercourse and obscene or pornographic photographing of a child engaged in sexual acts, and may include vague and undefined provisions, such as permitting or encouraging a child to engage in offenses against public morality. The neglect clauses of state statutes are often ambiguous. They typically define as neglected a child who does not receive proper care, supervision, or discipline from his or her parent, or who lives in an environment injurious to his or her health, and include failure to provide necessary medical care. Some state laws also include *emotional neglect* or *abuse,* which may be defined as the infliction of physical, mental, or emotional injury or the causing of the physical or emotional deterioration of a child.

Other elements commonly found in reporting laws require the following:

1. Reports are to be made only to a state department of social services (23 states) or to the police (26 states and the District of Columbia).[3]
2. Social service, law enforcement, and/or hospital personnel may take children into protective custody if there is reason to believe that a child will be endangered if left in or returned to his or her home (47 states and the District of Columbia).
3. X-rays and photographs may be taken and medical treatment authorized under emergency circumstances (37 states and the District of Columbia).
4. Criminal and/or civil penalties may be levied for failure to make a report. Criminal penalties, provided for in 43 states and the District of Columbia, allow for misdemeanor charges and a fine, while civil penalties, provided for in 10 states, create liability for damages caused to a child.

5. Those reporting in good faith are immune from liability in all states, but both civil and criminal charges may be lodged against persons who knowingly make a false report.
6. Privileged communication between husband and wife or between professionals and their clients is waived in most states.

All states provide time frames stating when investigations must begin (from 24 to 48 hours following receipt of a report) and when they must be concluded (from 30 days to 6 months following their commencement).

Protecting Children From Harm in Their Own Homes and Placement in Foster Care

Federal and state laws provide two approaches to protecting from harm children at risk of abuse or neglect and those who have been maltreated. On either a voluntary or an involuntary basis, children may be served in their own homes or placed in out-of-home care.

Federal law requires that states have programs to prevent family breakup when desirable and possible (42 U.S.C. Section 622). Prevention programs provide for services to children in their own homes to reduce the likelihood of abuse or neglect or a recurrence thereof. To ensure that states provide preventive services before placing a child in foster care, the law requires that a judicial determination be made, in writing, on a case-by-case basis, "that the continuation in the home would be contrary to the welfare of the child, and also to the effect that reasonable efforts were made to prevent or eliminate the need for removal . . . and to make it possible for the child to return home" (42 U.S.C. 671 [a][15], 1986). The judicial determination must be made for states to claim federal funds to defray the cost of maintaining children in out-of-home care.

All states have laws that permit placement in out-of-home care to protect children. When children are removed under emergency circumstances, eligibility for receipt of federal funds is contingent upon the court's finding that the lack of preventive efforts was reasonable. Failure to provide services is not necessarily reasonable in all emergency situations. If the emergency arose because services were not provided to a family whose case was open to the agency, the court may make a determination of no reasonable efforts (Stein & Comstock, 1987). Moreover, there are crisis intervention services that are designed specifically to be used to alleviate immediate danger to a child. When a child is removed from his or her home and retained in custody, most states require that a petition be filed with the juvenile court to initiate a custody hearing, often within 24 to 48 hours.

Protecting Children Through the Courts

Social workers are involved mainly with juvenile courts whose procedures are governed by civil law. Civil law involves disputes between individuals and organizations and is distinct from criminal law, which involves violations against the state.

When a child has been abused or neglected, a decision must be made on whether to bring the case to court. State law or agency policy may require workers to petition the juvenile court under certain circumstances, for example, whenever there is evidence of severe physical abuse or sexual abuse. In the absence of statutory or policy requirements, the decision to file a court petition may be made following consultation with agency counsel or may be left to worker and supervisory discretion. A decision to petition the court may be made if (a) parents will not cooperate with protective or preventive services, (b) there is reason to question whether parents who agree to work cooperatively will do so (for example, if agency records show that the parents have not been cooperative in the past), or (c) if clients withdraw from services and there is reason to think that withdrawal creates risk for a child.

Social workers may testify in court, presenting evidence to support a petition that a child be declared abused or neglected or to support a parent's request that the child be returned to his or her care. Regardless of whether a worker testifies in court, her or his case records may contribute evidence to the case that an attorney presents in court.

Standard of proof refers to the burden of proof required in a particular case, for example, the requirement that the prosecution in a criminal case prove beyond a reasonable doubt that the defendant committed a crime (Black, 1979, p. 1260). This standard of proof means that, to render a guilty verdict, the judge or jury must be fully satisfied or convinced the evidence shows that the accused committed a crime.

The standard of proof that is required in civil proceedings (a petition to sustain an allegation of child abuse or neglect, for example) is less stringent than that required in a criminal proceeding. Most states require that a "preponderance of the evidence" offered in support of an allegation be greater or more convincing than the evidence that is offered in opposition to it.

"Clear and convincing evidence" is a standard intermediate between "preponderance of the evidence" and "beyond a reasonable doubt." There is a lack of precision in defining this standard. *Black's Law Dictionary* (Black, 1979, p. 227), for example, in addition to referring to this standard as intermediate, notes also that it may be equated with proof beyond a reasonable doubt.

Evidence refers to the different kinds of proof that are admitted in court to convince a judge or a jury of the truth of the matter being heard.

Direct evidence comes from firsthand knowledge. It consists of facts describing what you heard, saw, said, and did. If you observed a parent strike a child, the statement, "I observed Mr. Kennedy hit his son with a belt," would be admissible in court as direct evidence.

Real evidence consists of documents and photographs. A copy of school attendance records showing a high rate of absenteeism and certified by school authorities is one type of real evidence that may be presented to the court to support an allegation of educational neglect. X-rays and photographs may be important evidence in substantiating allegations of abuse.

Circumstantial evidence consists of deductions that are drawn from other kinds of evidence. For example, real evidence may consist of photographs showing burns on an infant's buttocks. A physician may testify that the burns, in light of the child's age and their location, could not have been sustained accidentally. We might infer, from knowledge of who was taking care of the child at the time the injury was sustained, that the caretaker caused the child's injury.

Hearsay evidence is secondhand information whose truth cannot be ascertained through cross-examination. The person whose observation is being reported is either unable, unwilling, or unavailable to testify. If you were to testify that a neighbor of a family under investigation for physical abuse told you that he saw the child being beaten, this statement would be considered hearsay and would not be admissible in court. The statement may or may not be true. While true, it may exaggerate the situation and not accurately reflect the events that it purports to describe. There are exceptions to the hearsay rule that permit testimony that would otherwise be excluded.

Excited utterances are statements made while the declarant is under stress caused by a startling event or condition. An excited utterance is presumed to be reliable because it is spontaneous and uncalculated and may be reported in court by the person to whom it was made.

Medical exceptions permit the introduction of evidence given to a medical person for the purpose of receiving treatment. This form of hearsay, which may be entered through the testimony of a physician or nurse, is allowed because it is assumed that a person / would not lie to medical personnel if he or she needed treatment.

Prior recollections recorded permit you (or another witness) to enter into evidence information found in notes that were made at the time an incident occurred. These may be used in court if you cannot recall an event. Notes may be read aloud if you testify that (a) at one time, you had firsthand knowledge of the event; (b) you do not now remember the event; (c) the notes were made when your memory of the event was fresh; (d) the notes were accurate when they were made.

Admissions are statements made by a party to a legal action. A party is a person whose interests are at risk in the legal proceedings. If a parent tells you that he abused his son, you may repeat this statement in court. This admission is allowed as evidence to prove that the parent committed the act.

If a neighbor told you that she abused the child, her statement can not be repeated in court if she is not a party to the proceeding. An admission cannot be self-serving. The statement, "I did not abuse my son," would not be permitted under this exception.

Admissions by silence consist of statements made in the presence of an alleged perpetrator who chooses not to deny the allegation made. For example, if, in an interview with the parents of an allegedly abused child, the mother tells you that the father "always uses his belt to discipline their son," you could testify to this in court if (a) the statement was made in the father's presence and (b) it can be shown that he heard the statement, understood it, and did not object to it. His silence is construed as agreement with what was said by his wife. This testimony would not be admissible if (a) the father was not present, (b) did not hear the statement made, or (c) had consulted with an attorney and was acting on his attorney's advice not to talk about the incident.

Official records, such as birth and death certificates, information from a child abuse registry, and school or hospital records, are allowed into evidence. It is assumed that a public official has no motive to create a false record, because he or she has no personal connection to the people or events about which the records were created.

Catchall or residual exceptions permit a judge the discretion to allow the introduction of evidence that would otherwise be deemed inadmissable hearsay if the nature and circumstances under which a statement was made offer strong assurances of its accuracy. For example, in *State v. Sorenson* (1988), the court determined that a child's hearsay statements made to a social worker were reliable.[4]

Juvenile Court Jurisdiction

The jurisdiction of the juvenile court is specified in state statutes. In general, juvenile courts have jurisdiction over juvenile delinquents, status offenders, and children who are dependent, neglected, or abused.

Whereas juvenile delinquents and status offenders come before the court because of their own conduct, dependent, neglected, and abused children come before the court because of the behavior of their parents. Dependent children are those whose parents cannot afford to provide for them; neglected children are youngsters whose parents have engaged in acts of omission (such as failing to send a child to school or failing to provide medical care); and abused children are those who are said to suffer from parental acts of commission that cause children to suffer injuries.

Juvenile court hearings are divided into fact-finding stages (adjudicational or jurisdictional hearings) and decision-making stages (dispositional hearings). Prior to adjudication, a petition is filed. The petition states the facts of the case and requests a particular finding from the court. For example, a social worker, subsequent to investigating a report of child abuse, will describe in writing what he observed during the investigation (for example, bruises on a child's body or a child who was found unsupervised), and what he was told by the child and/or parent. Corroborating evidence may be presented by physicians, mental health experts who have examined the youngster, and school officials. At the adjudicatory hearing, the central question that a judge must answer is whether or not the facts of the case allow her to draw the conclusion that the court has jurisdiction over a young person.

Our system of jurisprudence assumes that a child's best interests are served by vesting custody with the child's biological parents (*Meyer v. Nebraska*, 1922; *Pierce v. Society of Sisters*, 1925; *Prince v. Massachusetts*, 1944). Thus the burden of proof is on the state to show, by a preponderance of the evidence, that a parent is unfit before the court may assume jurisdiction over a child.

If the facts do not support the request for jurisdiction, the case will be dismissed. If the child had been removed from her or his home, she or he will then be returned home. If the court assumes jurisdiction, a dispositional hearing will occur at which time social facts, which describe the circumstances in which the child was living, will be presented. Recommendations for services and living arrangements would then be made. Dispositional alternatives may differ state by state but generally include (a) leaving the child in her or his own home but granting the department of social services the right to supervise the child's care or (b) placing the child in a substitute care setting, such as a foster home, group home, or institution.

Dispositional alternatives are limited by the requirement in federal law that, consistent with the best interests and special needs of the child, children's placement be in the least restrictive and most familylike setting in close proximity to the parent's home (42 U.S.C. Section 675[1], 1980). This requirement places a responsibility on the courts to review whether the dispositional alternative under consideration meets this requirement and to overrule an agency's placement choice if it does not.

Representation to
Protect Children's Interests

For most of its history, a central premise of the juvenile court was that all parties were concerned with, and able to act in, the best interests of the child. There was no purpose to be served by appointing separate counsel for children.

In 1967, the U.S. Supreme Court ruled that juveniles have a right to counsel at the adjudicatory stage of delinquency proceedings (*In re Gault*, 1967). This ruling did not protect children in civil proceedings. Provisions in the federal Child Abuse Prevention and Treatment Act, however, require that a guardian ad litem be appointed to represent a child's interests in all judicial proceedings (42 U.S.C. Section 5103 [b][2][G]), thus extending a right to representation to all youth.

A guardian ad litem may be an attorney or a lay person. One who is acting in the role of guardian conducts an investigation of the child's situation and makes a recommendation to the court as to what, in his or her opinion, is in the child's best interests. Unlike the guardian who offers his or her own opinion to the court, an attorney, in the traditional role of counsel, represents the *expressed* wishes of his or her client.

The Testimony of Children

Available evidence may not be sufficient to sustain an allegation in court. This is especially so when allegations involve sexual abuse because (a) the child is likely to be the only eyewitness; (b) charges may not be brought until long after an incident occurred, thus eliminating the chances that medical evidence will be available; and (c) there may not be physical evidence unless the incident involved penetration or was accompanied by other forms of physical violence, such as battering.

For these reasons, children may be called upon to testify in court, especially when criminal charges are lodged against an alleged perpetrator. In recent years, professionals have struggled with the question of how to use a child's testimony without further victimizing the child by subjecting her or him to the rigors of providing testimony and being cross-examined (Bulkley, n.d.; California Child Victim Witness Judicial Advisory Committee, 1988; Eastman & Bulkley, 1986).

Issues that arise around child testimony include (a) competency to testify; (b) use of corroborating evidence, including evidence presented by experts; (c) protecting children from the effects of giving testimony about events assumed to be traumatic; and (d) protecting them from the effects of being cross-examined about evidence that is given.

Competency. Whether a person is competent to testify is determined by a two-part test that asks whether the witness (a) is intelligent enough to make his or her testimony worthwhile and (b) recognizes the need to testify truthfully (Horowitz & Davidson, 1984).

Most states assume that a child is competent to testify unless otherwise established (Henry, 1986). Competency may be established by a judge after questioning a child if the judge determines that the child (a) is capable of observing and recalling facts, (b) is able to relate facts to the judge or jury, and (c) has a moral sense of obligation to tell the truth (*Griffin v. State,* 1988). In *Griffin,* the Florida Court of Appeals overturned a conviction of sexual abuse ruling that the trial court had erred by not personally questioning the child to determine her competency to testify.

Concern with competency directs attention to whether a child's testimony is influenced by pretrial events. For example, parents accused of sexually abusing their children filed suit alleging, in part, that their children were "worn-down and brainwashed" into making accusations against them (*In re Scott County Master Docket,* 1985, supp. 1544). Defendants, including county attorneys, sheriffs, therapists, and social workers, were said to have coerced the children to give the responses that defendants desired.

Recognizing the various problems child victims face during child abuse investigations and in court, the California Child Victim Witness Judicial Advisory Committee made a series of recommendations to govern interviews of children alleged to be victims, including (a) holding interviews in special centers, (b) reducing the number of interviews, (c) requiring that interviews be conducted by "certified child interview specialists," (d) memorializing the information that is gathered by a child interview specialist, and (e) requiring that this information be used in lieu of additional interviews whenever possible (California Child Victim Witness Judicial Advisory Committee, 1988, p. 6).

Corroborating evidence supplements other evidence and is offered to strengthen other evidence. Corroborating evidence may take different forms. The following are examples.

1. The subsequent pregnancy and abortion of a minor were sufficient to corroborate an 11-year-old's out-of-court statements to her social worker in which she named her father as the abuser (*In the Matter of Joli M.,* 1986). There was no requirement of independent proof that her father was the perpetrator, said the court.

2. A child's out-of-court statement, coupled with *in camera* testimony (testimony given in the privacy of a judge's chambers or in the courtroom with witnesses excluded) and expert opinion that the child was sexually abused, when there was virtually no likelihood that the child was lying, was sufficient evidence (*In the Matter of Melissa M.,* 1987).

New York State's Family Court Act establishes a standard for corroborating testimony that is defined as "any other evidence tending to support the reliability of the [child's] statements" (New York State, Family Court Act, Section 1046, 1992). The testimony of the child is not necessary to make a factual finding of abuse or neglect. Applying this standard, the court ruled that expert validation, standing alone, may be sufficient corroboration of a child's out-of-court statement to a social worker (*In the Matter of E.M. et al.,* 1987).[5]

Expert testimony may be offered to (a) rehabilitate a child's testimony (when, for example, the child's behavior is at variance with adult expectations of how a sexually abused person would behave) and (b) to assist a judge or jury in understanding the general characteristics of those who suffer abuse.

Those whose testimony is offered as expert opinion must be qualified by the court and the theories to which experts refer, or the methods used to elicit information, must be reliable and accepted within the expert's profession or discipline. A judge has a great deal of latitude in determining who is an expert:

Experience with the subject matter and/or educational requirements are likely to be considered. "Usual education and experience" were sufficient for one court to qualify as an expert a social
worker who testified that a child was deprived (*In re RMB*, 1987).
The credentials of expert witnesses trained in nursing, psychology,
and social work were sufficient despite the fact that the witnesses
had only been in practice one year (*Westbrook v. State*, 1988).

A mental health expert may describe the behavior patterns of
sexually abused children to help the jury understand that certain
behaviors may be characteristic of children who have been
sexually abused. Without this explanation, behaviors such as
recanting of testimony and presenting conflicting versions of
events may be interpreted by the jury as reflecting inaccurate
recall or prevarication (*Allison v. State*, 1987; *State v. Bailey*,
1988; *State v. Lindsey*, 1985; *Ward v. State*, 1988). But expert
opinion may not be used to conclude that the victim was telling
the truth. Thus an expert may say that children who are abused
tend to act in certain ways but may not conclude that the actions
of the alleged victim should be interpreted as being truthful. The
determination of truthfulness lies solely within the province of the
judge or jury (*Commonwealth v. Ianello*, 1987; *Dunnington v.
State*, 1987; *State v. Lindsey*, 1985).

A variety of "syndromes" have been postulated to explain the
behavior of children who have been maltreated or the condition
of a child that leads an expert to conclude that she or he has
been physically or sexually abused. The *battered child syndrome*, defined as a "clinical condition in young children who
receive serious physical abuse" (Kempe, 1974, p. 174), is perhaps the most well known of these and one that the courts
accept as a basis for expert testimony because it has been
extensively studied by medical science and is accepted within
the medical profession (*Commonwealth v. Rogers*, 1987; *People
v. Jackson*, 1971). In determining whether to admit testimony
that rests on scientific methods of proof, the courts use a test
established by the Supreme Court, which requires that the
scientific methods used be "sufficiently established to have
gained general acceptance in the field in which it belongs" (*Frye
v. United States*, 1923). Evidence that a method is acceptable by
a professional community may be offered by introducing scientific or legal articles, by evaluating the reliability of the method-

ology used to arrive at the conclusions, or by presenting expert witness testimony concerning the reliability and general acceptance of the methodology.

An appellate court in California ruled that evidence presented by two psychologists about the "child molest syndrome" was inadmissible because the syndrome lacked acceptance in the professional community (*In re Sara M.,* 1987). For the same reason, courts have rejected testimony based on the use of anatomically correct dolls (*In re Amber B.,* 1987; *United States v. Gillespie,* 1988). The "child sex abuse accommodation syndrome" lacks acceptance by the scientific community and was deemed inadmissible as evidence to prove sexual abuse (*People v. Bowker,* 1988; *People v. Jeff,* 1988) but was admissible to rehabilitate the credibility of a child witness (*People v. Nelson,* 1990). While one court ruled that the "sexually abused child syndrome" was not admissible due to its lack of professional acceptance (*Lantrip v. Commonwealth,* 1986), another court reached the opposite conclusion (*People v. Koon,* 1986).

Testimony based on posttraumatic stress disorder was admissible (*State v. Allewalt,* 1986) while expert testimony that children were sexually abused, based on the experts' observations of the children's behavior, was deemed inadmissible because the testimony was not based on reliable and scientifically accepted measures and was thus considered prejudicial (*State v. Lawrence,* 1988).

A recent U.S. Supreme Court decision highlights the importance of experts using reliable methods to compile information. In *Idaho v. Wright* (1990), the Court upheld a state supreme court decision that overturned a mother's conviction for sexual abuse. During the mother's trial, her 2-year-old daughter's statements to a pediatrician were admitted under Idaho's "residual or catchall" hearsay exception as corroborative evidence that abuse had occurred. The appellate court ruled that the interview techniques used by the pediatrician were considered unreliable. He had not tape-recorded the interview, had used leading questions, and may have differentially reinforced (through the use of verbal and nonverbal behaviors) those statements most likely to support his conviction that the child was sexually abused.

The Court identified factors that should be used to determine whether hearsay statements made by a child in sexual abuse cases are reliable. The factors included (a) spontaneity, (b) consistent repetition, (c) the mental state of the child, (d) use of terminology unexpected of a child of similar age, and (e) lack of motive to fabricate. While the trial court had considered the child's age and motive to fabricate, it had failed to consider circumstances beyond the interview, thus not proving that the incriminating statements made by the pediatrician were trustworthy (Grimm, 1990).

Protective devices. Concern with protecting from harm child victims of physical and sexual abuse who testify in court in criminal cases has led to the use of protective devices, such as closed-circuit television and videotaped testimony. The statutes of 25 states allow the use of closed-circuit televised testimony. Videotaped testimony is permitted in 33 states (Demchak, 1988).

The use of protective devices for child witnesses raises the question: "Is a defendant's Sixth Amendment right to confront and cross-examine witnesses in a criminal trial violated?" Sixth Amendment protections are not generally applicable in civil procedures. The purpose of the "confrontation clause" of the Sixth Amendment is threefold: (a) to allow for effective cross-examination, (b) to allow the trier of fact to observe the demeanor of the witness, and (c) to impress upon the witness the requirement that the truth be told (*State v. Thomas,* 1988).

The courts have struggled with the need to create a balance between protecting children and upholding the constitutional rights of criminal defendants. A New York State court ruled that the confrontation clause was not violated by the use of closed-circuit testimony when (a) a prosecuting attorney and one defense attorney was in the room with the child, (b) another defense attorney was in the courtroom with the defendant, (c) the image and voice of the child and attorneys were transmitted live to the courtroom, (d) the voice of the judge and the images of the jury and defendant were transmitted to the testimonial room, and (e) a two-way private communication system was set up between the defense table and the defense lawyer in the testimonial room that allowed the defendant to participate in his defense (*People v. Algarin,* 1986).

In *Coy v. Iowa* (1988), a screen was placed between the defendant and two complaining child witnesses, which blocked the defendant from the view of the witnesses. The use of this protective devise was permitted by Iowa statute. Coy objected to the use of the screen on two grounds: first, that it prevented the witnesses from seeing him during their testimony, which he argued violated his Sixth Amendment right to face-to-face confrontation. Second, he claimed that use of the screen made him appear guilty to a jury. The judge had instructed the jury to draw no inference from use of the screen. Coy was found guilty.

Attorneys for the state of Iowa argued that the purpose of the statute was to protect children from trauma during courtroom testimony. The U.S. Supreme Court rejected this argument, ruling that the presumption of trauma was too generalized. Use of the screen violated Coy's rights under the confrontation clause.

Justice Sandra Day O'Connor, concurring with the majority, wrote a separate opinion in which she left open the door for use of other procedural devices to protect children. She recognized the "disturbing proportions of [child abuse] in today's society" and acknowledged the difficulty of detecting and prosecuting abuse because there are often no witnesses available. According to O'Connor, the right to face-to-face confrontation is not absolute. The confrontation clause reflects a preference that may be overcome if "close examination of competing interests warrants." Thus, while agreeing that the assumption in the Iowa law that a child witness will suffer trauma from testifying was too general, she suggested that case-by-case determinations of the necessity for protective devices may suffice.[6]

Conclusion

Child abuse reporting laws provide the basic legal framework sanctioning state action to protect children from abuse and neglect. These laws are broad and far reaching, providing a great deal of latitude to state agents to accept and to investigate reports. Most states (a) require investigations whenever known or suspected maltreatment is reported, (b) accept reports from professional and lay persons, (c) limit or preclude screening out of reports, (d) cover a wide range of physical and emotional conditions, and (e) do not define clearly the conditions covered. The breadth of child abuse reporting laws may mitigate somewhat their potential for protecting children from harm.

"Do child abuse reporting laws adequately protect children?" This is one question that has been raised (Besharov, 1990; Merriwether, 1986; Stein, 1984; Wald, 1976).

In 1987, the last year for which national data are available, states received 2,178,000 reports of child abuse and neglect, an increase of 225% from 1976 (American Association for Protecting Children, 1988, pp. 4, 5). The percentage of cases substantiated as valid incidents of maltreatment, however, is low (data provided by 27 states show a substantiation rate ranging from 37% to 40%; p. 10) and reflect a downward trend (Besharov, 1990, p. 12; Stein, 1984, p. 307). As the number of reports increases, the substantiation rate decreases.

The discrepancy between reported and substantiated cases may be the result of (a) ambiguous laws that encourage over-reporting (reporting all observations of injured children because what is to be reported is not clear) and underreporting (failing to report incidents because of uncertainty as to whether they are covered by the law); (b) weak investigatory practices due to lack of worker training and/or the inability of workers to conduct thorough investigations due to the volume of reports; (c) insufficient information to commence an investigation (e.g., family cannot be found); and (d) an unwillingness of workers to substantiate cases because services to assist families are in short supply.

Recommendations to deal with these problems include (a) defining more clearly reportable conditions, (b) restricting the focus of the law to child abuse only, (c) accepting reports from professionals only, (d) improved training of protective service staff, and (e) implementing procedures to screen out reports with a low probability of substantiation (see, for example, Besharov, 1990; Merriwether, 1986; Stein, 1984; Wald, 1976).

Notes

1. *Intrafamilial violence* consists of actions of a parent, guardian, or caretaker that cause harm or the failure of a parent, guardian, or caretaker to protect a child from known harm.

2. Child abuse reporting laws were not intended to protect children from violence committed by nonfamily members, absent a showing that a parent's negligence contributed to a child's injuries. Violence against children by nonfamily members may be prosecuted under a state's penal code.

3. New York State requires that reports be made to the "Central Registry."

4. The court considered 5 factors in determining whether the statements were reliable: (a) attributes of the child, such as age, ability to communicate, and ability to know the difference between truth and falsehood; (b) the relationship of the victim to the person told and the motivation of that person to "fabricate or distort" (p. 77) contents; (c) the circumstances of the disclosure; (d) the content of the statement (e.g., does it allude to knowledge of sexual matters not ordinarily known by children of the victim's age?); and (e) other corroborative evidence (e.g., physical evidence).

5. Referring to the corroboration requirement of the Family Court Act, the court said that the "validator" must (a) be highly qualified (in the *E.M.* case, the validators were a clinical psychologist and a psychiatrist); (b) use a reliable methodology or system of analysis (play therapy and the use of anatomically correct dolls as well as carefully phrased questions); and (c) be able to articulate precisely how the conclusions were a product of the methodology. In this case, the expert said that the child had a good capacity for accurate recall, her story was clear and coherent, she behaved in an age appropriate manner; her emotional reactions to the interview included manifestations of anxiety and shame consistent with posttraumatic stress. Other courts have ruled that expert testimony can suffice to corroborate a child's out-of-court testimony for making a prima facie case for maltreatment (*In the Matter of Dutchess County Department of Social Services,* 1987; *In the Matter of Linda K.,* 1987; *In the Matter of Meggan C.,* 1987).

6. In *Maryland v. Craig* (1990), the U.S. Supreme Court reaffirmed its ruling in *Coy v. Iowa* (1988), limiting constitutional protections to those enumerated in *Coy.* The Court vacated a decision of the Maryland Court of Appeals (*Craig v. State,* 1988), which, while correctly requiring an individual determination of necessity for the use of closed-circuit television, had added two requirements for the use of this protective device; first, that an attempt be made to question a child in the presence of the defendant and, second, that alternatives to the use of one-way closed-circuit television be considered to better protect the defendant's right to confront witnesses. The Court ruled that the Constitution did not require either of these protections.

References

Allison v. State (Ga. Sup. Ct., 3/17 1987).

In re Amber B., No. A035298 (1st App. Dist., April 19, 1987).

American Association for Protecting Children. (1988). *Highlights of official child neglect and abuse 1986.* Denver, CO: American Humane Association.

Besharov, D. J. (1990). *Recognizing child abuse: A guide for the concerned.* New York: Free Press.

Black, H. C. (1979). *Black's law dictionary.* St. Paul, MN: West.

Bulkley, J. (n.d.). *A report of the American Bar Association Child Sexual Abuse Law Reform Project.* Washington, DC: American Bar Association.

California Child Victim Witness Judicial Advisory Committee. (1988). *Final report.* Sacramento: California Attorney General's Office.

Child Abuse Prevention and Treatment Act, 42 U.S.C. § 5103(b)(2)(G).

Commonwealth v. Ianello, 401 Mass. 197, 515 N.E.2d 1181 (1987).

Commonwealth v. Rogers, 528 A.2d 610 (1987).

Coy v. Iowa, 108 S.Ct. 2798 (June 29, 1988).

Craig v. State, 544 A.2d 784 (Maryland App. 1988).

Demchak, T. (1988). Child victim-witness must be able to see sex abuse defendant in court. *Youth Law News, 9,* 10-12.

Dunnington v. State, 740 S.W.2d 896 (Tex. App. 1987).

In the Matter of Dutchess County Department of Social Services, N.Y.L.J., 12/18 1987, at 18, col. 5 (2d Dept.).

Eastman, R., & Bulkley, J. (1986). *Protecting child victim/witnesses: Sample law and materials.* Washington, DC: American Bar Association.

In the Matter of E. M. et al., N.Y.L.J. 11/9 1987, at 15, col 4. (Fam. Ct., N.Y. Co.).

Frye v. United States, 293 F. 1013, 1014 (D.C. Cir. 1923).

In re Gault, 387 U.S. 1 (1967).

Griffin v. State, 526 So.2d 752 (Fla. App. 1988).

Grimm, B. (1990). Supreme Court eases rules for testimony by child abuse victims. *Youth Law News, 11,* 7.

Henry, M. (1986). States act to protect child victim/witnesses. *Youth Law News,* 7, 1-4.

Horowitz, R. M., & Davidson, H. A. (1984). *Legal right of children.* New York: Sheppard's McGraw-Hill.

Idaho v. Wright, 110 S. Ct. 3139 (1990).

In the Matter of Joli M., N.Y.L.J. 6/30 1986, at 15 col. 1 (Fam. Ct. N.Y. Co.).

Kempe, C. H. (1974). Child abuse and neglect. In N. B. Talbot (Ed.), *Raising children in modern America.* Boston: Little, Brown.

Lantrip v. Commonwealth, Supr. Ct. of Kentucky, May 22, 1986; 713 SW2d 816 (Ky 1986).

In the Matter of Linda K., N.Y.L.J., 12/9 1987, at 1, col. 6 (2d Dept.) LA, 12/87.

Maryland v. Craig, 110 S. Ct. 3157 (1990).

In the Matter of Meggan C., N.Y.L.J., 12/17 1987, at 27. col. 4 (Fam. Ct., West. Co.).

In the Matter of Melissa M., N.Y.L.J., 7/23 1987, at 15, col. 5 (Fam. Ct. Suffolk Co.).

Merriwether, M. H. (1986). Child abuse reporting laws: Time for a change. *Family Law Quarterly, 20,* 141-171.

Meyer v. Nebraska, 262 U.S. 390 (1922).

Myers, J. E. B., & Peters, W. D. (1987). *Child abuse reporting legislation in the 1980s.* Denver, CO: American Humane Association.

New York State, Family Court Act, § 1046(a)(vi) (1992).

People v. Algarin, N.Y.L.J., 3/4 1986, at 12, col 5 (Sup.Ct. Bronx Co.). 49.

People v. Bowker, 249 Cal. Rptr. 886 (C.A. 4th Dist. 1988), Court of Appeals, Fourth District (July 29, 1988).

People v. Jackson, 18 Cal. App.3d 504 (1971).

People v. Jeff, 251 Cal. Rptr. 135 (C.A. 5th Dist. 1988).

People v. Koon, No. 84-CA017 (Colo. App. May 8, 1986).

People v. Nelson, Ill. App.3d, 561 N.E.2d 439 (1990).

Pierce v. Society of Sisters, 268 U.S. 510 (1925).

Prince v. Massachusetts, 321 U.S. 158 (1944).

In re RMB, 402 N.W.2d 912 (ND 1987).

In re Sara M., 239 Cal. Rptr. 605 (Cal. App. 3 Dist 1987).

In re Scott County Master Docket, 618 F. Supp. 1534 (D.C. Minn. 1985).

Social Security Act, 42 U.S.C. § 622 (1935).
Social Security Act, 42 U.S.C. § 471(a)(15),42 U.S.C. § 671(a)(15) (1986).
Social Security Act, 42 U.S.C. § 475(1), 42 U.S.C. § 675(1) (1980).
State v. Allewalt (MD. Ct. App. 11/25 1986).
State v. Bailey, 365 S.E.2d 651 (N.C. App. 1988).
State v. Lawrence, 541 A.2d 1291 (Me. 1988).
State v. Lindsey, No. 2 CA-CR 3600. Court of Appeals of Arizona, Division 1, Department A. (October 3, 1985).
State v. Sorenson, 421 N.W.2d 77 (Wis. 1988).
State v. Thomas, 425 N.W.2d 641, 144 Wis.2d 876 (1988).
Stein, T. J. (1984). The Child Abuse Prevention and Treatment Act. *Social Service Review, 58,* 302-314.
Stein, T. J., & Comstock, G. D. (1987). *Reasonable efforts: A report on implementation by child welfare agencies in five states.* Washington, DC: American Bar Association, National Legal Resource Center for Child Advocacy and Protection.
United States v. Gillespie, 87-5067 (9th Cir. July 22, 1988).
Wald, M. (1976). State intervention on behalf of "neglected" children: Standards for removal of children from their homes, monitoring the status of children in foster care, and termination of parental rights. *Stanford Law Review, 28*(4).
Ward v. State, 9 So.2d 1082 (Fla. Dist. Ct. 1988).
Weebs v. State, 0 S.E.2d 444 (Ga. App. 1988).
Westbrook v. State, 8 S.E.2d 131 (Ga. App. 1988).

• *CHAPTER 9* •

The Assessment and Treatment of Violent Families

GARY M. BLAU

MARY BUTTEWEG DALL

LYNETTE M. ANDERSON

Every 10 seconds, there is an episode of family violence in the United States (Stark & Flitcraft, 1987). An angry husband smacks his wife across the face, a frustrated stepfather throws his 6-year-old son through a wall, a betrayed woman stabs her boyfriend in front of her three children. Family members are often the target of each other's violence. The U.S. Department of Justice (1984) reported that nearly 20% of all murders are committed between family members and that almost 33% of all female homicide victims are killed by their husbands or boyfriends. Straus, Gelles, and Steinmetz (1980) estimate that more than 1.8 million women living in couples are abused each year in the United States, and the National Center on Child Abuse and Neglect (1988) has published data indicating that there are more than 1 million reports of child abuse or neglect every year. It is disconcerting, however, that family violence statistics are thought to grossly underestimate actual incidences (Emery, 1989).

Accurate statistics of violent incidences in families are difficult to obtain, for, as Emery (1989) points out, there are no consistent definitions of what constitutes family violence. Rather, each author may have a different perception of violent behavior (see Arias, Samios, & O'Leary, 1987; Berk, Berk, Loseke, & Rauma,

1983; Craft & Staudt, 1991; Gonzalez-Ramos & Goldstein, 1989; Jaffe, Wolfe, Wilson, & Zak, 1986; Muram, Miller, & Cutler, 1992; U.S. Department of Health and Human Services, 1991). Definitions of family violence are further complicated by political, legal, and cultural orientations. For example, some authors posit that family violence must be defined within the sexist organization of the society (Bograd, 1988). Other authors write that family violence must be defined within the context of cultural norms (Hampton, 1987; Sigler, 1989). Still other authors argue that family violence definitions must take into account the legal statutes that govern domestic behavior (Stark & Flitcraft, 1988).

A broad approach to the term considers *violence* to be "behavior that involves the direct use of physical aggression against other household members which is against their will and detrimental to their growth potential" (Lystad, 1986, p. xii). Blau and Campbell (1991) take this definition a step further by incorporating the idea that violent behavior can be described as a continuum ranging from acts of omission (e.g., failure to protect a child from witnessing violence) to acts of verbal commission (e.g., demeaning, threatening, and intimidating) to acts of physical commission (e.g., physical altercations, sexual victimization). The specific behaviors must first be identified so that the behaviors' relationship to societal standards may be assessed. Using this concept as a foundation, it is the purpose of this chapter to provide an overview of assessment and treatment issues for physically aggressive families. The first section discusses the assessment process, and the second section reviews current treatment approaches.

Assessment of Family Violence

Because decisions regarding the occurrence of violence within a family have substantial impact on children and their families, it is crucial that the development and use of assessment procedures serve as a means of facilitating treatment planning and monitoring client progress. There are two distinct types of assessment: "investigative" assessment and "interventive" assessment (Goldstein & Gonzalez-Ramos, 1989). Mouzakitis (1985) writes that an investigative assessment, often conducted by protective service or police personnel, must ascertain the severity and nature of the violent behavior. In doing so, a determination is made regarding the continued risk to the child within the home and the necessity of legal/court involvement (see Stein in this volume). Specifically, Mouzakitis (1985) writes that investigative personnel must be able to evaluate whether the perpetrators are capable of controlling their hostile and aggressive impulses, whether they recognize that their behavior is abusive or problematic, whether they demonstrate cooperation, and whether there is continued risk for additional violence. The investigative assessment is further encumbered by the crisis nature of the situation. The individuals are not participating on a voluntary basis; the circumstances may be potentially life threatening; and any diagnostic procedures may be viewed as intrusive.

Interventive assessment (also called continuous assessment) typically occurs after the crisis situation has stabilized (Goldstein & Gonzalez-Ramos, 1989). Asen, George, Piper, and Stevens (1988) and Belsky's (1980) research supports the use of an ecological approach to evaluation. Such an approach involves gathering data regarding the functioning of children, adults, and families as well as gaining an understanding of the impact of the social environment on these individuals and families. Individual assessments may be conducted to determine a person's physical, intellectual, emotional, developmental, and social status. The family system may be evaluated to gain an understanding of communication patterns, roles and structure, child-rearing practices, social integration, and resources (e.g., housing, financial). The assessment of the family must be made within its social and environmental context to address the family's stressors and support network.

In most cases, the assessment process is conducted by professionals, each of whom has his or her own *weltanschauung* or worldview (Sarason, 1981). Thus it is not surprising that family violence assessment is criticized as subjective. Interpretations, predictions, and decisions that rely on techniques such as interviewing and projective testing may be biased by the investigator's perceptions of "violence."

Standardized measurements have been developed in an effort to decrease such bias. These instruments seek to improve the validity of data collection procedures and to provide a strategy for evaluating prevention and intervention strategies. Standardized assessment methods include self-report inventories, behavior rating scales, structured interviews, and observational coding systems. These instruments may be used at multiple levels: individual, family, and environment. At the individual level, the association between violence and such factors as self-esteem, coping styles, depression, interpersonal relationships, and parenting skills are measured (Belsky, 1980; see also Milner & Crouch in this volume). Zuravin (1984), for example, in her study of the relationship between child abuse and neglect and maternal depression, found that mothers who were moderately or severely depressed were over 180% more likely to abuse their children than nondepressed mothers.

Individual inventories to assess such factors as depression, anxiety, self-esteem, and stress include the Beck Depression Inventory (Beck & Beamesderfer, 1974), the Children's Depression Inventory (Saylor, Finch, Spirito, & Bennett, 1984), the Revised Children's Manifest Anxiety Inventory (Reynolds & Richmond, 1978), and the Coopersmith Self-Esteem Inventory (Coopersmith, 1981). For issues of parental violence, a more specific individual assessment is the Parenting Stress Index (Abidin, 1983).

The Parenting Stress Index provides an assessment of parental frustration and self-esteem (Abidin, 1983). Using a 5-point Likert scale, a parent indicates his or her level of agreement from "strongly agree" to "strongly disagree" with 101 items. Subscales include measures of "parent depression" or "unhappiness," "parent attachment," "restrictions imposed by the parental role," and a "parent's sense of competence." Test-retest reliability correlations between .69 and .91 have been demonstrated depending on the length of time that has elapsed between test administrations (Grotevant & Carlson, 1989). Grotevant and Carlson (1989) also report that numerous studies have demonstrated the PSI's content, construct, and criterion-related validity. For example, Mash, Johnson, and Krovitz (1983) found that the PSI successfully discriminated between samples of physically abusive and nonabusive mothers.

For abusive mothers, the Maternal Esteem Scale has been used to provide specific information about an individual's feelings regarding her parental role (Koeske & Koeske, 1990). On this scale, a respondent rates herself as a mother on 15 trait adjectives using a 5-step Likert scale. A response of "5" to such traits as "sympathetic," "moody," or "ambitious" represents the mother's perception of the trait as "always or almost always true," while a response of "1" indicates that the respondent believes the trait to be "never or almost never true." High scores are interpreted as reflecting a positive sense of self-esteem as a mother. Although statistical information is not yet available, preliminary results indicate that low maternal self-esteem may be an important contributor to violence against children.

Standardized assessment instruments have also been developed to evaluate family interaction and relationships. Family measures can provide specific descriptions of dysfunctional processes (e.g., marital discord, reciprocal cycles of aversive behavior, reinforcement of inappropriate behavior, ineffective use of appropriate consequences). Researchers have found that abusive families display distorted patterns of parent-child interactions as well as dysfunctional marital relationships (see Milner & Crouch in this volume). Examples of instruments are the Parent-Child Behavioral Coding System (Forehand & McMahon, 1981), the Dyadic Adjustment Scale (Spanier & Filsinger, 1983), the Family Adaptability and Cohesion Evaluation Scale (Olson, 1986), the Index of Marital Satisfaction (Hudson, 1982), the Index of Spouse Abuse (Hudson & McIntosh, 1981), and the Adult-Adolescent Parenting Inventory (Bavolek, 1984).

One widely used self-report inventory is the Adult-Adolescent Parenting Inventory (AAPI; Bavolek, 1984). The AAPI consists of 32 statements reflecting perceptions of the parent's role and the child's role within the family. A parent is instructed to circle his or her level of agreement with each statement on a 5-point Likert scale ranging from "strongly agree" to "strongly disagree"; a respondent can also mark "uncertain."

An analysis of responses on the AAPI yields constructs of parenting attitudes, inappropriate expectations, empathy, corporal punishment, and role reversal. Scores, which have been standardized for white, black, Hispanic, and Asian parents, develop a profile that Grotevant and Carlson (1989) describe as having discriminant validity based on the instrument's ability to distinguish between abusive and nonabusive populations. Studies of internal reliability are in the adequate range (coefficients from .70 to .86), and validity studies are currently in progress

(Bavolek, 1984; Grotevant & Carlson, 1989). Responses on the AAPI, as with all self-report measures, may be susceptible to a social desirability effect and may therefore be a measure of a cognitive awareness of culturally determined expectancies rather than of actual parental behavior.

Recent studies on the association of parental attitudes and parenting behavior have focused on the "working model" concept of parental attachment. A parent's "working model" is conceptualized as the internalized thoughts and feelings (representations) regarding attachment. Based on Bowlby's theory, *attachment* is defined as an enduring bond between two individuals (Bowlby, 1969). As this process is reciprocal, a parent who is not positively attached to his or her child may be at greater risk for abusive behavior. The Adult Attachment Interview, developed by Mary Main, is a structured interview that seeks to understand the working model of an individual's attachment. The interview, which generally takes an hour to complete, is audiotaped and verbatim transcripts are then rated by trained coders on seven 9-point scales. An assessment of the parent's attachment is classified as "dismissing," "preoccupied," or "autonomous." These classifications correspond to Bowlby's conceptualization of infants' attachment as "avoidant," "ambivalent," and "secure," respectively (Benoit, Zeanah, & Barton, 1989). Such classifications may have implications for the assessment of the capacity to acknowledge and control aggressive behavior. In a study of adult attachment models, Haft and Slade (1989) concluded that one of the central ways secure adults differ from dismissing and preoccupied adults is in their ability to recognize and cope with negative affect.

An interview format such as the Adult Attachment Interview may present advantages over self-report questionnaires such as the AAPI. In Benoit et al.'s (1989) view: "Evaluating the mother's descriptions in interview format produces more valid measures of adult attachment than does merely accepting mother's reports of childhood experiences at face value, as in a questionnaire measure" (p. 194). Unlike self-report questionnaires, for which the association between attitudinal scales and parenting behavior has not been established, Crowell and Felman (1989) write of the Adult Attachment Interview: "The interview appears to be a reliable tool for . . . assessing the associations between subjective conceptualizations and parenting behavior, [for] exploring parental contributions to child behavior and outlining patterns of relationships" (p. 173).

Parent-child interactions also may be assessed through direct observation and the use of a standardized coding system. Two such systems of coding direct observations are the Nursing Child Assessment (N-CAST; Barnard, 1978) and the Massie-Campbell Scale of Mother-Infant Attachment Indicators During Stress (Massie & Campbell, 1983).

The N-CAST consists of two separate scales, the teaching scale, which scores the interaction of a parent while the parent teaches a simple age-appropriate task to his or her child (aged birth to 3 years), and the feeding scale, which assesses the interaction between a parent and child (aged birth to 1 year) while the parent feeds the child. Both N-CAST scales include subscales for parental "sensitivity to cues," "response to distress," "social emotional growth fostering," and "cognitive growth fostering." In addition, the child's behavior is scored in terms of "clarity of cues" and "responsiveness to parent." Scoring of observations requires specialized training.

The Massie-Campbell scale similarly requires specific training. The scale was devised to record observations of parent-child interactions during a medical examination or during naturally occurring events in which some tension predictably occurs (Massie & Campbell, 1983). The Massie-Campbell scale scores the reciprocity between parent and child as it is observed in behaviors of "gazing," "vocalizing," and "proximity." The Massie-Campbell scale has been used in both on-site assessment and in the coding of interactions recorded on film. One advantage of scoring filmed interactions is that the film recording provides reliable and accurate documentation that enables detailed analysis of complex behaviors.

Environmental measures take into account such factors as life stress and social support. Howing, Wodarski, Gaudin, and Kurtz (1989), for example, write that social isolation is one of the most powerful factors distinguishing maltreating from nonmaltreating families. Straus, Gelles, and Steinmetz (1988) write that personal life stress (e.g., loss of job, death of a family member) and the lack of effective social support tend to increase the likelihood of violence and child abuse. Examples of environmental measures can be found in the Family Inventory of Life Events and Changes (McCubbin & Patterson, 1983) and the Social Support Behaviors Scale (Vaux, Riedell, & Stewart, 1987).

The Social Support Behaviors Scale is a 45-item self-report inventory designed to measure five areas of support: emotional support, socializing, practical assistance, financial assistance, and advice/guidance. Respondents record the likelihood of receiving support on a 5-point scale (from "no one would do this" to "most family members/friends would certainly do this"). Another instrument that assesses the social support of a family is the Inventory of Socially Supportive Behaviors (Barrera, Sandler, & Ramsay, 1981). A 40-item self-report measure, the inventory provides an understanding of the frequency and source of an individual's available support. Respondents indicate, on a 5-point scale ranging from "not at all" to "about every day," the frequency with which support was obtained from specific people. In identifying sources of support, it may be possible to use those individuals as resources for the family during the treatment process.

Several measures have been developed that attempt to account for all levels of assessment. These ecological-type assessment devices include the Child Abuse Potential Survey (Milner, Gold, Ayoub, & Jacewitz, 1984), the Family Risk Scales (Magura, Moses, & Jones, 1987), and the Child Well Being Scales (Magura & Moses, 1986).

The ultimate goal of all assessment strategies, whether individual or family, subjective or objective, is to assist practitioners and researchers in screening, treatment planning, monitoring client change, and program evaluation. Of particular importance to clinical practitioners is the use of these devices in the development of treatment interventions.

Family Violence Interventions

Interventions for violent families include the provision of shelters or "safe houses," the removal of the perpetrator, and the placement of endangered children (Jennings, 1990). Therapeutic interventions are often employed as part of a rehabilitative process. Clinical interventions for violent families include treatment for abusive parents, therapy for victims, family therapy, and community-based therapy. For a comprehensive evaluation of treatment approaches specific to the battering male, the reader is directed to the chapter by Edward Gondolf in this volume.

Treatment for Abusive Parents

There are numerous strategies for working with violent parents. Research suggests that behavior therapy is particularly effective (Bornstein & Kazdin, 1985; Crimmins, Bradlyn, St. Lawrence, & Kelly, 1984; Howing et al., 1989; Trickett & Kuczynski, 1986; Wolfe et al., 1982). Behavioral methods are based on the assumption that violent behavior is learned through socialization. For example, a parent may be "rewarded" for spanking a child by the immediate cessation of the unwanted behavior. Behavioral treatment involves the teaching of new behavioral responses. A parent is taught to chart a child's behavior, to reward positive behaviors, and to practice nonviolent discipline procedures such as time-out, response cost, and withdrawing privileges. Behavioral strategies such as role-playing, modeling, and rehearsal may be employed (Bornstein & Kazdin, 1985). Behavioral techniques have been shown, by some studies, to increase knowledge of appropriate parenting and to reduce violent behaviors (Wolfe & Sandler, 1981). These strategies, however, have been criticized for failing to address the cognitions of abusive individuals (Gambrill, 1983).

The importance of modifying the cognitions of abusive parents has received considerable attention (Morton, Twentyman, & Azar, 1988). Berkowitz (1983), for example, argues that aggressive behavior occurs when an organism perceives a stimuli as aversive, a theory referred to as "aversively stimulated aggression" (Emery, 1989). When a negative perception is coupled with a history of reinforcement for violent behavior, aggressive behavior has a higher probability of occurrence (Vasta, 1982). This conceptualization suggests interventions using cognitive-behavioral strategies. Aversive stimuli may result from unrealistic parental expectations or the misattribution of negative intent to a child's behavior. For example, a young woman in therapy with one of the authors insisted that her 8-month-old was "violent," when, in fact, the infant was simply thrashing his arms in excitement. This young woman also stated that her baby, who was developmentally unprepared to walk, would be able to walk "if he weren't so lazy."

In an attempt to modify the negative cognitions of abusive parents, Whiteman, Fanshel, and Grundy (1987) used a cognitive-behavioral intervention. Participants were taught to reduce their feelings of anger and aversive arousal by attributing a less negative meaning to a potentially provoking situation. Participants were also taught to evaluate alterative response options. Results of this 6-session intervention were quite promising and the authors concluded that this methodology could greatly enhance clinical interventions for violent families (Whiteman et al., 1987).

Unfortunately, despite the numerous studies supporting the effectiveness of behavioral and cognitive-behavioral interventions, these approaches are criticized for failing to account for the complexity of violent behavior (Jennings, 1990). While observable expressions of violence may be eliminated in the short term, it is unlikely that the elimination of violent behavior will be maintained. Jennings (1990) states that therapy is expected to encourage the abuser to assume responsibility for his or her actions, assist in the development of peaceful alternatives to violent behavior (e.g., anger control procedures such as relaxation training and time-out), and develop empathy and sensitivity skills. Jennings (1990) further states that a short-term approach will only reach the "tip of the iceberg" (p. 50) and is simply unrealistic. In addition, if a perpetrator is assessed to have sociopathic or antisocial tendencies, treatment will most likely have no effect (see Gondolf in this volume).

As an alternative to short-term individual therapy, Jennings (1990) calls for a "lifelong" (p. 50) approach. Long-term monitoring and support (similar to the methods used in substance abuse recovery) are favored over brief involvement. Unfortunately, there are few long-term supportive programs and even fewer evaluation studies (Wesch & Lutzker, 1991). Abusers often drop out of treatment after a period of abstinence (or when legal proceedings have concluded). In addition, long-term approaches tend to be insight oriented, and this method has been criticized because many perpetrators do not have the verbal capacity, cognitive ability, or financial resources to benefit from this strategy (Howing et al., 1989).

More recent clinical interventions with abusive parents are based on a developmental model (Gondolf, 1987). For example, Kohlberg's (1981) conceptualization of the stages of moral reasoning and action is incorporated into the therapy. Kohlberg characterized moral thought as developing in three levels, each level having two stages. In Level I (preconventional), moral behavior is a response to the perceived threat of external consequences. In Level II (conventional), moral behavior is motivated by expectation or duty, and, in Level III (postconventional), moral behavior is dictated by values and ethical principles. Gondolf and Hanneken (1987) describe abusers as being unconcerned with anyone but themselves and only concerned about their own outcome (e.g., incarceration). This ideology corresponds to the most primitive level of Kohlberg's theory. The goal of therapy therefore is for the abuser to develop a higher level of moral functioning. Gondolf (1987) states that clinicians must first respond to the abuser's denial and egocentrism. The abuser often feels justified for using violence and is totally preoccupied with his or her own needs and wants. At this stage, it is important to identify parameters of acceptable behavior and to delineate the rewards and consequences of specific behaviors. External constraints may be the only motivating factor for abusers in this stage, and therapeutic confrontation may be essential to gaining the abuser's acknowledgment of the dysfunctional nature of the violent behavior. For example, Wolfe, Aragona, Kaufman, and Sandler (1980) and Irueste-Montes and Montes (1988) report that court orders may be needed to facilitate treatment participation. Protective service leverage also may be necessary to engage families in treatment.

Once an abuser has recognized that his or her behavior has caused severe harm to him- or herself and others, the next stage requires self-control, introspection, and relationship building (Gondolf, 1987). This corresponds to Level II of Kohlberg's theory in which behavior is performed out of conformity. The abuser becomes aware of other people's feelings and explores his or her own past as a means to understanding the root of the violent behavior. This insight becomes the foundation for the development of empathy.

In the final stage of treatment based on Kohlberg's developmental formulation, the abuser is encouraged to analyze violent behavior in terms of societal and cultural influences. This is thought to facilitate the development of Level III of Kohlberg's theory in which behavior is performed out of a sense of principle. Gondolf (1987) states that guiding abusers into community service or social action helps reinforce and maintain their attempts to change.

Despite evidence recognizing the importance of individual interventions for abusive parents, many authors (Feazell, Myers, & Deschner, 1984; Howing et al., 1989; Jennings, 1987; Rosenbaum, 1986; Steinfeld, 1989; Taubman, 1986) write that individual treatment is not sufficient to produce behavioral change and prevent future episodes of violence. For example, in a study of 19 federally funded demonstration projects, Daro (1988) concluded that individual therapy was less effective in reducing the propensity toward violence than all other treatment modalities. Thus, at the very least, individual interventions should be augmented by alternative approaches. One of the most popular alternatives to individual therapy is group work.

Group therapy for abusive parents. Groups are believed to provide a powerful impetus for change by incorporating peer feedback and allowing for the validation of feelings (Cohn & Daro, 1987). Howing et al. (1989) write that groups allow for the mutual sharing of coping strategies and serve in reducing the social isolation experienced by many abusers. A variety of groups have been developed to treat and prevent violent behaviors in families (see Gondolf in this volume). For abusive parents, parent training programs are often employed. The basic tenet of these programs is that abusive parents have unrealistic expectations of their children, lack sufficient child management skills, and lack basic knowledge about interaction and communication. Parent groups are typically time limited and didactic, and information is presented on child development, behavior management techniques (e.g., contingency contracting), stress reduction procedures, and family interaction patterns. These psychoeducational groups average between 6 and 12 sessions and usually last for a period of less than 3 months (Jennings, 1987). Using a problem-solving and discussion format, parents (or other adult perpetrators) are encouraged to develop alternatives to violent behaviors and are taught about the "cycle of violence" (Dodge,

Bates, & Pettit, 1990), which is the typical pattern of abusive behavior in families. In the first phase, there is increased tension and anger. In the second phase, emotions erupt into violent actions such as threatening, hitting, slapping, choking, throwing, and sexual assault. The third (and final) phase, referred to as the calm phase, is marked by apologies and promises. The abuser may blame the violence on external factors (e.g., alcohol) and reassure the victim that it "won't happen again." Unfortunately, not only does the violence typically happen again, but the length of time spent in phase 3 will decrease as the violence is repeated (Stark & Flitcraft, 1988).

Many psychoeducational programs have reported positive outcomes. Increases in knowledge and skills, as well as reductions in the overall propensity toward violence, have been demonstrated (Cohn & Daro, 1987). Of interest, Cohn and Daro (1987) report that adults who received educational group counseling were more likely to demonstrate progress in treatment than adults who did not receive these services. Most effectiveness studies, however, fail to assess the long-term impact of programs. This is unfortunate, because evidence suggests that abusive parents do not transfer their learning to home situations (Goldstein, Keller, & Erne, 1985).

Self-help groups have been found to be a successful adjunct in family violence treatment (Howing et al., 1989). The most widely known self-help group is Parents Anonymous. With more than 1,500 chapters nationwide, Parents Anonymous provides peer support for abusive parents through regular meetings and the use of a mentoring or sponsorship model. In this model, individuals who have been successful in controlling their violence become the support system for individuals who continue to struggle with their propensity toward violence. Although volunteer and professional sponsors are often difficult to obtain, the use of this strategy as a component in service delivery has been found to reduce overall recidivism rates in participants (Cohn & Daro, 1987). This model also has been applauded because it recognizes that perpetrators of violence need long-term assistance and support to remain in control of their behaviors (Jennings, 1990).

In addition, anger control groups have become an increasingly popular strategy in treating violent offenders. Many of these groups are based on cognitive-behavioral principles, although there is often an educational component. Edleson (1984) describes a program for battering males in which participants are taught to reduce violent behavior by learning to cope more effectively with anger. Initially, each group member is taught to become self-observant. The idea is for the participant to identify the physical, behavioral, and cognitive cues that are associated with feelings of anger. Participants are often asked to keep a "diary" or "anger log" to describe any anger-provoking situation, complete with a description of the thoughts and feelings associated with the incident and the recording of any coping strategy that led to the successful avoidance of violence. To facilitate successful coping, anger control groups often try to restructure irrational thoughts or faulty belief systems. For example, an individual who believes he or she must have control over everything needs to modify this belief to avoid unnecessary conflicts over such issues as child rearing and finances. Anger control groups also attempt to increase alternative responses to anger-producing situations. For example, conflict resolution skills and self-relaxation techniques may be taught as a more appropriate response to anger. Edleson (1984) and Deschner and McNeil (1986) have demonstrated that improving the ability to control anger significantly increases the possibility that conflicts can be resolved nonviolently.

Therapy for Victims

The needs and functioning of victims are also important when developing interventions for violent families. Individual and group treatment approaches have been used. Although insight-oriented therapies have been attempted with battered women, most theorists and practitioners advocate a cognitive approach to treatment (Cox & Stoltenberg, 1991). Insight approaches are based on pathology (e.g., inadequate personality), while cognitive approaches tend to focus on skill development. If the battered woman lacks the necessary skills to extricate herself from an abusive situation, she must be taught to identify alternative strategies. For victimized women, Stark and Flitcraft (1988) write that autonomy and empowerment are the most important therapeutic goals. The idea is to restore personal power so that the battered woman will be capable of acting in her own best interest. Many authors contend that victims of violence develop feelings of helplessness, which, in turn, undermine self-esteem and the ability to seek help (Hilberman, 1980; Stark & Flitcraft, 1988). The battered woman may feel trapped and subordinate; she may experience agitation, anxiety, and depression; and she may not have the resources or support to prevent future episodes of violence. Thus treatment must engender support and advocacy and facilitate the identification of alternatives and options.

A child's trauma is experienced in accordance with his or her developmental level. A child may feel intense rage, fear, and guilt and may exhibit withdrawn, aggressive, or defiant behaviors. A child may also develop interpersonal difficulties (e.g., poor attachment) and view him- or herself as "bad" or "worthless." These feelings may, then, be exacerbated by multiple placements or rejections.

Howing et al. (1989) state that individual therapy for abused children is often the preferred intervention. The use of behavior therapy has received the most empirical support (Burgess, Anderson, Schellenbach, & Conger, 1981). For example, the behavioral technique of contingency contracting has been shown to be effective for increasing the prosocial behavior of abused children (Howing et al., 1989). In addition to exhibiting observable behaviors, however, the abused child often internalizes the abuse and needs to communicate the trauma as a means of reworking, piecemeal, what was experienced as overwhelming (Mann & McDermott, 1983).

Play is a child's most natural form of communication, and a skilled therapist can facilitate an abused child's symbolic expression of feelings and fantasies in a safe manner. Mann and McDermott (1983) describe a four-phase framework for treating abused children. In Phase I, the goal is to establish rapport and learn how to play. In this stage, the therapist seeks to establish trust and to understand the metaphor of the youngster's play. In Phase II, the child explores the trauma through the process of disclosure. While some children may directly verbalize their experiences, others may communicate through art, story, or puppets. Mann and McDermott (1983) refer to this process as "regression and abreaction" (p. 293). This process involves the weakening of emotional tensions through reliving (via thoughts, feelings, actions, or imagination) the circumstances that created the conflict. As the child makes statements or develops play themes reflecting abuse, the therapist provides a corrective emotional experience and assists the child in establishing more functional coping mechanisms.

In Phase III of therapy, which Mann and McDermott (1983) call the testing of real relationships and the development of impulse control and self-esteem, the abused child is aided in developing empathy and is helped to identify his or her own strengths. Phase IV involves the process of termination. The therapist must slowly discontinue therapy, with respect for the child's feelings of rejection and abandonment. Although widely supported (Bixler, 1976; Ginott, 1976), there has been very little research on the effectiveness of play therapy with abused children. Green (1978) and Crenshaw, Rudy, Treimer, and Zingaro (1986), however, have found that play therapy improves the overall functioning of abused children.

Group therapy for victims. For victims, participation in group therapy has been widely supported in both the clinical and the research communities (Daro, 1988). In his seminal work, Yalom (1975) contends that involvement in groups is "curative" (p. 60), especially when compared with other forms of intervention. To demonstrate this, Yalom (1975), based on input from professionals, developed a list of potential curative factors (e.g., having people listen, finding out that other people have similar problems). Using a Q-sort procedure, Yalom (1975) then asked prior group participants to rank the relative importance of these curative factors. In sum, group involvement was deemed effective because it allowed participants to receive modeling and feedback from other group members who had similar experiences and needs. Groups were thought to help members gain insight, develop support, and increase hope. Thus, as Daro (1988) states, groups can often be a potent strategy when helping children and adults cope with their victimization.

Although long-term, analytically oriented therapy groups have been used with victimized populations (Blau & Campbell, 1990), cognitive and behavioral strategies are more common. Cox and Stoltenberg (1991) provide a good example of a group treatment program. These researchers, using a control group design, investigated the use of group procedures for battered women who had voluntarily sought protective shelter from their abusive situations. Women were assigned to either the experimental or the control group based on the time of the year they sought services. Women in the experimental condition received a group treatment program consisting of five modules: the cognitive module, the self-assertiveness and communication skills module, the problem-solving module, the vocational counseling module, and the body awareness module. The treatment program consisted of 12 hours (3 times a week for 2 weeks) as well as weekly individual counseling sessions. The findings of this investigation indicated that women in the experimental conditions demonstrated significant pre-post improvement on measures of affect (anxiety, depression, and hostility), assertiveness, and self-esteem. A major limitation of this study, however, is that there was no longer-term follow-up. Thus it is unknown whether the skills learned during group participation helped to prevent future episodes of victimization.

Perhaps the most recent advance for the treatment of victimized women is the use of mentoring or mutual-aid groups. Mentoring programs have assisted with the improvement of academic skills (peer tutoring) and the prevention of drug and alcohol abuse (peer counseling; Danish, 1991). For victimized women, the first step in developing a mentoring program is to train a group of peers to become advocates for women who are in abusive relationships. A professional facilitator is typically necessary and can provide technical and clinical assistance. Training involves educational information on such topics as the cycle of violence and the battering syndrome as well as facilitating the learning of listening skills and how to access resources. The peer advocates have often experienced their own victimization but have demonstrated some form of successful coping, thus becoming role models. The role of the peer advocate/mentor is to provide information and support so that the risk of family violence is decreased, stress factors are reduced, self-esteem and self-sufficiency are enhanced, and the appropriate use of community resources is increased.

In the mentoring program operated by Child and Family Agency of Southeastern Connecticut, the goal of the project is to recruit and train a neighborhood-based group of female peer mentors who can assist other women in developing more productive and proactive behaviors. The program is operated from an apartment in a low-income housing complex in southeastern Connecticut. This is an ideal location because it provides the warmth of a home environment as well as easy access. The "on-site" location also encourages participants to develop child-care and food co-op services.

Mentors are volunteers who receive 40 hours of training from domestic violence professionals at the local women's center. The mentor's role is to provide assistance and support during times of crisis in addition to helping with resource development (e.g., basic skills, educational opportunities, job training, child care). Each mentor is paired with up to two mentees. The ultimate goal of the project is to help all participants develop skills and improve functioning. Although no formal evaluation has been accomplished, anecdotal information has demonstrated significant success. For example, mentors and mentees both report positive attitudes toward the group, and many mentees have "graduated" to become mentors.

Group therapy has also been use to treat victimized children. Behavioral methods have received the most empirical support For example, social skills groups have been shown to help maltreated children overcome social deficits and improve peer relationships (Fantuzzo et al., 1988). These groups target specific social behaviors (e.g., making eye contact) and develop reward systems to increase the identified behavior. This technique may be particularly useful with younger, withdrawn children (Steward, Farquhar, Dicharry, Glick, & Martin, 1986). Similar to adult groups, the ability to share information about traumatic experiences also has been deemed a "curative factor" in children's groups.

Family Therapy

Interventions may be designed to involve, in varying degrees, both the victim and the abuser. One example is family treatment. Bowen (1976) describes a model for family therapy with abusive families. Conceptually, the idea is that family patterns, such as the intergenerational transmission of violent behaviors, must be understood and altered to prevent future episodes of violence. Although there is very little research on the effectiveness of this technique, many professionals now recognize family violence as a family systems problem (Bolton & Bolton, 1987). Problems in family structure, boundaries, and communication are all factors that give rise to the potential for violence. Therapeutic interventions include reorganizing the loyalties between generations, developing self-family differentiations, exploring family projection schemes, and improving communication and listening skills. Daro (1988) concluded that family therapy is particularly useful for neglectful families. Benefits also have been demonstrated, however, for physically abusive families. Assisting families in restructuring their interactions and relationships can facilitate improved functioning and reduce the chances for violence (Woods, 1988). One technique that has been proposed is the transgenerational themes strategy (Anderson, 1984). By this method, family members trace their family history back several generations to understand how the family of origin has affected current functioning. Once accomplished, the clinician can help the family alter maladaptive patterns through the development of new family themes.

Family therapy has received much criticism for not taking into account the potential for retraumatization of the victims (Mann & McDermott, 1983). In fact, inappropriately forcing victims to attend therapy with their abusers may create significant anxiety, fear, and guilt (Sigler, 1989). For example, an abusive, self-absorbed parent may be unconcerned if he appears threatening or intimidating in front of his victimized child. Howing et al. (1989) state, however, that family therapy can be particularly valuable in the later stages of treatment. Once individual and group therapy for the abuser, victim, and other family members has evolved, family therapy can be used to facilitate additional change. This can be done, for example, by allowing confrontations and the expression of feelings. Caution must be used, however, to ensure that this treatment approach respects the needs of all participants.

Community-Based Interventions

Perhaps the most recent advance in service delivery for violent families is the use of community-based interventions. The most common of these interventions is family support in the home (Roberts, Wasik, Castro, & Ramey, 1991). Although providing therapy in a family's home is not a new idea (tracing its history to the early roots of social work), the incorporation of this model is often seen as innovative (Woods, 1988). Home-based services combine the provision of concrete services, such as responding to a family's basic needs for food, clothing, medical services, and transportation, with other services, such as respite care and legal assistance (Roberts & Wasik, 1990; Zigler & Black, 1989). The belief is that providing service in a family's home will allow for more accurate assessment, provide the opportunity to model behaviors in the environment in which they will be adopted, and increase a family's feelings of empowerment by developing resources (Nelson, 1990). This, in turn, may serve to improve family functioning and reduce the probability of future violence (Halpern, 1986).

Home-based services, for example, Parent Aide programs, may be provided by volunteers or paraprofessionals. The development of Parent Aide programs has become widespread in North America. In fact, the U.S. Department of Health, Education, and Welfare has produced a manual on the subject (Gifford, Kaplan, & Salus, 1979). Parent aides may visit a home for 2-4 hours a week and are trained to provide emotional support for the abusive family, teach parenting skills, and assist in securing appropriate concrete resources such as medical care, food stamps, or Aid to Families with Dependent Children (AFDC). Parent aides may also help with concrete tasks such as improving nutritional habits and home cleanliness (Lines, 1987).

In a 5-year study of the effectiveness of Parent Aide programs, Lines (1987) compared a group of abusive mothers who received parent aide services with a group who did not: 36 clients received the services, and the average rate of monthly contact was 22 hours. Lines (1987) reports that the Parent Aide program was highly successful. Reabuse rates were less than 3% for program participants (1 in 36) compared with an average rate of 8% in the comparison group. Positive effects were also found in that the abusive mothers viewed their child or children more favorably, were able to identify appropriate resources, and felt more confident in their ability to cope with future crises. Parent Aide programs have also been found to be cost-effective (Daro, 1988; Miller, Fein, Howe, Gaudio, & Bishop, 1985). Halpern (1984) and Haynes, Cutler, Gray, and Kempe (1984), however, reported no differences in outcome when clients of a Parent Aide program were compared with a control group. In addition, Barth (1991), in his experimental evaluation of in-home child abuse prevention services, reported that the efficacy of paraprofessional services continues to be suspect. Therefore it is recommended that parent aides not be used in isolation but, instead, as part of a comprehensive treatment approach (Barth, 1991; Hornick & Clarke, 1986).

The need for home-based therapeutic services has also been advanced (Nelson, Landsman, & Deutelbaum, 1990; Woods, 1988). Being in the home, the clinician may gain a more complete understanding of a client's unique situation. The clinician can observe the physical characteristics of a family's home (e.g., cleanliness, furnishings, space), the dynamics of interaction patterns (e.g., family seating arrangements, behavioral roles), and a host of other factors such as emotional status, medical needs, and available resources and supports. Woods (1988) writes that a home-based therapist also sends a message to the family that the therapist is willing to reach out, thus facilitating the establishment of rapport. This may be particularly advantageous when a therapist's culture, ethnicity, or financial status differs from those of the client (Gray & Nybell, 1990).

Many authors currently are advocating for more in-home services, particularly for abusive families (Montalvo, 1986; Sefarbi, 1986; Simon, 1986; Woods, 1988). Home-based models are thought to enhance the probability of a successful outcome. It is rare, however, for a clinical treatment plan to include a strategy for any extended in-home services. Rather, home-based clinical interventions tend to be short term and crisis oriented (Wesch & Lutzker, 1991). Indeed, home-based clinical work that uses master's level professionals is the basis for many family preservation services.

Family preservation is the term ascribed to in-home interventions for families who are at imminent risk of having a child or children removed from the home due to abuse or neglect (Maluccio, 1991). Although there are several theoretical models for family preservation services (Barth, 1990), the basic program features include a crisis orientation, a focus on the family, the use of home-based service delivery, strict time limits (usually between 4 and 12 weeks), concrete objectives, intensive involvement (often as much as 20-25 hours per week), an emphasis on education and skill building, coordination, networking, and 24-hour accessibility (Maluccio, 1991). In an outcome study of family preservation programs, Pecora, Fraser, Haapala, and Bartlome (1987) evaluated the percentage of children who were able to remain safely in their home environments for a year following the initial referral into the preservation program. The results were startling. Almost 93% of the at-risk children receiving family preservation services remained with their families. Unfortunately, these results have been severely criticized. First, there has yet to be a systematic evaluation of family preservation programs that uses a randomly assigned control group. In addition, problems with outcome measures have been raised. For example, defining success as a child remaining with his or her family does not reflect the possibility that a foster placement may actually be in the child's best interest. Finally, program services (e.g., intake criteria, theoretical foundation) vary, and this has reduced the generalizability of results (Whittaker, Kinney, Tracy, & Booth, 1990). Despite these criticisms, however, this model is currently enjoying widespread support among professionals who treat abusive families.

Comprehensive Service Delivery

The most common criticism leveled against clinical interventions for violent families is lack of service integration (Emery, 1989; Helfer, 1991; Howing et al., 1989; Wesch & Lutzker, 1991). Indeed, studies of particular treatment modalities (e.g., groups for battered wives, anger control groups, parent aides) often cite the need to involve the abusive family's total ecological system in treatment planning. The complexity of violent behavior, and its association with poverty, drug, and alcohol use, societal standards, poor medical conditions, and mental illness, clearly suggest that single programs will likely fail to produce long-lasting change. Therefore a new focus is being directed to treatment models that offer comprehensive services.

One of these models is described by Wesch and Lutzker (1991). In a 5-year evaluation of Project 12-Ways, an ecobehavioral approach is used in which participants can receive parent-child training, basic skill training, social support, health maintenance and nutrition, home safety, problem-solving training, stress reduction counseling, money and time management training, job finding, self-control training, and alcohol counseling. Project 12-Ways is located in Carbondale, Illinois, and is operated as part of the Southern Illinois University at Carbondale. Referrals for the program come directly from the state protective service department (Illinois Department of Children and Family Services), and all families are identified as having problems with abuse or neglect. Although several methodological problems were noted in the study (e.g., use of recidivism rates as a measure of program success, lack of measures on factors associated with family violence), it was concluded that families served by Project 12-Ways had lower rates of child abuse and neglect, and lower incidences of child placements, than families who did not receive the services. Such results are quite promising and indicate that providing a range of services may be the necessary condition to increase positive outcomes for violent families.

All three authors of this chapter are involved in a Child and Family Agency's integrated service delivery program for the treatment of family violence. Blau and Campbell (1991) state that the Child and Family Agency's clinical interventions for violent families are best understood as a continuum of service approaches. On one end of the continuum is traditional outpatient therapy, followed by intensive outpatient therapy, short-term home-based services, and longer-term home-based services. The Family Violence Treatment Unit (FVTU) at the Child and Family Agency was established to provide direct access to intensive treatment and support services to individuals experiencing family violence. This program is funded by the Department of Children and Youth Services (DCYS) and involves close coordination between these two agencies as well as other service providers. For example, the FVTU works closely with the area Women's Center, which provides shelter and assistance for battered women and their children.

Through the provision of immediate, intensive treatment, the objectives of this program are to break the cycle of violence and to help families achieve a higher level of functioning. The goals are accomplished through specialized counseling and consultation, a multidisciplinary team approach, 24-hour availability, and an ongoing assessment of the family's status and needs. As an adjunct to traditional outpatient and case management services, intensive outpatient therapy can be offered in the form of multiple weekly appointments or the inclusion of additional outpatient strategies. For example, group programs (e.g., women's support group, men's support group, psychoeducational group on family violence) are also offered as well as a mentoring/self-help program that matches victimized women with other women who have learned to successfully cope with their own history of victimization. Home-based services are also available through the agency's Family Preservation and Family Stabilization programs. Family Preservation is a 4-6 week crisis intervention service, while Family Stabilization is a longer-term (12-week) home-based service. Networking and long-term resource development are also important goals of the program. The overall concept is that family violence cannot be treated in isolation, and each family has unique needs. By allowing a client to experience comprehensive services the possibility of eliminating violence and improving family functioning is greatly enhanced.

Conclusion

Despite some reports of success, there is a lack of methodologically sound evaluation of treatment procedures for violent families. Research must continue to address the relationship between a successful outcome and such factors as the type and degree of abuse, specific treatment components, and the setting and timing of clinical interventions. The literature in this area has blossomed in the past decade, however, and a variety of longitudinal projects are currently being evaluated. In addition, based on the current research, several conclusions have been made. One is that treatment cannot be isolated. The use of a single approach or intervention does not produce significant behavioral change (Daro, 1988). Therefore the current trend toward comprehensive service delivery is warranted. Perpetrators and victims of family violence must be able to access a continuum of interventions to appropriately meet their needs and improve functioning (Blau & Campbell, 1991). This also reduces the burden on individual clinicians and service providers. Professionals may become overwhelmed by the intensity of violent families, and the incorporation of a service network allows for peer consultation.

Another conclusion is that short-term models cannot be expected to have a long-term impact. Families may require ongoing therapeutic assistance to remain "violence free." Helfer (1991), in his article on the potential status of domestic violence in the year 2007, writes that professionals should endeavor to develop eight standardized therapeutic interventions that would be readily available and ongoing. The first interventions consist of services to meet families' basic needs. Helfer (1991) refers to these as logistical improvement services, which include helping families with food, shelter, heat, electricity, and transportation. The second interventions regard health care and the procurement of medical services. The third interventions are social and personal support services. These include such services as phones, parent aides, or big brothers. Fourth, families should have access to support groups (e.g., Parents Anonymous). Fifth, family-oriented counseling should be available. For example, parent groups and anger control groups would be standard components in service delivery. Sixth, Helfer (1991) believes that skills training programs must be included. For example, interpersonal, educational, and career development activities could be incorporated into treatment plans. Seventh, one-on-one therapy would be available when necessary; and, eighth, training programs and support would be offered to community professionals (e.g., foster parents, teachers) who work with violent families.

In addition to therapeutic interventions, there must be comprehensive service delivery to facilitate assessment, prevention, and training activities. There must also be a national commitment to address the societal problems that give rise to violent behavior (see Harrington & Dubowitz in this volume). Through these mechanisms, service delivery activity may be improved, and the continued development and implementation of successful programs will be enhanced.

References

Abidin, R. R. (1983). *Parenting Stress Index manual.* Charlottesville, NC: Pediatric Psychology Press.

Anderson, L. (1984). A systems theory model for foster home studies. *Child Welfare, 61*(1), 37-47.

Arias, I., Samios, M., & O'Leary, K. D. (1987). Prevalence and correlates of physical aggression during courtship. *Journal of Interpersonal Violence, 2,* 82-90.

Asen, K., George, E., Piper, R., & Stevens, A. (1988). A systems approach to child abuse: Management and treatment issues. *Child Abuse & Neglect, 12,* 45-57.

Barnard, K. (1978). *Nursing child assessment.* Seattle: University of Washington School of Nursing.

Barrera, M., Jr., Sandler, I. N., & Ramsay, T. B. (1981). Preliminary development of a scale of social support: Studies on college students. *American Journal of Community Psychology, 9,* 435-447.

Barth, R. P. (1990). Theories guiding home-based intensive family preservation services. In J. K. Whittaker, J. Kinney, E. M. Tracy, & C. Booth (Eds.), *Reaching high-risk families: Intensive family preservation in human services.* New York: Aldine.

Barth, R. P. (1991). An experimental evaluation of in-home child abuse prevention services. *Child Abuse & Neglect, 15,* 363-375.

Bavolek, S. J. (1984). *Handbook for the adult-adolescent parenting inventory.* Schamburg, IL: Family Development Associates.

Beck, A. T., & Beamesderfer, A. (1974). Assessment of depression: The Depression Inventory. In P. Pichot (Ed.), *Psychological measurements in psychopharmacology: Modern problems in pharmacopsychiatry* (Vol. 7). Paris: Karger, Basel.

Beloky, J. (1980). Child maltreatment: An ecological integration. *American Psychologist, 35,* 320-335.

Benoit, D., Zeanah, C. H., & Barton, M. L. (1989). Maternal attachment disturbances in failure to thrive. *Infant Mental Health Journal, 10*(3), 185-202.

Berk, R. A., Berk, S. F., Loseke, D. R., & Rauma, D. (1983). Mutual combat and other family violence myths. In D. Finkelhor, R. Gelles, G. Hotaling, & M. Straus (Eds.), *The dark side of families: Current family violence research.* Beverly Hills, CA: Sage.

Berkowitz, L. (1983). Aversively stimulated aggression: Some parallels and differences in research with animals and humans. *American Psychologist, 38,* 1135-1144.

Bixler, R. H. (1976). Limits of therapy. In C. E. Schaefer (Ed.), *Therapeutic use of child's play.* New York: Jason Aronson.

Blau, G. M., & Campbell, D. R. (1990, October). *Family violence: Theory, treatment and research.* Workshop presented at the annual convention of the Connecticut Psychological Association, Stamford, CT.

Blau, G. M., & Campbell, D. R. (1991, April). *Clinical interventions in the treatment of children who observe violence: Family assessment and clinical issues.* Workshop presented at the Connecticut Association of Mental Health Clinics for Children Conference, Hartford, CT.

Bograd, M. (1988). Feminist perspectives on wife abuse: An introduction. In K. Yllö & M. Bograd (Eds.), *Feminist perspectives on wife abuse.* Newbury Park, CA: Sage.

Bolton, F. G., & Bolton, S. R. (1987). *Working with violent families: A guide for clinical and legal practitioners.* Newbury Park, CA: Sage.

Bornstein, P. H., & Kazdin, A. E. (1985). *Handbook of clinical behavior therapy with children*. Homewood, IL: Dorsey.

Bowen, M. (1976). Use of family therapy in clinical practice. *Comprehensive Psychiatry, 7*, 345-374.

Bowlby, J. (1969). *Attachment and loss: Vol. 1. Attachment*. New York: Basic Books.

Burgess, R. L., Anderson, E. A., Schellenbach, C. J., & Conger, R. D. (1981). A social interactional approach to the study of abusive families. *Advances in Family Interventions: Assessment and Theory, 2*, 1-46.

Cohn, A. H., & Daro, D. (1987). Is treatment too late? What ten years of evaluative research tells us. *Child Abuse & Neglect, 11*, 433-442.

Coopersmith, S. (1981). *Coopersmith Inventory*. Palo Alto, CA: Consulting Psychologists Press.

Cox, J. W., & Stoltenberg, C. D. (1991). Evaluation of a treatment program for battered wives. *Journal of Family Violence, 6*(4), 395-413.

Craft, J. C., & Staudt, M. M. (1991). Reporting and founding of child neglect in urban and rural communities. *Child Welfare, 70*(3), 359-370.

Crenshaw, D. A., Rudy, C., Treimer, D., & Zingaro, J. (1986). Psychotherapy with abused children: Breaking the silent bond. *Residential Group Care and Treatment, 3*(4), 25-38.

Crimmins, D. B., Bradlyn, A. S., St. Lawrence, J. S., & Kelly, J. A. (1984). A training technique for improving the parent-child interaction skills of an abusive neglectful mother. *Child Abuse & Neglect, 8*, 533-539.

Crowell, S., & Felman, S. (1989). Assessment of mothers' working models of relationships: Some clinical implications. *Infant Mental Health Journal, 10*(1), 173-184.

Danish, S. J. (1991, June). *Go for the goal: A school-based prevention program*. Institute presented at the Biennial Hartman Conference on Children and their Families, New London, CT.

Daro, D. (1988). *Confronting child abuse: Research for effective program design*. New York: Free Press.

Deschner, J. P., & McNeil, J. S. (1986). Results of anger control training for battering couples. *Journal of Family Violence, 1*(2), 111-120.

Dodge, K. A., Bates, J. E., & Pettit, G. S. (1990). Mechanisms in the cycle of violence. *Science, 250*, 1678-1683.

Edleson, J. L. (1984, May-June). Working with men who batter. *Social Work*, pp. 237-241.

Emery, R. (1989). Family violence. *American Psychologist, 44*(2), 321-328.

Fantuzzo, J. W., Jurecic, L., Stovall, A., Hightower, A. D., Goins, C., & Schachtel, D. (1988). Effects of adult and peer social initiations on the social behavior of withdrawn, maltreated preschool children. *Journal of Consulting and Clinical Psychology, 56*(1), 34-39.

Feazell, C., Myers, R., & Deschner, J. (1984). Services for men who batter: Implications for programs and policies. *Family Relations, 33*, 217-223.

Forehand, R. L., & McMahon, R. J. (1981). *Helping the noncompliant child: A clinician's guide to parent training*. New York: Guilford.

Gambrill, E. D. (1983). Behavioral interventions with child abuse and neglect. *Progress in Behavior Modification, 15*, 1-56.

Gifford, C. D., Kaplan, F. B., & Salus, M. K. (1979). *Parent aides in child abuse and neglect programs* (#79-30200). Washington, DC: U.S. Department of Health, Education and Welfare, National Center on Child Abuse and Neglect.

Ginott, H. G. (1976). Therapeutic intervention in child treatment. In C. E. Schaefer (Ed.), *Therapeutic use of child's play.* New York: Jason Aronson.

Goldstein, A. P., Keller, H., & Erne, D. (1985). *Changing the abusive parent.* Champaign, IL: Research.

Goldstein, E. G., & Gonzalez-Ramos, G. (1989). Toward an integrative clinical practice perspective. In S. M. Ehrenkrantz, E. G. Goldstein, L. Goodman, & J. Seinfeld (Eds.), *Clinical social work with maltreated children and their families: An introduction to practice.* New York: New York University Press.

Gondolf, E. W. (1987). Changing men who batter: A developmental model for integrated interventions. *Journal of Family Violence, 2*(4), 335-349.

Gondolf, E. W., & Hanneken, J. (1987). The gender warrior: Reformed batterers on abuse, treatment and change. *Journal of Family Violence, 2,* 177-191.

Gonzalez-Ramos, G., & Goldstein, E. G. (1989). Child maltreatment: An overview. In S. M. Ehrenkrantz, E. G. Goldstein, L. Goodman, & J. Seinfeld (Eds.), *Clinical social work with maltreated children and their families: An introduction to practice.* New York: New York University Press.

Gray, S. S., & Nybell, L. M. (1990). Issues in African-American family preservation. *Child Welfare, 69*(6), 513-523.

Green, A. H. (1978). Psychopathology of abused children. *Journal of the American Academy of Child Psychiatry, 17,* 92-103.

Grotevant, H. D., & Carlson, C. I. (1989). *Family assessment: A guide to methods and measures.* New York: Guilford.

Haft, W., & Slade, A. (1989). Affect attachment and maternal attachment: A pilot study. *Infant Mental Health Journal, 10*(3), 157-172.

Halpern, R. (1984). Lack of effects for home-based early intervention? Some possible explanations. *American Journal of Orthopsychiatry, 54,* 33-42.

Halpern, R. (1986). Home-based early intervention: Dimensions of current practice. *Child Welfare, 63,* 387-398.

Hampton, R. C. (1987). *Violence in the black family: Correlates and consequences.* Lexington, MA: Lexington Books.

Haynes, C. F., Cutler, C., Gray, J., & Kempe, R. S. (1984). Hospitalized cases of nonorganic failure to thrive: The scope of the problem and short-term lay health visitor intervention. *Child Abuse & Neglect, 8,* 229-242.

Helfer, R. E. (1991). Child abuse and neglect: Assessment, treatment, and prevention, October 21, 2007. *Child Abuse & Neglect, 15,* 5-15.

Hilberman, E. (1980). Overview: The "wife-beater's wife" reconsidered. *American Journal of Psychiatry, 137,* 1336-1347.

Hornick, J. P., & Clarke, M. E. (1986). A cost/effectiveness evaluation of lay therapy treatment for child abusing and high risk parents. *Child Abuse & Neglect, 10,* 309-318.

Howing, P. T., Wodarski, J. S., Gaudin, J. M., & Kurtz, P. D. (1989, July). Effective interventions to ameliorate the incidence of child maltreatment: The empirical base. *Social Work,* pp. 330-338.

Hudson, W. W. (1982). *The clinical measurement package: A field manual.* Chicago: Dorsey.

Hudson, W. W., & McIntosh, S. R. (1981). The assessment of spouse abuse: Two quantifiable dimensions. *Journal of Marriage and the Family, 43,* 873-888.

Irueste-Montes, A. M., & Montes, F. (1988). Court-ordered vs. voluntary treatment of abusive and neglectful parents. *Child Abuse & Neglect, 10,* 309-318.

Jaffe, P., Wolfe, D., Wilson, S., & Zak, L. (1986). Similarities in behavioral and social maladjustment among child victims and witnesses to family violence. *American Journal of Orthopsychiatry, 56*(1), 142-146.

Jennings, J. (1987). History and issues in the treatment of battering men: A case for unstructured group therapy. *Journal of Family Violence, 2,* 193-213.

Jennings, J. (1990). Preventing relapse versus "stopping" domestic violence: Do we expect too much too soon from battering men? *Journal of Family Violence, 5*(1), 43-60.

Koeske, G. F., & Koeske, R. D. (1990). The buffering effect of social support on parental stress. *American Journal of Orthopsychiatry, 60*(3), 440-459.

Kohlberg, L. (1981). *The philosophy of moral development.* San Francisco: Harper & Row.

Lines, D. R. (1987). The effectiveness of parent aides in the tertiary prevention of child abuse in South Australia. *Child Abuse & Neglect, 11,* 507-512.

Lystad, M. (1986). *Violence in the home: Interdisciplinary perspectives.* New York: Brunner/Mazel.

Magura, S., & Moses, B. S. (1986). *Outcome measures for child welfare services: Theory and applications.* Washington, DC: Child Welfare League of America.

Magura, S., Moses, B. S., & Jones, M. A. (1987). Assessing risk and measuring change in families: The Family Risk Scales. In S. Magura & B. S. Moses (Eds.), *Outcome measures for child welfare services: Theory and applications.* Washington, DC: Child Welfare League of America.

Maluccio, A. N. (1991). Family preservation: An overview. In A. L. Sallee & J. C. Lloyd (Eds.), *Family preservation.* Riverdale, IL: National Association for Family Based Services.

Mann, E., & McDermott, J. F., Jr. (1983). Play therapy for victims of child abuse and neglect. In C. F. Schaefer & K. J. O'Connor (Eds.), *Handbook of play therapy.* New York: John Wiley.

Mash, E. J., Johnson, C., & Krovitz, K. (1983). A comparison of the mother-child interactions of physically abused and non-abused children during play and task situations. *Journal of Clinical Child Psychology, 12,* 337-346.

Massie, H., & Campbell, B. K. (1983). The Scale of Mother-Infant Attachment Indicators During Stress (AIDS scale). In J. Call, E. Galenson, & R. Tyson (Eds.), *Frontiers of infant psychiatry.* New York: Basic Books.

McCubbin, H. I., & Patterson, J. M. (1983). Stress: The family inventory of life events and changes. In E. E. Filsinger (Ed.), *Marriage and family assessment: A sourcebook for family therapy.* Beverly Hills, CA: Sage.

Miller, K., Fein, E., Howe, G. W., Gaudio, C. P., & Bishop, G. V. (1985). A parent aide program: Record keeping, outcomes, and costs. *Child Welfare, 44,* 407-419.

Milner, J. S., Gold, R. G., Ayoub, C., & Jacewitz, M. M. (1984). Predictive validity of the Child Abuse Potential Inventory. *Journal of Consulting and Clinical Psychology, 52,* 879-884.

Montalvo, B. (1986, January-February). Lessons from the past. *Family Therapy Networker*, p. 39.

Morton, T. L., Twentyman, C. T., & Azar, S. T. (1988). Cognitive-behavioral assessment and treatment of child abuse. In N. Epstein, S. E. Schlesinger, & W. Dryden (Eds.), *Cognitive-behavioral therapy with families.* New York: Brunner/Mazel.

Mouzakitis, C. (1985). Intake-investigative assessment. In C. Mouzakitis & R. Varghese (Eds.), *Social work treatment with abused and neglected children.* Springfield, IL: Charles C Thomas.

Muram, D., Miller, K., & Cutler, A. (1992). Sexual assault of the elderly victim. *Journal of Interpersonal Violence, 7*(1), 70-76.

National Center on Child Abuse and Neglect. (1988) *Study of national incidence and prevalence of child abuse and neglect: 1988* (Contract 105-85-1702). Washington, DC: U.S. Department of Health and Human Services.

Nelson, K. (1990, Fall). How do we know that family-based services are effective? *Prevention Report*, pp. 1-3.

Olson, D. H. (1986). Circumplex model seven: Validation studis and FACES III. *Family Process, 25,* 337-351.

Pecora, P. J., Fraser, M. W., Haapala, J. D., & Bartlome, J. A. (1987). *Defining family preservation services: Three intensive home-based treatment programs.* Salt Lake City: University of Utah, School of Social Work, Social Research Institute.

Roberts, R. N., & Wasik, B. H. (1990). Home visiting programs for families with children birth to three: Results of a national survey. *Journal of Early Intervention, 14,* 274-284.

Roberts, R. N., Wasik, B. H., Castro, G., & Ramey, C. T. (1991). Family support in the home: Programs, policy, and social change. *American Psychologist, 46*(2), 121-137.

Rosenbaum, A. (1986). Group treatment of battering men: Process and outcome. *Psychotherapy, 23,* 607-612.

Sarason, S. B. (1981). *Psychology misdirected.* New York: Free Press.

Saylor, C., Finch, A., Spirito, A., & Bennett, B. (1984). Children's Depression Inventory: A systematic evaluation of psychometric properties. *Journal of Consulting and Clinical Psychology, 52,* 955-967.

Sefarbi, R. (1986). To reclaim a legacy: Social rehabilitation. *Child and Adolescent Social Work Journal, 3,* 38-49.

Sigler, R. T. (1989). *Domestic violence in context: An assessment of community attitudes.* Lexington, MA: Lexington.

Simon, R. (1986, January-February). Across the great divide. *Family Therapy Networker*, p. 26.

Spanier, G. B., & Filsinger, E. E. (1983). The dyadic adjustment scale. In E. Filsinger (Ed.), *Marriage and family assessment: A sourcebook for family therapy.* Beverly Hills, CA: Sage.

Stark, E., & Flitcraft, A. (1987). Violence among intimates: An epidemiological review. In V. B. Van Hasselt, R. L. Morrison, A. S. Bellack, & M. Hersen (Eds.), *Handbook of family violence.* New York: Plenum.

Stark, E., & Flitcraft, A. (1988). Personal power and institutional victimization: Treating the dual trauma of woman battering. In F. M. Ochberg (Ed.), *Post traumatic therapy.* New York: Brunner/Mazel.

Steinfeld, G. (1989). Spouse abuse: An integrative-interactional model. *Journal of Family Violence, 4,* 1-23.

Steward, M., Farquhar, L. C., Dicharry, D. C., Glick, D. R., & Martin, P. W. (1986). Group therapy: A treatment of choice for young victims of child abuse. *International Group of Psychotherapy, 36,* 261-277.

Straus, M. A., Gelles, R. J., & Steinmetz, S. K. (1980). *Behind closed doors: A survey of family violence in America.* New York: Anchor/Doubleday.

Straus, M. A., Gelles, R. J., & Steinmetz, S. K. (1988). *Behind closed doors: Violence in the American family.* Garden City, NY: Anchor/Doubleday.

Taubman, S. (1986). Beyond the bravado: Sex roles and the exploitative male. *Social Work, 31,* 12-18.

Trickett, P. K., & Kuczynski, L. (1986). Children's misbehaviors and parental discipline strategies in abusive and nonabusive families. *Developmental Psychology, 22,* 115-123.

U.S. Department of Health and Human Services, Office of Human Development Services, Administration for Children, Youth and Families, Children's Bureau, National Center on Child Abuse and Neglect. (1991). *Family violence: An overview.* Washington, DC: Author.

U.S. Department of Justice. (1984). *Uniform crime reports for 1983.* Washington, DC: Government Printing Office.

Vasta, R. (1982). Physical child abuse: A dual-component analysis. *Developmental Review, 2,* 125-149.

Vaux, A., Riedell, S., & Stewart, D. (1987). Modes of social support: The Social Support Behaviors (SS-B) Scale. *American Journal of Community Psychology, 15,* 209-237.

Wesch, D., & Lutzker, J. R. (1991). A comprehensive 5-year evaluation of project 12 ways: An ecobehavioral program for treating and preventing child abuse and neglect. *Journal of Family Violence, 6*(1), 17-35.

Whiteman, M., Fanshel, D., & Grundy, J. F. (1987, November-December). Cognitive-behavioral interventions aimed at anger of parents at risk of child abuse. *Social Work,* pp. 469-474.

Whittaker, J. K., Kinney, J., Tracy, E. M., & Booth, C. (Eds.). (1990). *Reaching high risk families: Intensive family preservation in human services.* New York: Aldine.

Wolfe, D. A., Aragona, J., Kaufman, K., & Sandler, J. (1980). The importance of adjudication in the treatment of child abusers: Some preliminary findings. *Child Abuse & Neglect, 4,* 127-135.

Wolfe, D. A., St. Lawrence, J., Graves, K., Brehony, K., Bradlyn, D., & Kelly, J. A. (1982). Intensive behavioral parent training for a child abusive mother. *Behavior Therapy, 13,* 438-451.

Wolfe, D. A., & Sandler, J. (1981). Training abusive parents in effective child management. *Behavior Modification, 5*(3), 320-335.

Woods, L. J. (1988, May-June). Home-based family therapy. *Social Work*, pp. 211-214.

Yalom, J. D. (1975). *The theory and practice of group psychotherapy.* New York: Basic Books.

Zigler, E., & Black, K. B. (1989). America's family support movement: Strengths and limitations. *American Journal of Orthopsychiatry, 59,* 6-19.

Zuravin, S. J. (1984). *Child abuse, child neglect, and maternal depression: Is there a connection?* Unpublished manuscript.

• CHAPTER 10 •

Male Batterers

EDWARD W. GONDOLF

In the last 15 years, men who batter have emerged from the dark corners of society into the spotlight of public attention and mainstream treatment. The women's movement is largely responsible for initiating this exposure. In the late 1970s, it produced startling accounts of wife battering in such books as Del Martin's *Battered Wives* (1976) and Lenore Walker's *The Battered Woman* (1979). The men in these accounts appeared monstrous and even demonic in nature. The batterer Mickey Hughes, in the TV movie dramatization *The Burning Bed* (McNulty, 1980), was portrayed as an unemployed alcoholic with an uncontrollable vengeance.

Over the years, a barrage of studies have attempted to probe the men who batter (see Eisikovits & Edleson, 1989; Tolman & Bennett, 1990). What has emerged is a more sympathetic image of men crippled by a variety of psychological deficiencies and difficult experiences of their own. Ironically, the majority of batterers may not be that distinguishable from the normal "good guy"—in fact, many of them may be "good guys" on all other counts.

Counseling for men who batter began slowly and cautiously in the late 1970s. A handful of pioneering programs, such as EMERGE in Boston, RAVEN in St. Louis, and AMEND in Denver, employed consciousness-raising techniques to expose the sexist attitudes underlying male violence. Many battered women's advocates were concerned that batterer counseling programs might promote the illusion to battered women that batterers had changed. They were also concerned that batterer programs might divert funding and attention from battered women's shelters and victim services in general. By the mid-1980s, batterer counseling had caught the attention of social workers, psychotherapists, and even family counselors, who adapted their various therapies for psychopathology and family dysfunction to battering. In the process, cognitive restructuring and behavioral management began to dominate most counseling programs for batterers.

The late 1980s saw a surge in batterer counseling across the country as court-mandated counseling was encouraged by battered women's advocates. Wife battering had been "criminalized" in most states, where proarrest laws required arrest in battering cases. The courts, in lieu of open probation, have increasingly been diverting or sentencing men who batter to counseling. The current movement is toward establishing counseling for batterers as part of, or in conjunction with, a variety of other social services. Alcohol treatment, psychiatric care, and child protection services, for instance, often have the first contact with men who batter and could help initiate and contribute to their batterer treatment. Moreover, the courts continue to bring forth a greater diversity of men, some of whom bear a variety of compounding problems. More comprehensive and integrated treatment is ultimately needed for many of these cases.

The research and programs for men who batter have increasingly developed a context of their own. They are, in fact, a "special topic." Consequently, "men who batter" is a specialization adjacent to, but somewhat removed from, the topic of battered women. As men who batter have entered the spotlight, they have stolen some of the attention, if not the funds, as many battered women advocates initially feared. While the attention is not necessarily unwarranted, it may distract us from the social and personal experience of women and in the process end up "fixing" men rather than helping women.

As the expansion of batterer research and programs continues, so does the incidence of rape and female homicide. There are, as well, glaring attacks on women that range from the brutal beating of "the Central Park jogger" to the Senate questioning of Anita Hill. The climate of "hate crimes" has created wariness, fear, and even terror in the hearts of many women, some of whom have responded with suspicion or rage (Morgan, 1989). Moreover, Susan Faludi (1991) documents in her recent best seller, *Backlash: The Undeclared War Against American Women,* the insidious counter to women's progress in negative media images, misleading research studies, and lack of workplace supports. Programs for men who batter must attend to this larger social context, which current views and future directions must address. Men who batter as a distinct "specialization," however, runs the risk of separating itself from this context and losing its way.

In this chapter, I attempt to summarize the current efforts to determine who the men are who batter, why they batter, and what is to be done with them.[1] The first section discusses the inconclusive efforts to establish a profile of men who batter. Batterers may perhaps be more accurately represented in a typology indicating a range of batterers. Even with different types, there is some indication that men who batter may be similar in their justifications of battering. It remains, as a result, difficult to identify men who batter. The second section considers three micro-level theories that suggest why individual men commit an act of violence: the cycle of violence, the cognitive trigger model, and the wheel of control. The implications for treatment and the limitations of each of these theories are discussed as well. In the third section, I review the prevailing approaches of counseling programs for men who batter: anger control, skill building, and resocialization. Treatment issues such as denial and dropout, and men's pain and couples counseling, are also raised. The last section addresses the uncertain success rates of these programs and presents the rationale for more comprehensive services. To keep the now highly specialized subfield responsive to the concerns of women, battered women's advocates in several states have established state standards and guidelines for batterer programs.

Distinguishing Batterers

Accompanying the development of counseling programs for men who batter has been a progressively sophisticated line of research attempting to distinguish men who batter. A substantial portion of the recent research has attempted to establish a profile of batterers. This line of research—comparable to the psychological studies in the related fields of criminology, alcohol and drug abuse, and child abuse—has sought characteristics that would help identify potential batterers and aspects that warrant treatment. Contradictions and inconclusiveness in the profile research have prompted a turn toward more diverse representations of men who batter women. Several studies have substantiated the presence of different types of batterers, suggesting several different profiles.

Batterer Characteristics and Typologies

Clinical observations and preliminary studies have surfaced a profile of an inexpressive, impulse-driven, traditional, and rigid personality with low self-esteem and frequent drug and alcohol problems (Dutton, 1988). Much like the ongoing debate over the presence of an "addictive personality" in the alcohol field, the evidence suggests, however, that no conclusive "batterer profile" exists (Edleson, Eisikovits, & Guttman, 1985). Much of the profile research is either based on limited clinical samples or contradicts itself. A comprehensive review of profile studies using comparison or control groups showed that exposure to wife battering as a child, higher alcohol abuse, and lower socioeconomic status were the only consistent risk markers (Hotaling & Sugarman, 1986; see also Sugarman & Hotaling, 1989). Overall, the few studies with control groups suggest that, while batterers in treatment have more personality and alcohol problems than "nonbatterers," batterers as a group do not substantially differ from the general population of men (e.g., Hamberger & Hastings, 1991). Studies using personality inventories like the MMPI or MCMI indicate a variety of personality problems but no unified personality type (Hamberger & Hastings, 1988a). The personality inventories do not appear to distinguish batterers from other men with problems; nor are they predictive of violence.

Empirical research on batterer characteristics has recently moved to the formulation of a typology of batterers. One conception, based on batterers' behavior, suggests a continuum of sporadic, chronic, antisocial, and sociopathic batterers (Gondolf, 1988b). This typology is echoed in an additional study combining behavior indicators with several attitudinal scales. This later study found three similar batterer types: emotionally volatile, family only, and generalized aggressors (Saunders, 1992). The severity and extent of wife abuse is greatest among those batterers who are violent outside the home: These include antisocial and sociopathic batterers who also tend to have more criminal arrests and drug and alcohol problems. While this range of batterers may still hold a similar predisposition toward woman abuse, alcohol and drug abuse, psychopathology, and/or a violent subculture appear to exacerbate and complicate the battering—and the men's response to treatment. Several studies indicate, in fact, that men with alcohol and drug problems, criminal history, and antisocial personalities are more likely to drop out of programs and reoffend (Grusznski & Carrillo, 1988; Hamberger & Hastings, 1989).

Underlying Commonalty

Righteous crime. With the range of batterer types, one might assume that wife battering may be a composite of epiphenomena. That is, *wife battering* may be an umbrella term for the actions of men who are emotionally impulsive and men who are generally antisocial in nature as well as for men who have problems dealing with women. Regardless of the various manifestations, some underlying commonalities, however, may remain. All of the various manifestations or types of wife battering may be explained in terms of a belief system based on an egocentric perspective that holds one's needs and desires as primary (see Gondolf, 1987a). This belief system implies a moral order in which right and wrong are determined by one's own selfish interests and expectations. It is not that batterers are irrational or senseless. Their reasoning is often punishingly logical and value based. The problem is that their values are often distorted and their logic self-serving. As John Stoltenberg (1989) has claimed, wife battering is really an ethical issue as opposed to a psychological or psychiatric one.

Of interest, many criminologists attempting to revise the failed theories of deviance have pointed to a similar explanation for even so-called crimes of passion. Even the most emotion-filled homicides may be related to a "righteous" belief system, according to criminologist Jack Katz (1988). Katz studied the accounts of those who had killed a family member in a so-called crime of passion. He had not been directly involved in the domestic violence field, and he insists that he put aside theoretical biases to develop an explanation from the criminal's point of view. His relatively unbiased conclusion was that, whether the murder was highly planned or an explosive event, a righteous belief system was behind it. "These killers were defending both the morality of the social system and a personal claim of moral worth" (Katz, 1988, p. 19). The perpetrators basically saw themselves as justified. They acted in response to what they saw to be a violation of their moral order—or some greater good. In many cases, being apprehended made the men feel like martyrs. This mind-set may account in part for why batterers often appear so logical on the surface, full of justifications, and basically "normal," in comparison with the victims they have devastated.

Deniers and admitters. Many clinicians, nevertheless, encounter a contradictory picture when evaluating batterers. On one hand, there are men who could be described as "deniers." In so many words, they insist that they did not batter anyone. They were merely protecting themselves, doling out warranted punishment, or just making a point in a heated argument. The victim was asking for it or was not hurt, so therefore whatever the batterer was supposed to have done was not "battering." Another group of men appears more as "admitters." They tend to blurt out shameful confessions and wonder what is wrong with themselves. They search for clues in their alcohol abuse, stressed-out body, poor upbringing, or confused mental state. There is something wrong with them rather than—or as well as—the victim. It is therefore easy to be misled by either group. The deniers may so minimize and disavow the battering that its severity and duration become hard to assess and are consequently overlooked. The admitters may so redefine the battering as secondary to another disorder, like alcohol abuse, that the battering becomes secondary in diagnosis and treatment.

The deniers and admitters may both be doing the same thing in their accounts of battering. In fact, they may both be simply acting out of their sense of "righteousness" in different ways. A study of convicted rapists (n = 114) found a similar pattern of accounts (Scully & Marolla, 1984). The researchers interpreted both the denying and the admitting accounts as dismissing responsibility for the rape. The deniers did it through justifications and the admitters did it through excuses. Even after being convicted and jailed, the vast majority of the rapists basically deflected responsibility for their behavior. This finding lends some support to the notion that a belief system of "righteousness" underlies the attacks on women. The men basically do not see themselves at fault or as "wrong." Instead, they project or attribute the blame to some external factors rather than themselves (see Ptacek, 1988).

Implications of Batterer Research

Identification. The first and most fundamental step in intervention may be the identification of batterers. Therapists in a variety of fields argue that identification of a problem is the catalyst for behavioral change. Identification of batterers, however, is problematic given the inconclusive profiles and prevalent rationalization. This may contribute to the tendency for so many social services to overlook or neglect battering and batterers. It at least reinforces the institutional constraints, professional perspectives, or personal biases that compound batterer identification.

A number of different studies demonstrate the extent of the identification problems. For instance, we found in a study of substance abuse treatment programs that the vast majority of batterers were simply not identified. An inventory of assaultive behaviors was administered to alcohol inpatients (*n* = 218) and to a subsample of their wives or female partners (Gondolf & Foster, 1991a): 40% of the inpatients were admitted to the program for assault of their wife or partner in the previous year, and 80% of the women reported being assaulted. Only 5% of the clinical records indicated any form of wife assault ever in the past in response to a question on the intake forms about "domestic violence." Similarly, violence reported by individuals visiting a psychiatric emergency room was not systematically followed-up in evaluation interviews, reported in detail during staff discussions, or addressed in treatment recommendations or referrals (Gondolf, 1992). Moreover, Hansen, Harway, and Cervantes (1991) asked couples counselors (*n* = 362) to interpret two case studies of battering. They found that 41% of the counselors "missed obvious evidence of domestic violence" in responding to domestic violence case studies; 91% of those who did identify the domestic violence considered it mild or moderate, even though both cases were actually severe with one resulting in a murder.

Even in a domestic violence court, we found the majority of cases brought before the court on arrest were referred to drug and alcohol evaluation, mental health evaluation, or released on probation rather than referred to batterer counseling. This was the result even with a battered women's advocate and batterer counseling representative present in the court (Gondolf & Foster, 1993).

The largest percentage of men who batter and end up in treatment are identified by their partners, who report them to the police. Even by liberal estimates, those who are mandated to counseling by the courts account for less than 5% of the batterers in most cities. Batterers, however, are perhaps more likely to have first contact with alcohol and drug treatment, mental health programs, and other social services. Their victims are likely to have had contact with an emergency room of a general hospital. A study of the help-seeking behavior of battered women, in fact, indicated that the women had contacted an average of four different sources of help prior to their entering a shelter (Gondolf & Fisher, 1988).

It appears essential that a specific protocol for identifying and referring batterers be in place throughout the social service community. The research mentioned above suggests that using one of the several established behavioral screening devices with the high-risk populations in alcohol and drug treatment and mental health programs would substantially increase the identification of batterers (for examples, see Gondolf, 1990b; Gondolf & Foster, 1991a; McLeer & Anwar, 1989). Recognizing and investigating cues of wife battering would also increase identification. Indication of "angry outbursts" or "marital conflicts," for instance, warrant some follow-up. Assistance from victim advocates who interview battered women can also increase reporting and make available useful information (see Gondolf, 1990b).

Program development. The findings regarding batterer characteristics also have important implications for program development. First, the lack of a substantiated profile should help diffuse the tendency, particularly in the media, to promote the deviant "crazed killer" stereotype of batterers. The stereotype too easily reinforces the tendency of men to dismiss their abuse by insisting, "But I'm not one of *them*!" Similarly, women who encounter men who do not fit a batterer profile are more likely to have a false sense of safety or assurance. Second, the preoccupation with a "mild mannered" profile may divert programs from treating the real issues and sufficiently accounting for the compounding problems of some individuals.

In addition, the notion of a unified batterer profile furthers the pell-mell expansion of batterer counseling. As a result of greater public awareness and court-mandated counseling, a wider range of batterers are coming to batterer programs. Many batterers, however, simply do not belong there; the chances of antisocial and especially sociopathic batterers responding to counseling are low (Gondolf, 1988b). Some of these men are "system failures" who have been in and out of law enforcement programs, drug and alcohol treatment, and psychiatric care. Moreover, if these men do remain in the program, they are so resistant or deceptive that they often undermine the progress of those who have the potential to change.

Batterer programs need therefore to evaluate mental health, criminality, and alcohol and drug problems of batterers to sufficiently assess their suitability for batterer counseling (see Sonkin, 1987). This task carries some awkward compromises, however. To invest too much in batterer assessment may again divert the program emphasis on accountability for the woman abuse and open the door to psychiatric diagnoses that lead a program back to mainstream mental health treatment. An effective social history may be sufficient to surface troublesome and intransigent cases without undoing a program's objectives. Another alternative is to use orientation sessions to further assess men's motivation and their suitability for further counseling (Tolman & Bhosley, 1989).

Micro Theories of Battering

Macro Versus Micro Theories

As Chapter 4 discusses, there are several macro-level theories that offer explanations for why so many men batter women. The macro-level theories might be loosely categorized as sociocultural theories, which hold norms as fundamental to social stability, and sociopolitical theories, which suggest that power is central to the ordering of society. The sociocultural theories include normative theories asserting that violence has become the norm in American society in what might be termed a "culture of violence" (Stacey & Shupe, 1983), and those theories asserting that violence is a manifestation of the social breakdown or normlessness in society (Levine, 1986). The ambiguity, contradictions, and confusion caused by the lack of consistent norms lead to many "social diseases" including violence against women.

The sociopolitical theories include the feminist notion of a patriarchal social structure in which wife battering is merely another means to subject and control women in a male-dominated society (Schechter, 1982). Sex role socialization, another sociopolitical theory, suggests that men are educated through role models, sanctions, and overmothering to repress their feelings and "take charge" (Taubman, 1986). Wife abuse is an extension of what men learn about how to relate with others.

The macro theories best explain why so many men are predisposed to wife battering, but they say less about what compels individual men to commit a violent act. In a sense, the macro theories tell us how a gun is put in a person's hand but not why a person pulls the trigger. Several micro theories attempt to explain the compulsion in violent acts. These social-psychological theories see violence as a process rather than an isolated event. By describing this process, or the "dynamics of violence," the micro theories not only show how individuals become violent but also imply ways to interrupt and avoid violence.

The Cycle of Violence

Perhaps the most popular of these theories is the "cycle of violence" based on Lenore Walker's clinical observations in the late 1970s (Walker, 1979). The cycle of violence theory is implicitly derived from the frustration-aggression hypothesis that one becomes increasingly aggressive as one is frustrated. The theory is fundamentally an emotion-driven escalation model of violence. Tensions gradually mount until they explode in a violent incident. After the emotional release provided by the violent incident, a period of apologies, promises, and forgiveness begins. Tensions gradually rise again, however, and the cycle repeats itself. The implication of this theory is to teach men and women the cycle so that (a) they will not fool themselves into thinking the violence has been curtailed during the apology period and, (b) they will seek help at that point before tensions begin to build again. It also implies that one has to deal with the lack of conflict resolution and poor impulse control that underlie the escalation of tensions and explosion of violence. In addition, "time-outs" may be taught as a means to interrupt the cycle. When a man becomes aware of the "cues" associated with particular tensions, he can signal with a "T" sign that he needs to leave for a set period to cool down.

The cycle of violence has been increasingly qualified and revised over recent years, as empirical studies raise more contradictory evidence. In Walker's (1983) subsequent research on battered women, she found a substantial portion of her sample reporting an absence of the so-called apologetic/forgiveness or "honeymoon" phase. Many women in fact reported the batterer turned from apologizing to blaming the victim for the violent event over time. Similarly, the typologies of men who batter reveal a type of batterer who is violent sporadically in a pattern that approximates the cycle of violence (Gondolf, 1988b; Saunders, 1992). The majority of batterers, however, appear to be apologetic only occasionally and many are consistently controlling and abusive. The cycle of violence may therefore be more the exception than the rule.

The Trigger Model

Another widespread conception is the "trigger model" based on cognitive theories of anger (Dutton, 1984). This micro-level theory suggests that violence is the result of a progression of steps that are directed by our thought patterns and the expectations they imply. This is fundamentally a cognitively driven conception, as opposed to an emotionally driven one. An event occurs such as dinner being served late. The man interprets the event as a threat. It is seen as a violation of his expectations. There is then physiological arousal—a set of sensations as the body reacts to the perceived threat. Subsequently, the man labels the arousal "anger" and the emotion intensifies. Another cognitive step follows in which the man determines that the most appropriate response to the anger is to act violently. The violence releases the anger as well as neutralizes the perceived threat.

The implication of the cognitive trigger model is that a change in our thought patterns will interrupt and avoid violence. The violence is more the result of a series of bad choices. Therefore we can help men who batter recognize the steps toward violence and make different choices. For instance, a man might label a late dinner as a mistake rather than a threat, or the arousal as hurt or disappointment rather than anger. He may choose, as well, to withdraw and cool off rather than acting aggressively in response to his anger. This sort of choice making is frequently the basis of "anger control" programs that have emerged in the field. One becomes aware of the steps toward violence through "stop action" in recitations of recent violent events or close calls. A man begins to describe the circumstances that preceded the violence and is periodically interrupted by a counselor to identify what he was thinking and feeling at that particular moment and what he might have thought or done instead. Another technique is to use anger logs in which a man monitors his own triggers by writing the event that set the process in motion, his perceptions at the time, how he might have reinterpreted the event, and so forth.

The trigger model presents a relatively mechanistic view of violence that can be redirected by redirecting our thinking. One of the challenges to this conception, however, is that much of the violence against women is quite deliberate and intended. Several studies of batterer accounts have noted justifications and rationalizations of the abuse and violence that appear to go beyond a series of poor choices (Ptacek, 1988). In fact, the effort to identify "triggers" and "provocations" may bring yet another rationalization: "If only she would not do that, I would not react." Moreover, the trigger model does not appear to address the underlying need for power and control that is used to typify many batterers. In fact, it may inadvertently play into the control. The man simply "controls" himself rather than "letting go" of the excessive sense of responsibility and privilege he may bear.

Wheel of Control

A third micro theory of violence is the power and control theory that sees men acting violently toward women as part of an underlying belief system. The beliefs hold men as entitled to get their way with women and women as subordinate to men. The socialization of men and the male-dominated structures of our society ingrain and perpetuate this belief system. The dynamics of abuse, from this standpoint, are portrayed more as a "wheel of control" rather than an escalating cycle (see Pence, 1989). The violence is merely an extension of a persistent pattern of controlling behaviors like intimidation, threats toward the children, limiting access to funds, and isolating the victim from relatives and friends. The violence, then, becomes part of a reign of terror that subjects and debilitates the woman.

Feminists have exposed the systematic oppression of women—sexual harassment, acquaintance rape, as well as battering, along with economic and political discrimination—that persists in insidious forms (Faludi, 1991). The evidence that a sexist belief system is fundamental to battering is inconclusive, however. Several studies employing sex role and "attitude toward women" measures have failed to show that batterers are more sexist than nonbatterers (Hotaling & Sugarman, 1986). These results may reflect various types of batterers or the prevalence of a sexist belief system that make the nonbatterers a poor comparison group. At least one comparative study, which used the TAT (Thematic Apperception Test) to assess power needs, showed batterers to have higher power needs than nonbatterers (Dutton & Strachan, 1987). Also, a recently developed measure of beliefs about wife abuse also has been shown to differentiate batterers (Saunders, 1987).

The principal implication of the power theory is that the belief system of batterers needs to be confronted and exposed. Some programs address this objective through sex role education and cognitive restructuring. Sex role education attempts to alert men to the messages they have learned about how to treat women from their fathers, from the media, and from the "locker room" they share with their peers. The most touted batterer program model, "the Duluth Model," employs a series of filmed vignettes and role-plays that present different scenarios of power and control and has men in a group discuss or act out alternative behaviors (Paymar & Pence, 1993). This approach receives the most favorable support from battered women advocates, because it holds men directly accountable for their battering rather than allowing them to deflect responsibility for the violence by attributing it to some emotional deficiency or thoughtlessness.

Program Structure

The approaches, formats, and structure of batterer programs vary considerably nationwide, as program surveys (Feazell, Mayers, & Deschner, 1984; Pirog-Good & Stets, 1985) and program descriptions (Caesar & Hamberger, 1989) indicate. Some of the variation is a reflection of the different micro theories discussed above. The curriculum of batterer counseling programs might be loosely categorized as anger management, skill building, or resocialization (see Adams, 1988, for further discussion). Anger control programs tend to follow the micro theory of the "the cycle of violence," whereas resocialization programs comply more with the "wheel of control" notion of violence. There are now several published treatment manuals that set forth these various curricula in detail (see Edleson & Tolman, 1992; Gondolf, 1985; Kivel, 1992; Paymar & Pence, 1993; Sonkin, Martin, & Walker, 1985; Stordeur & Stille, 1989).

Anger Management

Anger management programs, as the description suggests, focus on identifying the "provocations" that contribute to anger, "cues" that precede angry outbursts, and strategies, such as "time-outs," to interrupt the escalation toward battering (see Sonkin et al., 1985). Anger management is a principal component of the majority of programs, even when accompanied by components that deal with sex roles and nonviolence education. Many of its proponents believe that it offers some practical steps to avoid battering and also some quick results that can motivate an individual to change further.

The underlying assumption, in this approach, is that battering is anger driven rather than an outgrowth of a sense of male privilege and control. Intentionally or not, many batterers may, as a result, project their battering and avoid confronting its roots by thinking: "My anger made me do it!" Furthermore, men with a penchant for control see themselves as controlling one more thing, their anger, rather than letting go of some responsibility and entitlement. Anger management too easily becomes a "quick fix" in some men's minds, as well. With a few convenient gimmicks, they assert that they are "cured" while not having to substantially change the underlying dynamics of their relationships (Gondolf & Russell, 1986).

Skill Building

Skill-building programs offer a sequence of psychoeducational sessions that attempt to address the psychological deficits associated with batterers; they rely on instruction, exercises, and discussion to improve communication patterns, stress reduction, and sex role images, with better conflict management, assertiveness training, and cognitive restructuring (Hamberger & Hastings, 1988b; Stordeur & Stille, 1989). This curriculum usually includes components that teach the kinds, dynamics, and consequences of abuse as well. Again, there may be a secondary effect to this "treatment": Batterers might easily construe their violence as some sort of psychological problem that they need to "fix," like a mechanic tinkering with a car. In some cases, programs inadvertently create "nonviolent terrorists" who simply learn new ways to get their way as part of their "skills" acquisition.

Profeminist Resocialization

The programs that align themselves most expressly with battered women's concerns tend to focus on what might be termed *accountability* education, which attempts to confront men's tendency toward power and control (Adams, 1989; Paymar & Pence, 1993). A substantial portion of these programs is used to expose the range of abusive behaviors—put-downs, ridicule, withholding money, social isolation, intimidation, threatening children, and sexual abuse—all parts of "the wheel of control." Also, "cost-benefit analysis," "safety plans," and "control logs" are frequently employed to focus on the behavior in question and point to safer alternatives. *Cost-benefit analysis* refers to a group exercise identifying the gains from and consequences of violent behavior and of nonviolent behavior. Safety plans are outlines of strategies and procedures to avoid being abusive and violent. In control logs, batterers record instances in which they attempted to control their partners or spouses during the previous week. They identify as well the circumstances of those instances and how the men might have handled them differently.

These "profeminist" programs attend to group dynamics as well as individual denial and rationalization. One of the feminist concerns is that an inadvertent tolerance of abusive thinking is often present in batterer groups. The male bonding that emerges in intense group sessions too easily becomes collusion. Two things therefore become essential in profeminist programs. One is confrontation, much as is done in many drug programs, to challenge the deep-seated tendencies in our society to justify and excuse abuse of women and violence in general. Another essential is to provide for monitoring by battered women's advocates (Hart, 1988). Having the advocates observe and evaluate group sessions, contribute to curriculum development, and colead or speak at group sessions helps keep women's concerns at the center of batterer treatment.

There are, of course, some criticisms and reservations regarding this approach (see Gondolf, 1988c). Some see the profeminist programs as too "ideological," attempting to impose a worldview on a captive audience. Others contend they smack of male bashing and push many already defensive men away. Still another group of critics suggest this approach is naive to the part women play in their abuse and battering. From the feminist viewpoint, what is important is the outcome in terms of achieving safety and justice for women, not in terms of the man feeling better about himself.

Treatment Issues

Resistance and dropout. Two of the most difficult issues that face batterer counseling, regardless of approach, are resistance and dropout. There are increased efforts to confront the denial, self-pity, evasiveness, and rationalization associated with so many batterers. Denial may be checked with elaborate behavioral inventories or checklists that identify the full continuum of abusive behaviors. The results of the checklist are reviewed with a batterer to illustrate his abusiveness. Many counseling programs attempt to challenge the evasiveness or rationalizations by dissecting weekly behaviors and group participation in terms of their potential abusiveness. A participant in a counseling group recounts episodes with his partner, and group members evaluate the degree of control, manipulation, disregard, or subjection of another person in the episode.

Many programs attempt to foster a commitment to long-term change in an effort to check the high dropout rates from batterer counseling. Men are encouraged to develop alternative support groups, follow-up or complementary treatment, and active self-monitoring. Batterer programs are increasingly using a phased approach to treatment that corresponds with a developmental course of change (Fagan, 1989; Gondolf, 1987a): (a) an orientation or didactic phase that teaches men about the dynamics and extent of their abuse, (b) an issues phase that discusses the obstacles to change and how to deal with them, and (c) a support phase that attempts to reinforce and extend alternative behaviors (e.g., Stordeur & Stille, 1989). Admittedly, few men complete what is conceived as an 8- to 12-month program, but the phased approach conveys the message that treatment is a long-term process. Men are therefore less likely to assume they are "cured" through brief attendance or piecemeal accomplishments.

Men's pain. Several peripheral issues press at the momentum of batterer counseling as it has been described here. In recent years, there has been an increasing turn toward "helping" the batterer—that is, focusing treatment on the individual man rather than specifically confronting his behavior. This has been boosted by the rise of the mythic-poetic men's movement with Jungian roots. This popularized stream of thought is epitomized in recent best sellers like *Iron John* (Bly, 1990), *King, Warrior, Magician, Lover* (Moore & Gillette, 1990), and *Fire in the Belly* (Keen, 1991). Also, the personal growth movement, which extends into Adult Children of Alcoholics (ACOAs) work, has promoted shame as a prime factor in dysfunctional behavior. John Bradshaw's crusadelike TV and public lectures have, in fact, made *shame* a household word (Bradshaw, 1988).

Much of the new men's movement and accompanying "shame doctors" attribute abuse and battering to childhood trauma, absent fathers, and emasculation experienced in the modern work world. In this vein, men are victims, too, who bear debilitating shame. There is research to substantiate at least that batterers have disproportionately experienced abuse as children (Hotaling & Sugarman, 1986; Sugarman & Hotaling, 1989). Some batterer programs have consequently devoted more attention to "men's pain" associated with the batterers' own victimization (see Dutton, 1988; Waldo, 1987).

While emotional distress is undeniable in many men, its relationship to battering and its role in counseling are not clear. The popular assertion, within the mythic-poetic men's movement, that "wounded men wound others" may be only partially true. Men who are victimized do not necessarily batter their partners, and many wounded men who do batter have stopped battering without first healing their wounds. In fact, the limitations of intergenerational theories of violence, which echo the sentiment of the "wounded men" assertion, have been empirically demonstrated in the criminology field in general (Widom, 1989). Given the tendency to minimize, justify, or rationalize battering, batterers are likely to use "men's pain" as an excuse, diverting them from fully accepting responsibility for their battering. As is generally the case in alcohol treatment, the issues of victimization may best be addressed much later in batterer counseling.

Couples counseling. Perhaps the most intense controversy is over the appropriateness of couples counseling for domestic violence cases. As suggested above, the vast majority of programs already employ a psychoeducational approach in a group format, and a movement toward establishing statewide standards for court-mandated counseling currently opposes or limits couples counseling for batterers. There are, of course, some obvious practical reasons for this. Many battered women are reluctant to confront the batterer or be in counseling with him for fear of reprisals, and many batterers are openly opposed to couples counseling because of their denial and projection of blame (Bograd, 1984). If couples counseling is to be introduced, it may be best after successful completion of a batterer program and after at least 6-12 months of nonviolence. Couples counseling may, however, be ineffective and even dangerous with a substantial portion of batterers considered to be antisocial or sociopathic.

If couples counseling is not appropriate, what then should be the relationship of batterer counseling to battered women? Should a program obtain the woman's assessment of the abuse to offset denial and monitor the man's progress? Should a program contact the woman to assess her sense of safety and independence to evaluate "success"? While some programs actively use the woman's input and evaluation in the course of treatment, others strongly oppose it. "Partner contact," as it is frequently called, can too easily become surrogate couples counseling. Program staff are inadvertently put in the middle of the couple and react to the expectations of the two individuals. Furthermore, there is concern, as with couples counseling in general, that the woman may be placed at risk by sharing information about the batterer. The partner contact, according to some shelter advocates, may also divert the battered women's attention away from her own recovery toward the man's.

The answer may be to use women's shelter staff or battered women advocates to offer guiding input and focus, rather than the immediate victims. The specific details about a particular batterer may not be that necessary. Staff can generally assume that he has been abusive simply by his referral to the program. There are other means to confront his denial and elaborate his abuse, as discussed above, without involving the woman (see Hutchinson, 1987). In addition, batterer programs cannot do much about a woman's report of abuse. Carefully monitoring the man through partner contact may, in fact, create an illusion of safety. The best position for the woman may again be paradoxical: Advising her forthrightly that the program cannot assure her safety may prompt her to seek more substantial help and thus keep additional pressure on the man to change.

Toward Comprehensive Services

Program Outcome

No doubt, the question asked most of batterer programs is this: "What is your success rate?" The implication often is that the program outcome can be compressed into some "bottom line" intelligible to consumers—and investors. The reality is not that clear-cut and skepticism about the contribution of batterer counseling to women's safety may be warranted. The outcome of batterer programs remains somewhat elusive because of the difficulty in measuring "success," numerous methodological short-comings, and high subject attrition in follow-up studies (Gondolf, 1987b, 1987c). Two recent reviews of single-site outcome studies, nevertheless, point to a few tendencies worth noting (Eisikovits & Edleson, 1989; Tolman & Bennett, 1990).

The batterer program evaluations suggest that approximately 60% of program completers are not physically assaultive at a 6-month follow-up, according to victim reports (Tolman & Bennett, 1990). There is some indication, however, that most batterers (60%) are verbally threatening and abusive during this time period (Edleson & Syers, 1990; Tolman & Bhosley, 1990). Moreover, the "success rates" do not account for the high dropout rate of most programs that average around 50% over the course of a prescribed program (Demaris & Jackson, 1987; Gondolf, 1990a). One extended dropout study revealed that, out of 200 men who initially phoned a program, approximately 50 appeared for an intake interview, 25 participated in more than one counseling session, 12 completed 3 months, and 7 completed 6 months. Only 2 of the original 200 callers completed the entire 8-month program (Gondolf & Foster, 1991b).

Unfortunately, there has not been a controlled study that effectively compares different curriculum approaches and con-clusively indicates which approach is generally most effective in reducing battering and with what type of batterers. Analysis of controlled comparison studies in the mental health field suggests that program curriculums or approaches do not substantially differ in short-term outcomes (e.g., Wilner, Freeman, Surber, & Goldstein, 1985). These studies suggest that the significant fac-tors influencing outcome may be in the process of treatment rather than in the content. For instance, a coherent message of change, alternative role models, and social support are shown to be related to a positive outcome irrespective of treatment mo-dality. A controlled comparison study has, however, demon-strated that a didactic format is more effective in reducing recidivism than self-help or guided discussion, at least in the short term (Edleson & Syers, 1990).

Batterer programs must increasingly identify their limits for a number of reasons. There are some men being "dumped" on batterer programs who would be better served by incarcera-tion, psychiatric hospitalization, or residential alcohol and drug treatment—or some combination of these. Batterer counseling might be established as an adjunct to these facilities, as is yet another trend in the making. Moreover, refusing to treat some men may paradoxically help women. One of the strongest predictors of a woman returning to her batterer is the batterer being in counseling (Gondolf, 1988a). Counseling is too easily taken as a potential "cure" in our society, and women understandably tend to hold great hopes for it. Moreover, their batterers tend to expect congratulations and reconciliation for submitting to counseling: "I've gone to counseling, now you should take me back." Women are less likely to put down their guard or return to a dangerous man if he has refused counseling.

Integrating Services

Most program evaluations do not weigh the contribution of a variety of social factors that may be in operation. Additional police action, an impending divorce, and participation in Alcoholics Anonymous are just a few of the factors that may account for the "success" programs claim (Cocozzelli & Hudson, 1989). A noted study of formerly battered women, moreover, demonstrates that a constellation of formal and informal interventions are associated with the cessation of violence (Bowker, 1983). Formerly battered women reported that a variety of personal strategies, informal help sources, and formal interventions contributed to stopping the battering.

These considerations point to the need for greater coordination among community services (e.g., Brygger & Edleson, 1987). The batterer programs cannot and do not stop battering by themselves. There needs to be collaboration with the courts that assures the programs' right to refuse certain court referrals as well as decisive action for delinquent court-mandated batterers (e.g., Soler, 1987). Compatible mental health and alcohol and drug facilities also need to be identified. Unfortunately, research indicates that staff at these facilities tend to underidentify woman battering and not specifically address battering in treatment (Gondolf, 1990b; Gondolf & Foster, 1991a).

Even with the increased number of batterer programs, the number of batterers that actually attend a program is still dismally low, considering the number of battered women in shelters and the estimates of abuse in the community as a whole. Men who batter women are much more likely to present their problems as related to alcohol, stress, unemployment, or marital conflicts, given the ambiguous sanctions for battering. As discussed above, a variety of studies have shown that so-called generalists (Foster & Gondolf, 1989), medical practitioners (Kurz, 1990), psychiatric staff (Gondolf, 1990b), drug and alcohol counselors (Gondolf & Foster, 1991a), family counselors (Hansen et al., 1991), and social workers (Borkowski, Murch, & Walker, 1983) have systematically neglected domestic violence in clinical assessments and treatment. Consequently, there is a heightened effort to train human service professionals to better recognize and address battering. Individual and couples counselors are advised to use abuse inventories or screening tests, investigation of control and anger cues, and victim reports to help expose abusive behavior. Referral to established domestic violence programs, to help assure that the abusive behavior will be confronted and monitored, is urged as well. If such a program is not available for batterers, one might consider establishing at least a batterer group drawing on the number of training conferences and program manuals now available (e.g., Gondolf, 1985; Sonkin et al., 1985; Stordeur & Stille, 1989).

Cooperation with shelter and victim services can additionally help give women the opportunities they need to empower themselves: transitional housing, available transportation, child care, job training, and legal council contribute to a woman leaving a dangerous batterer and also contribute to a batterer's behavioral change (Gondolf & Fisher, 1988). Finally, batterer counseling programs might do more case management and "after-care" planning to promote men's participation in a variety of social supports that maintain and further their change. In sum, batterer programs need to be more conscious and attentive to the community and social context in a way that incorporates and activates a diversity of community sanctions, resources, and services. As feminists—who tend to see battering more as a sociological problem—have long argued, reorganization and restructuring of the social context are ultimately needed.

Conclusion

Our overview of the field suggests that batterers may not easily fall into a composite profile and that batterer counseling is not a unified venture. Batterer counseling is, moreover, far from a "cure-all" and sometimes even a disservice to battered women. But, with appropriate cautions and collaborations, batterer programs offer an additional support to the efforts to stop wife battering. In sum, batterer programs do have a contribution to make as one facet of an ever widening campaign against woman battering. In addition to reinforcing the individual efforts of some men to change their behavior, batterer counseling programs also present a visible symbol to the community that men can and should change.

They, moreover, provide a laboratory for improving and shaping the direction of things to come. But, as in any laboratory, precautions must be taken to avoid inordinate risks. One of the lingering risks is that batterer counseling programs will succumb unwittingly to the insidious backlash against women, mentioned at the outset. Some battered women advocates feel that more attention to psychopathology, men's pain, and couples counseling are already signs that this risk is a reality. Consequently, there is an increasing effort, led largely by battered women's advocates, to establish statewide standards for batterer programs—ones that assure some "quality control" and proper representation of victim concerns. These standards take various forms in a handful of states: as legislated standards for court referrals, policy guidelines for state funding, or program requirements for shelter referrals. The standards usually prescribe an assumption that the batterer is accountable for his violence as well as checks on victim blaming and projection, curriculum components for stopping the violent behavior and promoting safety, and a didactic group format for the batterers (see Gondolf, 1991). The potential regulation, of course, has its critics, but regulation of related fields like mental health treatment and drug and alcohol treatment—and even dieting programs—suggests that some standards for batterer programs may be a matter of "catching up" to the general demand for quality control.

In sum, the special topic of men who batter has increased efforts to characterize and treat batterers. The rapid development of batterer counseling programs carries with it a proliferation of profiles, theories, and programs. More awareness, knowledge, and resources about and for batterers exist. We can take heart from this progress. The challenge now becomes to increasingly integrate what we know about batterers into the mainstream of human services. Identification of batterers and collaborative interventions are needed from a variety of services. This all needs to be done, however, with the needs of battered women still at the forefront—and that takes effort amidst the momentum of other services and the climate of social backlash.

Note

1. This chapter focuses on men who physically assault their wives or female partners. There are, as Chapter 4 suggests, some cases in which the man is physically assaulted by the woman as part of what is often referred to as "mutual combat" (Deschner, 1984). Numerous studies, however, counter this notion by showing the difference in motive and severity. The violence that is reported by women is much more likely to be in self-defense and the violence by men is more than 5 times more likely to lead to injury (Saunders, 1986). The psychological impacts are different as well, with men more likely to dismiss the attacks from women as a nuisance rather than being terrified by them. Moreover, psychological and emotional abuse of women is admittedly related to battering but is addressed more specifically in other chapters. In this chapter, *battering* refers to physical assault and *abuse* refers to the collection of psychological abuse and battering inflicted on women.

References

Adams, D. (1988). Treatment models of men who batter: A pro-feminist analysis. In K. Ylö & M. Bograd (Eds.), *Feminist perspectives on wife abuse* (pp. 176-199). Newbury Park, CA: Sage.

Adams, D. (1989). Feminist-based interventions for battering men. In P. L. Caesar & L. K. Hamberger (Eds.), *Treating men who batter: Theory, practice, and programs* (pp. 3-23). New York: Springer.

Bly, R. (1990). *Iron John: A book about men.* Reading, MA: Addison-Wesley.

Bograd, M. (1984). Family systems approaches to wife battering: A feminist critique. *American Journal of Psychiatry, 31,* 129-137.

Borkowski, M., Murch, M., & Walker, V. (1983). *Marital violence: The community response.* New York: Tavistock.

Bowker, L. (1983). *Beating wife beating.* Lexington, MA: Lexington.

Bradshaw, J. (1988). *Healing the shame that binds you.* Deerfield Beach, FL: Health Communications.

Brygger, M. P., & Edleson, J. L. (1987). The domestic abuse project: A multi-systems intervention in woman battering. *Journal of Interpersonal Violence, 2,* 324-326.

Caesar, P. L., & Hamberger, L. K. (Eds.). (1989). *Treating men who batter: Theory, practice, and programs.* New York: Springer.

Cocozzelli, C., & Hudson, C. (1989). Recent advances in alcoholism diagnosis and treatment assessment research: Implications for practice. *Social Service Review, 37,* 533-552.

Demaris, A., & Jackson, J. D. (1987). Batterers' reports of recidivism after counseling. *Social Casework, 68,* 458-465.

Deschner, J. P. (1984). *The hitting habit.* New York: Free Press.

Dutton, D. G. (1984). An ecological nested theory of male violence toward intimates. In P. Caplan (Ed.), *Feminist psychology in transition.* Montreal: Eden.

Dutton, D. G. (1988). Profiling of wife assaulters: Preliminary evidence for a trimodal analysis. *Violence and Victims, 3,* 5-30.

Dutton, D., & Strachan, C. (1987). Motivational needs for power and spouse-specific assertiveness in assaultive and nonassaultive men. *Violence and Victims, 2,* 145-156.

Edleson, J. L., Eisikovits, Z. C., & Guttman, E. (1985). Men who batter women: A critical review of the evidence. *Journal of Family Issues, 6,* 229-247.

Edleson, J. L., & Syers, M. (1990). The relative effectiveness of group treatments for men who batter. *Social Work Research and Abstracts, 26,* 10-17.

Edleson, J. L., & Tolman, R. M. (1992). *Intervention for men who batter: An ecological approach.* Newbury Park, CA: Sage.

Eisikovits, Z. C., & Edleson, J. L. (1989). Intervening with men who batter: A critical review of the literature. *Social Service Review, 37,* 385-414.

Fagan, J. (1988). Contributions of family violence research to criminal justice policy on wife assault: Paradigms of science and social control. *Violence and Victims, 3,* 159-186.

Fagan, J. (1989). Cessation of family violence: Deterrence and dissuasion. In L. Ohlin & M. Tonry (Eds.), *Family violence* (pp. 377-426). Chicago: University of Chicago Press.

Faludi, S. (1991). *Backlash: The undeclared war against American women.* New York: Basic Books.

Feazell, C. S., Mayers, R., & Deschner, J. (1984). Services for men who batter: Implications for programs and policies. *Family Relations, 33,* 217-223.

Foster, R., & Gondolf, E. (1989). From social worker to batterer counselor. *Response, 12*(3), 3-5.

Gondolf, E. W. (1985). *Men who batter: An integrated approach to stopping wife abuse.* Holmes Beach, FL: Learning Publications.

Gondolf, E. W. (1987a). Changing men who batter: A developmental model of integrated interventions. *Journal of Family Violence, 2,* 345-369.

Gondolf, E. W. (1987b). Evaluating programs for men who batter: Problems and prospects. *Journal of Family Violence, 2,* 95-108.

Gondolf, E. W. (1987c). Seeing through smoke and mirrors: A guide to batterer program evaluations. *Response, 10,* 16-19.

Gondolf, E. W. (1988a). The effect of batterer counseling on shelter outcome. *Journal of Interpersonal Violence, 3,* 275-289.

Gondolf, E. W. (1988b). Who are those guys? Towards a behavioral typology of men who batter. *Violence and Victims, 3,* 187-203.

Gondolf, E. W. (1988c). The state of the debate: A review essay on woman battering. *Response, 11,* 3-8.

Gondolf, E. W. (1990a). An exploratory survey of court-mandated batterer programs. *Response, 13*(3), 7-11.

Gondolf, E. W. (1990b). *Psychiatric response to family violence: Identifying and confronting neglected danger.* Lexington, MA: Lexington.

Gondolf, E. W. (1991). A victim-based assessment of court-mandated counseling for batterers. *Criminal Justice Review, 16,* 214-226.

Gondolf, E. W. (1992). Discussion of violence in psychiatric evaluations. *Journal of Interpersonal Violence, 7,* 334-349.

Gondolf, E. W., & Fisher, E. R. (1988). *Battered women as survivors: An alternative to treating learned helplessness.* Lexington, MA: Lexington.

Gondolf, E. W., & Foster, R. A. (1991a). Wife assault among V.A. alcohol rehabilitation patients. *Hospital and Community Psychiatry, 21,* 17-79.

Gondolf, E. W., & Foster, R. A. (1991b). Preprogram attrition in batterer programs. *Journal of Family Violence, 6,* 337-349.

Gondolf, E. W., & Foster, R. A. (1993). *Batterer characteristics and disposition in a family violence court.* Unpublished manuscript.

Gondolf, E. W., & Russell, D. (1986). The case against anger control for batterers. *Response, 9*(3), 2-5.

Grusznski, R. J., & Carrillo, T. P. (1988). Who completes batterer's treatment groups? An empirical investigation. *Journal of Family Violence, 3,* 141-150.

Hamberger, L. K., & Hastings, J. E. (1988a). Characteristics of male spouse abusers consistent with personality disorders. *Hospital and Community Psychiatry, 39,* 763-770.

Hamberger, L. K., & Hastings, J. E. (1988b). Skills training for treatment of spouse abusers: An outcome study. *Journal of Family Violence, 3,* 121-130.

Hamberger, L. K., & Hastings, J. E. (1989). Counseling male spouse abusers: Characteristics of treatment completers and dropouts. *Violence and Victims, 4,* 275-286.

Hamberger, L. K., & Hastings, J. E. (1991). Personality correlates of men who batter and nonviolent men: Some continuities and discontinuities. *Journal of Family Violence, 6,* 131-148.

Hansen, M., Harway, M., & Cervantes, N. (1991). Therapists' perceptions of severity in cases of family violence. *Violence and Victims, 6,* 225-235.

Hart, B. (1988). *Safety for women: Monitoring batterers programs.* Harrisburg: Pennsylvania Coalition Against Domestic Violence.

Hotaling, G. T., & Sugarman, D. B. (1986). An analysis of risk markers in husband to wife violence: The current state of knowledge. *Violence and Victims, 1,* 101-124.

Hutchinson, E. D. (1987). Use of authority in direct social work practice with mandated clients. *Social Service Review, 37,* 580-598.

Katz, J. (1988). *Seductions of crime: Moral and sensual attractions in doing evil.* New York: Basic Books.

Keen, S. (1991). *Fire in the belly: On being a man.* New York: Bantam.

Kivel, P. (1992). *Men's work: How to stop the violence that tears our lives apart.* Center City, MN: Hazelden.

Kurz, D. (1990). Interventions with battered women in health care settings. *Violence and Victims, 5,* 243-256.

Levine, E. M. (1986). Sociocultural causes of family violence: A theoretical comment. *Journal of Family Violence, 1,* 3-12.

Martin, D. (1972). *Battered wives.* San Francisco: Glide.

McLeer, S. V., & Anwar, R. (1989). A study of battered women presenting in an emergency department. *American Journal of Public Health, 79,* 65-77.

McNulty, F. (1980). *The burning bed.* New York: Harcourt Brace Jovanovich.

Moore, R., & Gillette, D. (1990). *King, warrior, magician, lover: Rediscovering the archetypes of the mature masculine.* New York: Harper Collins.

Morgan, R. (1989). *The demon lover: On the sexuality of terrorism.* New York: Norton.

Paymar, M., & Pence, E. (1993). *Working with men who batter: The Duluth Model.* New York: Springer.

Pence, E. (1989). Batterer programs: Shifting from community collusion to community confrontation. In P. L. Caesar & L. K. Hamberger (Eds.), *Treating men who batter: Theory, practice, and programs* (pp. 24-51). New York: Springer.

Pirog-Good, M., & Stets, J. (1985). Male batterers and battering prevention programs: A national survey. *Response, 8,* 8-12.

Ptacek, J. (1988). Why do men batter their wives? In K. Yllö & M. Bograd (Eds.), *Feminist perspectives on wife abuse.* Newbury Park, CA: Sage.

Saunders, D. G. (1986). When battered women use violence: Husband-abuse or self defense? *Violence and Victims, 1,* 47-60.

Saunders, D. G. (1987). The inventory of beliefs about wife beating: The construction and initial validation of a measure of beliefs and attitudes. *Violence and Victims, 2,* 39-58.

Saunders, D. G. (1992). A typology of men who batter: Three types derived from cluster analysis. *American Journal of Orthopsychiatry, 62,* 264-275.

Schechter, S. (1982). *Women and male violence: The visions and struggles of the battered women's movement.* Boston: South End.

Scully, D., & Marolla, J. (1984). Convicted rapists' vocabulary of motive: Excuses and justifications. *Social Problems, 31,* 530-544.

Soler, E. (1987). Domestic violence is a crime: A case study of the San Francisco Family Violence Project. In D. J. Sonkin (Ed.), *Domestic violence on trial* (pp. 21-35). New York: Springer.

Sonkin, D. J. (1987). The assessment of court-mandated male batterers. In D. J. Sonkin (Ed.), *Domestic violence on trial* (pp. 174-196). New York: Springer.

Sonkin, D. J., Martin, D., & Walker, L. E. A. (1985). *The male batterer.* New York: Springer.

Stacey, W., & Shupe, A. (1983). *The family secret: Domestic violence in America.* Boston: Beacon.

Stoltenberg, J. (1989). *Refusing to be a man: Essays on sex and justice.* New York: Meridian.

Stordeur, R. A., & Stille, R. (1989). *Ending men's violence against their partners: One road to peace.* Newbury Park, CA: Sage.

Sugarman, D., & Hotaling, G. (1989). Violent men in intimate relationships: An analysis of risk markers. *Journal of Applied Social Psychology, 19,* 1034-1048.

Taubman, S. (1986). Beyond the bravado: Sex roles and the exploitive male. *Social Work, 31,* 12-18.

Tolman, R. M., & Bennett, L. W. (1990). A review of quantitative research on men who batter. *Journal of Interpersonal Violence, 5,* 87-118.

Tolman, R. M., & Bhosley, G. (1989). A comparison of two types of pregroup preparation for men who batter. *Journal of Social Science Research, 13,* 33-43.

Tolman, R. M., & Bhosley, G. (1990). The outcome of participation in a shelter-sponsored program for men who batter. In D. Knudsen & J. Miller (Eds.), *Abused and battered: Social and legal responses* (pp. 116-138). New York: Aldine de Gruyter.

Waldo, M. (1987). Also victims: Understanding and treating men arrested for spouse abuse. *Journal of Counseling and Development, 65,* 385-388.

Walker, L. (1979). *The battered woman.* New York: Harper.

Walker, L. (1983). *The battered woman syndrome.* New York: Springer.

Widom, C. S. (1989). Does violence beget violence? A critical examination of the literature. *Psychological Bulletin, 106,* 3-28.

Wilner, D. M., Freeman, H. E., Surber, M., & Goldstein, M. S. (1985). Success in mental health treatment interventions: A review of 211 random assignment studies. *Journal of Social Service Research, 8,* 1-21.

CHAPTER 11

What Can Be Done to Prevent Child Maltreatment?

DONNA HARRINGTON

HOWARD DUBOWITZ

Interest in preventing child maltreatment has been increasing. Research findings indicate that maltreatment is related to harmful and expensive outcomes, including physical and emotional harm, the intergenerational transmission of abusive behavior (Kaufman & Zigler, 1989), and delinquency (Starr, MacLean, & Keating, 1991). Therefore it may be cost- effective to prevent maltreatment (Daro, 1988). The most compelling reason, however, is humanitarian: We can, and therefore should, attempt to avoid or diminish the potential suffering of children (Schorr, 1988).

The prevention of child maltreatment has been difficult for at least three reasons. First, the political will to prioritize the needs of children and families has been lacking (National Commission on Children, 1991). Many of the programs that have been found to help high risk families, such as Head Start and the Special Supplemental Food Program for Women, Infants, and Children (WIC), do not have sufficient funding to serve more than approximately half of eligible families (National Commission on Children, 1991). Second, it has been difficult to develop prevention programs because of limited information about the causes of child maltreatment. Without knowledge of the causes, it is difficult to know where or how to intervene. Third, there has been relatively little evaluation research on prevention programs (Dubowitz, 1987; Helfer, 1982).

Child maltreatment is thought to be the result of multiple interacting factors. The ecological theory of child maltreatment (Belsky, 1980) provides a useful framework for examining prevention efforts, integrating what is known of factors contributing to child maltreatment. This chapter examines some of the main factors that have been found to be related to child maltreatment and how they are being addressed. In addition, strategies that appear useful are suggested. This review cannot cover the full array of interventions but presents examples of prevention and early intervention programs. Schorr (1988), Simmons (1986), and the Massachusetts Committee for Children and Youth (1987) provide more detailed descriptions of prevention programs.

Prevention efforts for child sexual abuse are typically quite different than those aimed at other forms of child maltreatment and are not included in this review. Berrick and Gilbert (1991) and Fogarty and Conte (1991) have recently reviewed the literature on the prevention of child sexual abuse.

Types of Prevention

Prevention efforts occur at three levels (Dubowitz, 1990; Helfer, 1982; Newman & Lutzker, 1990). *Primary* prevention targets the general population such as public service announcements ecouraging parents to call a hot line if they feel they might lose control with their children. *Secondary* prevention is directed at groups thought to be at high risk for child maltreatment, such as home visiting programs for young unmarried mothers (e.g., Olds, Henderson, Chamberlin, & Tatelbaum, 1986). *Tertiary* prevention takes place after the abuse condition has occurred. In 1964, Caplan transferred this three-tier public health prevention model to the field of mental health. In the years since 1964, this model has been revised to efforts at the first tier (primary prevention). Primary prevention uses interventions aimed at groups that attempt to promote their health and eliminate or reduce their distress. Those interventions can be grouped into four categories. They are interventions that *educate,* that *promote social competency* (i.e., to increase feelings of self-worth, belonging, and community contribution), that encourage *social change* and increase *social networks* (Albee & Gullotta, 1986; Gullotta, 1987).

The Ecological Theory of Child Maltreatment

To understand and prevent child maltreatment, the entire context in which it occurs must be considered. Child maltreatment is not committed by a parent in isolation, independent of the parent's past experiences and current circumstances. Rather, child maltreatment is the product of factors within the individual parent, the family (including the child), the community, and the culture or society (Belsky, 1980). All four of these levels may contribute to the occurrence of child maltreatment.

Factors influencing the occurrence of maltreatment at the *individual* level include a person's characteristics and past experience. Abusive as compared with nonabusive parents tend to be more depressed and have more health problems (Wolfe, 1984). When people become parents, their personal histories influence the type of parents they will be. The type of parenting they themselves received provides a model for their new role as parents. There is a widely held belief that many abusive parents were themselves abused as children (Egeland, Jacobvitz, & Sroufe, 1988; Kaufman & Zigler, 1989; Main & Goldwyn, 1984), although many abused children do *not* necessarily become abusive parents. In her prospective study Widom (1989) found that adults who had been maltreated as children were *not* more likely to abuse their own children than adults who had not been previously maltreated. Therefore, whether or not people who were abused as children are more likely to be abusive parents, it is possible that many abused children will grow up to be adequate or good parents. The ecological theory suggests that other factors, such as social support, may influence how abused individuals will consequently treat their own children.

Parents function within a family. The *family* level of the ecological theory includes parents, children, grandparents, and other extended family members. The relationship between parents and children has been thought to be influenced by the traits of the parent (e.g., impulsiveness) and child (e.g., difficult temperament) that may contribute to the occurrence of maltreatment (Belsky, 1980). Two recent studies did not, however, find a relationship between child characteristics and maltreatment. Dodge, Bates, and Pettit (1990) examined a sample of 309 children and found that child temperament, as reported by parents, and health problems were not related to physical abuse. In home observations of 123 children with conduct problems, Whipple and Webster-Stratton (1991) found no differences in behavior between abused and nonabused children. These two studies suggest that child characteristics do not contribute significantly toward child maltreatment. Even if child characteristics do not have a direct effect, however, they may interact with parent characteristics, such as a child with a difficult temperament and parents with little patience; indirectly, this may influence the parent-child relationship, and parenting, and lead to child maltreatment.

The relationship between parents and children may also be influenced by other members of the family (Belsky, 1980). For example, the mother-child interaction may be influenced by the mother-father relationship. Because it may be easier to lash out at a child, parents may redirect their anger with each other toward the child. In contrast, a supportive grandparent can be a valuable buffer against the stresses a family is experiencing.

The family functions within the larger context of the *community.* The community influences maltreatment through work conditions, community resources, formal and informal social supports, or the lack thereof, and by providing role models for parents (Belsky, 1980).

Maltreating families are often socially isolated (Belsky, 1980; Garbarino, 1980; Polansky, Chalmers, Williams, & Buttenwieser, 1981), and this may be related to maltreatment in two ways. First, the family might not receive material and emotional support from the community (Garbarino, 1980). Second, contact with others in the community can provide role models for acceptable parental behavior and influence parents to conform to these standards. Isolated families may not have positive role models.

The *culture* within which the community resides is the fourth level in the ecological theory. Culture influences the occurrence of maltreatment through its "attitudes toward violence, corporal punishment, and children" (Belsky, 1980, p. 328; Garbarino, 1980). In the United States, violence is widely accepted, as evidenced by the amount of violence in television programming and the acceptance of physical punishment for disciplining children, including the legal use of corporal punishment by schools in many states (Holmes, 1987).

Ecological theory suggests that maltreatment is determined by some or all of the factors discussed above interacting with each other (Belsky, 1980). Some of these factors are difficult to change, such as parents' past experiences, although therapy might enable recovery from maltreatment. Many factors can be changed, however, and these are the focus of this chapter.

An understanding of the factors contributing to maltreatment is necessary for designing and implementing prevention and early intervention programs. While research on the etiology of child maltreatment has been limited by many methodological issues (Rosenberg & Reppucci, 1985), the ecological theory is widely accepted in the field of child maltreatment. Nevertheless, in many areas, our understanding of the roles of various contributing factors remains limited. For example, we still are uncertain exactly how poverty leads to child maltreatment.

Ecological theory is also useful because it suggests resources that may assist potentially maltreating families. For example, the availability of extended family members and social support from the neighborhood may be related to positive outcomes. Efforts may be directed at any or all of the four levels of the ecological theory. Ideally, interventions should be comprehensive and address as many underlying risk factors as possible. This may not be essential, however; for example, giving a mother antidepressants might enable her to cope better with difficult circumstances while the contributory stresses remain.

Prevention and
Early Intervention Strategies

Many families are routinely challenged by circumstances that make it difficult to adequately care for children and that have been associated with child maltreatment. As discussed below, poverty, unemployment, lack of support for families and working parents, lack of health care, poor nutrition, substance abuse, and society's acceptance of violence are all related to child maltreatment. Examples of the current efforts aimed at each of these factors, as well as additional interventions that may be useful, will be discussed.

Poverty and Unemployment

The problem. Poverty and unemployment have been associated with maltreatment (Dodge et al., 1990; Gelles, 1989; Halpern, 1990; Volpe, 1989). Currently, 1 in 5 children in the United States live in poverty (National Commission on Children, 1991); *half* of black children under 6 live in poverty (National Center for Children in Poverty, 1991). Not all families living in poverty have an unemployed or single head of household; a mother working full-time at a minimum wage job may not earn enough to keep herself and a single child above the poverty line (National Commission on Children, 1991). Poverty, per se, constitutes a form of maltreatment (e.g., environmental hazards such as lead, inferior educational opportunities, and inadequate food and shelter) by directly and indirectly harming the health and well-being of children. Poverty has been thought to burden a family with a variety of stresses (e.g., housing problems) that contribute to abuse (Halpern, 1990; Volpe, 1989). Any strategy to prevent child maltreatment needs to address the problem of poverty.

Studies of the incidence and prevalence of child maltreatment have consistently found the involvement of a disproportionately high number of low income families, including a study based on parents' self-reports of how they resolve conflicts in their families (Straus, Gelles, & Steinmetz, 1988). It is also evident, however, that many poor people are very good parents.

Gelles (1989) examined the effects of parent absence and economic deprivation in more than 6,000 households. He found children from single-parent households were more likely to be abused than those from two-parent households. It was the poverty of families headed by a single mother, however, that was more strongly associated with abuse than was single parenthood.

Prevention efforts have primarily focused on problematic parental behavior as the cause of child maltreatment. Less attention has been given to broader aspects of society that harm children, where responsibility or culpability is more difficult to pinpoint (e.g., poverty).

Current strategies. Several programs are designed to reduce the impact of poverty, including Aid to Families with Dependent

Children (AFDC), Special Supplemental Food Program for Women, Infants, and Children (WIC), food stamps, school lunch and breakfast, and medical assistance. Although these programs were not designed to prevent child maltreatment, they provide crucial assistance to low income families and thus support the functioning of these families. Many eligible families do not, however, receive these benefits. Further, for many other families, the benefits they receive are inadequate.

A study by Barth (1989) evaluated a task-oriented prevention program: 97 women at high risk for child maltreatment were recruited while pregnant. Each mother was provided with a parent aide who provided in-home services. The mothers helped identify various goals, such as contacting community service agencies, taking care of themselves and their children, and providing food. Barth found that the mother's achievement of these goals was associated with reduced scores on the Child Abuse Potential Inventory (Milner, 1980, cited in Barth, 1989), but the amount of contact between parent aides and mothers did not make a difference. Although this intervention was not designed to reduce poverty, many of the tasks helped reduce the impact of poverty, such as contacting community agencies for assistance and food. Barth cautions that this intervention was not effective for the highest risk families.

This study has several methodological limitations. First, accomplishment of tasks was rated by the parent aides and therefore may have been biased. Second, a comparison group of mothers not receiving the intervention was not included. Third, the potential for child abuse, rather than actual abuse, was measured; therefore it is unknown whether the intervention really reduced maltreatment rates. Nevertheless, Barth's findings suggest that parent aides using a task-oriented approach may be effective. Additional research in this area is needed.

Recommended strategies. Poverty is a complex problem for which there is no simple solution. Several aspects of poverty are amenable to change, however, such as increasing the availability of low income housing, reducing unemployment, and improving the minimum wage and benefits for those who are employed. Funding for programs that provide crucial support to low income families, such as Head Start, WIC, Food Stamps, and Medical Assistance, should be increased so that all eligible families can receive these services or benefits. Fuchs and Reklis (1992) suggest that children could be helped by child allowances and tax credits provided by the government. Reducing poverty should substantially reduce the incidence of child maltreatment (Olds & Henderson, 1989; Wolock & Horowitz, 1984).

In addition to providing increased benefits to more families, several other factors should be addressed. Federal programs, such as the Job Opportunities and Basic Skills Training Program, should be expanded to serve more families (National Commission on Children, 1991). There also could be more emphasis placed on encouraging adolescents to remain in school and providing them with basic job skills.

Support for Working Parents

The problem. Several factors make it difficult for many parents to maintain jobs that can financially support their families. Child care is needed by all families with young children and a working single parent or two working parents. Good quality child care is often unavailable for several reasons. First, the quality of child care is often poor or variable. Second, child-care providers are greatly undervalued in this society. Potentially good providers may not enter or stay in the field because of limited recognition and remuneration of their work. Third, good child care is relatively expensive. If good and affordable child care is not available, parents may be unable to work or may leave their children in marginal or inadequate arrangements; child neglect and abuse are possible concerns.

Part-time, flexible employment opportunities, parental leave for new babies or family illnesses, and adequate basic benefits, such as health coverage, are not available for many parents. Working parents without access to these benefits face increased stress and financial hardship as they try to provide for their families. As mentioned earlier, the current minimum wage is frequently inadequate to support even a single child.

Public policies, such as those concerning parental leave, influence the fundamental relationships within families. Policies that do not allow parents to spend time with newborn children may interfere with bonding. Bonding leads to a process of attachment between the infant and parent. Many child development specialists believe that the time soon after birth is especially important for bonding between parents and children (White, 1985). Secure attachment in turn is important for developing a sense of security and an ability to trust others. Maltreated children have been found to be less securely attached to their parents than nonmaltreated children (Egeland & Sroufe, 1981).

Current strategies. Recently, several public policy changes have enhanced support for families. The minimum wage has been increased. The new Federal Child Care and Development Block Grant will provide money for states to provide "low- and moderate-income families [with] increased access to affordable care" and improved referral and resource systems (Children's Defense Fund, 1991). In addition, corporations have been showing more sensitivity to the needs of families, such as the increased availability of child-care facilities at work sites. The Family and Medical Leave Act providing up to 12 weeks of unpaid leave per year for parents of a new infant or in the event of illness of a family member has recently been signed into law by President Clinton.

Recommended strategies. A new baby requires an adjustment by the family and this may be stressful. Parents may be overwhelmed with their new roles and this transition could be enhanced by providing them with pregnancy/family leave. Ideally, this leave would be at least partially paid and jobs would be protected.

The quality and availability of child care could be improved in several ways. First, to ensure good quality child care, standards should be established by the federal government. Second, salaries for child-care providers should be increased. Third, employers and governments need to subsidize child care. Fourth, flexible work schedules could also help some families obtain child care.

Health Care

The problem. Recent estimates indicate that almost 11 million children, or 16.9%, have no health insurance, or their insurance status was unknown (Children's Defense Fund, 1991). The problem is most prevalent among low income and minority families. For example, only 62% of children in African American families earning less than 200% of the federal poverty level were insured.

Access to and use of health care are clearly linked to insurance status. In 1988, 92% of insured children had a regular source of health care compared with only 79% of those without insurance.

Adequate prenatal care and health of the mother are also important for the health of a newborn child. More than 9 million women of childbearing age had no insurance in 1985, and another 5 million lacked maternity benefits (Children's Defense Fund, 1991). Again, minority and low income women were most likely to be uninsured. Being employed does not always assure health benefits; among women of childbearing age, 9% of those working full-time and 20% of women working part-time were not insured (Alan Guttmacher Institute, 1987). Of note, health insurance hardly guarantees health care. It has been estimated that more than 20 million women of childbearing age and children live in medically underserved areas (National Association of Community Health Centers, 1991).

Limited access to health care is compounded by the increased health problems confronting those least likely to be insured. Consequently, many families are at high risk for poor health, which can further stress the functioning of these families. For example, the poor health of a child increases the demands on parents who might be unable to obtain health care and pay for necessary medications. Important health care needs might be neglected, and, more indirectly, other forms of maltreatment might occur (Sherrod, O'Connor, Vietze, & Altemeier, 1984).

Current strategies. A number of recent reforms in the Medicaid program should substantially expand the availability of health care to children in low income families. For example, states are now required to cover all pregnant mothers and children under 6 with family incomes below 133% of the federal poverty level (Omnibus Budget Reconciliation Act, 1989); states are mandated to phase in coverage of children between 6 and 19 years of age in families with incomes less than 100% of the federal poverty level (Omnibus Budget Reconciliation Act, 1990); and states have the option to cover pregnant women and infants under 1 with family incomes below 185% of the federal poverty level (Omnibus Budget Reconciliation Act, 1987). Fully implemented, these reforms would extend Medicaid coverage to an additional half-million pregnant women and 4 million children.

Concerned with the spiraling costs of health care, there has been considerable national debate on the need to reform the health care system. Although there is an emerging consensus on the need to ensure universal health care, there is little agreement as to how this should be achieved. For example, the National Commission on Children (1991) majority recommendations included development of community-based health programs, a "universal system of health insurance coverage for pregnant women and for children through age 18" (p. xxiii), increased volunteer efforts from health and other professionals, and the expansion of federal and state health care programs. A minority of members felt, however, that these recommendations would be "inflationary, result in substantial job losses or reduced wages, and encourage discrimination against employees with families" (p. xxv) and recommended against increased funding of federal and state health care programs. Instead, they suggested that primary responsibility for health care resides with the individual, and insurance could be obtained through employer-employee negotiations and a "private-public partnership."

Recommended strategies. Universal health care for children and pregnant women, among others, should be a major priority for the federal government. A comprehensive system of health care delivery, based on the principle that health care is a right rather than a privilege, is needed to prevent the many gaps that now exist. A detailed approach to this complex problem is beyond the scope of this chapter.

There are a number of additional measures that would partially alleviate the current crisis. Increased support to the National Health Services Corps would enhance care in medically underserved areas. In addition, the Title V Maternal and Child Health Services Block Grant, which helps states develop health services for low income women and children and children with special health care needs, should be increased as should the federal Childhood Immunization program.

Nutrition

The problem. Adequate nutrition is crucial, particularly for pregnant women and children. Poor nutrition compromises the potential growth and development of children. Maternal nutritional status during pregnancy is related to birth weight, which is related to later social and developmental functioning (Parker, Greer, & Zuckerman, 1988). Malnutrition can lead to stunted growth and poor health and developmental outcomes (Frank & Zeisel, 1988).

Current strategies. WIC provides nutritional supplements to approximately half of eligible families nationwide (U.S. House of Representatives, 1989). School lunch and breakfast programs also supplement children's diets; however, they are not available for large numbers of eligible families (National Commission on Children, 1991). The food stamps program provides a maximum of $300 per month for a family of four (in 1989); however, 30% of a family's income is expected to be used for food; therefore many families do not receive the maximum benefit of $300 (U.S. House of Representatives, 1989). Even families that receive all of these food benefits might still have hungry children. A recent study in Massachusetts found that the combined benefits enabled families to obtain approximately two thirds of their food requirements (Wiecha & Palombo, 1989).

Recommended strategies. There are several ways to improve the nutritional status of women and children. As the National Commission on Children (1991) suggested, the WIC program should be expanded to reach all eligible families. Similarly, the Food Stamp and School Breakfast and School Lunch programs should be expanded. In addition, schools should provide nutritional education for students, to improve their knowledge of nutrition and eating habits.

Increased Family Support Services

The problem. Being a parent can be difficult and often requires support. The factors discussed above are among the difficulties faced by many parents. Parents who have been maltreated as children may need help and support so that they do not maltreat their own children (Egeland, Jacobvitz, & Sroufe, 1988; Kaufman & Zigler, 1989). Poverty is a major obstacle to obtaining adequate food, shelter, and health care. Although research findings have been mixed, parental lack of knowledge concerning child development may also contribute to child maltreatment (Taylor & Beauchamp, 1988). In addition, a lack of alternative child care means that stressed parents may have little time to themselves, without respite from the demands of parenting. Consequently, angry, impulsive behavior or neglect of children's needs might arise.

Current strategies. Several recent studies have examined programs offering support for parents; these include small group meetings, extensive psychotherapy, and home visiting programs. Egeland et al. (1988) studied mothers who reported being maltreated as children. These mothers were divided into two groups: those who had abused their children and those who had not. The mothers who did not abuse their own children were more likely than the others to report having had a "supportive relationship with some adult in their own childhood and having undergone extensive therapy" (p. 1085). These findings suggest that therapeutic services for maltreated children and the availability of a supportive parent or adult may reduce future maltreatment.

Several studies suggest that home visiting may be effective in reducing the incidence of child maltreatment. Olds, Henderson, Chamberlin, and Tatelbaum (1986) conducted a randomized study of home visitation designed "to prevent a wide range of childhood health and developmental problems, including child abuse and neglect" (p. 66). Women who were pregnant for the first time could participate in the study; in addition, young (less than 19 years), single, and low income women were actively recruited. Women were enrolled into the study prior to the 30th week of pregnancy and were randomly assigned to one of four interventions. Children in one group received developmental screenings at 1 and 2 years of age, and those with problems were referred for intervention. Families in the second group received the screening provided to the first group as well as transportation for prenatal and well-child care. Families in the third group received the transportation and screening services as well as an average of 9 nurse home visits during pregnancy. Families in the fourth group received the services provided to the third group as well as nurse home visits until the child was 2 years old. The postnatal visits focused on infant development education, informal support, and health and human services linkages. It should be noted that all families could have obtained standard prenatal care and pediatric primary care, aside from the intervention.

The children of poor, unmarried teenagers were considered to be at greatest risk for child maltreatment. Of these highest risk children, 19% of the group receiving developmental screening only were abused or neglected compared with 4% of the group who received the most comprehensive services. There were also several related differences between these two groups. Compared with the developmental-screening-only group, the latter group of mothers reported that their infants were happier and less irritable; the mothers were more concerned about their children's behavior problems; they had more positive interactions with their children and more toys available; and there was a trend toward higher developmental scores in their infants. In general, among the highest risk mothers, those who received the most comprehensive intervention appeared to be functioning significantly better as parents than the mothers whose children received developmental screenings only (Olds et al , 1986).

Unlike the Olds et al. study, the Good Start Project has found that families at moderate risk of child maltreatment are most amenable to improvement with a variety of services, including developmental assessments, counseling, medical care, social advocacy, and parent-child enrichment sessions in both clinic and home settings (Ayoub & Jacewitz, 1982; Kowal et al., 1989; Willett, Ayoub, & Robinson, 1991). Certain types of problems were more amenable to change than others. For example, more than half the families showed improvement in the areas of parent-child interaction during play, communication, and encouragement of the child. Little improvement was achieved with families that initially had problems with discipline, difficult child behavior, learning disabled children, or parent-child conflict. Less than 7% of the families with substance abuse problems improved (Kowal et al., 1989). The findings of the Good Start Project are limited by at least two methodological problems. First, the ratings of family functioning were made by the interventionists working with the family. Second, no comparison group was studied. This project does, however, provide an example of how a variety of services can be integrated to support families.

Another study of home visiting was done in Hawaii (Amundson, 1989). The Family Crisis Care (FCC) project, based on the

Homebuilders model, was designed to serve "families at immi-nent risk of child placement out of the home for child abuse and neglect" (p. 286). The FCC was a tertiary prevention program for families identified for child maltreatment, providing inten-sive services in three phases. The first phase was intensive crisis intervention over 6 weeks, during which time problems and goals were identified and families were referred for appropriate services. The second phase was 2 to 6 weeks of regular in-home visits by therapists with master's degrees. Families were pro-vided with support and concrete services, such as food, cloth-ing, and shelter. The third phase was 4 to 12 weeks of follow-up services including therapy and assistance obtaining services from community agencies; the therapists were on call 24 hours a day.

Of the 42 families followed for 6 months after treatment, 90% of the families that received services were able to keep their children at home, avoiding out-of-home placement. Communica-tion and problem-solving skills, as rated by the therapists, were improved for 80% of the families; 95% of the families had reduced rates of physical punishment and other problem behav-iors. Further, 85% of the families had used suggested community resources (Amundson, 1989). Amundson concluded that "home-based, intensive services delivered by interdisciplinary cother-apists are an effective alternative to out-of-home placement for many abused children" (p. 295). The findings of this study, however, are limited by the lack of a comparison group, making it difficult to assess how the families might have done without intervention.

In another study, 32 first-time mothers over the age of 18 participated in a hospital-based primary prevention program that addressed parenting skills, mother-infant interaction, child-rearing attitudes, and knowledge of child development (Taylor & Beauchamp, 1988). Half of the women were randomly as-signed to receive a home visitor/parent aide and the other half received standard postnatal hospital services. The student nurse home visitors met with the mothers in the hospital and in their homes at 1, 2, and 3 weeks postpartum. The women who met with the home visitors displayed more knowledge of children's per-sonal-social and physical-motor development, reported a more appropriate attitude toward child discipline, provided more verbal stimulation of their infants, were more sensitive and reciprocal in their interactions with their infants, and had improved problem-solving abilities. These outcomes were assessed by independent ratings of videotaped behavior and self-report (Taylor & Beauchamp, 1988). No assessment of child maltreatment was made.

Taylor and Beauchamp's (1988) sample size was small and the follow-up was at 3 months. This study did, however, include random assignment to comparison and intervention groups and employed independent ratings of behavior. This study suggests that changes in mothers' parenting knowledge, attitudes, and behavior can be improved, at least in the short term, with a relatively brief (four 90-minute visits) intervention.

Parenting education has also been effectively provided in a group setting. Thirty families with children involved with protective services were randomly assigned to two groups (Wolfe, Edwards, Manion, & Koverola, 1988). Half the families participated in an informational group that met for 2 hours twice a week for an average of 18 weeks; there were informal discussions on family and health-related topics and social activities. The other half of the families attended these group meetings and received additional training in child management skills, including videotaped sessions of mother-child interactions allowing the mothers to critique their own behavior. Training lasted an average of 20 weeks.

At the 3-month follow-up, the mothers who received the additional training reported less intense and fewer child behavior and adjustment problems than did the women who received the more limited intervention (Wolfe et al., 1988). Direct observation using the Home Observation for Measurement of the Environment (HOME), however, did not reveal significant differences between the two groups. Wolfe et al. concluded that the combination of training in child management techniques and family support can address the needs of families at risk for child maltreatment. This conclusion is uncertain, however, given that the differences were only found with parental self-report and not by more objective, direct observation.

Recommended strategies. These studies suggest that home visiting may be effective primary prevention and early intervention strategies for reducing child maltreatment, particularly for certain types of families, such as poor, unmarried first-time teen mothers (Olds & Henderson, 1989) or families with young children (Nelson, Landsman, & Deutelbaum, 1990). Home visiting might be effective in that it assists families at several levels (of the ecological theory). At the individual level, the home visitor can provide support and counseling and model good parenting approaches. At the family level, the involvement of extended family members in the care of a child might be enhanced. At the community level, the home visitor can make suitable referrals, helping the family obtain assistance from local resources. While not all studies have found home visitors to be effective (U.S. General Accounting Office, 1990), overall, home visiting appears to be a promising strategy for serving high risk families and preventing child abuse and neglect (Cohn Donnelly, 1991; Garbarino, 1986).

Substance Abuse Treatment

The problem. Based on a review of the literature on prenatal drug exposure and the National Institute of Drug Abuse's 1990 household survey, Gomby and Shiono (1991) estimate that nationally 2%-3% of newborns are cocaine exposed, 3%-12% are marijuana exposed, and 0.3%-4% are opiate exposed; many newborns have been exposed to more than one drug. Reddick and Goodwin (1991) estimate that illicit drugs are being used by 11% of all pregnant women. Another study found 73% of women drank alcohol during pregnancy, with 3%-4% drinking excessive amounts of alcohol (Gomby & Shiono, 1991).

Drug use during pregnancy can be associated with low birth weight, impaired fetal growth, microcephaly, lethargy, poor responsivity, irritability, abnormal reflexes, and poor muscle tone (Deren, 1986; Zuckerman, 1991) as well as prematurity, developmental delay, and child maltreatment (Deren, 1986; Merrick, 1985). In addition, parents who abuse alcohol or drugs may be substantially impaired in their parenting ability. It is estimated that 30%-90% of all substantiated child maltreatment reports involve families with some degree of adult alcohol or drug abuse (McCullough, 1991). In a study of 78 families with an alcohol- or drug-addicted parent, Mayer and Black (1977) found 13% had physically abused a child, 31% reported angry, impulsive behavior indicative of a high potential for abuse, and 63% were identified as high risk for problems in parenting.

Current strategies. The Institute of Medicine Committee on Substance Abuse Treatment found that drug treatment is needed for approximately 105,000 pregnant women each year; of these, only about 30,000 receive any treatment (Kumpfer, 1991). The special needs of pregnant women, and women with children, are very seldom addressed by treatment programs (Kumpfer, 1991). A 1989 survey found that two thirds of the hospitals in 15 cities did not have a place to refer pregnant addicts for treatment (Kumpfer, 1991). In the child welfare system, the fastest growing foster care population is that of drug-exposed infants and children of alcohol- or drug-addicted parents, further overwhelming an already stressed system (McCullough, 1991).

Recommended strategies. Deren (1986) suggests that pregnant women may be more likely to seek treatment for their addiction because of concern for the fetus. Substance abuse needs to be addressed through a variety of strategies. Primary prevention should be occurring in the schools, through public service announcements, and as a part of routine health care services, especially in obstetric clinics. In addition, greater efforts are needed to address the underlying factors that contribute to substance abuse. Screening measures need to be developed so that secondary prevention can target those at high risk. The availability of all types of substance abuse treatment programs, including outpatient and residential programs with child-care facilities, needs to be greatly expanded, especially for pregnant women.

Societal Attitudes Toward Violence

The problem. As a society, the United States sanctions the use of physical punishment of children (Belsky, 1980; Helfer, 1982; Stein, 1984). Hitting children is still allowed in schools in 28 states (National Child Abuse Coalition, 1991). Teachers are considered to be experts in understanding and teaching children. When they hit children, this serves as a negative role model for parents. Belsky suggests that maltreatment may occur as an escalation of "acceptable" levels of physical punishment. The message often communicated to parents is that it is all right to hit children, as long as no bruises are left. As a society, our attitudes toward the physical punishment of children need to change (Belsky, 1980; Helfer, 1982; Stein, 1984). There are many more effective ways than physical punishment to teach and socialize children.

Current strategies. A bill recently has been introduced in the U.S. Congress that would prohibit the use of "corporal punishment in any school receiving federal funds" (National Child Abuse Coalition, 1991, p. 3). Also currently, at the state level (e.g., Maryland), child advocacy groups and legislative efforts are aiming to prohibit corporal punishment in schools. In many states that still allow corporal punishment, individual counties and cities have banned the practice.

Recommended strategies. Teachers and schools should set an example by rejecting the use of corporal punishment, using preferable forms of discipline and teaching parents how to effectively deal with problem behaviors without using physical punishment. A long-term goal is the prohibition against hitting children *anywhere,* including at home.

Conclusion

Child maltreatment is associated with risk factors at each level of the ecological theory: for example, poor parenting skills at the individual level, conflict between parents at the family level, social isolation at the community level, and acceptance of hitting children at the societal level. In many cases, maltreatment is the result of the interaction of factors at various levels. Clearly, the problem of child maltreatment needs to be addressed through a variety of prevention strategies; no single approach will be sufficient.

Examination of the development of the field of child maltreatment over the past decade suggests that several advances have been made. In 1982, Helfer reported that only three studies of child abuse and neglect prevention *research* could be located. In 1987, Dubowitz reported on several research projects but concluded that most of these had been poorly evaluated. Dubowitz suggested that the existing evaluations provided little information on "what works, for whom, and under what circumstances" (p. 46).

Research in the prevention field has progressed. More research is being done with more rigorous, longer-term evaluation components as the sample projects in this chapter indicate. The research is also beginning to provide answers about targeting specific types of prevention strategies to specific types of families. For example, the home visitors provided by Olds et al. (1986) were more effective for poor, single, teenage mothers.

Although progress has been made, much remains to be done. There needs to be a national commitment to addressing the underlying problems that contribute to child maltreatment, such as poverty and attitudes toward hitting children. To develop prevention programs, research is needed to understand the relationships between maltreatment, development, socioeconomic status, and child-rearing styles (Trickett, Aber, Carlson, & Cicchetti, 1991). Much more information is needed about what prevention strategies are most effective, including most cost-effective, for which families. Although some families may be adequately served with programs that focus on one problem, such as substance abuse, many families require comprehensive services that address their multiple needs.

References

Alan Guttmacher Institute. (1987). *Blessed events and the bottom line.* New York: Author.

Albee, G. W., & Gullotta, T. P. (1986). Facts and fallacies about primary prevention. *Journal of Primary Prevention, 6*(4), 207-218.

Amundson, M. J. (1989). Family crisis care: A home-based intervention program for child abuse. *Issues in Mental Health Nursing, 10,* 285-296.

Ayoub, C., & Jacewitz, M. M. (1982). Families at risk of poor parenting: A descriptive study of sixty at risk families in a model prevention program. *Child Abuse & Neglect, 6,* 413-422.

Barth, R. P. (1989). Evaluation of a task-centered child abuse prevention program. *Children and Youth Services Review, 11,* 117-131.

Belsky, J. (1980). Child maltreatment: An ecological integration. *American Psychologist, 35,* 320-335.

Berrick, J. D., & Gilbert, N. (1991). *With the best of intentions: The child sexual abuse prevention movement.* New York: Guilford.

Caplan, G. (1964). *Principles of preventive psychiatry.* New York: Basic Books.

Children's Defense Fund. (1991). Child care in the states: New plans promise better care for children. *CDF Reports, 13*(3), 1-3.

Cohn Donnelly, A. H. (1991). What we have learned about prevention: What we should do about it. *Child Abuse & Neglect, 15,* 99-106.

Daro, D. (1988). *Confronting child abuse: Research for effective program design.* New York: Free Press.

Deren, S. (1986). Children of substance abusers: A review of the literature. *Journal of Substance Abuse Treatment, 3,* 77-94.

Dodge, K. A., Bates, J. E., & Pettit, G. S. (1990). Mechanisms in the cycle of violence. *Science, 250,* 1678-1683.

Dubowitz, H. (1987). *Child maltreatment in the United States: Etiology, impact, and prevention* (Contractor document). Washington, DC: U.S. Congress, Office of Technology Assessment, Health Program.

Dubowitz, H. (1990). Pediatrician's role in preventing child maltreatment. *Pediatric Clinics of North America, 37,* 989-1002.

Egeland, B., Jacobvitz, D., & Sroufe, L. A. (1988). Breaking the cycle of abuse. *Child Development, 59,* 1080-1088.

Egeland, B., & Sroufe, L. A. (1981). Developmental sequelae of maltreatment in infancy. In R. Rizley & D. Cicchetti (Eds.), *New directions for child development* (pp. 77-92). San Francisco: Jossey-Bass.

Fogarty, L., & Conte, J. R. (1991). Sexual abuse prevention programs for children. *Violence Update, 2*(1), 1 ff.

Frank, D. A., & Zeisel, S. H. (1988). Failure to thrive. *The Pediatric Clinics of North America, 35,* 1187-1206.

Fuchs, V. R., & Reklis, D. M. (1992). America's children: Economic perspectives and policy options. *Science, 255,* 41-46.

Garbarino, J. (1980). What kind of society permits child abuse? *Infant Mental Health Journal, 1,* 270-280.

Garbarino, J. (1986). Can we measure success in preventing child abuse? Issues in policy, programming and research. *Child Abuse & Neglect, 10,* 143-156.

Gelles, R. J. (1989). Child abuse and violence in single-parent families: Parent absence and economic deprivation. *American Journal of Orthopsychiatry, 59,* 492-501.

Gomby, D. S., & Shiono, P. H. (1991). Estimating the number of substance-exposed infants. *The Future of Children, 1*(1), 17-25.

Gullotta, T. P. (1987). Prevention's technology. *Journal of Primary Prevention, 7*(4), 176-196.

Halpern, R. (1990). Poverty and early childhood parenting: Toward a framework for intervention. *American Journal of Orthopsychiatry, 60,* 6-18.

Helfer, R. E. (1982). A review of the literature on the prevention of child abuse and neglect. *Child Abuse & Neglect, 6,* 251-261.

Holmes, C. P. (1987). Prevention of child abuse: Possibilities for educational systems. *Special Services in the Schools, 3,* 139-153.

Kaufman, J., & Zigler, E. (1989). The intergenerational transmission of child abuse. In D. Cicchetti & V. Carlson (Eds.), *Child maltreatment: Theory and research on the causes and consequences of child abuse and neglect.* New York: Cambridge University Press.

Kowal, L. W., Kottmeier, C. P., Ayoub, C. C., Komives, J. A., Robinson, D. S., & Allen, J. P. (1989). Characteristics of families at risk of problems in parenting: Findings from a home-based secondary prevention program. *Child Welfare, 68,* 529-538.

Kumpfer, K. L. (1991). Treatment programs for drug-abusing women. *The Future of Children, 1*(1), 50-60.

Main, M., & Goldwyn, R. (1984). Predicting rejection of her infant from mother's representation of her own experience: Implications for the abused-abusing intergenerational cycle. *Child Abuse & Neglect, 8,* 203-217.

Massachusetts Committee for Children and Youth. (1987, November). *Preventing child abuse: A resource for policymakers and advocates.* Boston: Author.

Mayer, J., & Black, R. (1977). Child abuse and neglect in families with an alcohol or opiate addicted parent. *Child Abuse & Neglect, 1,* 85-98.

McCullough, C. B. (1991). The child welfare response. *The Future of Children, 1*(1), 61-71.

Merrick, J. (1985). Addicted mothers and their children: A case for coordinated welfare services. *Child: Care, Health, and Development, 11,* 159-169.

Milner, J. S. (1980). *The Child Abuse Potential Inventory: Manual.* Webster, NC: Psytec Corporation.

National Association of Community Health Centers. (1991). *Access to community health centers.* Washington, DC: Author.

National Center for Children in Poverty. (1991, Fall). Number of poor children growing. *News and Issues,* p. 1.

National Child Abuse Coalition. (1991, June 28). Federal bill to prohibit corporal punishment. *National Child Abuse Coalition Monthly Newsletter,* pp. 3-4.

National Commission on Children. (1991). *Beyond rhetoric: A new American agenda for children and families: Final report of the National Commission on Children.* Washington, DC: Government Printing Office.

Nelson, K. E., Landsman, M. J., & Deutelbaum, W. (1990). Three models of family-centered placement prevention services. *Child Welfare, 69,* 3-21.

Newman, M. R., & Lutzker, J. R. (1990). Prevention programs. In R. T. Ammerman & M. Hersen (Eds.), *Children at risk: An evaluation of factors contributing to child abuse and neglect.* New York: Plenum.

Olds, D. L., & Henderson, C. R. (1989). The prevention of maltreatment. In D. Cicchetti & V. Carlson (Eds.), *Child maltreatment: Theory and research on the causes and consequences of child abuse and neglect.* New York: Cambridge University Press.

Olds, D. L., Henderson, C. R., Chamberlin, R., & Tatelbaum, R. (1986). Preventing child abuse and neglect: A randomized trial of nurse home visitation. *Pediatrics, 78,* 65-78.

Omnibus Budget Reconciliation Act. (1987). Section 4104.

Omnibus Budget Reconciliation Act. (1989). Section 6401.

Omnibus Budget Reconciliation Act. (1990). Section 4601.

Parker, S., Greer, S., & Zuckerman, B. (1988). Double jeopardy: The impact of poverty on early child development. *The Pediatric Clinics of North America, 35,* 1227-1240.

Polansky, N. A., Chalmers, M. A., Williams, D. P., & Buttenwieser, E. W. (1981). *Damaged parents: An anatomy of child neglect.* Chicago: University of Chicago Press.

Reddick, S., & Goodwin, D. (1991, September). *A community response to drug affected babies: A cooperative effort.* Paper presented at the Ninth National Conference on Child Abuse and Neglect, Denver, CO.

Rosenberg, M. S., & Reppucci, N. D. (1985). Primary prevention of child abuse. *Journal of Consulting and Clinical Psychology, 53,* 576-585.

Schorr, L. B. (1988). *Within our reach: Breaking the cycle of disadvantage.* New York: Anchor/Doubleday.

Sherrod, K. B., O'Connor, S., Vietze, P. M., & Altemeier, W. A. (1984). Child health and maltreatment. *Child Development, 55,* 1174-1183.

Simmons, J. T. (1986). *Programs that work: Evidence of primary prevention of child abuse.* Houston, TX: Greater Houston Committee for Prevention of Child Abuse.

Starr, R. H., Jr., MacLean, D. J., & Keating, D. P. (1991). Life-span developmental outcomes of child maltreatment. In R. H. Starr, Jr., & D. A. Wolfe (Eds.), *The effects of child abuse and neglect: Issues and research*. New York: Guilford.

Stein, T. J. (1984, June). The child abuse prevention and treatment act. *Social Service Review*, pp. 302-314.

Straus, M. A., Gelles, R. J., & Steinmetz, S. K. (1988). *Behind closed doors: Violence in the American family*. Garden City, NY: Anchor/Doubleday.

Taylor, D. K., & Beauchamp, C. (1988). Hospital-based primary prevention strategy in child abuse: A multi-level needs addressment. *Child Abuse & Neglect, 12*, 343-354.

Trickett, P. K., Aber, J. L., Carlson, V., & Cicchetti, D. (1991). Relationship of socioeconomic status to the etiology and developmental sequelae of physical child abuse. *Developmental Psychology, 27*, 148-158.

U.S. General Accounting Office. (1990, July). *Home visiting: A promising early intervention strategy for at-risk families* (Report GAO/HRD-90-83). Washington, DC: Author.

U.S. House of Representatives Select Committee on Children, Youth, and Families. (1989, September). *U.S. children and their families: Current conditions and recent trends, 1989*. Washington, DC: Government Printing Office.

Volpe, R. (1989). *Poverty and child abuse: A review of selected literature*. Toronto: Institute for the Prevention of Child Abuse.

Whipple, E. E., & Webster-Stratton, C. (1991). The role of parental stress in physically abusive families. *Child Abuse & Neglect, 15*, 279-291.

White, B. (1985). *The first three years of life* (rev. ed.). New York: Prentice-Hall.

Widom, C. S. (1989). Child abuse, neglect, and adult behavior: Research design and findings on criminality, violence, and child abuse. *American Journal of Orthopsychiatry, 59*, 1-13.

Wiecha, J. L., & Palombo, R. (1989). Multiple program participation: Comparison of nutritional and food assistance program benefits with food costs in Boston, Massachusetts. *American Journal of Public Health, 79*, 591-594.

Willett, J. B., Ayoub, C. C., & Robinson, D. (1991). Using growth modeling to examine systematic differences in growth: An example of change in the functioning of families at risk of maladaptive parenting, child abuse, or neglect. *Journal of Consulting and Clinical Psychology, 59*, 38-47.

Wolfe, D. A. (1984, August). *Behavioral distinctions between abusive and non-abusive parents: A review and critique*. Paper presented at the Second Family Violence Research Conference, University of New Hampshire.

Wolfe, D. A., Edwards, B., Manion, I., & Koverola, C. (1988). Early intervention for parents at risk of child abuse and neglect: A preliminary investigation. *Journal of Consulting and Clinical Psychology, 56*, 40-47.

Wolock, I., & Horowitz, B. (1984). Child maltreatment as a social problem: The neglect of neglect. *American Journal of Orthopsychiatry, 54*, 530-543.

Zuckerman, B. (1991). Drug-exposed infants: Understanding the medical risk. *The Future of Children, 1*(1), 26-35.

· *CHAPTER 12* ·

Substance Abuse
and Family Violence

HEATHER R. HAYES
JAMES G. EMSHOFF

Interest in and response to the issues of the use and abuse of drugs and alcohol have increased in the United States in the last 10 years. As treatment and prevention programs have focused on the chemically dependent person, professionals have also turned their attention to the physical and emotional health of children born and raised in addicted family systems (Bays, 1990).

Simultaneously, both professionals and the general public are increasingly alarmed by the apparent growth of violent behavior in this country, particularly with respect to the wide range of what can be considered family violence. The battering of women, child abuse and neglect, and sexual abuse have high visibility not only in the media but also in the concerns of the social service and legal systems.

While interest in substance abuse and family violence have grown independently, there is a gradual but steady recognition that many social and human problems are not independent but highly related. Comprehensive, multidisciplinary collaborative approaches to these issues are developing in response to the understanding that violence may lead to substance abuse, substance abuse may lead to violence, and environmental pathologies may result in either or both behaviors.

This chapter will examine the phenomena of substance abuse and family violence and their comorbidity, present a variety of

281

theoretical and empirical explanations of the relationship between these behaviors, and conclude with implications for prevention, identification, assessment, and treatment.

Etiology

Substance Abuse

Chemical dependence is a primary, chronic, progressive, and potentially fatal disease. The development and manifestation of chemical dependence is influenced by genetic (Eskay & Linnoila, 1991; Tarter, 1991a), psychosocial (Funkhauser, Goplerud, & Bass, 1992), and environmental factors (Talbott, 1991). Diagnostically, it is considered the intermittent and progressive compulsive use of the drug or drugs (including alcohol) with loss of control. Of every 10 Americans, 2 are social users, 5 are drug and/or alcohol abusers, and 1 suffers directly from the disease of chemical dependence (Talbott, 1991). Despite overwhelming scientific evidence that addiction is a primary disease, it continues to be poorly understood even among some professionals.

Historically, the compulsive use of drugs by drug addicts and alcoholics was interpreted as being secondary to a primary psychiatric disorder. Psychiatrists traditionally treated this assumed underlying pathology only to find little change in the chemically dependent person's pattern of use or loss of control (Alcoholics Anonymous, 1939). It is difficult to estimate the exact number of strictly chemically dependent versus dually diagnosed patients early in the recovery process because reliably separating the comorbid conditions is problematic (Dinwiddie & Reich, 1991). Estimates of dually diagnosed chemically dependent persons range from 10% to 75%. Studies by Cadoret, Troughton, and Widmer (1984), Hesselbrock, Meyer, and Kener (1985), and Ross, Glaser, and Germanson (1988) estimate an average of 40% of males hospitalized for chemical dependence are also diagnosed with antisocial personality disorder. Dinwiddie and Reich (1991) report that three fourths of the patients hospitalized for alcoholism and half of the alcoholic population in general suffer from additional pathology.

When in active addiction, the chemically dependent individual will do anything to survive, including risking the loss of his or her job, family, money, health, morals, or values. Chemically dependent individuals experience emotional and social/spiritual cultural consequences. Emotionally, many addicts experience low self-esteem, loss of impulse control, a decrease in frustration tolerance, lack of inhibitions, lability, anger, guilt, anxiety, and depression. The socio/spiritual cultural consequences are evaluated by identifying the impact of addiction on the individual's job, family, legal, financial, community, and spiritual life. Denial and ignorance of the disease often lead the chemically dependent individual to falsely believe that he or she uses excessively because of these stressors. For many individuals, stressors such as financial, cultural, and familial problems may be present regardless of their use of chemicals. The abuse of drugs and alcohol does not serve as an appropriate coping mechanism and, in many cases, often increases rather than reduces stress levels.

Chemically dependent persons may experience negative consequences that they do not remember. Drug-induced amnesia or blackouts are characteristic of the disease of addiction. Drug amnesia is differentiated from toxic drug unconsciousness or passing out. While in a state of drug-induced amnesia, the addict may appear to be in a state of consciousness varying from sober to extremely intoxicated. When the addict becomes sober, he or she has no recollection of episodes that happened while intoxicated (Altman, 1986; Smith & Wesson, 1985; Wallace, 1986). The phenomenon of blackouts may contribute to the addict or alcoholic's denial of the recognition of the incidence and devastating impact of his or her behavior on others.

Family Violence

Family violence has been in existence since the dawn of written history. Greek and Roman mythology, as well as the Bible, refer to child abandonment and sacrifice. Freud, in his paper "A Child Is Being Beaten," described a universal, unconscious impulse to destroy or hurt children. Even legislation against cruelty to animals preceded legislation on cruelty to children by 75 years (Smith & Kunjukrishnan, 1985). Our understanding of the etiology, intergenerational transmission, and developmental sequelae of abuse has been only recently heightened by systematic inquiry and research. The result of this research has been a shift in the country's perspective and tolerance for child abuse and family violence.

Prior to the 1960s, the medical profession failed to acknowledge the existence of child abuse (Dubowitz & Newberger, 1989). In 1946, John Caffey, a pediatric radiologist, suggested that fractures associated with intercranial bleeding might be the result of parental abuse or neglect (Smith et al., 1985). Caffey's description of this "new syndrome" helped to initiate the medical profession's recognition of abuse in recent years. In 1953, another radiologist, F. Silverman, reported on the high incidence of infant and childhood physical injury. He suggested that parental abuse was the cause of such childhood trauma and criticized his colleagues for their reluctance to consider this possibility (Cicchetti & Olsen, 1990). In 1955, two pediatricians, Wooley and Evans, pointed out for the first time that a child's parent was responsible for child abuse (Smith & Kunjukrishnan, 1985).

In 1961, C. Henry Kempe became alarmed at the number of children admitted to pediatric clinics for the care of nonaccidental injuries. Kempe conducted a symposium at the annual national meeting of the American Academy of Pediatrics. Kempe and his colleagues coined the dramatic term *battered child syndrome,* which has helped to increase the public's awareness to the harsh realities of child abuse. As a direct result of the work by Kempe and his colleagues, legislative activity increased, resulting in mandatory reporting laws in all 50 states by 1970 (Cicchetti & Olsen, 1990; Kempe, Silverman, Steele, Droegemueller, & Silver, 1985). Despite the heightened awareness and attention that resulted from Kempe and his colleagues' work, negative consequences ensued. The adoption of the term *battered child syndrome* connoted a model of a psychologically disturbed adult perpetrator. This etiological view narrowed the perspective of abuse, virtually absolving society from any responsibility. Furthermore, the treatment preceeding from this perspective focused on supplying treatment to the perpetrator without focusing on the need to provide concomitant intervention for the abused child (Cicchetti & Olsen, 1990; Smith & Kunjukrishnan, 1985).

In the following decade, the reporting laws were modified. The Child Abuse Prevention and Treatment Act of 1974 expanded the definition of child abuse to include neglect, mental/emotional injury, deprivation of medical services, and sexual abuse (Cicchetti & Olsen, 1990; Smith & Kunjukrishnan, 1985). In addition to this modified view of abuse, social factors began to be taken into account. The work of David Gil (1975) delineated five causal dimensions: (a) society's definition of childhood, including the rights and expectations of children; (b) society's social philosophy, its dominant values, its concepts of humans, and the nature of its institutions; (c) the societal acceptance of the use of force or violence to meet one's needs; (d) stressful contexts, which include poverty, overcrowding, lack of resources, large numbers of children, and social isolation; and (e) various forms of psychopathology (Cicchetti & Olsen, 1990; Pagelow, 1984). Malicious parental intent was no longer the primary genesis for child abuse.

As the etiological models became less focused on the psychopathology of the perpetrator, increasing attention was placed on prevention, research, and treatment of the childhood victims of abuse. Models explaining abuse have shifted to include high risk factors, transgenerational transmission, and the sequelae of maltreatment.

This perspective on the genesis of family violence necessitates evaluating the relationship between family violence and substance abuse. Parental substance abuse has been linked to family violence as a high risk factor and as an element in transgenerational transmission.

For the purpose of this chapter, family violence will include (a) physical abuse of children, (b) sexual abuse of children, (c) physical and emotional neglect of children, (d) verbal and emotional abuse, and (e) spousal abuse. These conditions often coexist and may somewhat overlap in definition.

*Physical ab*use is defined as the intentional, nonaccidental use of force by a parent or caretaker toward a child or adolescent. The use of force is aimed at hurting, injuring, or destroying the child (Gil, 1970; Pagelow, 1984). Physically abusive behaviors include acts that leave signs of physical trauma (i.e., broken bones, burned skin, bruises, and so on) as well as hitting, slapping, shoving, and beatings that leave few external signs of the abuse.

Sexual abuse is defined as an adult or older person's use of a child or adolescent for sexual relations and sexual gratification. The perpetrator may or may not be a family member. For the purpose of this chapter, the term *sexual contact* includes intercourse, masturbation, hand-genital or oral-genital contact, sexual fondling, exhibitionism, pornography, voyeurism, or sexual propositioning (Bass & Davis, 1988; Pagelow, 1984; Peters, Wyatt, & Finkelhor, 1986).

Physical and emotional neglect is a condition in which the caretaker responsible for the child fails to provide the essentials necessary for physical, emotional, and intellectual development. This neglect may include lack of adequate food and nutritional requirements, lack of proper medical care, ignoring a child, isolating a child, and lack of appropriate supervision and limits (Pagelow, 1984).

Verbal and emotional abuse takes the form of the degradation, humiliation, terrorizing, and threatening of an individual with the goal of the abuse being the destruction of the individual's (adult's or child's) sense of self-worth. This abuse includes the following behaviors: (a) rejecting an individual by verbally degrading her or him, calling her or him names, or not talking to him or her; (b) terrorizing a person by having him or her witness violence, using verbal threats, intentionally creating a climate of intense fear and unpredictability, and setting unrealistic goals that are followed by punishment when they are not obtained; (c) ignoring a child or spouse, including not protecting her or him from dangerous situations, leaving a child unsupervised, refusing to discuss the child's interests; (d) isolating a child or spouse from normal opportunities for social interaction and relationships, for example, not allowing friends or playmates to one's home, withdrawing a child from interaction to perform household duties such as cleaning or caring for siblings; and (e) corrupting a child by teaching her or him deviant or antisocial behaviors such as selling drugs or by rewarding a child for aggressive behavior (Garbarino, Guttman, & Seeley, 1986).

Spousal abuse is defined as the incidence of intentional force to cause pain or injury between two persons involved in a relationship that often includes sexual intimacy (Pagelow, 1984).

Incidence

Bays (1990) reports there are approximately 10 million adult alcoholics, 500,000 heroin addicts, and between 5 and 8 million regular cocaine users in the United States. A study by Thomas

(1989) in conjunction with juvenile and family court judges estimates between 20% to 50% of the total population is at risk of "serious dysfunction" from the misuse of drugs. A survey of college students, high school seniors, and young adults (Johnston, O'Malley, & Bachman, 1990) reported that 29% of the high school seniors interviewed had smoked marijuana and 10% had used cocaine 30 days prior. In addition, 13% of the eighth graders, 23% of the tenth graders, and 30% of the high school seniors had binged on alcohol (5 or more drinks) in the 2 weeks prior to the survey. The National Institute of Drug Abuse household survey revealed that, in 1991, 6% of the population admitted to having used an illicit drug in the previous month. The National Committee for the Prevention of Child Abuse (1989) estimates that 10 million children are being raised by addicted parents and that at least 675,000 children are seriously mistreated by an alcoholic or addicted caretaker annually.

Discrepancies in identification tools and definitions of abuse and violence, as well as limited access to the appropriate population, make prevalence and incidence rates difficult to determine in the study of family violence and childhood abuse (Bays, 1990; Finkelhor, 1988; Finkelhor et al., 1986; Herman, 1981; Smith & Kunjukrishnan, 1985). In addition, cases of family violence are frequently not reported or recognized.

A study by Straus, Gelles, and Steinmetz (1980) obtained estimates of family violence through a national survey of family members. In this study, 12% of the spouses reported acts of violence directed at them from their spouses in the previous year and 28% reported that there had been at least one violent act in the course of their marriage. Finkelhor and Yllo (1985) and Russell (1982) estimate from community surveys that anywhere from 1 in 10 to 1 in 7 wives were raped or otherwise sexually abused by their partners.

The National Committee for the Prevention of Child Abuse and Neglect annually conducts surveys in all 50 states. Results of the 1991 survey estimated 2.694 million reported cases of child and adolescent victimization: 25% were reports of physical abuse; 15%, sexual abuse; 48%, neglect; 6%, emotional abuse; and 10% fell into an "other" category (Daro & McCurdy, 1991).

The first national survey of sexual abuse incidence, conducted in 1985, found 27% of the women and 15% of the men had been

abused as children (Finkelhor, 1988). Prevalence studies estimate that approximately one third of women and one tenth of
men in North America are sexually victimized before their
midteens (Briere, 1989). A study done by Russell (1982) sampling women in the San Francisco area found that 38% recalled
an incident of childhood sexual abuse. Of these women who
recalled abuse, 18% reported the abuse had happened within
their family (parent or stepparent). Finkelhor and Baron (1986)
and associates surveyed college students in the United States and
found that 19% of females and 9% of males reported abuse by the
age of 6. Children are abused within as well as outside of the
family. Boys are molested outside of the family 11 times more
than girls (McNamara & McNamara, 1990).

Estimates of childhood physical abuse vary widely. According
to the National Center on Child Abuse and Neglect, between
100,000 to 200,000 children are abused each year (Pagelow,
1984). The Children's Defense Fund (1989) reported that in
1986, 2.2 million children were reported to protective services
for child abuse, neglect, or both. In addition, the number of
cases reported increased 90% between 1981 and 1986. A national survey of parents carried out by Straus and Gelles (1986)
estimates that 10.7% of the parents admitted to having committed a "severe violent act" against their children in the previous
year. And, in the study previously cited by Straus et al. (1980),
4% of the parents surveyed admitted to having used severe
violence against their children in the previous year. Physical
violence is frequently accompanied by psychological abuse such
as name calling or terrorizing. Emotional battering is difficult to
estimate. Emotional abuse is probably reported the least unless
accompanied by neglect, physical, or sexual abuse.

Comorbidity

Increasing emphasis has been placed on the association between chemical use (including alcohol) and family violence
(Bays, 1990). It is imperative to recognize the reality of the
frequency of the coexistence of chemical dependence and incest, battering, neglect, and emotional and physical abuse. The
National Council on Alcoholism and Drug Abuse predicts that

as many as 60% of the chemically dependent families now in treatment have experienced domestic violence. Black (1981) reports that 66% of the children raised in alcoholic homes are either physically abused or witness family violence and 26% of the children raised in alcoholic families are sexually abused. In one third of these families, the abuse occurs on a regular basis. Studies of physical abuse (Leonard & Jacob, 1988), sexual abuse (Aarens et al., 1978; Morgan, 1982; Rada, 1976), and spousal abuse (Van Hasselt, Morrison, & Bellack, 1988) have shown that alcohol involvement frequently accompanies abuse; that is, either the offender was either an alcoholic or drinking at the time of the offense.

Alcohol is consistently implicated in wife abuse by male batters (Van Hasselt et al., 1985). Abuse of a spouse is more likely to occur when intoxication is present (Kantor & Straus, 1989). In cases of extreme violence (e.g., fractures, violently induced abortions, and murder), the abuser is frequently a chronic drinker or drug user (Shapiro, 1982).

In families that abuse alcohol and drugs, violence is increased (Bays, 1990). Alcoholics are more hostile, aggressive, and impulsive than nonalcoholics (Williams, 1976). The National Institute on Alcohol Abuse and Alcoholism (NIAAA; 1984) reports that families in which one or both parents are chemically dependent are at high risk for child abuse. In families with an addicted female caretaker, the children seem to be at greater risk of abuse than in those with nonaddicted female caregivers. Often in systems where there is a woman who is addicted, the partner or spouse is also likely to use drugs or alcohol, which leaves the children to be raised by two caretakers who are intoxicated.

In 1976, a survey of heroin-addicted parents self-reported abusing or neglecting their children 4 to 5 times more than the comparison families. In addition, teachers working with the children of addicted parents reported a need for protective services 3 times more than for nonaddicted families (Bays, 1990).

Leonard and Jacob (1988) reviewed five studies from 1968 to 1979 that suggest a link between child abuse and alcoholism. A study done in 1968, looking at childhood victims of physical violence, found that one fourth of their fathers drank to excess. An archival study done in Canada in 1979 found that 31% of the cases reported for child abuse or neglect to the Alberta Registry for Child Abuse and Neglect mentioned alcohol use. Neglect or abuse was more likely to be substantiated in cases where alcohol was mentioned (84%) than in cases where it was not mentioned (65%). In 83% of those cases where alcohol was mentioned, it was suspected that the abuser was intoxicated at the time of the reported incident (Leonard & Jacob, 1988).

Child welfare agencies have begun keeping records and publishing studies that examine the incidence of substance abuse in child abuse and neglect cases (Bays, 1990; Smith & Kunjukrishnan, 1985). One half of child abuse and neglect cases in New York City in 1987 were linked to parental illicit chemical use (Chasnoff, 1988). Children placed as wards of the court were surveyed in 1986 and the surveys revealed that more than half came from chemically dependent families (Chasnoff, 1988).

Many studies show that the offender was using alcohol or drugs at the time of the offense. Smith and Kunjukrishnan (1985) report that alcoholism is a problem associated with childhood sexual abuse in 71% of families and in 56% of families in which the sexual abuse was accompanied by physical abuse. Aarens et al. (1978) reviewed studies done in the United States and in two foreign countries. They found that alcohol accompanied the abuse in 30%-40% of the cases. They also found that an average of 45%-50% of those studied had histories of drinking problems (ranging from as low as 8% to as high as 70%). In a review of the literature, Finkelhor et al. (1986) found that female-object pedophiles tended to be more alcohol involved than male-object pedophiles. Aarens et al. (1978) and Morgan (1982), in a review of relevant studies, concluded that incest offenders appear to have the most extensive histories of alcohol involvement of all the sexual offenders. They found that incestuous child molesters were more likely to be characterized by larger proportions of alcoholism and alcohol use at the time of the offense than nonincestuous child molesters.

A study by Roy (1988) was based on a sample of 146 children ranging from 11 to 17, who were either living at a battered women's shelter with their mothers or in protective homes. All of the children had a mother who was battered by her spouse; 48% of the children had been physically abused by either parent. The fathers tended to be physically abusive and the mothers neglectful when the families were intact. The children reported that 41% of the fathers had a drinking problem and the abuse was exacerbated by the drinking; 8% reported that their fathers smoked marijuana; and 2% believed their fathers did other illicit drugs. They also reported that 24% of their mothers also drank.

Theories of Comorbidity

Although there are many theories delineating the causes of family violence, thorough exploration and definition of these theories are outside the realm of this chapter. We intend to examine the dynamics and interaction between substance abuse and family violence including risk factors, drugs and alcohol as a disinhibitor, family communication dynamics, the violent adolescent, other family dynamics, and in utero and postpartum violence.

Risk factors. Violence and substance abuse share many common risk factors: individual, familial, and environmental. While few studies use the appropriate statistical techniques needed to separate causation from coincidence (Bays, 1990), it would appear that some of the causes and certainly the correlates of substance abuse and family violence overlap. Research in these fields suggests a relationship between the risk factors of both. The interaction between the risk factor, substance abuse, and family violence is not clear. There are, however, three possible ways in which risk factors may be precursors to dysfunction in families: (a) The risk factor may lead to substance abuse, which in turn leads to violence; (b) the risk factor may lead to violence, which in turn contributes to abuse of substances; (c) the risk factors may independently manifest themselves as either substance abuse or family violence. Additional research examining the nature of these interactions is needed to facilitate appropriate prevention and early intervention aimed at decreasing the risk factor and ultimately lowering the individual's vulnerability to substance abuse and family violence.

Individual factors. Personality and behavioral correlates of substance abuse and family violence that overlap include hyperactivity (Garbarino et al., 1986; Gittelman, Mannuzza, & Bonagura, 1985), "difficult" temperament (Lerner & Vicary, 1984), impaired attachment to mother (Bays, 1990), early sexual activity

(Browne & Finkelhor, 1986a; Dryfoos, 1987), antisocial and/or runaway behavior (Robins & Przybeck, 1985; Windle, 1990), lack of social confidence, difficulty with peer relationships, social isolation, and social deprivation (Browne & Finkelhor, 1986a; Finkelhor et al., 1986; Garbarino et al., 1986; Hawkins, Lishner, Jenson, & Catalano, 1987; Kandel & Yamaguchi, 1984; Peters et al., 1986; Robins & Przybeck, 1985). In addition, children with frequent moves during childhood are at greater risk for family violence, substance abuse, and parental addiction (Berndt, 1987; Browne & Finkelhor, 1986b; Finkelhor et al., 1986; Hawkins et al., 1987; Steinberg, 1987).

Familial factors. Researchers have suggested that the factors that show the strongest connection to family violence and substance abuse are those relating to parents and family (Baumrind, 1985; Finkelhor & Baron, 1986; Sgroi, 1985). Parental/familial factors that may contribute to these two issues are parenting behaviors and family structuring, including parental inconsistency, poor limit setting, excessively severe disciplinary tactics (deMarsh & Kumpfer, 1985; Finkelhor et al., 1986; Friedman, 1989; Garbarino et al., 1986; Hawkins et al., 1987; Jessor & Jessor, 1977; Kline, Canter, & Robin, 1987), parental conflict (Finkelhor et al., 1986; Rhodes & Jason, 1990), poor communication (Black, 1981; Finkelhor & Baron, 1986; Peters et al., 1986), parental absence and unavailability (Bays, 1990; Black, 1981; Finkelhor & Baron, 1986; Peters et al., 1986; Weigsheider, 1981), and familial social isolation (Emshoff & Anyan, 1991; Finkelhor & Baron, 1986; Garbarino, 1976). The presence of a stepfather has been found to significantly increase the risk of sexual abuse for female children (Finkelhor & Baron, 1986). It could be speculated that the high rate of marital discord and conflict in substance-abusing families may contribute to divorce, which may lead to the introduction of a stepfather into the addicted family system.

Environmental factors. While most attention in the areas of substance abuse and family violence has been given to individual and micro-environmental (family) risk factors, macro-level variables clearly play a role in both (Bays, 1990; Cicchetti & Olsen, 1990; Funkhouser, Gopler, & Bass, 1992; Pagelow, 1984). These include community norms (Hawkins et al., 1987; Johnston et al., 1990), neighborhood disorganization (Wilson & Hernstein, 1985), cultural disenfranchisement (Pagelow, 1984), and the availability of community education on both substance abuse and family violence.

Poor school performance, truancy, and early dropping out are factors that increase the risk of alcohol and drug use in adolescence. These factors also correlate with children who have been abused and who come from addicted families (Bachman, Johnston, & O'Malley, 1987; Gottfredson, 1986; Herman, 1981; Jessor & Jessor, 1977; Peters et al., 1986; Sher, 1991; Steinberg, 1987).

Alcohol and other drugs as disinhibitors. Researchers agree that chemical dependence does not totally explain molesting or other forms of violence; rather, it is a contributing factor. Alcohol and drugs have the potential to exacerbate any psychiatric disorder or emotional instability within the chemical user, including conditions such as poor impulse control, bipolar disorder, characterological disorders, low frustration tolerance, and violent behaviors (Cicchetti & Olsen, 1990; Curtis, 1986). Alcohol and drugs lower the inhibitions that keep people from acting upon violent or sexually aggressive impulses (Finkelhor et al., 1986). It appears that, if a person has the tendency to behave in a pedophilic, violent, or acting-out manner, alcohol and/or drugs may act as a direct psychological disinhibitor, enabling the person to engage in these behaviors. Furthermore, alcohol and/or drugs may act to enable the offender to disregard or disavow the societal taboos against incest and child abuse. Frustration tolerance may also be lowered by alcohol and drugs, leaving a parent more likely to strike out against a child when intoxicated than when sober. Alcohol and/or drug consumption may also act to diminish or anesthetize any shame or guilt the perpetrator may experience after the offense. This lack of experiencing negative emotions or internal inhibitors may further perpetuate abuse by defending the abuser from his or her own internal process.

McCagy (1968) explains uncharacteristic violent behavior that occurs after consuming alcohol with the Disavowal Theory. This theory states that the drinker uses alcohol as an excuse to neutralize any deviant behavior by evading or disavowing her or his own responsibility and blaming the intoxication. Gelles

(1974) contends that the offender may disown her or his behavior by actually using the drink or the drug to gain the courage to carry out a violent act. An example of this would be a spouse who drinks so as to beat his or her partner with minimal guilt.

Family Communication Problems

Communication within the addicted family system becomes distorted and dysfunctional (Dulfano, 1985). Often, the spouse will try to control the alcoholic's or addict's behavior by nagging, pleading, or expressing disappointment (Lindquist, 1986). As the addict's disease progresses, communication may become inconsistent, unrealistic, paranoid, or literally unintelligible (i.e., slurred speech). When intoxicated or hung over, the addict may make damaging judgmental comments or become verbally abusive. If the addict is experiencing drug-induced amnesia (a blackout), verbal abuse or promises that are made may not be remembered. Dysfunctional communication adds additional tension to the couple and family system, exacerbating a climate in which violence may occur. The parents' frustrations may potentially be misdirected at the children or lead to violent interactions between the couple. Inconsistent communication may also leave children confused about family rules and disappointed about parental broken promises (Zimberg, Wallace, & Blume, 1985).

Couples may blame each other for their problems. They project onto each other, which keeps either partner from seeing his or her own contribution to the problems, thus eliminating the possibility of change. Patterns of avoidance and withdrawal are often used as a defense against confronting the partner (Grisham & Estes, 1986). Avoidance may involve long periods of tense silence that further exacerbate negative feelings and distrust. The tension of avoidance and withdrawal has the potential for eventual eruption, with the explosive expression of pent-up anger being either physical or verbal.

Closely related to communication problems, the addict's relationship is rarely free of sexual problems (Black, 1981; Grisham & Estes, 1986; Strack & Dutton, 1971; Wegscheider, 1981). Acute ingestion of alcohol or prolonged alcohol use is a frequent factor in the onset of secondary impotence in men (Forrest, 1983; Masters & Johnson, 1970) and in infrequent orgasm in women (Schuckit, 1971; Wilsnack, 1984). The spouse of the addict often struggles with the inability to respond to the addict's sexual advances while the addict is intoxicated or sober. The addict may experience this as rejection and may often interpret it as a reflection of his or her inadequacies. Poor sexual relations further stress and frustrate the couple. This frustration and stress may be manifest as violence toward the children or the spouse and/or exploitation of children to fulfill adult sexual needs.

Aggressive behavior in children of substance abusers. Another dynamic that links violence and substance abuse concerns the behavior of children of substance abusers (COSAs). The literature suggests that COSAs have a specific temperamental vulnerability (Tarter et al., 1985). These children, as a group, have less ability to recover from emotional distress and increased emotional lability ("hot temper").

Another explanation for deviance and aggression in COSAs comes from the popular literature description of common roles adopted by COSAs as a means of coping with parental substance abuse (Black, 1981; Wegscheidcr, 1981). According to this proposition, some children have become scapegoats by exhibiting antisocial or aggressive behavior to distract attention from the central focus of the addicted family: the addict.

Whether this behavior is the result of temperament, is a coping strategy, or is both, there is little doubt that children in alcoholic homes are more likely to engage in antisocial, delinquent, and problem behaviors, including more frequent arrests, suspensions, and counseling for disciplinary reasons (Bennett, Wolin, & Resii, 1988; Rimmer, 1982; Schuckit & Chiles, 1978; Zucker & Lisansky-Gomber, 1986). While not all of these behaviors are violent, it is likely that as a group these children are predisposed toward violent behavior, thus helping to perpetuate the familial cycles of both substance abuse and violence.

Other family issues. In addition to children of substance abusers, the partners of substance abusers may be prone to violent behavior. In chemically dependent families, the nonaddicted spouse may overcompensate for the addicted partner's lack of functioning (Grisham & Estes, 1986). For instance, the nonaddicted spouse may assume the responsibilities abdicated by the addict. These additional responsibilities, as well as the chemically dependent person's chaotic and inconsistent behaviors, are stressful. In response to this stress, the nonaddicted spouse may become frustrated and angry, which frequently can be misdirected at the children in the family. Children whose emotional and physical needs are not being met within the family system may act out, be demanding of parental attention, or engage in power struggles with their parents. Tension between the parents and child will further stress both the addicted and the nonaddicted parent, which may potentially result in physical violence or verbal abuse (Garbarino et al., 1986).

Parental preoccupation with chemical use may also lead to neglect or emotional abuse. Physically, the children's needs may be neglected because of the parents' inability to feed children appropriately, attend to medical needs, or provide an environment conducive to appropriate sleep. Parents may ignore or reject their children, resulting in inadequate limit setting and supervision. Emotionally, the child may be void of a safe, loving, and nurturing environment due to parental fighting, verbal abuse, and/or parental emotional unavailability.

While this parental neglect is abusive in and of itself, parental absence or unavailability is also one of the factors that has been found to correlate with sexual abuse (Finkelhor & Baron, 1986). A study cited by Finkelhor and Baron (1986) and associates that looked at father-daughter incest found significantly more mothers of abused daughters were sick with disabling diseases including alcoholism, depression, and psychoses. Mothers also may be absent from the home because of a spouse's drinking or drug habit. It is not uncommon for a wife to work outside the home to compensate for an addicted partner's lack of financial support.

Spouses of chemically dependent persons tend to be isolated from outside support (Black, 1981; Wegscheider, 1981). As a result, children in the family may be used by the nonaddicted parent for support and as confidants. Children may begin to serve a surrogate spousal role for the nonaddicted parent. This form of role reversal places additional, inappropriate adult functioning on the child and can be considered abusive (Grisham & Estes, 1986).

The children within the family system may also absorb responsibilities neglected by either parent. In some homes, children may be expected to meet parental needs that are not age appropriate.

The responsibilities these parentified children may incur include taking care of their parents emotionally and physically, taking care of younger siblings, and performing household duties.

In Utero and Postpartem Violence

The link between substance abuse and violence has implications not only for the female partners of users and their children but for the unborn children. The incidence of battering is increased with pregnancy; victims of violence have a higher rate of pregnancy. Violence toward the pregnant mother is traumatizing and potentially damaging to the fetus (Kantor & Straus, 1989; Thomas, 1988).

Infants born into substance-abusing families often experience the consequences of their parents' use while in the womb. Polydrug use is common in addicted women. As many as 93% of the women in methadone treatment programs also report using cocaine and other drugs in addition to opiates (Bays, 1990). Chasnoff (1989) reports that at least 11% of the pregnant women nationwide are using illegal drugs. More that 300,000 infants are born annually to women using crack/cocaine (Chasnoff, 1989; NCPCA, 1989). The perinatal effects of opiate, marijuana, phencyclidine, alcohol, and amphetamine ingestion include spontaneous abortion, mental retardation, birth defects, premature labor, fetal distress, growth retardation, and withdrawal symptoms at birth. The long-term effects of drug and alcohol use while in utero include impulsivity, learning disabilities, antisocial behavior, neurological deficits, and sudden infant death syndrome (Bays, 1990). Furthermore, the addicted mother rarely stops her drug use after the birth of her child. Many of these babies are visited infrequently by their mothers in the hospital and others are abandoned altogether.

A study by Hurt, Salvador, and Brodsky (1989) of toddlers of addicted mothers suggested that toddlers who are raised in environments in which drugs and alcohol continue to be abused are more insecurely attached than the toddlers of addicted mothers who are raised in non-drug-abusing environments, that is, in extended or foster families. Toddlers of abusing mothers are also more likely to have abnormal affect and play behaviors. This may be due in part to the drug-using mothers' inability to pay attention to their children and help the children adequately develop (Black, Mayer, & Zaklan, 1981; Rodning, Beckwith, & Howard, 1989).

The behaviors exhibited and difficulties experienced by the infant born to a mother who used alcohol and/or drugs may interfere with the parent-child attachment. Exacerbating this tendency is the fact that many infants who were exposed to drugs and alcohol in utero are separated from their mothers at birth because of withdrawal, prematurity, birth defects, or infection. Difficulty with parent-child attachment may place children at greater risk of abuse.

Identification and Assessment

Chemical dependence and family violence have both been unduly neglected by clinicians (Bratton, 1992; Pagelow, 1984; Shapiro, 1982). Research, clinical training, assessment tools, and treatment programs have traditionally focused on chemical dependence, childhood abuse, and marital violence separately. The possibility of the co-occurrence of each should always be taken into account. Every chemically dependent family should be assessed for the possibility of violence; conversely, the violent family should have a chemical dependence assessment.

Multiple issues make the topic of sexual, physical, and/or emotional abuse, as well as substance abuse, difficult for families and individuals to discuss. Addicted and violent family systems tend to be closed, rigid, and shame based, making them difficult for clinicians to penetrate (Dulfano, 1985; Finkelhor et al., 1986; Nathanson, 1989). Substance abuse and violence are often denied and minimized by family members. The dynamic of secrecy is powerful in childhood sexual abuse and is often accompanied by threats (Bass & Davis, 1988; Finkelhor & Baron, 1986; Sgroi, 1985). Children and spouses may fear retribution by the abuser or addict for disclosure of violence and/or substance abuse (Bass & Davis, 1988; Black, 1981, 1990; Lindquist, 1986; Sgroi, 1985). Similarly, issues of family loyalty also make disclosure difficult for families.

Identities of the family members involved in alcohol and drug use, as well as violence, should be ascertained rather than inferred. Families may include several alcoholics/addicts and offenders as well as persons (adults and children) being abused

(Emshoff & Anyan, 1991; Goodwin, 1985; Shapiro, 1982; Wegscheider, 1981). For this reason, each family member in both the addicted and the violent system should have an age-appropriate assessment independent from other family members. The timing of the assessment of family members should be at the clinician's discretion. For example, when a couple is in marital crisis, it may be expedient to see the husband and wife first and the children soon after.

The way in which an individual or family arrives for treatment will influence the evaluation and assessment. Persons who come to a specific agency or organization, such as an addiction treatment center or a shelter for abused women and children, are at least able to admit the existence of substance abuse and violence in their family. The therapist will be able to enter into the system around the presenting problem. Assessment will be more difficult with families that are resistant to revealing information around either of these issues. Evaluation of each family member individually may facilitate a safe environment for family members to discuss secrets. Issues of family loyalty or fear of retribution and safety need to be discussed after disclosure of violence and addiction (Gil, 1988; Herman, 1981; Sgroi, 1985; Shapiro, 1982). One way to begin to uncover information about substance abuse in resistant families is to ask questions related to the negative behavioral consequences of chemical dependence. For example, questions about personality changes while drinking or using drugs, time loss and lack of remembering when intoxicated (drug-induced amnesia), legal problems, and changes in or loss of interests may be helpful in gathering information about the impact of addiction on the family. Addicts tend to minimize their use (Talbott, 1991), therefore specific questions about the quantity of drugs and/or alcohol used should be pursued rather than simply accepting broad answers such as "a couple of drinks." Emotional states and behavior, particularly in children, may be symptomatic of the presence of family violence or substance abuse. Anxiety, panic attacks, acting-out behavior, running away, depression, phobias, change in school performance, low self-esteem, and isolation may be warning signs of violence or addiction (Bass & Davis, 1988; Briere, 1989; Cicchetti & Olsen, 1990; Finkelhor et al., 1986; Garbarino et al., 1986; Wegscheider, 1981).

An early determination of the severity and chronicity of the substance abuse and the violence is importance. Chronicity relates to resistance. The family that has tolerated addiction and violence for many years may have more difficulty with change. In such cases, removal from the family system and inpatient treatment may be necessary (Grisham & Estes, 1986; Pattison & Kaufman, 1982; Shapiro, 1982; Talbott, 1991).

In addition to evaluating the presence of addiction and/or violence within the family system, other family dynamics need to be explored. These dynamics include communication patterns, interactional sequences, family rules and roles, power differentials, hierarchies, and the matrix of relationships (Black, 1981, 1990; Dulfano, 1985; Pattison & Kaufman, 1982; Wegscheider, 1981).

Treatment/Prevention

The treatment of both the addicted and the violent client must be designed to address both issues. In the past, treatment was compartmentalized, with clinicians exclusively focusing on the issues most familiar to their field (Pagelow, 1984; Shapiro, 1982). Both the violent family and the chemically dependent family are characterized by denial and shame, which makes the therapist's entering into either system and facilitating change difficult (Nathanson, 1989). Both the violent client and the chemically dependent client can be challenging and resistant to treatment. The difficulty is only compounded when families have dual problems. Both populations may elicit countertransference issues of anger, frustration, and fear. For example, untreated addicts can be irresponsible, hostile, and/or resistant, making them poor prospects for psychotherapy (Grisham & Estes, 1986; Shapiro, 1982; Talbott, 1991). Working with the violent client may be equally as difficult with the issue of violence eliciting anxiety and fear in the therapist.

Because alcohol and drug use play a role in physical, emotional, and sexual abuse, it is vital that the two issues be treated independently. Treatment of one does not supplant treatment of the other. The belief that the treatment for chemical dependence will extinguish violence is unsound and potentially dangerous.

The disease model explains inappropriate behavior while intoxicated as a product of one's compulsion (Talbott, 1991). Controversy exists as to whether the disease model excuses one's responsibility for behaviors when using (Shapiro, 1982). Regardless of the therapist's belief about responsibility when intoxicated, an addict or alcoholic should always be held responsible for her or his recovery, including changing dysfunctional behaviors.

Issues of addiction and violent behavior must be addressed if the chemically dependent individual is to recover and her or his family members are to heal. While it is nearly impossible for the active addict or alcoholic to work on issues around managing power, control, and violence while drinking, it is equally as difficult for a sober addict/alcoholic to remain in recovery while continuing violent/abusive behaviors.

The treatment of chemical dependence begins with total abstinence from all mood-altering chemicals (Zimberg et al., 1985). Due to the lethality of withdrawal from certain types and amounts of drugs and alcohol, the chemically dependent person should always be evaluated by a physician to determine whether a medical detoxification is necessary (Pattison & Kaufman, 1982). Removing the addict from the family system and her or his environment may be necessary based on the quantity and duration of drug use as well as the severity of negative consequences suffered. Availability of chemical dependence treatment programs for special groups such as pregnant woman, abuse survivors, or dual-diagnosed individuals are available and should be considered in determining appropriate treatment.

Evaluation and assessment of underlying psychopathology such as bipolar disorder, organic brain dysfunction, and characterological disturbances may necessitate a primary mode of psychiatric treatment. In addition, psychopharmacological intervention may be appropriate (Talbott, 1991).

Nonchemical coping skills must be acquired to help the newly sober individual appropriately process feelings (including anger), increase frustration tolerance, and handle uncomfortable situations that exacerbate stress. Other necessary coping mechanisms include relaxation techniques, assertiveness training, leisure skills, communication training, and social skill building (Broderick, Friedman, & Carr, 1981; Carr & Binkoff, 1981; Goldstein, 1981; Morrison, Hayes, & Knauf, 1989). Group therapy has been found

more effective as a treatment modality for confronting the alco-
holic/addict's denial than individual psychotherapy (Flores, 1988).
Education about the disease process for the addict and her or his
family members is imperative. In addition, ongoing support from
a 12-step program such as Alcoholics Anonymous, Narcotics
Anonymous, or Cocaine Anonymous is vital for continued sobri-
ety (Grisham & Estes, 1986; Talbott, 1991; Zimberg et al., 1985).
The 12-step groups give the addict and alcoholic ongoing support as well as a device with which to find meaning or spiritu-
ality in her or his life.

Early treatment for chemical dependence focuses on decreasing the client's denial and helping her or him to recognize the
consequences of use. Given this insight, the client is responsible
for learning and eliciting more appropriate, less destructive
behaviors (McCarthy, 1985). The same reality-oriented therapy
is vital for the violent client who needs to assume responsibility
for her or his actions rather than disavowing responsibility.

Family therapy is essential in the treatment of addiction (Black,
1981; Dulfano, 1985; Wegscheider, 1981). Each family member
must address her or his role in maintaining the dysfunctional family
system. This includes addressing ineffective communication and
interactional sequences. Direct, honest communication between
family members will help decrease triangulation and role reversal with children. Marital problems, including sexual dysfunction, need to be addressed by the couple. In addition, the addict
needs to assume the responsibilities she or he once abdicated.
These responsibilities include financial support, providing emotional and physical parenting needs, and equal distribution of
household duties. This redistribution of responsibilities helps to
lessen stress placed on the spouse and decreases parentification
in children. Treatment for additional behavioral problems and
other disorders in family members, including violence and aggression in children, needs to be constantly monitored with
therapy/treatment referrals being made when appropriate.

Twelve-step programs for family members are available as
additional support. Alanon, Naranon, Adult Children of Alcoholics, Alateen, and Alatot are available in most communities.

The key to the development of effective prevention programs lies
in our further understanding of the etiology of both substance
abuse and family violence and particularly their comorbidity. Sub-

stance abuse prevention programs, and, to a lesser extent, violence prevention, have increasingly focused on the reduction of risk factors and the enhancement of resiliency or protective factors (Hawkins et al., 1987).

Some of these prevention strategies, especially those focused on the development of social competence, have been employed for the prevention of both substance abuse and family violence. For instance, the enhancement of problem solving and decision making is seen as an effective way of reducing stress and conflict—two antecedents to substance abuse and violence (Botvin & Wills, 1985). As pointed out earlier, poor communication may result in either substance abuse and/or violence. Therefore communication skill building also may be seen as preventive in terms of both behaviors. A third example is the use of conflict resolution skill building, which is most clearly seen as a violence prevention strategy but also may reduce the incidence of substance abuse, which often occurs as a dysfunctional response to conflict.

Early identification and assessment of either substance abuse or violence may serve as a means of preventing the further development of these behaviors (secondary prevention) or any incidence of the behavior not initially identified.

Conclusion

The dynamics involved in chemical dependence and family violence are complex. Clearly, the combination of the two behaviors can be devastating to family members and challenging for both researchers and clinicians.

Our understanding of the dynamics linking substance abuse and family violence is far from complete. Much more research is needed to illuminate the relationship between the two. Does substance abuse lead to violence? Does violence lead to substance abuse? Do other common factors cause them both? The answer to all of these questions is probably yes, but we must understand the specific conditions under which each is true. Such progress would have practical implications for the development of prevention and treatment strategies as well as for improving our theories of etiology. Most promising in this regard is the continued focus on risk factors and the causal modeling of these phenomena.

While further understanding of the exact linkage between substance abuse and family violence is clearly desirable from both theoretical and intervention perspectives, these problems continue to take their daily toll on victims. We cannot wait for full understanding. Interventions designed to prevent either substance abuse or violence, as well as aid their victims, are consistently in short supply and must become a social priority.

References

Aarens, M., Cameron, T., Roizen, J., Room, R., Schneberk, D., & Wingard, D. (1978). *Alcohol, casualties and other crime.* Berkeley, CA: Social Research Group.

Alcoholics Anonymous World Service. (1939). *Alcoholics Anonymous* (No. 76 4029). Washington, DC: Library of Congress.

Altman, G. B. (1986). Care of persons with alcohol problems of an episodic nature. In N. J. Estes & M. E. Heinemann (Eds.), *Alcoholism: Development, consequences, and interventions* (pp. 334-352). St. Louis: MO: C. V. Mosby.

Bachman, J., Johnston, L., & O'Malley, P. (1987). *Monitoring the future: Questionnaire responses from the nation's high school seniors.* Ann Arbor, MI: Institute for Social Research.

Bass, E., & Davis, L. (1988). *The courage to heal: A guide for women survivors of child sexual abuse.* New York: Harper & Row.

Baumrind, D. (1985). Familial antecedents of adolescent drug use: A developmental perspective. In C. L. Jones & R. Battjes (Eds.), *Etiology of drug abuse: Implications for prevention* (NIDA Monograph 56, pp. 13-45). Rockville, MD: NIDA.

Bays, J. (1990). Substance abuse and child abuse: Impact of addiction on the child. *Pediatric Clinics of North America, 37*(4), 881-904.

Bennett, L. A., Wolin, S. J., & Resii, D. (1988). Deliberate family process: A strategy for protecting children of alcoholics. *British Journal of Addictions, 83,* 821-829.

Berndt, T. (1987, March). *Changes in friendship and school adjustment after the transition to junior high school.* Paper presented at the biennial meeting of the Society for Research in Child Development, Baltimore, MD.

Black, C. (1981). *It will never happen to me.* Denver, CO: M.A.C.

Black, C. (1990). *Double duty.* New York: Ballantine.

Black, R. M., Mayer, J., & Zaklan, A. (1981). The relationship between opiate abuse and child abuse and neglect. *Drugs and the Family NIDA Research Issue, 29,* 74-75.

Botvin, G. J., & Wills, T. A. (1985). Personal and social skills training: Cognitive-behavioral approaches to substance abuse prevention. In D. S. Bell & R. Bettes (Eds.), *Prevention research: Deterring drug abuse among children and adolescents* (pp. 8-49). Rockville, MD: NIDA.

Bratton, M. B. (1992, March/April). Sexual abuse survivors: The initial intervention. *The Counselor,* pp. 22-23.

Briere, J. (1989). *Therapy for adults molested as children.* New York: Springer.

Broderick, J. E., Friedman, J. M., & Carr, E. G. (1981). Negotiation and contracting. In A. Goldstein, E. Carr, W. S. Davidson II, & P. Wehr (Eds.), *In response to aggression: Methods of control and prosocial alternatives* (pp. 66-109). New York: Pergamon.

Browne, A., & Finkelhor, D. (1986a). Impact of child sexual abuse: A review of the research. *Psychological Bulletin,* 66-77.

Browne, A., & Finkelhor, D. (1986b). Initial and long-term effects: A review of the research. In D. Finkelhor (Ed.), *Sourcebook on child sexual abuse* (pp. 143-179). Newbury Park, CA: Sage.

Cadoret, R., Troughton, E., & Widmer, R. (1984). Clinical differences between antisocial and primary alcoholics. *Comprehensive Psychiatry, 25*(1), 1-8.

Carr, E., & Binkoff, J. A. (1981). Self-control. In A. Goldstein, E. Carr, W. S. Davidson II, & P. Wehr (Eds.), *In response to aggression: Methods of control and prosocial alternatives* (pp. 110-158). New York: Pergamon.

Chasnoff, I. J. (1988). Drug use in pregnancy: Parameters of risk. *Pediatric Clinics of North America, 35,* 1403.

Chasnoff, I. J. (1989). Drug use and women: Establishing a standard of care. *Annual of New York Academy of Science, 562,* 208.

Children's Defense Fund (1989). *A vision for America's future.* Washington, DC: Author.

Cicchetti, D., & Olsen, K. (1990). The developmental psychopathology of child maltreatment. In M. Lewis & S. M. Miller (Eds.), *Handbook of developmental psychopathology* (pp. 261-280). New York: Plenum.

Curtis, J. M. (1986). Factors in sexual abuse in children. *Psychological Reports, 58,* 591-597.

Daro, D., & McCurdy, K. (1991). *Current trends in child abuse reporting and fatalities: The results of the annual fifty states survey.* Chicago: National Committee for the Prevention of Child Abuse.

deMarsh, J., & Kumpfer, K. (1985). Family-based interventions for the prevention of chemical dependency in children and adolescents. *Journal of Children in Contemporary Society, 18*(1-2), 117-152.

Dinwiddie, S. H., & Reich, T. (1991). Epidemiological perspectives on children of alcoholics. In M. Galanter (Ed.), *Recent developments in alcoholism: Vol. 9. Children of alcoholics* (pp. 287-299). New York: Plenum.

Dryfoos, J. D. (1987). *Youth at risk: One in four in jeopardy.* Unpublished report submitted to the Carnegie Corporation, Hastings-on-Hudson, New York.

Dubowitz, H., & Newberger, E. (1989). Pediatrics and child abuse. In D. Cicchetti & V. Carlson (Eds.), *Child maltreatment: Theory and research on the causes and consequences of child abuse and neglect* (pp. 76-94). New York: Cambridge University Press.

Dulfano, C. (1985). Family therapy of alcoholism. In S. Zimberg, J. Wallace, & S. B. Blume (Eds.), *Practical approaches to alcoholism psychotherapy.* New York: Plenum.

Emshoff, J., & Anyan, L. (1991). From prevention to treatment: Issues for school-aged children of alcoholics. In M. Galanter (Ed.), *Recent developments in alcoholism: Vol. 9. Children of alcoholics* (pp. 327-346). New York: Plenum.

Eskay, R., & Linnoila, M. (1991). Potential biochemical markers for the predisposition toward alcoholism. In M. Galanter (Ed.), *Recent developments in alcoholism: Vol. 9. Children of alcoholics* (pp. 41-49). New York: Plenum.

Finkelhor, D., & Baron, L. (1986). High-risk children. In D. Finkelhor (Ed.), *Sourcebook on child sexual abuse.* Newbury Park, CA: Sage.

Finkelhor, D. (with Hotaling, G., & Yllö, K.). (1988). *Stopping family violence: Research priorities for the coming decade.* Newbury Park, CA: Sage.

Finkelhor, D., & Yllö, K. (1985). *License to rape: Sexual abuse of wives.* New York: Holt, Rinehart & Winston.

Finkelhor, D. and Associates. (1986). *Sourcebook on child sexual abuse.* Newbury Park, CA: Sage.

Flores, P. J. (1988). *Group psychotherapy with addicted populations.* New York: Haworth.

Forrest, G. G. (1983). *Alcoholism and human sexuality.* Springfield, IL: Charles C Thomas.

Friedman, A. (1989). Family therapy vs. parent groups: Effects on adolescent drug abusers. *American Journal of Family Therapy.*

Funkhouser, J. E., Goplerud, E. N., & Bass, R. D. (1992). Current status of prevention strategies. In M. A. Jansen, S. Becker, M. Klitzner, & K. Stewart (Eds.), *Promising future: Alcohol and other drug problem prevention services improvement* (OSAP Prevention Monograph 10-A, pp. 17-82). Rockville, MD: OSAP.

Garbarino, J. (1976). A preliminary study of some ecological correlates of child abuse: The impact of socioeconomic stress on mothers. *Child Development, 47*(1), 178-185.

Garbarino, J., Guttman, E., & Seeley, J. W. (1986). *The psychologically battered child.* San Francisco: Jossey-Bass.

Gelles, R. J. (1974). *The violent home: A study of physical aggression between husbands and wives.* Beverly Hills, CA: Sage.

Gil, D. (1970). *Violence against children.* Cambridge, MA: Harvard University Press.

Gil, D. B. (1975). Unraveling child abuse. *American Journal of Orthopsychiatry, 45,* 346-356.

Gil, E. (1988). *Treatment of adult survivors of childhood abuse.* Walnut Creek, CA: Launch.

Gittelman, R. S., Mannuzza, R. S., & Bonagura, N. (1985). Hyperactive boys almost grown up: I. Psychiatric status. *Archives of General Psychiatry, 42,* 937-947.

Goldstein, A. P. (1981). Social skill training. In A. Goldstein, E. Carr, W. S. Davidson II, & P. Wehr (Eds.), *In response to aggression: Methods of control and prosocial alternatives* (159-218). New York: Pergamon.

Goodwin, D. W. (1985). Alcoholism and genetics. *Archives of General Psychiatry, 12,* 937-947.

Gottfredson, G. D. (1986). An empirical test of school-based environmental and individual interventions to reduce the risk of delinquent behavior. *Criminology, 24,* 705-731.

Grisham, K. J., & Estes, N. J. (1986). Dynamics of alcoholic families. In N. J. Estes & M. N. Heinemann (Eds.), *Alcoholism: Development, consequences, and interventions* (pp. 303-314). St. Louis, MO: C. V. Mosby.

Hawkins, J. D., Lishner, D. M., Jenson, J. M., & Catalano, R. F. (1987). Delinquents and drugs: What the evidence suggests about prevention and treatment programming. In B. S. Brown & A. R. Mills (Eds.), *Youth at risk for substance abuse* (pp. 81-231). Washington, DC: Government Printing Office.

Herman, J. L. (1981). *Father-daughter incest.* Cambridge, MA: Harvard University Press.

Hesselbrock, M. N., Meyer, R. E., & Kener, J. J. (1985). Psychopathology in hospitalized alcoholics. *Archives of General Psychiatry, 42*(11), 1050-1055.

Hurt, H., Salvador, A., & Brodsky, N. L. (1989). Infants of cocaine abusers have fewer parent contacts (PC) during hospitalization than controls. *Pediatric Research, 25.* (*Pediatric Research Abstracts,* 1989, Abstract No. 254A)

Jessor, R., & Jessor, S. L. (1977). *Problem behavior and psychosocial development: A longitudinal study of youth.* New York: Academic Press.

Johnston, L. D., O'Malley, P. M., & Bachman, J. G. (1990). *Drug use among American high school seniors, college students, and young adults: 1975-1990* (Vol. 1, DHHS Pub. No. [ADM] 91-1813). Washington, DC: Government Printing Office.

Kandel, D. B., & Yamaguchi, K. (1984). Patterns of drug use from adolescence to young adulthood: Sequences of progression, part III. *American Journal of Public Health, 74*(7), 673-681.

Kantor, G. K., & Straus, M. A. (1989). Substance abuse as a precipitant of wife abuse victimizations. *American Journal of Drug and Alcohol Abuse, 173,* 214-230.

Kempe, C. H., Silverman, F. N., Steele, B. F., Droegemueller, W., & Silver, H. K. (1985). The battered-child syndrome. *Child Abuse & Neglect, 9,* 143-154.

Kline, R. B., Canter, W. A., & Robin, A. (1987). Parameters of teenage alcohol use: A path analytic conceptual model. *Journal of Drug Education, 20*(1), 77-94.

Kumpfer, K. L. (1987). Special populations: Etiology & prevention of vulnerability to chemical dependency in children of substance abusers. In B. S. Brown & A. R. Mills (Eds.), *Youth at high risk for substance abuse* (DHHS Pub. No. [ADM] 87-1537, pp. 1-72). Washington, DC: Government Printing Office.

Kumpfer, K. L., & DeMarsh, J. P. (1986, March). *Prevention strategies for children of drug-abusing parents.* Paper presented at the 34th Annual International Congress on Alcoholism and Drug Dependence, Calgary, Alberta.

Leonard, K. E., & Jacob, T. (1988). Alcohol, alcoholism and family violence. In V. B. Van Hasselt, R. I. Morrison, & A. S. Bellack (Eds.), *Handbook of family violence* (pp. 383-406). New York: Plenum.

Lerner, J. V., & Vicary, J. R. (1984). Difficult temperament and drug use: Analyses from the New York longitudinal study. *Journal of Drug Education, 14,* 1-8.

Lindquist, C. L. (1986). Battered women as coalcoholics: Treatment implications and case study. *Psychotherapy, 23,* 622-628.

Masters, W. H., & Johnson, V. E. (1970). *Human sexual inadequacy.* Boston: Little, Brown.

McCagy, C. H. (1968). Drinking and deviance disavowal: The case of child molesters. *Social Problems, 16*(1), 43-49.

McCarthy, J. C. (1985). The concept of addictive disease. In D. E. Smith & D. R. Wesson (Eds.), *Treating the cocaine abuser* (pp. 21-30). Center City, MN: Hazelden.

McNamara, B. & McNamara, J. (1990). *The SAFE-TEAM curriculum: Preparation and support for families adopting sexually abused children.* Ossining, NY: Family Resources.

Morgan, P. (1982). Alcohol and family violence: A review of the literature. In *National Institute of Alcoholism and Alcohol Abuse, Alcohol Consumption and Related Problems* (Alcohol and Health Monograph 1). Washington, DC: U.S. Department of Health and Human Services.

Morrison, M. A., Hayes, H. R., & Knauf, K. (1989). Progression of chemical dependence and recovery in adolescents. *Psychiatric Annals, 19*(12), 666-671.

Nathanson, D. L. (1989). Understanding what is hidden: Shame in sexual abuse. *Psychiatric Clinics of North America, 12*(2), 381-388.

National Committee for the Prevention of Child Abuse (NCPCA). (1989, October). The substance abuse and child abuse connection. In *The NCPCA Memorandum.* Chicago: Author.

National Institute on Alcohol Abuse and Alcoholism (NIAAA). (1974). *An assessment of the needs of and resources for children of alcoholic parents* (PB-241 119). Rockville, MD: Author.

National Institute on Alcohol Abuse and Alcoholism (NIAAA). (1984). *Children of alcoholics: A special report.* Rockville, MD: Author.

National Institute of Drug Abuse. (1991). *National drug control strategy: Vol. 1. A national response to drug use* [NIDA household survey]. Washington, DC: Government Printing Office.

Pagelow, M. D. (1984). *Family violence.* New York: Praeger.

Pattison, E. M., & Kaufman, E. (1982). *The encyclopedic handbook of alcoholism.* New York: Gardner.

Peters, S. D., Wyatt, G. E., & Finkelhor, D. (1986). Prevalence. In D. Finkelhor and Associates, *Sourcebook on child sexual abuse* (pp. 15-59). Newbury Park, CA: Sage.

Rada, R. (1976). Alcoholism and the child molester. *Annals of the New York Academy of Science, 273,* 492-496.

Rhodes, J. E., & Jason, L. A. (1990). A social stress model of substance abuse. *Journal of the American Medical Association, 24,* 2-7.

Rimmer, J. (1982). The children of alcoholics: An exploratory study. *Children and Youth Services Review, 4,* 365-373.

Robins, L. N., & Przybeck, T. R. (1985). Age of onset of drug use as a factor in drug and other disorders. In C. L. Jones & R. J. Battjes (Eds.), *Etiology of drug abuse: Implications for prevention* (Research Monograph No. 56, DHHS Publication No. [ADM] 85-1335, pp. 178-1192). Washington, DC: Government Printing Office.

Rodning, C., Beckwith, L., & Howard, J. (1989). Prenatal exposure to drugs and its influences on attachment. *Annual New York Academy of Science, 562,* 352.

Ross, H. E., Glaser, F. B., & Germanson, T. (1988). The prevalence of psychiatric disorders in patients with alcohol and other drug problems. *Archives of General Psychiatry, 45*(11), 1023-1031.

Roy, M. (1988). *Children in the crossfire.* Deerfield, Beach, FL: Health Communications.

Russell, D. (1982). *Rape in marriage.* New York: Macmillan.

Schuckit, M. A. (1971). Sexual disturbance in the woman alcoholic. *Medical Aspects of Human Sexuality, 6,* 44-45, 48-49, 53, 57, 60-61, 65.

Schuckit, M. A., & Chiles, J. (1978). Family history as a diagnostic aid in two samples of adolescents. *Journal of Nervous and Mental Disease, 166,* 165-176.

Sgroi, S. M. (1985). *Handbook of clinical intervention in child sexual abuse.* Lexington, MA: Lexington.

Shapiro, R. (1982). Alcohol and family violence. In J. Hansen & L. Barnhill (Eds.), *Clinical approaches to family violence* (pp. 69-89). Rockville, MD: Aspen Systems Corporation.

Shapiro, R. J., Hansen, J., & Barnhill, L. (Eds.). (1982). *Alcohol and family violence: Clinical approaches to family violence.* Rockville, MD: Aspen Systems Corporation.

Sher, K. (1991). Psychological characteristics of children of children of alcoholics: Overview of research methods and findings. In M. Galanter (Ed.), *Recent developments in alcoholism: Vol. 9. Children of alcoholics* (pp. 301-327). New York: Plenum.

Smith, D. E., & Wesson, D. R. (1985). *Treating the cocaine abuser.* Center City, MN: Hazelden.

Smith, S. M., & Kunjukrishnan, R. (1985, December). Child abuse: Perspectives on treatment and research. *Psychiatric Clinics of North America, 8*(4), 685-684.

Steinberg, L. (1987). *Adolescent transitions and substance abuse prevention.* Contract paper prepared for the Office for Substance Abuse Prevention, Alcohol, Drug Abuse and Mental Health Administration, Public Health Service, U.S. Department of Health and Human Services (Contract No. 283-87-0010), Rockville, MD.

Strack, J. H., & Dutton, L. A. (1971, September). *A new approach in treatment of the married alcoholic.* Paper presented at the 22nd Annual Meeting of the Alcohol and Drug Problems Association of North America, Hartford, CT.

Straus, M. A., & Gelles, R. J. (1986). Change in family violence from 1975 to 1985. *Journal of Marriage and the Family, 48,* 465-479.

Straus, M. A., Gelles, R., & Steinmetz, S. (1980). *Behind closed doors: Violence in the American family.* Garden City, NY: Anchor/Doubleday.

Talbott, G. D. (1991, June). Alcoholism and other drug addictions: A primary disease entity, 1991 update. *Journal of the Medical Association of Georgia,* pp. 337-342.

Tarter, R. E. (1991a). Developmental behavior: Genetic perspective of alcoholism etiology. In M. Galanter (Ed.), *Recent developments in alcoholism: Vol. 9. Children of alcoholics* (pp. 71-73). New York: Plenum.

Tarter, R. E. (1991b, October). *Risk for alcoholism: New cobehavioral perspective.* Paper presented at the National Consensus Symposium on COA & Co-dependence.

Tarter, R. E., Alterman, A. E., & Edwards, K. L. (1985). Vulnerability to alcoholism in men: A behavior-genetic perspective. *Journal of Studies on Alcoholism, 46,* 329-356.

Thomas, D. (1988). Infants of drug addicted mothers. *Australian Pediatric Journal, 24,* 16.

Thomas, J. N. (1989). Triple jeopardy: Child abuse, drug abuse and the minority client. *Journal of Interpersonal Violence, 4,* 351.

Wallace, J. (1986). Alcoholism from the inside out: A phenomenologic analysis. In N. J. Estes & M. E. Heinemann (Eds.), *Alcoholism: Development, consequences, and interventions.* St. Louis: C. V. Mosby.

Wegscheider, S. (1981). *Another chance: Hope and health for the alcoholic family.* Palo Alto, CA: Science and Behavior Books.

Wilsnack, S. C. (1984). Drinking, sexuality, and sexual dysfunction in women. In S. C. Wilsnack & L. J. Beckman (Eds.), *Alcoholism problems in women.* New York: Guilford.

Wilson, J. Q., & Hernstein, R. J. (1985). *Crime and human nature.* New York: Simon & Schuster.

Zimberg, S., Wallace, J., & Blume, S. (1985). *Practical approaches to alcoholism psychotherapy.* New York: Plenum.

Zucker, R. A., & Lisansky-Gomber, E. S. (1986). Etiology of alcoholism reconsidered: The case for a bio-psychosocial process. *American Psychologist, 41,* 783-793.

Index

About the Editors

Gerald R. Adams is Professor in the Department of Family Studies at the University of Guelph, Ontario, Canada. He is a Fellow of the American Psychological Association and has been awarded the James D. Moran Research Award from the American Home Economics Association. He currently has editorial assignments with the *Journal of Adolescence, Journal of Primary Prevention, Journal of Early Adolescence,* and *Social Psychology Quarterly.*

Thomas P. Gullotta is CEO of the Child and Family Agency in Connecticut. He is currently Editor of the *Journal of Primary Prevention,* serves as a general series book editor for *Advances in Adolescent Development,* and is the senior book series editor for *Issues in Children's and Families' Lives.* He also serves on the editorial boards of the *Journal of Early Adolescence* and *Adolescence,* and is an adjunct faculty member in the psychology department of Eastern Connecticut State University. His 59 published works include 2 textbooks, 4 edited books, 4 contributed chapters, 27 published papers, and 22 requested book/film reviews for professional journals.

Robert L. Hampton received his A.B. degree from Princeton University, his M.A. and his Ph.D. from the University of Michigan. He is Professor of Sociology and Dean of Connecticut College in New London; a Research Associate in the Family Development Program, Children's Hospital Center, Boston; and a Research Associate in Medicine (General Pediatrics), Harvard Medical School, Boston. He has published extensively in the field of family violence including two earlier books: *Violence in the Black Family: Correlates and Consequences* and *Black Family*

Violence: Current Research and Theory. His research interests include interspousal violence, family abuse, community violence, stress and social support, and institutional responses to violence.

Earl H. Potter III is Professor of Management and Associate Dean for Academic Affairs at the United States Coast Guard Academy. He received his Ph.D. in organizational psychology from the University of Washington in 1978. His research on leadership has been published in the *Journal of Applied Psychology,* the *Academy of Management Journal,* and the *Journal of Personality and Social Psychology.* As a Fellow of the American Council on Education, his work on improving quality in undergraduate education has had a significant impact on universities across the county. A specialist in community development, he has made major contributions to the development of effective systems for the delivery of human services.

Roger P. Weissberg is Professor of Psychology at the University of Illinois at Chicago. He has published more than 60 research articles and chapters focusing on issues related to preventive interventions with children and adolescents. He has also cowritten 9 curricula on school-based programs to promote social competence and prevent high risk, antisocial problem behaviors. Formerly, he was director of Yale University's NIMH-funded Prevention Research Training Program for Predoctoral and Postdoctoral Trainees (1989-1993). His is a recipient of the William T. Grant Foundation's 5-year Faculty Scholars Award in Children's Mental Health, the Connecticut Psychological Association's 1992 Award for Distinguished Psychological Contribution in the Public Interest, and the National Mental Health Association's 1992 Lela Rowland Prevention Award.

About the Contributors

Lynette M. Anderson (A.C.S.W.) is currently a social worker at Child and Family Agency of Southeastern Conneticut. A graduate of the Smith College for Social Work in 1959, she developed and ran a foster care program for emotionally disturbed children at the Baird Children's Center in Burlington, Vermont, from 1968 to 1981. While in Vermont, she ran a training program for State Protective Service workers. She has taught Family Therapy courses at Mitchell College in New London, Conneticut and at University of Conneticut School of Social Work and has been a field instructor for interns from the Adelphi School of Social Work, UCONN School of Social Work, and Connecticut College's M.A. Psychology program. In 1981, she wrote "A Systems Approach to Foster Home Studies" published in *Child Welfare.* Arriving at Child and Family Agency in 1981, she has been actively involved in the Family Violence Program since it started.

Jo-Ellen Asbury received her B.S. in Elementary Education from Indiana University of Pennsylvania in 1978. After 2 years as an elementary school teacher, she entered the Social-Personality Psychology program at the University of Pittsburgh, where she received her M.S. in 1983 and Ph.D. in 1985. Since completing her doctorate, she has worked both in academe and in government. Currently, she is Assistant Professor in the Psychology Department at Bethany College (Bethany, West Virginia), where she continues to pursue her interests in applying psychological research to real world problems.

Gary M. Blau (Ph.D., clinical psychology) is currently Director of Clinical Services at Child and Family Agency of Southeastern Connecticut. Since receiving his degree from Auburn University

(Auburn, Alabama) in 1988, he has worked in children's mental health with a primary emphasis on victimized children, child custody and permanency planning, and emotional trauma. He joined Child and Family Agency's staff as Director of Clinical Services in 1990 and has responsibility for Outpatient and Home-Based Clinical Services, the Family Violence Treatment Unit, and the School-Based Health Centers. He serves on the editorial board of the *Journal of Primary Prevention,* and he has published and presented in the areas of child custody, primary prevention, and clinical service delivery.

Frances A. Boudreau received her B.A. and M.A. degrees from the University of Rhode Island and a Ph.D. in sociology from the University of Connecticut. She is coauthor of an introductory text *Understanding Social Life* (West, 1992), coeditor and author of *Sex-Roles and Social Patterns* (Praeger, 1986) as well as a contributor of book chapters and essays focusing on issues in social psychology, family, and gender studies. She is currently Associate Professor of Sociology at Connecticut College, where she teaches Aging in American Society.

Mary Butteweg Dall (L.C.S.W., B.C.D.) is Clinical Coordinator at Child and Family Agency of Southeastern Connecticut. In addition to the direct treatment of children and their families, she supervises the outpatient clinical staff in both the child guidance and the family violence programs. Prior to joining the staff of Child and Family Agency, she worked directly with victimized children in rural areas of California and Alaska. She has served as a consultant to clinics on California Indian reservations and in native villages in Alaska. As a member of the Smith College School for Social Work part-time faculty, she teaches a course on the treatment of children. She serves as a field supervisor for the Connecticut College graduate program in psychology and the Smith College School for Social Work master's program and is a faculty field adviser for Smith's doctoral program. She received her M.S.W. from Smith College in 1974, where she is currently a Ph.D. candidate in clinical social work.

Michele Cascardi is a doctoral candidate in clinical psychology at the State University of New York at Stony Brook and a psychology intern at the Medical College of Pennsylvania. She has conducted research on the psychological impact of battering on women as well as gender differences regarding the impact and context of marital aggression. In addition, she spent 2 years working at the Nassau County Coalition Against Domestic Violence. Last summer, she interned at the National Woman Abuse Prevention Project in Washington, DC, where she drafted a chapter on how to work with victims of domestic violence. In addition, she has worked toward the passage of family violence legislation.

Alice F. Washington Coner-Edwards received her B.S. degree in psychology from Southern University in 1969, her M.S.W. degree in 1977 and her Ph.D. from Harvard University in 1985. She has conducted research studies in the areas of strategies of learning in children, race and memory ability, relationship satisfaction, employment and relationship conflict, mate selection, and marital expectation. She has published in professional journals and in 1988, edited a volume on black families. She has presented numerous papers and research reports in professional meetings and conferences. She has extensive knowledge of social systems based on theory and experience. She has traveled extensively, both nationally and abroad, in more than 15 countries. In 1985, she studied the social welfare system in the former Soviet Union, comparing and contrasting this system with that in the United States. She currently practices psychotherapy with individuals and couples. She is also studying public administration and marketing at Southeastern University.

Jon R. Conte is Associate Professor in the School of Social Work at the University of Washington. He is also the editor of the *Journal of Interpersonal Violence* and *Violence Update* and is a member and past president of the American Professional Society on the Abuse of Children. He is the author of numerous publications dealing with various aspects of child sexual abuse and is a frequent lecturer at national and international meetings. His current work deals with child abuse ethics and countertransference in the lives of trauma therapists. He has conducted research on the effects of childhood sexual experiences on child and adult survivors, the etiology of sexual violence, and the effects of programs to prevent the sexual victimization of young children. A clinical social worker and researcher by training, he maintains a private practice working with victims of interpersonal violence and consults with treatment providers and other private and public agencies.

Julie L. Crouch is a graduate student in the doctoral program in Clinical Psychology at Northern Illinois University. She is currently a Research Associate in the Family Violence Research Program. Her research interests include the study of physical and sexual child abuse victim effects and the description of factors that might buffer the effects of child maltreatment.

Howard Dubowitz (M.D.) is Assistant Professor of Pediatrics at the University of Maryland School of Medicine and Director of its Child Maltreatment Program. He is involved in clinical work, teaching, and research in the area of child maltreatment. He directs an interdisciplinary clinic for the evaluation of children alleged to have been sexually abused. He also directs the hospital's Child Protection Team, which provides consultation on children where there is a concern about possible abuse or neglect. His primary research interests are currently a longitudinal study of child neglect, home intervention and failure to thrive, and the health and educational status of children in kinship care—an arrangement where children are placed in the care of a relative. He is a member of the Parents Anonymous Board and the Family Preservation Advisory Committee in Maryland, the North American Kinship Care Policy and Practice Committee, and the board of the National Child Welfare Center of Foster Care at East Michigan University.

James G. Emshoff has a Ph.D. and M.S. in community psychology from Michigan State University. He is currently Associate Professor of Psychology at Georgia State University and the Director of Research at EMSTAR Research, Inc. He has directed five federally funded research projects. One of these grants was to develop, administer, and evaluate a preventive intervention for children of alcoholics, which was administered in middle schools and won the 1989 American Medical Association Substance Abuse Prevention Award. During a leave from his academic position, he worked at the Office for Substance Abuse Prevention (OSAP), where he concentrated on evaluation issues and the creation of OSAP's grant program for substance-abusing pregnant and postpartum women and their infants. He is currently evaluating three of OSAP's grantees as well as numerous other substance abuse prevention programs at the local, state, and national levels and provides technical assistance in prevention and evaluation to many organizations. Approximately 100 of his publications and professional presentations focus on a variety of prevention and evaluation issues.

Richard J. Gelles is Professor of Sociology and Anthropology and Director of the Family Violence Research Program at the University of Rhode Island. He has published extensively on the topics of child abuse, wife abuse, and family violence. His most recent books are *Intimate Violence* (Touchstone, 1989), *Physical Violence in American Families: Risk Factors and Adaptations in 8,145 Families* (Transaction, 1990), *Intimate Violence in Families* (Sage, 1990), and *Sociology: An Introduction* (4th edition, McGraw-Hill, 1991).

Edward W. Gondolf (Ed.D., M.P.H.) is Professor of Sociology in the Graduate Human Service Program at Indiana University of Pennsylvania (IUP). He is Research Director of the Mid-Atlantic Addiction Training Institute (MAATI) and Adjunct Professor at Western Psychiatric Institute and Clinic, University of Pittsburgh Medical School. He is also affiliated with the Domestic Abuse Counseling Center for men who batter in Pittsburgh and is a consultant to the batterers clinic of the Veterans Affairs Medical Center, Pittsburgh. He has written several books on domestic violence and community development issues, including *Men Who Batter* (Learning Publications, 1985), *Battered Women as Survivors* (Lexington Books, 1988), and *Psychiatric Response to Family Violence* (Lexington Books, 1990).

Donna Harrington (Ph.D.) is a Developmental Psychologist and Instructor at the University of Maryland School of Medicine. She is involved in research in the longitudinal study of child neglect, children's cognitive development, and the health and educational status of children placed in the care of a relative (kinship care). She also teaches at the University of Maryland, Baltimore County. She has worked with families and young children both in clinical and in educational settings, including directing the education component of the ParentInfant Center at Towson State University.

Heather R. Hayes (M.Ed., NCACII) is a master's level counselor/therapist working for Georgia Alcohol and Drug Associates. She works with adults and adolescents in a private practice setting, specializing in the treatment of chemical dependency, posttraumatic stress disorders, and anxiety disorders. She is currently doing graduate work toward a Ph.D. in clinical psychology, child and family track, at Georgia State University, Atlanta. In addition, she has trained in psycho motor oriented Integrative Group Psychotherapy for 2 years. She has written several articles on the progression of chemical dependency and recovery in adolescents. She and Dr. Martha Morrison have published a comprehensive model program for successful treatment and recovery of young adults from chemical dependency. Her current research is exploring the relationship and dynamics of physical and sexual abuse in adolescents being treated for chemical dependency.

Joel S. Milner (Ph.D.) is a Presidential Research Professor of Psychology and Coordinator of the Family Violence Research Program at Northern Illinois University. Currently, he is serving as member (1988-1993) and Chair (1990-1993) of the Violence and Traumatic Stress Review Committee at the National Institute of Mental Health (NIMH) and is Associate Editor of *Violence and Victims.* He has received several family violence research grants from federal agencies, such as the NIMH and the National Center on Child Abuse and Neglect. He is the author of more than 90 book chapters and articles, most of which are in the area of family violence. His current scholarly interests include the description and prediction of intrafamilial sexual child abuse and the application of a social information processing model to physical child abuse.

Christopher M. Murphy, a clinical psychologist, is Assistant Professor at the University of Maryland, Baltimore County. He has cowritten papers on the assessment, etiology, and social context of wife battering and on the relationship between marital discord and children's problems. He maintains active involvement in batterers' treatment through work at the House of Ruth in Baltimore.

Theodore J. Stein is Professor of Social Welfare at the School of Social Welfare, State University of New York at Albany. He was Director of the Alameda Project, an experimental effort to counter foster-care drift, and of the Illinois/West Virginia Project, in which procedures for decision making at child welfare intake were developed and tested. His publications include "Children in Foster Homes: Achieving Continuity in Care" (with Eileen D. Gambrill & Kermit T. Wiltse), "Decision Making in Child Welfare Services: Intake and Planning" (with Tina L. Rzepnicki), and *Child Welfare and the Law*.